THE INSTITUTIONALIZATION OF EUROPE

The Institutionalization of Europe

EDITED BY

Alec Stone Sweet

Wayne Sandholtz

and

Neil Fligstein

OXFORD

UNIVERSITY PRESS

OXFORD

UNIVERSITY PRESS

Great Clarendon Street, Oxford OX2 6DP

Oxford University Press is a department of the University of Oxford.
It furthers the University's objective of excellence in research, scholarship,
and education by publishing worldwide in

Oxford New York

Athens Auckland Bangkok Bogotá Buenos Aires
Cape Town Chennai Dar es Salaam Delhi Florence Hong Kong Istanbul
Karachi Kolkata Kuala Lumpur Madrid Melbourne Mexico City Mumbai
Nairobi Paris São Paulo Singapore Taipei Tokyo Toronto Warsaw

and associated companies in Berlin Ibadan

Oxford is a registered trade mark of Oxford University Press
in the UK and in certain other countries

Published in the United States
by Oxford University Press Inc., New York

British Library Cataloguing in Publication Data

Data available

Library of Congress Cataloging in Publication Data

Data available

ISBN 0-19-924795-1
ISBN 0-19-924796-X (Pbk)

1 3 5 7 9 10 8 6 4 2

Typeset by Hope Services (Abingdon) Ltd.

Printed in Great Britain by
Biddles Ltd., Guildford & Kings Lynn

PREFACE

This book is the result of an intensive, three-year collaboration among a small group of social scientists. The project partly extends the 1998 *European Integration and Supranational Governance* project (edited by Wayne Sandholtz and Alec Stone Sweet), but it also charts its own course, given the addition of new members, talents, and perspectives. The group met in four workshops: three in Laguna Beach, California, and one in San Domenico di Fiesole, Italy. In March 2000 we presented penultimate versions of papers at the final meeting of the group, a conference held at the Robert Schuman Centre for Advanced Study, European University Institute, San Domenico di Fiesole.

Collaborative research of this duration and scope proceeds only through the goodwill and generosity of others. We owe an enormous debt to a number of institutions and individuals. As with the *European Integration and Supranational Governance* project, a multi-year grant from the University of California (Berkeley) Center for German and European Studies provided basic funding; we thank the Center's Bev Crawford in particular for her encouragement. The University of California (Irvine) Center for Global Peace and Conflict Studies, under the directorship of Patrick Morgan, also provided substantial support over several years. Yves Mény, the Director of the Schuman Centre, organized funding of a workshop, through the Italian Ministry of Foreign Affairs; and the Schuman Centre sponsored a final conference. Monique Cavallari provided tireless logistical support in Italy.

Individual members of the group have acknowledged, in their own ways, the contributions of those who have made their respective chapters better. As a group, we are collectively grateful to friends and colleagues who participated at various stages of the project. We thank Harry Eckstein (in memoriam), Paul Pierson (Harvard), Martin Rhodes (EUI), and Dorothy Solinger (UCI) for joining in workshop sessions, and Berthold Rittberger (Nuffield), Margaret McCown (Nuffield), and Ron Jepperson (EUI) for acting as discussants at the conference. We appreciate the many important comments and criticisms these and other scholars have raised, even though our responses to them surely remain inadequate and incomplete. Michael Struett (UCI) helped to get the manuscript in shape.

Finally, we thank our editors, Dominic Byatt and Amanda Watkins at Oxford University Press, and our copy-editor, Michael James. In so many secret and (almost) invisible ways, these three made the final stages of a book project (almost) enjoyable.

Alec Stone Sweet
Neil Fligstein
Wayne Sandholtz

November 2000

CONTENTS

LIST OF CONTRIBUTORS

James A. Caporaso
Department of Political Science, University of Washington

Rachel A. Cichowski
Department of Political Science, University of California, Irvine

Neil Fligstein
Department of Sociology, University of California, Berkeley

Adrienne Héritier
Max Planck Project Group on Common Goods: Law, Politics and Economics, Bonn

Patrick Le Galès
Centre d'Étude de la Vie Politique Française, Centre National de la Recherche Scientifique; Institut d'Études Politiques

Sonia Mazey
Hertford College, Oxford

Kathleen R. McNamara
Woodrow Wilson School and Department of Politics, Princeton University

Jeremy Richardson
Nuffield College, Oxford

Wayne Sandholtz
Department of Political Science, University of California, Irvine

Martin Shapiro
Boalt Hall School of Law, University of California, Berkeley

Michael E. Smith
Department of Political Science, Georgia State University

Alec Stone Sweet
Nuffield College, Oxford

Penelope Turnbull
Institute for German Studies, University of Birmingham

LIST OF FIGURES

LIST OF TABLES

1

The Institutionalization of European Space

ALEC STONE SWEET, NEIL FLIGSTEIN, AND WAYNE SANDHOLTZ

IN 1950, a European political space existed in roughly the same sense as any other international political space, as an arena in which sovereign nation-states interacted to forward their interests. This arena was only a very primitive site of collective governance. It was also a space that had organized a disastrous intergovernmental politics, producing two devastating wars in less than 30 years. European states could have reproduced this system, locking themselves into another round of intergovernmental relations, and potential disputes, following World War II. But this is not what happened. Instead, they negotiated the Treaty of Rome and began a process of building a different kind of European political space, or, more accurately, a set of political spaces.

We know that the negotiators did not fully understand what kind of political space would evolve under the Treaty of Rome, although some of its visionaries, like Monnet and Schuman, clearly had high aspirations. Nonetheless, the Treaty created the possibility for new forms of political cooperation between European governments, firms, non-governmental organizations, and other private actors. It provided a set of rules and permanent organizations—the Council and the Commission—to facilitate cooperation. It made possible the emergence of multiple political arenas, a 'Brussels complex', that organizes ongoing, open-ended negotiation around a large number of common issues. It established a Court of Justice to interpret both the Treaty and the subsequent collective agreements.

Fifty years later, the European Union governs in an expanding number of policy domains, producing rules that are authoritative for both states and persons. Increasingly dense networks of transnational actors comprised of people who are representatives of Member State governments, firms, lobbying organizations, and members of the European Union organizations—mainly the Commission, the Court of Justice, the Parliament, and now the Central Bank—operate in political spaces that are best described as supranational in character. Various actors work to attain their goals, and vie with each other to influence policy outcomes that apply to all of Europe. European organizations and rules both enable and constrain these actors, providing opportunities for purposive action, and shaping goals and strategies. As jurisdiction has moved from the national to the EU level, complex, often unintended, linkages and tensions between modes of supranational and national governance have developed. The myriad processes through which these tensions are revealed, exploited, exacerbated, or resolved are today at the core of European politics. In a phrase, we have witnessed the emergence and institutionalization of European space.

There was no necessary reason for all of this to happen. The activities of the Brussels complex and the Luxembourg Court required that many actors, operating in pre-existing social and political spaces, had to figure out how to turn black-letter treaty provisions into organizations and practices. The move to European governance has been driven by firms trading more across national borders, by the economies of Europe becoming increasingly interdependent in other myriad ways, and by actors gradually finding that the forms and methods of supranational governance served their evolving conception of interests. The creation of organizational capacity to govern, in Brussels, Luxembourg, and now Frankfurt, and the expansion of transnational society are interrelated processes. As we showed in *European Integration and Supranational Governance*, these processes have tended to feed one another, transforming how governments and other political actors operate and relate to one another (Sandholtz and Stone Sweet 1998).

European Integration and Supranational Governance proposed two sets of arguments to explain the trajectory of European integration. The most fully elaborated argument offered a theory of why law-making competences tended to migrate, from the national towards the EC level, faster and further in some policy domains than in others. We identified two logics (Stone Sweet and Sandholtz, 1998: 7–15; Stone Sweet and Caporaso 1998a). First, rising levels of cross-national exchange would pressure public authorities to develop modes of supranational governance, and would undermine relevant national modes of governance, making the latter more costly to maintain. Actors engaged in, or contemplating, transnational exchange would seek to eliminate national barriers to their activities. Second, these and other actors, such as individuals and interest groups interested in policy reform more generally, would lobby in national political arenas, putting pressure on governments to design or support the expansion of European policies in EC policy domains. They would also work to access EC organizations, especially the Commission and the European Court of Justice, in order to activate rule-making processes that might escape the control of any single national government or consortium of governments. They would do so to the extent that they had an interest in undermining established national regulatory regimes or law. We expected to observe outcomes that competing approaches could not readily explain, namely, the development of EC rules and policy arenas that the Member States acting in a purely intergovernmental mode would not have negotiated on their own. The empirical chapters identified clear confirming instances.

Complex modes of supranational governance have developed, especially in those domains in which there have been relatively high levels of transnational activity, and once developed, EC rules have been enforced against those national governments that had most opposed them, even governments of the most powerful states.

We also proposed that once supranational rules were in place and new policy spaces had been organized, institutions and the EC's organizations would structure the further expansion of cross-border exchange, transnational policy networks, and the EC's authority to govern (Stone Sweet and Sandholtz 1998: 16–20). We labelled this dynamic process 'institutionalization', and noted that it often produces outcomes that actors could not expect or foresee. One of the more remarkable features of the development of the European Union is the degree to which ongoing processes of institutional innovation have facilitated the shift from a primary emphasis on negative integration, the elimination of 'national restraints on trade and distortions of competition', to positive integration, the making of 'common European policies to shape the conditions under which markets [and other forms of human activity] operate' (Scharpf 1996: 15). That is, in addition to removing national barriers to exchange, the EU produces common policies. It has done so in a growing number and variety of domains, including agriculture, environmental protection, social security, consumer health and safety, labour relations, gender equity, administrative law, justice and home affairs, foreign policy, and monetary policy.

1. The Institutionalist Challenge

This project focuses on the sources and consequences of institutionalization, that is, on the process through which European political space—supranational policy arenas or sites of governance, structured by EU rules, procedures, and the activities of the EU's organizations—has evolved. In *European Integration and Supranational Governance*, the question of how supranational arenas emerged and were institutionalized claimed a good deal of our collective attention (Stone Sweet and Sandholtz 1998: 16–20; 22–4). In this volume, our focus is on institutionalization of Europe *per se*.[1]

What has happened is not well understood. This is both a theoretical and an empirical problem. It is an empirical problem because the European Union is an unusual political entity. No existing supranational political system matches its organizational complexity, the density of its substantive and procedural law, or the extent of its impact on national structures. As a result, political scientists (for example, Sbragia 1992; 1993) and legal scholars (for example, Lenaerts 1990) have come to characterize the EU with reference to existing models, like federalism, or to characterize it as a new form of governance altogether (for example, Héritier1999; Marks, Hooghe, and Blank 1996; Wessels and Rometsch 1996).

[1] A recent study that adopts an institutionalist framework is Armstrong and Bulmer (1998).

Understanding, let alone explaining, the EU's emergence as a system of governance poses fierce theoretical difficulties. The EU may be unique when viewed as a particular set of institutions, organizations, and other arrangements. But most social scientists would agree that these arrangements ought to be the outcome of more conventional social and political processes, however uniquely these processes work their way out in the end. If the challenge is to use and develop theoretical tools that help us to explain how such institutions evolve, the question is: which tools? We do not believe that traditional approaches to international regimes (Keohane 1984; Krasner 1983), and even to European integration—for example, intergovernmentalism—are up to the task of explaining the institutionalization of Europe, or of how and with what effects European political spaces evolve. These theories were simply not designed with such purposes, or objects of inquiry, in mind. Instead, the appropriate theoretical materials are surely of a more abstract nature, in particular, ideas about how institutions are formed and evolve over time. Such materials must help us to understand the role of actors, rules, and organizations in the emergence and expansion of political spaces in general. Once developed, we can begin to apply them to the situation of Europe.

A concern for institutions has informed a great deal of recent theoretical work across the social sciences. Unfortunately, the ways in which new social and political spaces are constructed, and existing spaces develop, remain largely mysterious. Cultural theorists (for example, Eckstein 1988), neo-rationalist political scientists (for example, Taylor 1989), organizational sociologists (for example, Powell and DiMaggio 1991), and economic institutionalists (for example, North 1990) all agree that our understanding of institutional change, of how the rule systems that underpin social life evolve over time, and how—at least quasi-autonomous—rule systems interact dynamically with one another, remains primitive. We use terms like 'strategic action', 'cultural framing', 'path dependence', and 'unintended consequences' to capture the complexity of these processes and outcomes, but these terms are often used in a more descriptive than analytic guise.

Institutionalists better understand the logic of inertia. Rules facilitate exchange among individuals, and create opportunities for collective action. They often define who an actor is, how actors can express and pursue their interests, and the limits of action. One may be reasonably successful at predicting the behaviour of various groups if one knows the rules of a particular social space and the groups' relative positions in such an arena, and if one can infer interests from these positions. Both rationalist and structuralist accounts apply most easily to these situations. Behaviour that responds to these opportunities, whether conceived of as sunk costs, political coalitions, or taken-for-granted standards of conduct, ends up reinforcing existing social structure (for example, Pierson 1993; Weingast and Marshall 1988; Scott 1996).

Neo-rationalists proceed from theoretical micro-foundations that take stable cooperation among individuals to be inherently problematic (for example, Axelrod 1984; 1986). Not surprisingly, they have focused on the problem of constructing institutions, but not much on their subsequent evolution. Their approach is a useful starting point for any analysis because the outcome, such as a set of rules or organizational capacities, will organize strategic interactions to come. But there are deep problems with these analyses. As applied to the EU, for example (such as Garrett 1992; Moravcsik 1991), the functional regime theory of the international relations scholar (for example, Keohane 1984) downplays or ignores altogether the dynamics of intra-institutional, regime evolution (for critiques, see: Sandholtz 1996; Pierson 1998; Stone Sweet and Sandholtz 1998). In classic applications of principal-agent (p-a) models of delegation politics (see Kiewiet and McCubbins 1991), the analyst 'reads' backwards from the activity of the organization—the agent—to the control of the entity that has delegated rule-making power—the principal. This kind of analysis, too, has come under a great deal of constructive criticism (for example, Moe 1987; Pierson 1998; Pollack 1998; Stone Sweet and Caporaso 1998a), because it assumes that the institutional environment governing the p-a relationship is static, not malleable by the agent's activities, and continuously constituted by the principal's revealed preferences.

For their part, game theorists explicitly assume fixed rule structures, in order to build and test theories of strategic interaction. Institutionalization is largely conceived as the process through which stable, self-reproducing social systems—equilibria—are achieved (Calvert 1995). Game theorists admit that they have barely begun to theorize the dynamics of institutional change (Tsebelis 1990: Ch. 4), and that no satisfying means of endogenizing rule innovation within specific games yet exists (Vanberg 1998). Game theoretic models only begin when the analyst believes that rules are fixed and clear, and preferences are formed and known. Such models begin to break down if preferences are endogenized, or when actors begin to make sense of how rule evolution can alter interactions and outcomes (Stone Sweet 1998).

Most sociologically-oriented institutionalists (for example, March and Olsen 1989) and constructivists (for example, Giddens 1984; Onuf 1989; Sewell 1994) focus their analyses on dense and fully articulated social structures that are already in place. These structures are often understood to be in a dialectical relationship with individual identities. Sociological analysts emphasize that the production and reproduction of these structures always depends on agency, that is, on the actions of real actors. But these theories quickly reestablish the dominance of structures by arguing that, because the rule systems in place give meaning to action and frequently reflect the power differentials of actors, such structures are difficult to change by way of action. The tendency of social structures, once in place, is towards reproduction, not transformation. Explaining social change or the emergence of new institutions remains difficult for these theories, even where actors are taken seriously. Most theories that try to do so rely on a combination of political opportunities—that is, crises—and the ability of actors to construct new political 'frames' to organize identities and engage in collective action. Notwithstanding many crucial differences that separate them, both rational choice and more sociological institutionalists agree that the reproduction of particular ways of doing things is the 'normal' state of human community.

In this project, the institutionalization of new political space is our core concern, and the European Union is our empirical focus. Europe provides a politically important and intellectually challenging setting for engaging the topic, since the development of European policy arenas has been dramatic, and the construction of the EU's capacity to govern has taken diverse trajectories, with varied consequences. In the remainder of this chapter, we discuss how we conceive of actors, rules, and organizations. We argue that these are the constituent elements of any dynamic account of institutions. We advance some initial propositions concerning the relationships between these three basic units of analysis based on rationalist and sociological approaches to institutions. We then move from the abstract to the particular, discussing the major institutional characteristics that define the EU polity, and the likely consequences of these characteristics for the evolution of supranational governance. Last, we provide a summary and assessment of the substantive chapters to come.

It is important to be clear at the outset that this volume does not constitutes an 'anti-rationalist' project, any more than it is 'anti-constructivist'. We seek to build bridges and draw connections, by asking a specific set of theoretical questions, about what is going on in a specific set of empirical domains. Each member of the group sees actors' interests as fundamental to their engagement in producing the European Union. At the same time, we have all been drawn to the study of European integration and supranational governance because of its dynamic and multidimensional character. And, in our own individual research projects, each of us has been sensitive to how Europeanization has shaped the behaviour and interests of actors in fundamental ways.

2. Institutions and Institutionalization

For our purposes, an institution is a complex of rules and procedures that governs a given set of human interactions. We follow the now generally agreed upon distinction (see North 1990; 1995; Hall and Taylor 1996) between:

- rule systems: *institutions*, the macro level;
- groups of individuals, more or less formally constituted, who pursue a set of collective purposes: *organizations*, the meso level; and
- individuals who act with some purpose in mind: *actors*, the micro level.

Rules prescribe appropriate behaviour in particular settings and thus are collective attributes. Procedures are those rules that determine how actors and organizations make all other rules. At this level of abstraction, rules vary along three important dimensions:

1. *Precision of the prescription.* Rules vary in the specificity of the behavioural guidance they provide the individual or organization. In some situations, they

provide broad latitude for behaviour; in others, rules tightly prescribe highly specific actions.

2. *Formality*. Rule systems relevant to a given social setting range from relatively informal, customary standards of conduct to codified systems of law, and most rule systems embody complex—and scarcely understood—relationships between relatively formal and relatively informal rules. A rule can be said to be more formal to the extent that it has been made according to established procedures, by a body whose rule-making authority is explicitly recognized. Thus, certain elements of rule systems enable us to recognize the relative formality of others.

3. *Authority*. The obligatory or compulsory nature—what one might call the normative weight—of rules varies. Rules differ in the extent to which transgressions of them trigger social sanctions or other enforcement mechanisms. Sanctions—penalties attached to non-compliance with rules—also vary in their relative formality. Non-compliance with some rules carries no formal sanctions at all; in other cases, rules specify enforceable penalties for violation.

Institutions provide the structure in which social interaction—as opposed to random encounters—takes place; they tend to pattern behaviour in particular ways. Institutionalists offer varying accounts of how these regularities are produced. Neo-rationalists see institutions as structures of incentives and constraints, an opportunity set for collective action, to which rational individuals will adapt in predictable ways (Shepsle 1989; Tsebelis 1990). Sociologically inspired theorists suggest that institutions provide opportunities and more, affecting behaviour through shared cognitions, categories, paradigms, and beliefs (March and Olsen 1989), or even through 'performance scripts' that people internalize and enact (Burke 1969; Jepperson 1991). Both camps agree that institutions make purposive action possible by providing individuals with a framework of shared expectations. People can expect that the actions of others, within given contexts, will generally fit within certain ranges, and adapt their own behaviour accordingly.

Organizations are specific in time and place, with identifiable members and usually some kind of material presence—buildings, offices, records, assets. Most human activity takes place in or through organizations. Individuals construct organizations in order to pursue collective goals. In political spaces—see below—organizations are designed, among other things, to perform functions related to governance. By 'governance' we mean the authority to make, interpret, and enforce rules in a given social setting. Conceived in this way, political organizations are mechanisms of coordinating rule systems, on an ongoing basis, to the needs and purposes of those who live under them (Stone Sweet 1999). This function can be described, as Haas (1961) did in his discussion of the dynamics of regional integration, in terms of dispute resolution (see also March and Olsen 1989: Ch. 2). When organizations interpret (existing) or establish (new) rules to settle pre-existing disputes, they behave in a judicial mode. When they work to structure the social expectations and behaviour of individuals in the future, thereby seeking to reduce conflict in advance or to channel it down specific paths, they behave in a legislative mode. Often these two modes are blended. In any event, organizations are a critical locus of political life because of their inherent capacity to bridge the macro and the micro levels, by coordinating one with the other.

Individuals constitute the micro level. We recognize three models of individual action; the three differ in vital respects but are not mutually exclusive. That is, people behave in ways that fit all three models, in differing contexts. The first model is that of rational choice, which sees actors as seeking to maximize their own well-being, as they define it. Institutions establish the constraints within which actors choose their strategies. We expect that calculated rational action of this sort is ubiquitous, but rationalist approaches work best when institutions are known and interests are stable. In the EU context, it is useful to stipulate basic categories of actors and their underlying interests. By specifying broad types of interests, we identify the motives that draw different groups of actors into EU policy-making. How the EU resolves the tensions that inevitably arise between divergent interests may decisively shape subsequent interactions and institutional development.

We assume, for example, that bigger firms with cross-border business activities in the EU will come to Brussels in search of larger, liberalized markets. In general, they seek the removal of national barriers and in some cases the creation of common standards. Interest groups and associations frequently enter EU arenas in order to push for regulation of the European market in accordance with their conceptions of the larger social or public interest. Environmental, consumer, and women's groups thus seek rules that regulate the market in favour of environmental protection, consumer rights and safety, and gender equity. Member-State governments bring complex interests and goals into EU policy-making, but these include satisfying key domestic constituents or pressure groups so as to enhance their electoral prospects and domestic autonomy (see Moravcsik 1993). Finally, we assume that EU organizations will generally push to expand their own capacities and authority, and to increase the reach of supranational governance within and across policy domains.

The second model of action is grounded in a logic of appropriateness. That is, actors link specific actions to specific situations via rules that identify the range of suitable behaviour. Action is the result of matching situations to behaviours that fit them. The rules of appropriateness are transmitted through socialization (March and Olsen 1989), and through more formal, organizationally grounded processes that adapt rule structures to behaviour. Behaviours rooted in logics of appropriateness are bound to be ubiquitous as well; wherever people interact, they develop standards of acceptable conduct.

The third model focuses on a specific type of actor, namely, the skilled social actor. Skilled social actors are those who mobilize cooperation among others by generating and propagating cultural frames. Cultural frames are representations of collective problems and solutions that help other actors to link their own interests and identities to a collective purpose (Fligstein 1997*b*). Policy entrepreneurs are skilled social actors, and have to convince others that a set of policy decisions makes sense and can be construed as consistent with their basic interests or identities.

3. Institutional Change

Institutions are human artefacts; people make them. At the same time, institutions constitute community, shaping how individuals see themselves in relation to others, and providing a foundation for purposive action. Some contributors to this volume see the dynamic relationship between individuals and institutions as one of co-constitution, and institutionalization as a process that binds together, into a system of tight interdependence, the domain of social structure and the domain of agency (for example, Sandholtz 1998*a*; M. Smith 1998*b*; Stone Sweet 1999). Others sometimes prefer to begin with a more neo-rationalist orientation: at any given moment in time, one can observe individuals adopting the strategies that they believe will best enable them to maximize their utility given the relevant institutional constraints in place at that moment. One can then proceed to evaluate the consequences of this behaviour on subsequent decision-making (for example, Héritier 1997; Sandholtz 1998*b*; Stone Sweet and Caporaso 1998*a*).

We see no reason to impose one style of analysis. The participants in this group agree that how, or whether, one cuts into the feedback loops that connect institutions, organizations, and actors should depend not on *a priori* theoretical commitments, but on what one seeks to explain. Further, each of us has typically focused empirical attention on the interaction between intentional action—of lobbies, political parties, policy entrepreneurs, and so on—and the work of governmental organizations—of the Commission, the Court, governments, national parliaments, and so on—within policy processes broadly conceived. Put more abstractly, this project seeks to understand the complex processes through which rules and social interaction, structure and agency, are coordinated over time.

Our focus on institutional evolution and change nevertheless raises questions that most institutionalist theories are not well equipped to address. The more we design our research to respond directly to questions posed by the institutionalization of Europe, the more we will likely be pushed to move beyond traditional forms of analysis. This difficulty accepted, we need to take cognizance of those ideas about institutional change that have been offered. We see four families of approaches, families that are distinguished from each other by their relative emphasis on common factors, and not necessarily by their respective explanatory structures. That is to say, these propositions are not 'rival' explanations so much as complementary approaches to similar phenomena. At this point, we survey these materials only in their most abstract form. In the rest of the chapter, we will connect some of these ideas to the group's agenda.

The first approach asserts that institutions change as a function of how organizations and individuals respond to exogenous changes or shocks. A dramatic change in relative prices, for example, can change people's tastes and therefore destabilize the underlying basis of stability (North 1990). The process through which people adapt to changes in the relative costs of doing things, especially if new behaviours are then developed and locked in, itself constitutes a process of institutional evolution. Organization theorists have noted the capacity of external shocks and perceptions of crisis to alter how organizational performance is evaluated and to weaken standard routines in place (Fligstein 1991). Such perceptions may also provoke outsiders to search for organizational alternatives, thus provoking inter-organizational competition for survival and incremental evolution in structure (Hannan and Freeman 1984; North 1995). Of course, in explaining the specific forms taken by the responses to shocks and crises, the analyst cannot avoid ideational and discursive factors. Changes in the external environment seldom have a clear, self-evident meaning; actors seek ways to interpret and understand crises and shocks. One must determine what the problem is before one can begin to assess alternative responses to it. Shocks and crises sometimes trigger a search for new models, theories, or policy innovations (Sandholtz 1992). Actors will therefore be engaged in a competition of ideas, as they seek to persuade others that their understanding of the problem, even if self-interested, is the most accurate, and that their policy models are therefore the most appropriate.

A second approach sees rule innovation as endogenous to politics that take place within existing spaces of governance. As interactions within a given policy arena increase, for example, actors may reach the limits of existing rules, and seek new ones. For instance, as the EU generates an increasing volume of rules, through legislation and jurisprudence, and as it expands its authority to new domains, tensions between policy domains become increasingly likely. In fact, there has often been little coordination in constructing EU domains. Separate policy domains may have emerged as responses to separate sets of societal demands, and may be placed on quite different legal bases. As integration proceeds, tensions between domains are to be expected. Given the principle that goods shall move freely throughout the Union, for example, how far can the EU legislator go in regulating health and safety standards? Actors within domains in tension may be unable to conduct their activities until the contradictions have been resolved, which entails further clarification and elaboration of the rules. Or, as actors pursue their own policy goals, they may generate conflicts about the meaning of existing procedures, such as those that govern decision-making, access, and participation, in the hopes that the resolution of such disputes will lead to new, or revised, rules of the game. The rules and procedures of the EU, for instance, constitute the framework of constraints and opportunities for actors who want to enhance their social, economic, or political positions. Self-interested actors will exploit what they can in EU rules and arenas—for example, by taking their concerns to the Commission, the Court, the Parliament, and urging them to act. The struggle to influence policy outcomes will inevitably lead to the clarification and modification of existing rules and to the generation of new ones.

These dynamics are well-known to students of judicial and administrative rule-making (Shapiro 1988; Stone Sweet 1999), but the point has also been taken up by certain brands of new institutionalism to explain behaviour within complex organizations (for example, March and Olsen 1989). In any case, actors pursuing their interests within an institutionalized setting are not just competing on the basis of relative powers or access to resources. They are forced also to battle, in self-interested ways, over the meaning of rules and over the most appropriate ways to resolve conflicts among rules. Again, these contests involve the strategic deployment of ideas and persuasion.

A third approach to institutional change focuses on relationships at the meso level, between organizations, as they develop within a specific kind of environment called an 'organizational field'. Organizational fields are constituted by linkages, more or less institutionalized, between those actors and organizations that regularly interact with each other within specific kinds of social processes. The argument is that institutional change is partly brought about by the diffusion of organizational repertoires of behaviour and models of action (Fligstein 1991; Levitt and March 1988). In the literature (DiMaggio and Powell 1983; 1991), three mechanisms of such change have been identified: coercive—for example, the rules of the game change in one arena as a result of rule change in another; mimetic—for example, innovation results from one organization copying the ways of doing things in place in a more successful organization; and normative—for example, change occurs with the consolidation of the social power of certain types of knowledge-based elites. With mimetic and normative mechanisms at least, what is being transferred from one organization to another are models, principles, and truth claims. In that sense, skill in the manipulation of ideas and discourses will be crucial in the actual processes by which the transfers take place.

A fourth approach pays attention to the effects of 'skilled action', or policy entrepreneurship, on the part of specific actors. Skilled actors are those who find ways to induce cooperation amongst disparate individuals or groups by helping them to form stable conceptions of roles and identity (Fligstein, forthcoming). Institutional entrepreneurs respond to questions of group membership, procedures for participation, and how issues are to be approached. They seek to construct, or revise, cultural—or 'policy'—frames, collectively held sets of meanings, that (1) engage other actors and define new relationships between them, and (2) chart courses of action that make sense to this group and to others (Glenn 1999; Snow and Benford 1988; Tarrow 1998). Crises and breakdowns within organizations and institutions frequently provide skilled social actors the opportunity to generate and sell new frames, to redefine the grounds for cooperation. The policy entrepreneur generates and attempts to propagate ideas that will define problems and solutions in ways that other actors find convincing and useful. To the extent that such actors are successful at constructing new frames, we can expect to find changes at the micro-level that will provoke evolution at the meso and the macro levels.

We see these approaches as sharing some basic assumptions. First, institutions provide organizations and individuals with opportunities for purposive action. Second, organizations often know that they are in competitive environments, and know that their survival and prosperity may partly depend on how they perform their tasks and achieve their goals—one basis of their legitimacy. Third, 'strategic' actors go to organizations because they know that organizations are privileged sites of institutional innovation, not least because one of the social functions of organizations is to help adapt rules to practice. Generally, institutional evolution results from relationships that develop among three units of analysis—actors, organizations, and institutions—over time.

We also suggest that the concepts of skilled social actors and framing can usefully link the four approaches. Skilled social actors are crucial to institutional change because of their ability to generate or manipulate frames that make sense of institutional or policy problems and offer persuasive solutions. Frames can help mobilize cooperation among diverse actors by linking their interests and identities to a set of ideas—symbols, theories, models—that allow for further institutional development. We see skilled action, and sometimes new frames, in many situations, such as when the Commission produces new procedures to enable interest groups to participate in rule-making processes, the Court finds principles of mutual recognition in the Rome Treaty, the prime minister of a Member State government brokers a compromise in the European Council, thus breaking a long-standing deadlock, or the recommendations of a group of European central bankers focuses deliberations on the economic and monetary union (EMU).

4. Social and Political Space

Social spaces are arenas, or recurrent situations, wherein actors orient their actions to one another repeatedly. We call a social space 'institutionalized' when there exists a widely shared system of rules and procedures to define who actors are, how they make sense of each other's actions, and what types of action are possible. Institutionalization is the process by which a social space emerges and evolves. It is important to emphasize that a social space can be fully institutionalized, despite the fact that it has not developed formal and binding rules. As game theorists have it—the literature on the folk theorem in repeated games—in continuous interactions among individuals, within a unidimensional issue-space, institutionalization and the achievement of Nash equilibrium are one and the same thing. Rules and behaviour mutually reinforce each other, and further clarification of the rules, or the development of third party enforcement, is not needed (Fudenberg and Levine 1986; Kandori 1992; Calvert 1995). Put in different terms, in social settings where interactions are almost always face-to-face, and in which a system of informal norms is robust, well-known, and deeply-embedded, there is no social logic for movement to higher levels of formality and authority. Informal norms are precise enough and informal sanctions, like exclusion or banishment, are effective enough to enable communities to reproduce themselves (see Ellickson 1991; Collier 1973; Stone Sweet 1999). In Europe, the main outcome has generally been more rules—of greater precision and authority—more procedures, and more formal sanctions, discussed below. Along with these rules, of course, there has been the development of informal understandings within supranational policy domains.

Political spaces are social spaces wherein actors meet to make, apply, interpret, and enforce rules; they are thus sites of collective governance. They are distinguishable from other kinds of social spaces in that their purpose is to enable actors to produce rules—policy—governing subsequent interactions involving people connected to the political space, either by virtue of citizenship—which can be 'functional' in the sense that it implies belonging to a particular collectivity or engagement in a particular activity—or by presence in a geographical territory. The 'market' for corporate control, or a hobby group that collects mushrooms, are two examples of social spaces where actors meet to engage in actions under a set of rules. In these arenas, rules, procedures, and understandings usually build up over time. Actors will come to know their places in the system and interactions will proceed according to the rules of the game. But the participants in either of these spaces do not claim the right to make rules for actors in all other social spaces. Political spaces are characterized by having formalized structures and procedures that define how authoritative rules are to be created and enforced. They give actors formal 'roles' in the political process and define how that process produces outcomes.

5. Institutions and Power

Institutions define arenas, but in doing so they privilege some actors over others. Institutionalization is therefore never neutral: it is partly a process by which powerful actors seek to shape the rules of the game in their favour. The construction and development of institutions therefore has consequences for who will accumulate wealth and influence, and who will not. Actors deploy whatever forms of power they possess in order both to obtain policy outcomes they prefer and to shape the institutions themselves.

Powerful actors seek to establish rules that favour their own interests. But a system of rules can constrain as well as empower actors. Often rules reflect compromises between actors such that the powerful do not always get their own way. Once institutions—rules and procedures—are in place, they can be exploited or developed in ways that the founding powers did not foresee and cannot control. Other actors—including agencies and especially courts—apply, interpret, and clarify the rules in ways that alter the context for subsequent action. Thus, in a rule-of-law system such as the EC has become, powerful actors cannot simply do what they want. They, like other actors, must frame their claims in terms of existing laws, as these have been elaborated and interpreted by other agents. In the courts, for example, the objectively weaker party frequently wins because the ability to persuade others that one's claims are valid on the basis of the law does not depend just on the possession of power resources. Furthermore, institutions determine which political resources can be used, where, when, how, and by whom. In other words, power resources are not simply attributes of individuals; they are attributes of social—or institutional—structures. In order to understand the exercise of power, we argue, one must understand the institutional environment in which power operates.

In the EU, supranational political spaces produce authoritative rules that apply to certain kinds of actors and transactions—mostly economic—across and within national borders, and certain kinds of regulatory practices, for example, environmental and consumer protection. The procedures through which they do so now typically provide for the participation of the nation states, firms, and representatives of groups who feel that they will be most affected by the deliberations. Not surprisingly, it has been repeatedly found that these groups, along with representatives of the Member-State governments, matter most in these deliberations (for example, the chapters in Wallace and Young 1997).

6. Rule-making and Legitimacy

The linked problems of sovereignty and legitimacy have haunted political spaces since their inception in ancient Greece. One core attribute of the Westphalian state is the claimed authority to make and enforce all of the rules in a given territory. This claim has been resisted, and the degree to which any state has actually been able to make it stick has been relative (Krasner 1989). Legitimate governance implies that those who are governed believe that the procedures by which rules are generated are accepted or justified. To the extent that the governed do so, they will consider those rules to be binding, even if they dislike the content of some rules produced.

The problem for the EU, of course, is that most of the actors for whom such collective governance may have effects—that is, EU citizens—are not part of the rule-making process. Many, if not most, EU policies and rules are the product of negotiations among representatives of the states, the Commission, and interest groups. These negotiations can seem quite closed, even secret, especially when compared with domestic policy-making processes that are reasonably transparent, based as they are on electoral competition and parliamentary debate. Although public opinion studies have shown that citizens desire and expect the EU, not the nation state, to regulate certain kinds of activities (Dalton and Eichenberg 1998), governments nevertheless sometimes find it difficult to explain why certain kinds of decisions are being made at the

European level. Perhaps the most prominent recent example of this difficulty was the Maastricht Treaty provisions on EMU. In a number of Member States, notably Denmark, France, and Germany, large segments of the public reacted with suspicion and hostility to an agreement that was seen as a product of closed-door elite bargaining. Of course, the ratification process invoked traditional domestic procedures for expressing, or manufacturing, assent. Even so, the EMU debates called out the ever-present question of legitimacy: the procedures that led to the EMU agreement clearly did not enjoy the same legitimacy among publics that national policy-making did.

Naturally, many citizens attach fundamental legitimacy to national modes of governance, that is, policy-making through national parliaments and elected representatives. In Europe, people tend to see domestic modes of governance as fundamentally legitimate because they involve procedures that are known and accepted, and in which all citizens can in principle participate. In polities where legitimacy is broadly shared and deeply ingrained, people accept policy outcomes with which they disagree because they accept the established process that produced those outcomes. Unfavourable policies do not lead citizens to conclude that they should withdraw from or work to overthrow the regime. By comparison, policy-making at the EU level in working groups, committees, the Court, or even inter-state summits and conferences seems more opaque and less accessible.

Ordinary citizens feel that they have fewer chances to influence policy debates, or to express agreement or disagreement at the EU level compared with national levels of government. To the extent that legitimacy stems from the citizen's belief that she has a chance to influence the policy process, to express assent or disapproval, the EU at present can generate at best a thin or second-hand legitimacy. EU legitimacy is thin because although groups that exercise a voice in policy-making at the Commission, the Parliament, or the Court may thereby accept the process as legitimate, the broader populace may not feel that it has a voice. The EU may enjoy a second-hand legitimacy for the citizens of the Member States in that they are represented in Union deliberations through their elected governments.

It is this peculiar dynamic, the pooling of sovereignty at the Brussels level and the representation of self-interested parties in Brussels and Luxembourg in the construction of new rules, that is at the heart of present legitimacy debates. Yet it is exactly this dynamic that allows the Brussels complex to work in a legitimate way, at least from the perspective of governments and the organized interests who are most directly affected by EU rule-making.

Institutional change may proceed from perceived breakdowns in legitimacy, and also tends to provoke new problems in search of solutions. Institutionalists have always, at least implicitly, recognized the legitimacy problems associated with institutional evolution. Skilled social actors, for example, build into their cultural frames auto-legitimizing elements, to the effect that a group or organization ought to do things differently because it will better represent 'who we are', or produce better outcomes with fewer trade-offs in other, economic or symbolic-cultural, areas . Those who have studied the process through which new 'policy frames'—or, more generally, those ideas embedded in discourse generated among knowledge-based elites or epistemic communities—come to replace older ones within a specific policy arena (for example, Hall 1992; Mazey and Richardson 1998; MacNamara 1998) refer to the wider, social legitimacy of the 'winning' frame relative to rivals. When the European Court revises the Treaty of Rome—changing the rules of the game in the EC—in a direction that benefits some and hurts others, the judges give reasons for their decision, laying down principles that will guide litigation and their own decision-making in the future. Case law is itself a rule-oriented, and therefore formal, response to legitimacy problems generated by rule-innovation. 'Mimetic' and 'normative' mechanisms of organizational change identified by sociologists (DiMaggio and Powell 1983; 1991; see also Meyer and Rowan 1977) are explicitly animated by an organization's quest for legitimacy.

7. Explaining Institutional Change in the EU

One of the central puzzles of the EU is why supranational governance has expanded at all. Even if the integration project were narrowly restricted to the construction of a common market, huge and potentially insurmountable obstacles would still be confronted. We mention three of these here. First, the Rome Treaty is a vague document, like many constitutions, in that it declares the high aspirations of the Member States, and fixes mundane organizational procedures, but barely touches on the precise modalities of achieving market integration. With few exceptions, the rules enable actors to take certain kinds of decisions but leave the contents of decisions to future rule-makers. In the 1960s, as in successive decades, it has not always been clear what elements of agreement or rules would be necessary to promote market integration. The creation of a free trade area—the removal of tariffs and quotas—might have been the end point of a market integration project. The fact that maternity leave, environmental protection, and monetary union, to mention a few policy domains, are now also considered to be part of that project shows how fundamental is the political determination of what constitutes the central mission of supranational governance. Somehow, actors have constructed supranational governance creatively, giving life and agency to the black-letter provisions of treaty law.

Second, for much of the history of the EU, the formal decision-making rules for adopting legislation have been relatively restrictive, requiring unanimity for most important initiatives. Given that policy-making styles differ across nation states and the interests of governments on an issue-by-issue basis contradict one another as frequently as they line up, we might expect the Brussels complex to be primarily a site of deadlock and 'joint decision traps' (Scharpf 1988). But inertia and anomie have not been the most prevalent outcomes of integration. Instead, the EU has become a powerful regulatory state. Somehow, deadlocks have been avoided or broken, and supranational competences to govern have, almost continuously, expanded.

Third, any particular elaboration of an EU rule or regulatory capacity is likely to engender societal supporters and opponents. Firms and industries are differentially dispersed across Europe; and their national, European, or global market orientation varies as well. Thus, the interests of business do not neatly line up. Governments, to the degree that they are responsive to different fractions of business, can find themselves not being able to form policies because of these contradictory interests. Like business, public interest groups may oppose replacing national with 'harmonized', European rules, reinforcing whatever government opposition may exist. The treaties make no provision for the consultation of interest groups, yet interest groups have been integrated into policy processes in diverse ways. Somehow, a wide range of societal groups have been induced to orient their activities to arenas organized by supranational rules and procedures.

Each of these problems was overcome, partly because actors have taken the elements of the Treaty and turned them into arenas for governance. But it also required constructing a whole set of worlds and meanings, organizations, and practices. Actors come into situations with some conception of interest, but the problem of creating institutions from documents turns on actors becoming a member of a 'new' world. If one considers how daunting the real task of cooperation across states and their conflicting groups is, one could easily conclude that an organization like the European Union would be doomed to failure.

Yet we know that supranational spaces have evolved and that they have enabled actors to overcome their political differences and cooperate. Moreover, they have created a set of understandings, both formal and informal, that allow cooperation to continue to expand. At the core of all of this is the sense that actors have not just been rational but have behaved strategically in the broadest sense of the term. They have taken advantage of political opportunities to create rules, procedures, and practices that reflect not just particular interests of government or business. That is, they have created general institutions to govern European space.

8. Research Questions and Strategies

Implicit in our discussion of institutions and institutionalization so far is the idea of path-dependence, and therefore a particular notion of causality. For a given set of conditions, it is not always possible to predict outcomes, only that the outcomes that do emerge will be powerfully conditioned by the process through which they were generated (Arthur 1990). We know that action is easiest to predict in stable institutional domains where constraints are fixed, meanings are collectively understood, and actors' preferences and resources are well known. Actors will defend their interests and recognize the limits on their capacities to do so. But in less institutionalized domains, or in domains where institutions are just forming or in flux, the problem of action is more difficult, and paths that institutionalization will take may just be forming. When an institutional or organizational solution to a particular problem emerges and stabilizes into accepted rules and procedures, it will shape subsequent expectations, interactions, and institutional innovation. Once such developments come to follow a specific track, shifting to another track will be increasingly difficult, for reasons that have been theorized (North 1990; Pierson 2000; Stone Sweet and Sandholtz 1998: 22–4). Unravelling institutions, let alone starting over again, can be costly or impossible to the extent that actors have invested resources, and adapted their routines, expectations, and relationships with one another, in step with how institutional arrangements have evolved.

The path-dependent nature of institutions inevitably poses difficult questions bearing on method and research design. This project did not settle on one set of methods, nor did it impose a specific design. Instead, the group elaborated a set of basic, *a priori*, orientations to the problem of institutionalization, derived largely from institutionalist theory, and a set of questions that we left to the members of the group to answer in their own way. In the discussion that follows, we briefly lay out the group's perspectives on two general issues: (1) how new institutional arenas of governance are likely to emerge and develop; and (2) how the extent of institutionalization of any arena or organized field ought to be evaluated.

9. Institutional Innovation

The creation of new political arenas is innovation. It means establishing rules and procedures where none existed before, and it means adapting them, periodically or on a relatively continuous basis. Though the products of innovation are at least partially unpredictable from initial conditions, it is still possible to construct causal, process-oriented, explanations of institutionalization. In order to do so, we suggest, explanations must contain a number of crucial elements. The analyst must identify the relevant actors in terms of their underlying interests and motivations—the micro level. We earlier sketched broad categories and some of their fundamental interests in EU policy-making. These descriptions can be useful as a starting point, but analyses of specific domains need to specify more carefully the actors and interests in play in that area. Further, the analyst must indicate why actors may support or oppose institutional innovation, in terms of the perceived function of the existing institution in place or in terms of perceived problems that are taken to demand institutional solutions.

Most theories of the formation of new fields or the transformation of existing fields start with some conception of crisis or dysfunctionality; the literature on the Single European Act (SEA) provides good examples (Moravscik 1991; Fligstein and Mara-Drita 1996; Sandholtz and Zysman 1989). Exogenous shocks that originate outside of the policy space may produce the perception that change is needed. Perceived crises can also be caused by actions, whether intended or unintended, originating in other policy spaces, or from fields located entirely outside of existing political spaces. Such events can have the effect of bringing new groups or coalitions of groups together, for a common purpose: to design a new political space to respond to the shock. In already existing policy spaces, such shocks can unhinge the perceived efficacy or legitimacy of existing sets of rules and procedures governing interactions. Groups may begin to consider renewing their institution-building efforts.

Institutional-building can also be endogenous to 'normal' politics within particular policy spaces. Groups may become convinced that the current rules as they are being applied need clarification, or extension to new or novel situations. These types of innovations can be distinguished from the more normal politics of policy spaces because they focus on rewriting the rules that guide interaction. If successful, the result is a shift in the rules by which the policy space is constituted, as well as a shift in the goals of that arena. In research on European integration, we now have a small pile of studies that demonstrate the extent to which actors can successfully provoke profound institutional change by exploiting existing EU rules, procedures, and access points (for example: Héritier 1997, 1999; O'Reilly and Stone Sweet 1998; Stone Sweet and Brunell 1998a; Mazey and Richardson 1998; Sandholtz 1998b).

Spaces rarely emerge and institutionalize without a concomitant development of organizations. Accordingly, the analysis should identify the state of development of the relevant organizations and networks—meso level factors. Ongoing interactions between EU organizations and interest groups constitute most of the action of day-to-day politics. Whether we call them policy communities or networks, they produce rules.

In addition, the analyst must identify the raw materials—existing rules, procedures, and organizational forms—that could be accessed by those who construct new institutional spaces—the macro level. Where in the institutional structure do actors seek to build new spaces? Are there existing norms, procedures, practices, and organizational forms that could be borrowed from other settings? We can take some cues in this respect from the 'new institutionalism' in organizational theory in sociology (Powell and DiMaggio 1991). Institutional forms tend to diffuse, by way of mimetic, coercive, or normative mechanisms. The underlying problem facing actors is to determine which course of action makes sense in a particular situation, given existing institutions. In our context, this approach helps us to begin to understand where actors constructing new policy spaces look for rules to govern their interactions. One way that institution-building episodes proceed is when actors decide to mimic what they perceive to be successful political models, borrowing elements that have proved useful in other institution-building projects. Organizational actors may also be sufficiently constrained by external forces that they must choose to organize in a particular way across policy spaces. Finally, professional experts of various kinds can be used to tell actors how to organize themselves and write rules.

Finally, the analysis should identify the innovators, or those individuals who can persuade a sufficient number of relevant actors to support a set of institutional changes. Innovators take opportunities and mechanisms that are present in existing institutions and combine them, sometimes with elements from other institutional contexts, in new ways. They then provide new frames, or manipulate existing ones, in order to persuade others that the innovations suit their interests and are normatively appropriate. In social science literatures, the concepts of 'policy entrepreneurs' and 'skilled social actors' refer to those who perform these functions.

This orientation may need a more explicit defence. In standard game-theoretic approaches, institutions comprise the equilibrium outcome of a given configuration of (fixed) rules and preferences. Not only do such approaches almost always lead to a static view of institutions, they are also deterministic, if not teleological: institution-building episodes could not have turned out any other way. It may be the case that some episodes have this quality, but this is not the only way in which institutional design and innovation occur. Existing rules are not always unambiguous, and actor preferences are not always clear or stable. Or prior rules and conceptions of interest may offer inadequate guidance for action in the face of problems that are new in kind or magnitude. Even where rules and preferences are clear and stable, and innovation is minimal, and even when many of the building blocks of institutional *bricolage* already exist, they can be put together in different ways, as institutions must be adapted to the specific context and substantive issue area in which they are being put to use.

Actors with social skill work to construct the identities and interests of collectivities, and thus work to define the social space. In any particular situation, they have to link their current conception of those identities and interests to the concrete issue at hand. Since identities and interests are abstract, they are at least partially open to spin and interpretation. This gives leaders some leeway when it comes to determining which groups should be brought into discussions about how to organize a particular policy arena.

Skilled actors use cultural frames because they provide narratives that help them articulate what the collective interest will be in a particular situation. Such frames may be merely 'window dressing' for what leaders want to do. But to the extent that they are important to justifying action, maintaining unity within existing groups, resolving disputes real and potential, and bringing a new groups together, we need to take them seriously. Interests, conceptions of interest, and discourses about how things ought to be done become embedded in organized settings in this way. Leaders who face crises that seem to require new institution-building need to be able to justify their participation in the new arrangements to the members of their groups. The use of framing is a powerful tool to do this.

10. Assessing Institutionalization

So far, we have referred to European political space as a complex of policy arenas, structured by rules and managed by EU organizations. We view European political space as becoming more institutionalized as the capacity of European organizations to govern is consolidated. Given our theoretical priorities, we can be clear about the nature and scope of institutionalization as a dependent variable, which varies across policy domains and across time in any single domain. Generally, as institutionalization proceeds in any supranational arena, we expect that (1) procedures governing the interactions that take place in that arena will be generated and formalized; (2) private actors and groups will orient their lobby activities to the EU level; and (3) pressures will mount to co-ordinate what goes on in that arena with what goes on in others, at the national or supranational level. Although we do not rule out the possibility that 'de-institutionalization' can occur or that institutionalization in Europe can accommodate a great deal of deregulation and decentralized administration, we are sceptical of roll-back (see also Fligstein and Stone Sweet, this volume).

There are a number of reasons why institutionalization in Europe has generally meant more rules, more procedures, and more formality. One central mission of the EU is to provoke and sustain transnational exchange relationships; yet impersonal exchange, across jurisdictional boundaries, is problematic for reasons that institutionalists have explored at some length (see Greif 1989; 1993; North 1990; Stone Sweet 1999; Stone Sweet and Brunell 1998a). The EU's success has depended heavily on the extent to which it could develop its own organizational capacity to guarantee property rights, enforce competition rules, and adjudicate EU law claims. The development of this capacity has indeed constituted a European space, one in which EU organizations, private actors, and national public officials interact to determine, implement, and enforce EU law. The development of a rule of law system for Europe constitutes, by definition, profound institutionalization in a formal direction.

Second, the EU has moved into regulatory rule-making as the common market has been consolidated (Fligstein and McNichol 1998; Majone 1993). One striking feature of EU politics is the high degree to which EU organizations govern by promulgating rules—directives, regulations, and decisions—and drawing other actors into deliberative procedures—comitology processes and consultation. The functions of administering and enforcing EU rules are largely left to various Member-State authorities, although these functions are partially supervised by EU organizations. Because modes of supranational governance tend to be heavily rule-oriented, legalistic, and demanding of coordination among relatively autonomous governmental entities, they are also expansionary and potentially subversive of national practices. Indeed, as specific modes of governance are consolidated within European policy arenas, actors operating at regional, national, and sub-national levels tend to be pulled into the kinds of rule-making practices and discourses under way in European spaces (see Le Galès, this volume).

Third, integration processes have consistently produced powerful spillover effects, and these have eventually implicated even core aspects of state sovereignty. Foreign policy, policing, and welfare state policies may have remained largely outside of the jurisdiction of the EU until recently, and their development within the EU has been modest compared with other policy domains. Yet it is no longer evident, if it ever was, that there are any 'natural', functional limits to the integration project. The desire to complete the single market and to dismantle border controls raised the issue of controlling illegal aliens and activities, leading governments to propose more cooperation on policing issues (see Turnbull and Sandholtz, this volume). Similarly, free movement of labour has brought issues of social welfare on to the bargaining table. In the security area, the increasingly frequent interaction and cooperation among government ministries, both through the Brussels complex and on a direct face-to-face basis, has encouraged cooperation of other ministers (M. Smith 1998*b* and this volume).

Assessing the extent of institutionalization, we suggest, requires addressing the following sets of questions.

1. Exactly what is being or has been institutionalized? Is it an arena of governance, a mode or technique of governance, a set of linked processes, or new policy ideas, networks of associations, or cultures of technical or scientized expertise?

2. Degrees of institutionalization can be assessed in several—overlapping—ways. First, to what extent are the processes in question likely to be reversed or rolled-back? The more institutionalized the arena or mode of governance or process, the less likely it is that roll-back will occur, and the greater the collective action problem facing those actors who would wish to reverse institutionalization. Second, to what extent are the modes of governance stable, that is, likely to reproduce themselves over time? Institutionalization implies not only the emergence but the stability of forms. Third, how much of the future is determined by what has been decided in the past? The more past decisions tend to structure future ones, the more an arena or mode of governance can be described as institutionalized.

3. Through what mechanisms or processes has institutionalization taken place? The analyst should be as clear and precise as possible about the logic of action—micro-foundations—proposed, and the asserted relationship between this logic of action and the social environment—meso- and macro-foundations—in which it takes place. How much dynamic adjustment has taken place? The extent to which actors, public and private, come to adjust their expectations, decision-making, and investments to the arena or mode of governance under study, as it develops, is a measure of institutionalization.

11. Overview of the Book

The chapters of the book form three groups. The first set addresses general processes of institutionalization in the European Union. Neil Fligstein's and

Alec Sweet's chapter takes the most macro perspective on institutionalization in the book. The chapter, which builds on the theoretical materials developed in *European Integration and Supranational Governance*, examines the extent to which linkages between rule-making, dispute resolution, and different forms of transnational activity have created a dynamic, inherently expansionary system. The authors present comprehensive data on trading, legislating, litigating, and lobbying within the context of the Treaty of Rome. After a slow start, these activities began to grow steadily; after the Single European Act, they exploded. Econometric techniques are used to test hypotheses about how these four processes are interconnected. The analysis shows that a complex set of feedback loops binds these processes together in a self-reinforcing system that broadly determines the course of integration.

Adrienne Héritier's chapter concerns decision-making in the EU, given the ever-present threat of deadlock. She begins with the observation that the formal institutional structure of the European Union, combined with the diversity of Member States' interests, should regularly lead to an impasse in decision-making in the Council of Ministers. She argues that a set of informal tactics, serving to facilitate rule-making, has evolved to deal with this problem. First, the Court or the Commission may enact straightforward changes in the guise of interstitial rule-making through interpretation. These changes tend to extend EU rules, such as secondary legislation, in ways that were previously not foreseen or intended. Second, the Commission may develop, explicitly or implicitly, new soft or informal institutions that share information with, and monitor, mobilize, or network lobby groups. Again, the goal is often to expand EU competences and activity. Third, all EU officials may use more covert means to overcome formal institutional obstacles to decision-making and to attain agreements. For example, actors may seek to pre-commit others to policy decisions or procedures the implications of which are not spelt out in advance. Planned or ongoing changes are often concealed from the general public. Issues are re-labelled or re-contextualized in order to embed them in a different choice situation, in order to overcome resistance and deadlock. Héritier provides a wealth of examples of initiatives that were initially blocked by the Council, but eventually became EU law and policy.

Sonia Mazey's and Jeremy Richardson's paper explores the relationship between the European Commission and the various lobbying groups in Brussels. Mazey and Richardson argue that there is now a 'mature' institutionalized policy-making style governing interactions between the Commission and interest groups. The authors catalogue the formal and informal rules by which the Commission receives and seeks to organize lobbyist's views, and interest groups influence the Commission's development of legislative proposals. There has been a steady evolution of some formal, but more often informal, rules and procedures for lobbying organizations. These include: willingness to participate in early discussions; presenting rational/technical arguments based on reliable data; viewing European policy as an opportunity, not a threat;

formulating European, not national or particularistic, solutions; understanding the problems and perspectives of other stakeholders in the process; and investing in the entire policy-making process. The development of a stable system of interest group representation for the EU, sited in Brussels, impinges heavily not only on policy processes and outcomes, but on how democracy in the EU will be conceived and debated.

A second set of chapters explores how specific European policy spaces have emerged, mutated, and stabilized over time through what we called (see above) 'endogenous' processes of institutionalization. In these processes, the interactions of specific actors, pursuing specific interests within European policy space, generated problems of governance that came to be resolved by increasingly formal exercises of interpretation, resulting in the 'hardening' of EU law. Indeed, these three chapters demonstrate the extraordinary extent to which the European polity has been 'judicialized'.

Martin Shapiro examines one of the least visible or understudied, but most important, outcomes of integration: the development of an administrative law for the EU. As positive integration came to constitute a central priority for the EU's organizations, the Commission's administrative responsibilities and capacities multiplied. The Commission is expected not only to monitor and enforce compliance with an increasingly dense and technical body of supranational rules, but to determine how that law is to be applied to specific individuals and situations. It could not perform either task without appropriating a great deal of discretionary authority. Shapiro argues that, in Western democracies, the problem of controlling rising administrative discretion has inevitably been felt, and has typically been dealt with through the development of judicial mechanisms. Using the American experience as a comparative backdrop, he shows that once judges require that administrators furnish formal justifications for their actions, the judicial review of the 'reasonableness' of administrative acts follows. Shapiro then traces how these and other forms of judicial control of the EU's administrative acts developed through litigation and the rule-making of the ECJ and the Court of First Instance, despite the absence of explicit Treaty provision. Today, the basic foundations of EU administrative law are in place, and routinely impact on the day-to-day work of EU officials.

Rachel Cichowski's chapter explains how adjudication transformed the principle of 'equal pay for equal work' between men and women contained in Art. 119 of the Rome Treaty. Until 1976, the provision simply expressed one part of an intergovernmental bargain, and exerted no practical legal effects. In that year, however, the ECJ ruled that the provision bestowed upon women rights that national law must protect, through national courts if necessary. A rising tide of litigation in the area followed, leading the Court to construct Art. 119 as a general right for women to be free of discrimination in the workplace, notably as regards maternity issues and benefits. Cichowski shows: that a symbiotic relationship between litigant networks and the Court has developed; that this relationship has served to sustain an ongoing process of revising the Treaty article; and that these revisions have provoked not only a steady stream of litigation, but the continuous adaptation of national and supranational regimes to the evolving dictates of the Court's case law. As important, her analyses of the data on litigation in the area demonstrate that the preferences of national governments have not effectively constrained the Court's rule-making, even when these preferences have been clearly expressed.

In his chapter, Patrick Le Galès examines how tensions that develop between supranational and national governance structures are resolved, given institutionalization taking place at the European level. Focusing on two national policy domains—state aids and regional development—Le Galès explains how, since the mid-1980's, EU officials have succeeded in inducing their French counterparts to alter legislation and administrative practices once assumed to be fundamentally immune to external influence. The chapter thus provides a valuable and much-needed account of what is increasingly referred to as the Europeanization of the nation state. In his view, Europeanization took place in an series of 'rounds' that have followed a common sequence: disagreement about the nature and scope of EU rules in national regimes; open contestation between supranational and national officials; the fixing of a new or clarified rule on the part of EU officials; and, finally, the grudging acceptance of the rule by the French. After each round, new patterns of French resistance emerge. But the rules of the game governing these interactions are fixed by the results of previous rounds, and come to be more or less taken by granted by actors at both levels. The overall process, Le Galès argues, tends to favour the expansion and diffusion of EU modes of governance, and the weakening of specifically national modes.

The third group of chapters shares a concern with processes of institutional innovation, that is, the creation of new policy spaces. The substantive domains addressed cover the new institutional spaces created by the Treaty on European Union: monetary union, common foreign and security policy, and justice and home affairs. Intergovernmental bargains established each of these spaces but, the authors show, pre-existing rules, procedures, and shared understandings shaped these bargains, and structured subsequent, endogenous, institutional reform.

Kate McNamara analyzes the creation and development of 'rules governing the organizational form and the policy content' of the European Central Bank. The establishment of the ECB and the launching of the Euro constitute an extraordinary innovation, one that opens and organizes a new institutional space in Europe. McNamara assesses the ECB system in the light of three broad theoretical approaches emphasizing, respectively, power politics, institutions as rational solutions to collective problems, and pre-existing normative structures. She finds that the power politics and functional rationality approaches fail to account for important aspects of the ECB's rules and policy mandates. In contrast, a sociological emphasis on institutional context is useful in explaining the continuities linking the ECB to the normative structure that had previously developed, largely within the network of central-bank governors, and diffused throughout the organizational field in which monetary policy-making was embedded. It was the need to legitimize the new Central Bank in terms of these broader norms that shaped the ECB's organizational structure and governing rules. In particular, pre-existing norms influenced three key aspects of the ECB: its political independence, its criteria for membership, and its rules for price stability.

Michael Smith's chapter focuses on the institutionalization of a space for common foreign and security policies (CFSP), and on efforts since the signing of the Maastricht treaty to link the CFSP with other EU domains under a principle of coherence. Smith argues that the institutionalization of a foreign and security policy domain has been driven by both external factors—the collapse of the Soviet Union, the Gulf War, Bosnia—and endogenous institutional development. He begins by examining institutional gaps and contradictions created by the Maastricht provisions. The difficulties arose with respect to decision-making procedures, external representation, financing of external actions, relations with the Western European Union, and democratic oversight. The Maastricht treaty left open important questions regarding the legal status of the EU regarding international agreements, compliance, and the role of the European Court of Justice. These institutional deficiencies sometimes led to problems in specific EU foreign policy areas. Actors sought to resolve the institutional dilemmas by increasing the coherence among the EU's external policy domains—security, economic, development—through both informal and formal, treaty-revising, means.

Penelope Turnbull and Wayne Sandholtz analyze the creation of new EU spaces for cooperation in policing and immigration policies. The Treaty of Rome was silent on both topics. Prior to the Maastricht treaty, EC states had begun to coordinate their responses to specific problems—such as terrorism, drugs, and asylum seekers—usually on a bilateral basis. Multilateral forms of cooperation were fragmented, ad hoc, and outside of EC structures. Turnbull and Sandholtz argue that a combination of external shock and endogenous institutional development, coupled with policy entrepreneurship from Germany's Chancellor Helmut Kohl, led to a broad reframing of policing and migration issues. Both were linked to the EC's central project, namely, the completion of the internal market. As the single market proceeded, both publics and policy-makers became concerned about the implications of removing border controls for regulating immigration from outside the EU and transnational crime. The external shock was the collapse of the Soviet bloc, which triggered massive migrations from the east, especially into Germany. Chancellor Kohl became a policy entrepreneur, seeking EU solutions to an obstinate domestic political problem regarding immigrants. The result was the Third Pillar of the Maastricht Treaty, on Justice and Home Affairs (JHA). The Amsterdam Treaty (1996) then partially separated policing and migration again—but with a completely different institutional structure, within the European Union.

12. Conclusion: The Dynamics of Institutionalization and the Future of the EU

The European Union is now a set of institutionalized political and legal struc-tures, where Member States, the EU's organizations, and representatives of interest groups work to make Europe-wide rules, interpret and enforce existing rules, and expand European governance. With its own legal system, adminis-trative capacity, a central bank, and a single currency, what goes on in European space inevitably impacts upon national regimes, administrations, and ways of doing things that have previously been taken for granted. This impact is further reinforced by the growing strength of transgovernmental and transnational society. People who work in governments frequently come into contact with their counterparts across Europe. Centre-left and centre-right parties around most of Europe, if not Great Britain and Denmark, are united in their support of the European project. Those involved in European production and trade are well-organized, knowing that their well-being depends heavily on how supranational governance operates. In turn, people throughout Europe have found employment in firms that export across national borders. Consumers have also benefited from the integration of the European market by getting a wider selection of goods and services at lower prices. And even public interest groups less supportive of the market-building component of integration have found it in their interest to invest in the Brussels complex.

One of the major, non-economic side effects of EU cooperation is the high level of cooperation among governments. Indeed, given what national gov-ernments have already accepted—for example, the doctrine of supremacy of EC law, a central bank—it is impossible to predict 'natural limits' to integra-tion from current understandings of sovereignty and statehood. While the increases in cooperation over policing and defence have been thus far modest, even on security issues European governments view themselves as collabora-tors, not competitors, and worries mount about the lack of coherence in for-eign policies, not about excessive Europeanization.

Given this high level of institutionalized cooperation, it is interesting to consider what might cause crisis or de-institutionalization in the future. In general, we believe that rolling back important parts of these institutionalized arenas is unlikely. Indeed, all institutional theories agree: a system of institu-tions and organizations with legitimacy for those who participate in them is likely to maintain itself in the face of both endogenous and exogenous shocks. We consider three kinds of crises that potentially could undermine or produce further transformations in the institutional structure of the EU, and offer some predictions based on the institutional theory developed here.

The proposed expansion of the EU to include countries in eastern Europe could block further change in political and legal institutions. An increase in membership from 15 to 25 states may overload formal and informal rule-making structures in the Council, the Commission, and the Court. Given our institutional theory, we would expect that pre-existing institutions will play a critical role in constraining and informing how political elites respond to these problems. It could be that the existing structure will continue to be used, but would strain and groan under the burden, perhaps even grinding to gridlock and precipitating a crisis. But such a crisis would lead elites to reconsider and reconfigure EU institutions. More likely, the Member State governments would anticipate these problems and produce a new set of rules to solve them in the general framework of the existing treaties before enlargement took place.

A second crisis could be precipitated by the monetary union. The monetary union that created the Euro could come under attack because of, for example, persistent difficulties of coordinating monetary policies across national economies at different points in the business cycle. In this scenario, one or more of the larger Member States will face an economic crisis that will push them to want to have more national control over monetary policy. For instance, a country like Spain or France might try to leave the Euro in the face of an economic downturn where the Central Bank kept interest rates high. We think that such a crisis is not likely to result in exit from existing commitments. If it were deemed necessary to run temporarily higher budget deficits, Member States would be allowed to do so. But the locus of decision-making would, nonetheless, remain the Central Bank.

Third, there is a general problem that goes under the label of the 'democratic deficit'. Under this scenario, the people of Europe—or, more likely, the electorate of one of the larger states—will tire of having so much decision-making ceded to the Brussels complex, or become unhappy with specific outcomes. This could bring to power a political party oriented towards less cooperation in Europe. Such a crisis could alter the relationship between a particular Member State and the EU. Still, the EU has always accommodated different Member State arrangements with the EU. The EU could preserve the overall institutional structure, but change some of the substantive arrangements that affect a given Member State.

Finally, there could be a de-institutionalization and rollback, but we think this is the least likely scenario (see also Fligstein and Stone Sweet, this volume). There are clear economic and political gains from the institutionalization of the EU. Current institutional arrangements are set up to meet the needs of governments, firms, and citizen groups, which in turn have invested resources in EU rules and policies. Threats to those arrangements would entail costs for numerous actors. Even hostile political actors would have to confront the existing configuration of institutions and interests. The most likely response is therefore the preservation or even expansion of current institutions, rather than their contraction. As in the past, European actors are likely to find creative ways to adapt and modify EU institutions to better meet the challenges they face.

2

Institutionalizing the Treaty of Rome

NEIL FLIGSTEIN AND ALEC STONE SWEET

1. Introduction

WITH the Treaty of Rome, European states designed a set of policy domains related to trade and the regulation of markets, a complex of governmental organizations, and a binding set of substantive and procedural rules to help them achieve the construction of a European Economic Community (Fligstein and McNichol 1998). Although the Treaty traced the broad outlines of this new Community, it was the purposeful activities of representatives of national governments (Moravcsik 1998), of officials operating in the EC's organizations, like the Commission (Pollack 1998) and the Court (Burley and Mattli 1993; Stone Sweet and Brunell 1998a; Weiler 1990; 1994), and of leaders of transnational interest groups (Mazey and Richardson 1993) that subsequently produced the extraordinarily dense web of political and social networks that now functions to generate and sustain supranational governance (Wallace and Young 1998; Héritier 1999; Sandholtz and Stone Sweet 1998).

The overall process by which these actors have produced this dense structure is only partly documented and variously understood. From some perspectives, the building of the European polity looks to be full of starts and stops (for example, Moravscik 1991; Taylor 1983). From others, integration[1] appears remarkably steady and cumulative (for example, Pierson 1998; Stone Sweet and Caporaso 1998a). But over time, distinct modes of supranational governance[2] have gradually emerged, been institutionalised, and come to be

---

[1] By 'integration' (see Stone Sweet and Sandholtz 1998: 9) we mean the processes through which the horizontal and vertical linkages between actors—social, political, and economic—emerge, organize, and are stabilized by rules and procedures. *Vertical linkages* are the relationships—patterned interactions—that develop between actors organized at the EC level, and actors organized at or below the Member-State level. *Horizontal linkages* are the relationships—patterned interactions—between actors organized in one Member State with actors organized in another. We understand these linkages to be *institutionalized* to the extent that they are constructed and sustained by EC rules (see Stone Sweet, Fligstein, and Sandholtz, this volume). Thus, *European integration* and the *institutionalization of the EC* refer to the same process.

[2] We use 'supranational governance' as the term was defined in Sandholtz and Stone Sweet (1998; see also the discussion in Sandholtz and Stone Sweet 1999). In those policy domains in which a mode of supranational governance has been established, the EC's organizations possess jurisdiction, and EC rules authoritatively govern, throughout EC territory.

taken for granted by an ever greater range of actors, public and private, whose orientations are increasingly European.

Two premises of this project (see Stone Sweet, Fligstein, and Sandholtz, this volume) are that institutions not only provide opportunities for actors to act collectively, but condition how they actually do behave. Once established, rule systems push towards certain solutions and away from others. This push, in turn, entails certain consequences for how new institutional arrangements evolve or are generated over time. In the original neo-functionalist literature (Haas 1958; 1961; Schmitter 1969; 1970), the dynamics of integration were theorized under the label 'spillover'. In the European Integration and Supranational Governance project (Sandholtz and Stone Sweet 1998: 5–7, 11–15), we accepted important elements of neo-functionalism, especially its emphasis on institutionalization,[3] and we reconceptualized spillover.

In the earlier volume, we hypothesized that, under certain conditions, three sets of variables—the development of transnational society, the capacity of supranational organizations to pursue integrative agendas, and the structure of European-level rules—would bind together, within complex systems of mutual interdependence, and that this interdependence would, in turn, broadly determine the course of European integration (see also Stone Sweet and Brunell 1998a). The explanatory status of these three variables—actors, organizations, rule structures—within institutionalist theory has been elaborated on at length in Stone Sweet, Fligstein, and Sandholtz (this volume), and underpins the project (see also North 1995; Stone Sweet 1999).

In this chapter, we continue the effort to develop and test a macro theory of how the institutionalization of the EC has proceeded. We take up three different but well-known stories that scholars have told about European integration. We show how they are linked together, theoretically and empirically. The first story focuses attention on the consequences, for the development of supranational governance, of rising economic transactions across borders. The more goods, services, investment, and labour flow across national boundaries, the more governments and the EC's organizations are pushed to remove national barriers to further exchange—negative integration—and to regulate, in the form of European legislation—positive integration—the emerging Single Market (Moravscik, 1998; Stone Sweet and Sandholtz 1998).

The second story traces the causes and effects of the constitutionalization of the Treaty of Rome, the transformation of the EC from an international regime to a federalized polity through decisive moves on the part of the European Court of Justice (Burley and Mattli 1993; Weiler 1999). Constitutionalization has profoundly altered, within domains governed by EC law, how individuals and firms pursue their interests, how national judiciaries operate, and how policy is made (Slaughter, Stone Sweet, and Weiler 1998; Dehousse 1994). And the operation of the legal system, through Art. 177 procedures (De La Mare

---

[3] Haas (1961) theorized that integration would construct complex, positive feedback loops linking the development of supranational institutions, organizational capacities, and the self-interested behaviour of individuals.

1999; Stone Sweet and Brunell 1998*b*), has pushed the integration project a great deal further than Member State governments, operating under existing legislative rules, would have been prepared to go on their own (Stone Sweet and Caporaso 1998*b*; compare with Héritier, this volume).

Our third integration narrative traces the multidimensional causes and consequences of the growth of interest group representation at the supranational level. As interest groups and Commission officials have interacted in specific directorate generals and within ongoing policy processes, the Commission has worked to develop procedures and other arrangements for consultation within the Brussels complex (Richardson and Mazey, this volume). Further, a wide range of policy outcomes, from the form and content of directives to the specifics of administrative rules taken pursuant to secondary legislation, can be understood only by taking account the work of lobby groups (Andersen and Eliasson 1991; 1993; Greenwood and Aspinwall 1998; Mazey and Richardson 1993) and the emergence and consolidation of comitology processes (Dogan 1997; Joerges and Neyer 1997).

To tie these three stories together, it is necessary to be more specific about what we are trying to explain. We are interested in a specific form of institutionalization, the process through which actors come to constitute political arenas, or what our project calls 'European space'. Individuals organize these arenas in order to express their interests through collective activities, to orient their behaviour towards others operating in the same arena and, potentially, within a greater organizational field, and to produce specific outcomes. We will focus on four types of indicators of integration and institution building: cross-national trade within the European common market; the production of EC secondary legislation; the litigation of disputes involving EC law by judges operating within the framework of Art. 177 (EEC); and the growth and activities of lobbying groups operating within the Brussels complex. These four indicators, of course, are end results of the three integration narratives to which we have just referred.

It is our view that the process through which a European political space emerged and was institutionalized has been provoked, in the first instance, by non-state actors, particularly, but not exclusively, those representatives of firms or industries seeking to further their own sectoral interests by exploiting opportunities provided for by the Treaty of Rome. Such actors often proceeded by trial and error. They had to determine which issues could, or should not, be raised, and to devise methods of attaining agreement; and they had to develop strategies for effective lobbying of the Commission and Council, and for litigating matters of EC law before national and European judges. Of course, European organizations took part in, and helped to structure, this learning process, as EC officials figured out ways to respond to the demands placed upon them, by interpreting treaty rules, by developing lower-order norms and procedures, and by defining their own roles within new policy processes. Put simply, European political space evolved as an emerging transnational society and a new governing elite came to a set of agreements about how to use the overarching architecture of the Rome Treaty.

In this chapter, we attempt to evaluate this process from the standpoint of institutionalist theory, by testing specific hypotheses against relatively comprehensive quantitative measures of integration. We begin by elaborating on institutionalization more generally, before turning to how we expect the peculiar EC structure to have evolved over time. We then present several propositions about how the various processes of integration have interacted with one another to produce the current structure. Finally, we present quantitative analyses of the data. Our main finding is that (1) increasing economic transactions (2), the construction of the Brussels complex, (3) the capacity of supranational authorities to produce legislation, and (4) the operation of the EC legal system have become linked. Indeed they came about through self-reinforcing processes. Although our perspective is a macro one, we emphasize actors and agency. As increasing numbers of actors learn how to be effective in the EC, they build and consolidate new arenas for political activity, thereby bolstering the centrality of supranational governance.

2. Theoretical Considerations

We now discuss our theory and derive hypotheses from this discussion. To begin, two theoretical issues need attention. The first concerns micro-foundations. How do we view actors and the nature of agency within the processes of institutionalization analyzed? The second concerns the specific macro context of these processes, namely, the supposed interaction of the Treaty of Rome with previously organized political, social, and economic organizations and arenas. Why did Europe provide new opportunities for actors to pursue their interests and to construct themselves collectively, and why might we expect supranational governance to be pushed down certain paths rather than others?

The problem of what actors want and what they can get is central to making sense of institutions. As soon as actors—individuals operating in firms, non-governmental organizations, or parts of the state apparatus—sustain contact with one another in a specific context, the issue of collective governance is raised. We assume that all actors prefer rules that favour them—that is, rules that are likely to make the actor at least as well off as another posited set of rules. But we know that such a calculus depends entirely on whether actors can determine exactly what their interests are. Once they are able to do so, they will then need to decide how to attain their goals, who their allies might be in such a project, and whether or not it is possible to attain cooperation with those actors with whom they may be in conflict or competition. It is frequently the case that, even if actors have a clear view as to what their interests are, it is difficult to create collective institutions in a particular arena.

These issues of collective governance can be dealt with in a number of ways. First—assume large asymmetries in actors' resources and capabilities—powerful actors may be able to impose their will on others by coercion, or through the use of rules they create in their own interest and image. Second—assume a relatively equal distribution of power—actors may be able to negotiate collective solutions to their governance problems. Third, actors may resort to an outside party to help them resolve their differences, to construct negotiating space, or to propose or enforce an institutional solution. Fourth, actors may not be able to solve problems of collective governance at all, and anarchy, or a situation of permanent conflict and stasis, might result. Finally, some skilled social actors may be able to forge new political coalitions that transform actors' interests and identities (see Stone Sweet, Fligstein, and Sandholtz, this volume). These political or social entrepreneurs are able to promote a new institutional order by convincing others that their interests will be served in the creation of new arrangements of collective governance.

In all cases, individuals are key to whatever happens in creating new institutions or transforming old ones. We assume that actors are interested in gains from forms of collective governance and this convinces them to invest in institution-building projects. Further, we assume that actors will normally respond to situations considered to be suboptimal, or in crisis, with an eye towards resolving them. How they do so is heavily shaped, of course, by existing institutions and actors' relative position in organized systems of power. Existing institutions provide actors with powerful tools to innovate, and a legitimizing logic for constraining others. If actors have a position of power in an existing system of institutional arrangements, we generally expect them to reproduce that position of power, and to do so by employing repertoires of action and discourse whose legitimacy is more or less settled.

To apply a general view of institution-building to the EC, one must carefully identify the organizational contexts relevant to who the various actors are and what their project might be. One must also provide links between institutional spheres to suggest why actors in one sphere might try to influence action in another. We believe that the institutionalization of the Rome Treaty has been a process driven by the construction of feedback loops and other connections between relatively autonomous spheres of action in the EC. For our purposes, we identify three sets of interactions: between firms engaged in cross-border trade; between litigants, national judges, and the European Court; and between lobby groups and EC officials in Brussels.

2.1. Traders and exchange

The biggest 'black box' in our analysis is the firms that engage in trade across Europe. Social scientists have been slow to study in any systematic way how business has provoked and adapted to Europeanization. Large European corporations have an interest in selling their goods and services across Europe in order to expand their size and profits. Large firms learn how, and are only able, to utilize economies of scale and scope by expanded economic activities, for example, through finding new markets. Of course, one could argue that firms that trade would prefer one set of rules to protect the home market and another to allow them to invade markets in other societies. The problem is that if the first set held sway over the second, trade would be stifled. The firms who are the most likely winners in a move to creating a common market are the ones who will support common market rules the most. In practice what this has meant is that the integration of markets across national borders has been led by firms who will be net gainers and opposed by firms who are net losers (Fligstein and Brantley 1995). So, we observe that some goods and services are highly traded while others are not. This often reflects the relative power of national firms to block moves to establish or enforce such an order.

In our model, those who engage in economic transactions across borders influence the institutionalization of European governance, but they are also effected by it. Such transactors are the most likely benefactors and users of EC law, and the most likely to attack national rules and practices as violations of EC law. They are also the most likely to lobby their governments and the Commission for favourable rules to liberalize markets, or to replace national standards with European ones. But the character and scope of transnational exchange are also shaped by EC legislation and the results of litigating EC law. EC rule-making—case law and secondary legislation—that promotes market-opening projects, for example, by producing opportunities for traders to expand their activities, to lower their transaction costs, and thus to increase their size and profitability. We have good reason to expect that transnational exchange, like trade, will favour the development of European institutions, but we also expect institutions that do develop to favour more export activity.

Thus we propose the following hypothesis: increases in transnational exchange, especially economic, will provoke increases in litigation of EC law, increases in lobbying activity in Brussels, and the adoption of EC legislation by the EC's legislative bodies.

Firms involved in cross-national exchange will have the greatest interest in removing national barriers to exchange—negative integration—and in shaping the development of supranational regulation and standard-setting—positive integration. They will have a powerful interest in enforcing Treaty rules related to the Common Market through the courts, and they will have the money to use litigation as a means of evolving these rules in pro-integrative directions. They will feel compelled, or find it useful, to establish a lobbying presence in Brussels, to insure that the Euro-wide trading rules that are established do not injure their interests. And they will encourage the EC's legislators to adopt rules that will expand rather than restrict markets and trade.

2.2. Legal elites and litigation

Unlike certain 'hard law' rules governing the Common Market, such as those related to the free movement of goods or workers, the EC's legal system was only partly sketched out by the Treaty of Rome. The system actors produced came about through practice: interactions between lawyers, national judges, and the European Court of Justice (ECJ), and through the feedback of the ECJ's case law on subsequent litigation. That is, legal elites—lawyers activated by their clients, and judges activated by lawyers—had to figure out exactly how to make use of European law. They were confronted with, and ultimately succeeded in resolving, complicated problems of who could litigate EC law, under what conditions, and with what effects within national legal orders. And national judiciaries had to negotiate their relationship to the European Court of Justice through a set of multi-dimensional, intra-judicial, 'constitutional dialogues' (Slaughter, Stone Sweet, and Weiler 1998; Stone Sweet 2000: Ch. 6).

Legal integration has facilitated both the expansion of transnational society and supranational authority to govern (Stone Sweet and Caporaso 1998a), a result that depended critically on the development of a system through which individual litigants could pursue their private interests, in their own national courts, through rules and procedures provided by EC law and by the rule-making of the European Court. One does not have to assume that the Court has acted self-consciously to promote European integration to make sense of the result. Once the ECJ had announced, and national judges had accepted, the 'constitutional' doctrines of the supremacy,[4] and the direct effect,[5] of EC law—within national legal orders—the legal system became a privileged site of negative integration. The doctrine of direct effect enabled private actors to bring actions against their own governments in national courts, and the doctrine of supremacy meant that national judges had to resolve these conflicts with reference to EC law. Through litigation, judges became deeply involved in conflicts pitting transnational actors—and other people who could claim that their rights under the Treaty of Rome were being violated by existing national law or administrative practice—against national legal regimes and those actors, public and private, advantaged by national rules and practices.

In the Common Market for goods, foreign firms and importers will use this system to liberalize national markets—that is, to enforce EC law against conflicting national regulation. If the legal system operates with reasonable effectiveness, some firms, usually the largest and most export-oriented, will benefited from litigating, while others will lose out. In fact, we know that governments discovered that litigation in the free movement of goods area was punching large 'holes' in national regulatory frameworks, exposing to possible attack virtually any national rule that might have an adverse effect on intra-EC trade (Poiares Maduro 1998). As negative integration proceeds, then, we expect mounting pressure on governments to replace national regulatory regimes with supranational ones.

We therefore propose a second hypothesis: increases in the litigation of EC law will provoke more intra-EC trade, and pressure the EC's legislature to replace national regulatory frameworks with supranational ones. Litigation

---

[4] First articulated in the *Costa* judgement (ECJ 1964), the doctrine of supremacy asserts the principle that in *any* conflict between an EC legal rule and a rule of national law, or a practice sanctioned by national law, the EC rule must be given primacy by the national judge.

[5] First articulated in the *Van Gend en Loos* judgement (ECJ 1963a), the doctrine of direct effect asserts the principle that, under certain conditions, the provisions of EC law—including directives (*Van Duyn*, ECJ 1974)—confer upon private individuals legal rights that public authorities must respect and that national courts must enforce.

will increase as a function of exports and the production of new legislation. Thus we have put forward an argument to the effect that the legal system and transnational exchange will develop along mutually reinforcing paths. Initially, at least, firms most likely to take advantage of EC law are those who export and those who import goods from other EC markets. As trade rises, these actors will increase in number and, therefore, so will the numbers of potential conflicts between EC rules governing the Common Market and national regulatory regimes governing product standards, consumer safety, and environmental protection.

At the same time, we know (for example, Greif 1989; 1993; North 1981, 1990) that the expansion of markets depends heavily on (1) the construction of robust institutions, to encourage impersonal exchange and to protect traders from illiberal state action, and (2) the establishment of effective court systems to resolve disputes and to enforce legal rules. Thus, we have good reason to suppose that negative integration, through litigation activity, will lead to an expansion in transnational exchange. Further, the more effective negative integration is, the more costly it will be for various actors, including government, not to legislate common European rules governing economic activity.

2.3. The Brussels complex and legislating

Although the Treaty of Rome outlined a political structure for the EC, based in Brussels, it did not envision how this process would actually work. There were two problems. First, the Commission is a small organization. Given the potentially huge scope of its jurisdiction and responsibilities, the organization possesses relatively little capacity to generate, on its own, serious study of complex issues in order to facilitate agreements, and even less capacity to enforce and administer European rules once they are adopted. Second, the Treaty did not design a system of accommodating lobbying organizations in Brussels, nor did it outline procedures for incorporating them into the policy process. The Treaty did create an Economic and Social Committee to act as a sounding board for the Commission and Council in order to gather opinions. But that organization never exerted much influence over legislative processes. Lobbying groups formed at the very beginning of the EU and they chose to directly discuss matters of interest with members of the Commission and Council.

The central priority of the people who work at the Commission is to build Europe by finding new and innovative ways to attain cooperation. Of course, the Commission studies and proposes new legislative measures; in most areas, at least in the first instance, the Commission cannot legislate on its own. Instead, it typically must convince the Member-State governments—a majority, a qualified majority, or even all of them—and the European Parliament of the virtue of a proposal. The Commission's success in doing so, as Haas (1958) understood very well, depends heavily on its ability to enlist the support of non-governmental actors and groups who express their opinions to the Member State governments.

Lobbying groups have an interest in pushing Brussels for more legislation. The Rome Treaty suggested a means of attaining a Common Market, and thus for expanding economic activities. As trade increases, and as the negative integration project proceeds, firms' interest in setting up shop in Brussels is likely to increase as well. Many will want European-wide rules to govern their members' activities. Further, groups whose orientations had been largely or exclusively national, such as those organized to protect labour, consumers, the environment, and health and safety, may discover that joining free traders in Brussels makes sense because it potentially increases their political impact. In any given policy domain, the costs of failing to organize effectively at the supranational level will rise as the scope of supranational governance in that domain expands.

We see the growth of the Brussels complex partly as the development of a pervasively symbiotic relationship between the Commission and lobbyists. We assume that, at a first point in time, the Commission has an interest in coopting 'experts'—knowledge-based and industry-specific elites—into the policy process, to help draft new and assess existing legislation and to help legitimize legislation that is proposed. But as the scope and density of European legislation increases, more and more lobby groups will discover that it is in their interest to be consulted as well, and they will push, without prompting from the Commission, for more political voice in Brussels.

We therefore propose a third hypothesis: the founding of new lobbying groups will be provoked by increased trade and the fact that legislation is being produced in a domain.

As the number of NGOs and interest groups increases in a particular domain, we expect them to push for European legislation. Further, increases in trade will present the Community legislature with new problems of governance, and lobbyists and NGOs will wish to play a role in framing how these problems are understood, as well as in constructing the menu of policy responses to be put into play.

Thus, we propose a fourth hypothesis: increases in exports, lobbying groups, and litigation will provoke more legislation.

Finally, the production of European rules must also have a role in structuring institutionalization processes—feedback again. We have just suggested that as the institutional structure of the EC becomes more articulated, so will the interests of lobbyists to locate in Brussels. Yet the production of new rules also increases the opportunities that actors have to litigate. As European rules come to cover more and more interactions, they will generate, or at least become the context for, more and different kinds of litigation. Last, we expect positive integration to lower transaction costs further, thus expanding trade.

We therefore offer a final hypothesis: the increasing density and scope of European rules will stimulate more litigation of EC law and transnational exchange.

2.4. Summary

Our view of institutionalization is dynamic. The Treaty of Rome opened up the possibility for more cooperation between governments over economic issues, and created vast potential for European firms to derive benefits associated with larger and more open markets. It created two sets of organizations, one legislative and one judicial, to help governments and other actors achieve their goals. Private actors began to take decisions in light of this new institutional structure and to orient themselves to emerging European spaces; the EC legislative organs began to operate; and the EC's legal system began to take shape. These processes, we hypothesize, do not take place in isolation from one another but, in fact, are deeply embedded in one another. Each process at least partly conditions the other two.

3. Data

One of the most important problems in doing this research is selecting the units of observation. We are fortunate that the EC has created an organizational structure and language to guide us. Fligstein and McNichol (1998) have analyzed the Treaty of Rome as a set of issue arenas that were institutionalized, if in different ways, across time. Institutionalization is partly the formalization of these arenas in terms of organizational capacity to generate rules. The Directorate Generals of the Commission and the Council were divided into subunits to legislate and administer along these lines. The EC classifies legislation according to these issue arenas, and the European Court of Justice uses a slightly different, if adaptable, system of classification. Groups tend to lobby those parts of the Commission and Council that are relevant to their interests, thereby helping to make these policy domains real by linking what goes on in EC organizations with organized interests. In this project, we have defined a policy domain as an arena where political actors interested in a particular issue meet to forge agreements. In the Commission, domains are delineated by the competences conferred on particular Directorate Generals. The EC also uses these 'categories' to code litigation and legislation, thereby reinforcing their nature as policy arenas.

The data sets that we have constructed contain information on EC policy domains from 1958–94; because the data on interest groups, references, and legislation run beyond 1994, our tables, but not the statistical analyses, use data through 1996. The Commission and the Court specify, if somewhat differently, 18 important arenas or competencies of the EC: financial/institutional; customs/taxation; agriculture; fisheries; employment/social policy; right of establishment; transport policy; competition policy; economic and monetary policy; external relations; energy; internal market and industrial policy; regional policy; environment, consumers, and health; science/information/culture; competition law; justice/home affairs; people's Europe

(Fligstein and McNichol 1998). There are almost no legislation, court cases, or lobbying groups for justice/home affairs and the 'people's Europe', which are essentially domains located outside of the first pillar. Although the tables run through 1996, we were able to obtain usable data for the years 1958–94. Thus, for each data set, we have 36 years of information coded into 16 domains.

The data were compiled from various sources. The data on legislation comes from the Directory of Community Legislation in Force (European Union 1995). The directory includes all forms of legislation, but we analyzed only the data on regulations and directives here, after coding it into the domain specified by the EC. The measure we use is the total number of directives and regulations passed in a particular domain in a particular year.

We use the Data Set on Preliminary References in EC Law 1958–98, compiled by Stone Sweet and Brunell (1999) for data on litigation. Among other information, Stone Sweet and Brunell coded each reference by the domain or domains of EC law being litigated, as indicated by the referring question of the national judge to the ECJ. References contain as few as one and as many as five different domain codings. This information was then mapped directly on to our 16 policy domains.

The data on lobbying groups was obtained from a volume published by Philip and Gray (1997). They mailed out a survey to almost 1,000 lobbying organizations in Brussels and received answers from about 700. They collected information on each organization's name, size, location, founding date, and purposes, and on the Directorate-Generals with whom they had contact. On the basis of this data, we were able to code 586 organizations. We used the data on founding dates and the information on whom they lobbied to attach them to a policy domain.

Some groups tended to participate in more than one domain. If organizations claimed to lobby more than one part of the Commission, we counted that organization multiple times. So, for example, if the organization claimed it lobbied in the agriculture domain and the single market domain, in the year it was founded we counted it as a founding in both domains. The 586 organizations lobby in an average of 3.5 domains for a total of 2,059. We created two different measures of lobbying presence. For some of the analysis, we use the total number of lobbying groups founded in a particular year by domain. We also create a measure that cumulates the number of lobbying groups in each domain. Our theoretical argument suggests that both lobbying group foundation and the number of groups that come to exist in a domain might effect outcomes.

The data on trade is more aggregated. There are two problems. First, exports for particular industries do not neatly correspond to our policy domains. Categories like 'customs/taxation' cut across industries. Second, the EC has expanded from six to twelve and now to 15 nation states. Data on exports that measured only trade within the EC zone would show big jumps as soon as the EC zone widened. We decided to use trade data for exports for all of Western Europe that originated in Western Europe and ended up in Western Europe during 1958–94.

4. Methodology

Examining the trends in the data provides some feel for what has occurred in the EC. Institutionalization took time. The activities of lobbyists, litigators, legislators, and judges began slowly, but took off around 1970. In the early 1980s, the activities that we associate with institutionalization slowed. The integration project appears to have reached, or had nearly reached, its outward limits, given existing institutional arrangements. After the 1986 Single European Act (SEA), activity intensified, and integration was, in fact, 'relaunched'.

We believe that the EC has experienced two fundamental shifts in the level of institutionalization. We date the first shift roughly in 1970, and the second in 1985. If we are right, then it makes sense to analyze the dynamics of institutionalization of the Community in terms of three periods: 1958–69; 1970–85; 1986 to the present. We are not arguing that in 1970, and again in 1985, everything that matters suddenly changed. European integration has been a messy process from the beginning, and much of that process will not be captured by schema that aggregate complex phenomena across time and policy arenas. Nevertheless, we do argue that how (1) transnational activity like cross-border trade and the activities of supranational interest groups, (2) the litigation of EC law, and (3) the rule-making capacities and activities of EC organizations interact with each other causally, altered from one period to the next.

We have constructed two dummy variables designed to capture the effects of these three different periods. The two dummy variables index whether or not an observation occurred in 1970–85 or 1986–94. Coefficients from these dummy variables show the average difference between these periods and the period omitted, that is, 1958–69). Theoretically, we expect that the two latter periods index the effects of the institutionalization of the EC that began in the 1960s. Thus, we expect that both periods will have higher levels of changes in the various dependent variables associated with them.

We use two strategies to analyze the data. First, some of the data contains information on cross sections over time—that is, domains by years. There are two potential econometric problems in such data. First, if there are unspecified causes in the regression, then the errors will tend to be correlated. Second, the use of data on the same units of analysis—that is, domains—may also effect the correlations between the errors. One standard econometric approach for dealing with these problems is to estimate a random effects error components regression model (Ameniya 1985). We use the XTREG procedure in the computer program Stata 6.0 to do this estimation. We have constructed a series of equations where the independent variables are lagged. We lag the variables one year in order to untangle 'cause' from 'effect'. Different lag structures were tried, but the one-year lag produced stable and interpretable results.

We also analyzed data predicting changes in trade over time. The econometric problem presented by time-series analysis is autocorrelation. Here, the errors from one period are correlated with errors from adjacent observations. For this problem, the standard procedure is to do a Durbin-Watson test to see if there is evidence of autocorrelation. When we did the test, we found that there was evidence of autocorrelation. To solve this problem, we used a procedure that corrected for autocorrelation in time series data. The ARIMA procedure in Stata 6.0 was used for this estimation.

5. Results

Figure 2.1 depicts the annual level of exports within the EC from 1958 to 1994. There was a slow increase from 1958 to 1970. After 1970 trade rose steadily, and then accelerated following 1982. The figure shows that trade within the EC went from about $10 billion to almost $900 billion over the period in constant dollars.

Figure 2.2 presents the number of claims invoking European law contained in preliminary references to the ECJ from national courts pursuant to Art. 177 (EEC). Such claims averaged 6.1 per domain over the period. Although the Court's announcements of direct effect and supremacy date from 1963 and 1964 respectively, it took several years before the European Court received significant levels of references. The result is unsurprising since most of the rules governing the Common Market, such as those concerning the free movement

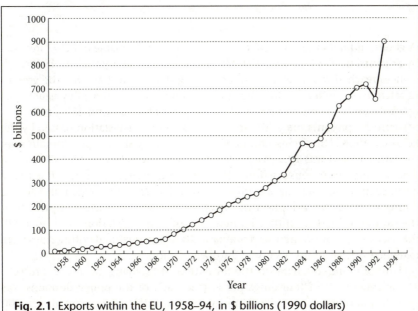

Fig. 2.1. Exports within the EU, 1958–94, in $ billions (1990 dollars)

Source: Eurostat (1997)

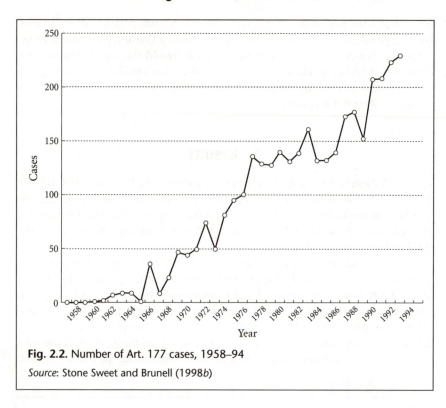

Fig. 2.2. Number of Art. 177 cases, 1958–94

Source: Stone Sweet and Brunell (1998*b*)

of goods, did not enter into effect, and thus were not capable of being invoked by litigants, until 1 January 1970. The figure shows that, by the late 1970s, references reached well over 100 a year. During the decade 1976–85, the growth in references stabilized. After the entry into force of the SEA, they again shot upwards, and are now being sent at an average of well around 250 a year.

Figure 2.3 presents the yearly total of all secondary legislation passed by the EC since 1958. The average number of pieces of legislation per domain over the entire period was 19.1, with a large standard deviation of 63.6. There is a gradual and continuous rise until 1977, when legislative production actually declines and then stabilizes until roughly 1985. The SEA, which altered the voting rules for the adoption of directives necessary for the completion of the Common Market, initiated a new explosion of legislation. Around 1990, the pace of legislation increased dramatically again: qualified voting rules were extended further in the Treaty of European Union.

Figure 2.4 presents data on the formation of lobbying groups in Brussels. The average level of foundings per year in each of the policy domains was quite low at only 1.2. But, over time, we were able to code data on almost 600 significant lobbying groups. At the beginning of the EC, there was a flurry of founding of lobbying groups in Brussels. This activity decreased during the

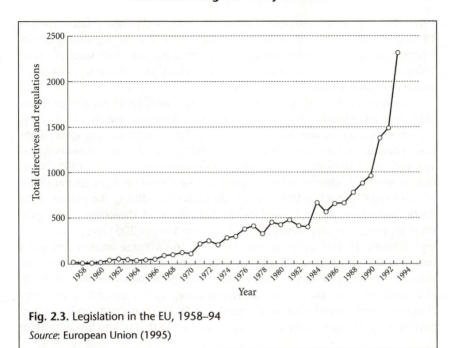

Fig. 2.3. Legislation in the EU, 1958–94

Source: European Union (1995)

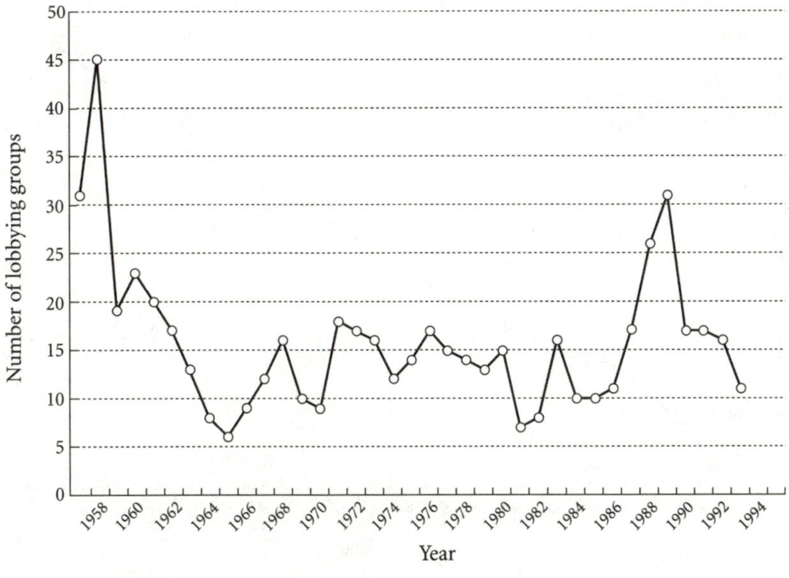

Fig. 2.4. Lobbying groups founded in the EU, 1958–94

Source: Philip and Gray (1997)

1960s. The number of foundings rose in the 1970s, and began to fall in the late 1970s and early 1980s. Following the passage of the SEA, the registering of new lobbying groups in Brussels shot upward, to their highest levels since the early 1960s. Figure 2.5 presents the cumulative growth of pressure groups in the EC, which mirrors the trends in Figs 2.1–2.3.

We now break these patterns down by domain in order to get a better sense of the relative importance of the various policy domains rose over time. Table 2.1 presents data on the legislative activity, by domain, during each of the three periods. The most striking result in the table is the sheer dominance of agricultural legislation in the EC. This is not surprising: as late as 1992, 70 per cent of the EC budget was being spent on the Common Agricultural Policy (Fligstein and McNichol 1998). The table shows that during the period of the 1960s, legislative output was relatively tiny, about 25 directives and regulations adopted annually. Legislative output rose to over 200 pieces a year during 1970–85. In the latest period, 1986–96, the average annual legislative output is almost 600 pieces. Positive integration—the replacement of national rules by supranational ones—now clearly constitutes the major activity of the EC. Further, the substance of rule-making has changed over time. Financial/institutional matters, the right to establish firms and services, transportation, and competition were more important early on, and less important

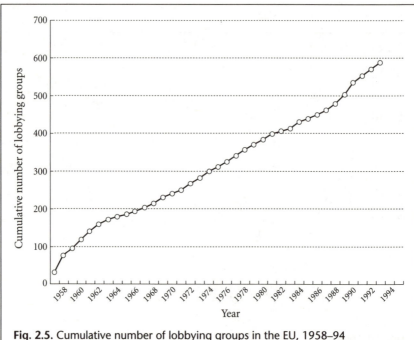

Fig. 2.5. Cumulative number of lobbying groups in the EU, 1958–94

Source: Philip and Gray (1997)

Table 2.1. EC secondary legislation by policy domain, 1958–96

Domain		1958–96	1958–69	1970–85	1985–96
Financial,	%	2.4	8.2	2.2	2.3
institutional	n	230	21	69	140
Free movement	%	8.3	0	9.8	9.0
goods/customs union	n	780	0	313	467
Agriculture	%	52.7	45.9	51.5	53.6
	n	4,950	118	1,642	3,190
Fisheries	%	3.3	0.8	2.1	4.1
	n	314	2	67	245
Free movement of	%	1.8	2.3	2.3	1.5
workers/social policy	n	170	6	72	92
Establishment/	%	2.3	13.2	2.0	2.0
services	n	217	34	64	119
Transport	%	2.6	5.1	2.1	2.8
	n	245	13	66	166
Competition	%	0.6	4.3	0.3	0.6
	n	56	11	11	34
Taxation	%	1.2	2.7	1.6	0.9
	n	112	7	52	53
Economic/monetary	%	0.1	0.4	0.2	0.1
policy	n	14	1	1	7
External relations	%	8.4	3.9	6.7	9.5
	n	793	10	215	568
Energy	%	0.6	3.1	0.9	0.3
	n	54	8	30	16
Internal market/	%	9.0	8.2	12.2	7.3
industrial policy	n	845	21	389	435
Regional policy	%	0.5	0.0	0.7	0.4
	n	45	0	21	24
Environmental/health	%	5.1	1.6	4.3	5.7
consumer protection	n	479	4	136	339
Science/information/	%	0.6	0.0	0.8	0.5
education/culture	n	56	0	24	32
Undertakings	%	0.4	0.4	0.4	0.4
	n	39	1	12	26
TOTAL	%	99.9	100.1	100.1	100.1
	n	9,399	257	3,189	5,953

Note: Data compiled by the authors from European Union (1995). Column percentages may not add up to 100 due to rounding up or down.

as time passed—even as the absolute amount of secondary legislation adopted increased in all domains. The domains of free movement of goods/customs union, internal market, external relations, fisheries, and environment/-health/education/culture have become more important over time.

Table 2.2 shows patterns for Art. 177 references. Litigation of EC law during the 1960s, as indicated by references, was very low: fewer than ten cases a year. The number of domains invoked in references rose over 100 year during the 1970–85 period, and increased to almost 300 cases a year between 1986 and 1996. The bulk of questions targeted the free movement of goods/customs union domain, followed by agriculture and free movement of workers/social policy. Some domains declined in importance over time, particularly competition policy, financial/institutional, agriculture, and free movement of workers/social policy—again even as Art. 177 references increased. There were also relative increases in cases in establishment/services, internal market/industrial policy, and environment/health/education/culture. The results in Tables 2.1 and 2.2 show that both legislation and litigation rose together over time. But the patterns of litigation changed as more directives were written in domains such as internal market/industrial policy and environment. These patterns are consistent with what we know about the process through which successful negative integration, in any given domain, tends to push for positive integration in that domain; new EC rules then provide the basis for further litigation (for further discussion, see Stone Sweet and Caporaso 1998a).

Table 2.3 sorts the data on founding dates of interest groups by domain. The patterns revealed do not mirror those found in the other areas of activity. It appears that when the Brussels complex was being formed, a wide range of interest groups believed it important to establish a presence at the supra-national level, which helped to legitimize and to institutionalize the Community. Undoubtedly, the creation of the Commission, the Council of Ministers, and the Court also encouraged interested groups to notice and then invest in the Brussels complex. The period 1970–85 witnessed new foundings, but on a per capita basis the 1986–96 period registered even more.

What issues were the lobbying groups most interested in? At the beginning, the overwhelming number of groups represented business groups as indicated by the high percentage of groups who joined the internal market/industrial policy domain and the agricultural domains—confirming findings of Cowles (1998). Over time, however, business became less important as a source of new groups. The largest increase in foundings occurred in the regional policy, environment/health/consumer protection, and science/information/educa-tion/culture domains. The rise in interest group activity in these sectors shows again the steady consolidation of the EC's role in positive integration processes. The negative integration project, centred in the legal system, steadily removed barriers to exchange, but left important holes in national legal frameworks that promoted important and legitimate concerns of public policy, such as protection for the environment, the consumer, and health. Clearly, in the past 20 years an increasing number of groups have decided to

Table 2.2. Art. 177 (EEC) references by legal domain, 1958–96

Domain		1958–96	1958–69	1970–85	1985–96
Financial,	%	4.1	2.1	· 5.2	3.5
institutional	n	189	2	85	102
Free movement	%	26.8	26.8	26.9	26.8
goods/customs union	n	1,242	26	437	779
Agriculture	%	17.3	13.4	26.8	12.1
	n	801	13	436	352
Fisheries	%	0.8	0.0	1.2	0.6
	n	38	0	20	18
Free movement of	%	17.6	27.8	16.3	18.0
workers/social policy	n	816	27	266	523
Establishment/	%	5.7	1.0	2.8	7.5
services	n	263	1	45	217
Transport	%	1.7	0.0	1.5	1.8
	n	77	0	25	52
Competition	%	6.1	10.3	5.1	6.5
	n	282	10	83	189
Taxation	%	8.9	14.4	4.8	11.0
	n	412	14	78	320
Economic/monetary	%	1.1	0.0	0.4	0.8
policy	n	29	0	7	22
External relations	%	2.4	1.0	3.1	2.0
	n	109	1	50	58
Energy	%	0.0	0.0	0.0	0.0
	n	1	0	0	1
Internal market/	%	5.1	1.0	3.4	6.1
industrial policy	n	234	1	55	178
Regional policy	%	0.0	0.0	0.0	0.0
	n	1	0	0	1
Environmental/health	%	2.9	2.1	2.5	3.1
consumer protection	n	132	2	40	90
Science/information/	%	0.0	0.0	0.0	0.0
education/culture	n	1	0	0	1
Undertakings	%	0.0	0.0	0.0	0.0
	n	0	0	0	0
TOTAL	%	100.5	99.9	100.1	100.1
	n	4,627	97	1,627	2,903

Note: Data compiled by the authors from Stone Sweet and Brunell (1999). The data set and accompanying codebook are accessible at the homepage of the Robert Schuman Centre for Advanced Study—the website of the European University Institute—and at Stone Sweet's homepage—the website of Nuffield College, Oxford. Column percentages may not add up to 100 due to rounding up or down.

Table 2.3. Founding dates of EC interest groups by policy domain, 1958–96

Domain		1958–96	1958–69	1970–85	1985–96
Financial,	%	0.9	0.7	1.1	0.9
institutional	n	18	6	7	5
Free movement	%	3.5	3.5	2.7	4.5
goods/customs union	n	72	31	17	24
Agriculture	%	6.7	9.2	5.5	3.7
	n	138	83	35	20
Fisheries	%	1.0	0.8	1.2	0.9
	n	20	7	8	5
Free movement of	%	8.5	6.6	10.8	8.8
workers/social policy	n	174	59	68	47
Establishment/	%	5.9	5.5	6.0	6.4
services	n	121	49	49	34
Transport	%	4.1	3.9	3.5	4.3
	n	80	35	22	23
Competition	%	5.1	4.3	2.5	6.0
	n	94	39	33	32
Taxation	%	3.4	3.6	2.5	3.9
	n	69	32	16	21
Economic/monetary	%	2.7	2.7	3.3	2.1
policy	n	56	24	21	11
External relations	%	2.3	2.2	2.4	2.2
	n	47	20	15	12
Energy	%	2.5	2.1	2.1	3.6
	n	51	19	13	19
Internal market/	%	21.5	26.7	20.2	14.5
industrial policy	n	443	238	128	77
Regional policy	%	1.7	1.3	1.9	2.3
	n	36	12	12	12
Environmental/health	%	11.5	9.7	12.1	13.6
consumer protection	n	237	87	77	73
Science/information/	%	12.0	10.3	11.9	15.1
education/culture	n	248	92	92	81
Undertakings	%	7.0	6.5	7.4	7.5
	n	145	58	47	40
TOTAL	%	100.3	99.6	97.1	100.2
	n	2,059	891	632	536

Note: Data compiled by the authors from Philip and Gray (1997). Column percentages may not add up to 100 due to rounding up or down.

orient themselves toward Brussels, in order to help shape the growing legislative agenda.

These four remarkable time series depict the macro-processes through which the EC emerged as a highly differentiated, multi-dimensional political system. There was a gradual process by which European organizations started to work, in tandem with interests and national officials, like judges. This included the construction of the organizations of the community, but it also witnessed the emergence of lobbying groups, primarily those concerned with business issues. At the same time, trade was growing slowly but steadily. Beginning in the 1970s, integration processes took off with some force. Litigants and national judges learned to use Art. 177 to push the negative integration project along, and the Commission and lobbying groups in Brussels begin to push the positive integration agenda. These linked projects reduced the transaction costs facing firms that traded, by replacing the kaleidoscope of national regulatory frameworks that faced cross-border trade with a set of unified rules. Further, the take-off in trade in the 1970s raised the costs of maintaining disparate national rules for policy-makers at all levels of government.

By the late 1970s, the EC had reached a stage where the demand for EC rules outpaced the supply. The Commission experienced difficulties in getting governments to cooperate with one another to produce legislation. We believe that integration began to reach its limits, given existing institutions. Legislative, lobbying, and litigation activities levelled off. The SEA reversed these trends. During the 1980s and 1990s, the SEA and the Treaty on European Union provoked groups to set up shop in to Brussels—see the anecdotal evidence in Hull (1993)—and to lobby for issues such as in the domains of environmental (Webster 1998) and consumer (Young 1998) protection. From our tables, it appears as if they have found some success.

Tables 2.1–2.3 are descriptive rather than analytic, and our discussion so far has been somewhat impressionistic. In order to test our hypotheses, it is necessary to present the results from the regression analyses. Table 2.4 presents the means and standard deviations used in the data analysis. These numbers

Table 2.4: Mean and standard deviations of variables

Variable	Mean deviations	Standard deviations
Legislation	12.7	46.5
References	6.1	12.8
Foundings, lobbying groups	2.8	5.2
Cumulative number of lobbying groups	5.6	8.3
Exports	261.5	248.8
Dummy variable for 1970–85	0.37	
Dummy variable for 1986–96	0.34	

See text for explanations of variables.

reflect the average values for each of the variables across domains and across time. Thus, there were, on average, 10.1 pieces of legislation passed in each domain over the 1958–94 period. The export data refer to years, not domains. Exports from European national markets to other European national markets averaged $265 billion over the period.

Earlier in the chapter, we proposed five hypotheses. Table 2.5 contains the results of the random effects error components model analysis of the data, which we use as one means of testing the first four. Our hypotheses suggest that each of the dependent variables is the outcome of previous levels of some of the other variables. So, for example, we argued that litigation is a function

Table 2.5: Results of random effects error components models

Independent variables	Legislation				References			
	b	SE(b)	b	SE(b)	b	SE(b)	b	SE(b)
1970–85	5.1**	2.0	−0.08	2.0	0.79*	0.34	0.63	0.46
1986–99	1.5**	2.9	4.4	3.6	1.1*	0.51	0.82	0.56
Lag-Legislation	0.84**	0.21	1.02**	0.16			0.21*	0.1
Lag-Cases			0.18*	0.07	0.89**	0.17	0.92**	0.19
Lag-Foundings lobbying groups			0.2	0.14				
Lag-Cumulative lobbying groups			0.05**	0.02				
Lag Exports			0.03**	0.01			0.03**	0.01
Constant	−3.2*	1.5	0.84	1.5	0.19	0.46	−0.12	0.38
R-squared	0.64		0.91			0.79		0.87

Independent variables	Foundings of lobbying groups			
	b	SE(b)	b	SE(b)
1970–85	0.48**	0.20	0.46**	0.19
1986–99	0.57**	0.20	0.90**	0.33
Lag-Legislation			0.41*	0.21
Lag-Cases			0.01	0.01
Lag-Foundings lobbying groups	0.45**	0.12	0.54**	0.14
Lag-Cumulative lobbying groups			0.10**	0.01
Lag Exports			0.01	0.01
Constant	0.72**	0.16	0.22	0.20
R-squared	0.54		0.55	

* p< .05, ** p<.01

See text for explanation of technique and variables.

of exports and the amount of legislation being produced. Our strategy in the analyses is to consider each of the dependent variables from the perspective of our hypotheses. We include lag levels of each of the dependent variables in the model. In essence, we are explaining the change in the level of the dependent variable each year.

Table 2.5 presents two sets of regression results. The first reports results on the attempt to predict changes in each of the outcome variables with effects that capture the three periods of institutionalization discussed above. Our purpose is to establish whether the periods in fact differ according to how much change occurs on the dependent variables. Then we add the relevant independent variables in order to see if the effects of the independent variables are in fact driving the changes in the dependent variables.

The first column of Table 2.5 presents results on the determinants of changes in legislation by domain. Hypotheses 1, 2, and 4 suggest that relative levels of exports, cases, and the founding of lobbying groups ought to explain changes in the number of pieces of secondary legislation produced in policy domains. The first column shows that the two periods—1970–85 and 1986–94—produced higher levels of secondary legislation than the period 1958–69. This is evidence that the negative integration project is slowly being replaced by a positive integration project. The second column in the table shows that the period effects disappear when the other variables are added to the equation. This implies that the lagged levels of the other variables are the causes of changes in legislation. We observe that the number of cases filed under Art. 177 in a particular domain, the cumulative number of lobbying groups in a domain, and the overall value of exports produce pressure for more legislation. This is in line with our hypotheses. The founding of lobbying groups was not a determinant of legislation, suggesting that having a critical mass of lobbying organizations is what is important to producing new legislation in policy domains.

We consider the causes of Art. 177 references to the European Court of Justice. Hypotheses 1, 2, and 5 suggest that reference activity in a particular domain will change as the result of two factors: increases in export and the production of directives in that domain. The first column shows that the periods 1970–85 and 1986–94 have higher levels of change in references than the earlier period. When the other variables are added to the equation, the period effects disappear. At the domain level, increases in exports appear to be one of the main causes of Art. 177 references. As trade increased over time, litigation increased as well—confirming Stone Sweet and Brunell's (1998a) results using a different measure. The production of legislation also stimulates litigation, as our hypothesis suggested. One way of stating this is that as rules increase, the opportunities for actors to use them to protect themselves from national rules that might exclude them from markets increases. But that is not the only logic. As the institutional structure of the EC becomes increasingly articulated in statutory rules, more and more actors are provoked and able to use the legal system to effect policy change, whether or not they are engaged in cross-border economic activities. Such is the case, for example, with women claiming rights under non-discrimination directives, or of environmental interest groups suing national governments in their own courts for failing to properly transpose a directive in the environmental field.

The last columns of Table 2.4 present findings on the determinants of the foundings of lobbying groups in policy domains. Hypotheses 1, 2, and 3 imply that lobbying groups will form as exports go up, as successful negative integration provides pressure or opportunities to legislate, and as legislation increases over time. The first columns of the table capture the effect of periods. Both of the latter periods have a positive effect on the founding of new organizations. When the other variables are put in the model, these effects remain statistically significant. In this case, there was less support for our hypotheses. Exports did not appear to be directly driving the founding of pressure groups. Neither did opportunities to legislate brought on by litigation. The most important determinant of the founding of lobbying groups was the cumulative number of lobbying groups already in the domain. This suggests that outsiders felt compelled to found new organizations when others were already participating in lobbying. Earlier the results suggested that the cumulation of lobbying groups produced changes in the production of legislation in a sector. That result, along with this one, implies that the cumulation of groups in a domain stimulates both legislation and the founding of new groups. In our view, groups who were not represented in Brussels came to realize that those groups who were had more legislative influence, and decided to join them.

We now test hypothesis 5. Does the institutionalization of the political and legal processes in the EC affect trade? We argued that litigation, legislation, and possibly the presence of lobbying groups in domains would signal to firms that there existed new opportunities to export. The regression analysis presented in Table 2.6 looks at changes in the level of exporting for all of the EC as a function of the overall level of these other factors. The first column reports these results with just the lag dependent variable and the dummy variables for the periods 1970–85 and 1986–94. There were large period effects, consistent with the tables presented earlier, showing a take-off in exports in the 1970s and 1980s. When the other variables are added to the equation, the period effects disappear. There is only one variable that is significantly related to exporting: the production of legislation. This is strong evidence that if one changes the rules of trade, one increases the opportunities for exporters. This is an important and plausible result.

At this level of aggregation, and with the use of these kinds of techniques, litigating EC law does not seem to cause increases in exporting. That said, we know that the legal system has done the lion's share of negative integration, and that much of what the Court did in the second period was to remove national barriers to trade and to construct the context for the move to mutual recognition and the SEA (Alter and Meunier-Aitshalia 1994; Stone Sweet and Caporaso 1998a). Similarly, our analysis does not show that the founding and

Table 2.6: Determinants of exports using first order autoregressive process (N=36)

Independent variables	Exports			
	b	SE(b)	b	SE(b)
Lag-Exports	0.87**	0.25	0.63**	0.21
1970–85	13.7*	6.2	4.2	4.8
1986–94	28.4**	8.4	13.6	8.4
Lag-Legislation			0.2**	0.05
Lag-Cases			0.8	1.2
Lag-Foundings lobbying groups			0.2	0.2
Lag-Cumulative lobbying groups			0.32	0.44
Constant	30.4	55.5	37.6	54.8

* p< .05, ** p<.01

See text for explanation of technique and variables

cumulation of interest groups in Brussels leads economic actors to increase their export. Our results show that the variable that best predicts changes in exports is the number of EC rules; traders see opportunities in EC legislation that harmonizes standards or newly regulates markets.

It is useful to revisit our hypotheses in light of the results. Our results provide strong evidence for a complex, yet theoretically specifiable, explanation for the dynamics of European integration. Hypothesis 1 suggested that exports drove litigation, the founding of pressure groups, and legislation. Our results show evidence that references and legislation were related to increases in exporting, but not to the creation of lobbying groups. Hypothesis 2 suggested that judicial rule-making would influence trade and legislation. Our results show that it does affect legislation, but not trade. Hypothesis 3 proposed that lobbying groups were founded when legislative opportunities arose, which the analysis confirms. Hypothesis 4 linked the growth in lobbying groups to increases in legislation, which our results also confirm. Finally, hypothesis 5 proposed that increased legislative activity would generate higher levels of trade and litigation. Both of these effects were observed.

We draw to two other important conclusions from our analyses. First, the period effects we postulated were generally due to changes in the other independent variables. The first period, 1958–69, was a period of institution-building in the EC. During the second period, once the Brussels-Luxembourg complex had been consolidated, the activities of litigating, lobbying, and legislating expanded, and linked with one another into a causal system. The final period, which we characterize more in terms of the primacy of positive integration, features growing levels of all three activities.

The other intriguing result concerned the growth of lobbying groups and their effects. It was the density of lobbying groups in a domain that produced legislation, and similarly encouraged other organizations to set up shop in Brussels. This is a relatively pure indicator of the political success, and the legitimacy, of the EC. As groups gathered and achieved legislative outcomes that may have favoured them, other groups perceived the necessity of going to Brussels. As the density of groups and the density of legislation increased over time across domains, a clear logic of increasing returns asserted itself. This reinforced the centrality, and we would argue the legitimacy, of the policy arenas and the rules and procedures that have developed in Brussels. The success of the positive integration project created a powerful 'bandwagon' effect, so that actors across Europe felt increasingly compelled to join.

In summary, cooperation in the EC took between ten and 15 years to develop. It moved forward as opportunistic actors organized as lobbying groups, and as the Commission and governments learned how to construct and to use new European arenas to their advantage. Intra-European trade stimulated litigation—negative integration—and legislation—positive integration. The demand for new and more rules was partly driven by interest group activity, and by the operation of the legal system. Increases in legislative rulemaking fed back on private actors, expanding opportunities for exporters to grow markets and for other individuals and groups to pursue their interests. Our results thus show that a particular dynamic of institutionalization—a virtuous circle of relationships between analytically separable but causally linked processes—developed, and that these relationships defined and have redefined the very nature of the Community.

6. Conclusion

The institutionalization of the Treaty of Rome has proceeded now for more than 40 years. The process, in retrospect, has been punctuated by discrete and significant events registered on political, economic, and legal orders. But these events have been embedded in a larger flow. Europeanization is about how a large number of actors, operating in a number different arenas, have produced new forms of governance for themselves. They have used the existing structures to identify and exploit opportunities for cooperation. Once successful, this has pushed along the construction of other structures which have produced new opportunities. Strategic actors in firms, lobbying organizations, governments, the European Commission, the legal profession, and the courts have found themselves having to confront one another in market, legal, and political arenas. They have managed to attain their interests by building institutions and organizational capacity, thus ratcheting up cooperation. In this way, European markets are integrated, market rules reflect European rules, European law holds sway over national law, and interested parties continue to push for new rules in Brussels. Is there a limit to this process? Is there a way in which national governments will choose to opt out and push things back towards less cooperation? These are highly speculative issues, but our results actually suggest some insights.

One potential limit can be found in the very success of integration. As European political space has been constructed so have the webs of constraints that all actors face in seeking to pursue their interests. The new powers given to the European Parliament with legislative processes is an indicator of institutional development, but could also effect the production of legislation by making the process less efficient. Some lobbying groups may have already attained their main ends, and act mostly to block new legislation. Governments may seek to reassert some of the dominance that they have lost. The European Commission is a relatively small organization that is stretched thin, and has been demoralized by recent events. As in 1980, perhaps some of the limits of the current institutions have been or will soon be reached. If the EC goes forward with enlargement, these institutional problems threaten to bog down the possibility for reaching any agreement. Finally, it is possible that anti-EC governments could come to power across Europe and push the process in this direction.

Yet there are powerful countervailing forces. European economies are now highly integrated, and exports are now critical to economic growth. Almost half of world trade occurs within the borders of the EC. The EU, for all intents and purposes is a single economy. Firms presumably tell their governments and Brussels officials that European rules and institutions are generally a good thing because they promote economic growth and work for them. Most European governments realise this. European administrative and legal systems are increasingly integrated as well. Legal systems are in some ways the backbone of European integration. National courts enforce EC law alongside national law, and national bureaucracies implement EC legislation into their procedures and practices. It would take a major economic or political crisis for actors to want to extricate themselves from these linkages. Far more likely, if limits are reached, the main actors will again find creative institutional solutions to their problems.

The institutionalization of European arenas of governance has occurred through self-reinforcing processes. As one set of European institutions has grown up, it has induced integration elsewhere. Actors across many of the important political, legal, and market structures are now living in worlds where their activities are strongly oriented towards Europe. It is difficult to imagine what would cause them to recast their interests in another way. Institutionalization is a powerful force because it serves to embed interest and identities. Today, European institutions do so by connecting arenas for economic, political, and legal decision-making, giving each of them strength and resilience.

3

Overt and Covert Institutionalization in Europe

ADRIENNE HÉRITIER

1. Introduction

OBSERVERS of the European policy-making process are inevitably struck by the contrast between cumbersome decision-making processes on the one hand and simultaneous swift policy developments on the other. Many policies seem to be stuck for long periods in the Council, while at the same time similar measures are introduced under a different guise along a different path. A case in point is European anti-poverty policy. At the very time when this measure was bogged down in a Council deadlock, it was reintroduced by the Commission, couched in different terms in a new political context. In the end it was elevated to official status in the Amsterdam Treaty. A further example of a similar process was in European telecommunications policy, which initially met with strong resistance from Member States. As a result of the Commission's skilful use of all kinds of soft measures, such as offering research funds to industry and actively creating a supportive policy network, it finally became established as a regular European policy.[1] Or, to cite an example from general procedure: the main avenue of European policy-making in the Council often stalls because of the need for consensus, whereas Court rulings and Commission decisions are not hindered by this requirement. Consequently, the emphasis of European policy expansion has often shifted to the European Court of Justice's and the Commission's legal interpretation of rules which exist under the Treaty of Rome. This has given European policies a bias in favour of free trade and free competition (Scharpf 1999). At the same time market-correcting measures and the pursuit of distributive goals remain entangled in the gridlock of Council decision-making processes and are pushed into the background. Again, however, theyre-emerge in bits and pieces and under a different guise in new contexts as a result of successful circumvention

---

[1] This was not exclusively the result of the application of informal soft measures, but also of the use of Article 90,3—now 86,3—by the Commission, which was subsequently confirmed by the ECJ (Héritier 1999).

of Council deadlocks (Héritier 1999). Why is it that European policies which stagnate in the main political arena materialize in other shapes and forms elsewhere? And what are the typical escape routes when the main political avenue is blocked? I argue that the formal institutional structure of the European Union together with the diversity of Member States' interests would regularly lead to an impasse in decision-making were it not for the existence of different paths of institutionalization which have emerged to circumvent impending deadlock. This overt and covert institutionalization creates a European political space, meaning 'a widely shared system of rules and procedures to define who actors are, how they make sense of each other's actions and what types of actions are possible' (Stone Sweet, Fligstein, and Sandholtz, this volume: p. xx). It has developed in three different ways: first, straightforward changes made to existing rules as a result of interpretation and negotiated modifications; second, the explicit and implicit development of new soft or informal institutions, such as information and monitoring, mobilization, and network building, and the spontaneous emergence of social conventions, as a way of expanding the areas of European activity; and third, 'kitchen politics', that is, more covert ways of overcoming formal institutional obstacles to decision-making. Such covert ways involve committing actors to policy decisions, the implications of which are not spelt out in advance, by concealing planned or ongoing changes from the general public, as well as by re-labelling and re-contextualizing issues in order to embed them in a different choice situation which helps overcome a deadlock. These three different modes of effecting change, as will be shown in this chapter, can be observed in the most diverse areas of European policy-making and generally result in a widening of European policy activities. They constitute the ways in which the rule structures governing the European policy space are elaborated, or adapted, through interpretation, legislation, and the development of shared understandings of norms and procedures, but also by committing unwitting actors to a subsequent widening of European activities: they are is the central theme of this volume as indicated by Stone Sweet, Fligstein, and Sandholtz (this volume). Since modes of institutionalization where there is Member-State resistance to the introduction of more European activities are of particular interest in this chapter, by logical implication the question also arises as to the conditions under which deepening institutionalization does *not* occur, and a development in the opposite direction takes place, narrowing the scope of European activities. In other words, the systematic points where turns in the other direction occur—steps of de-institutionalization, as it were—have to be identified as well.

In this chapter, the three basic modes of overt and covert institutionalization and their theoretical foundations are discussed, each illustrated by empirical examples of European policy-making. Then the question is raised as to consequences of the different modes of institutionalization and the conditions under which these different paths of deepening European institutionalization do *not* normally occur.

2. Sources and Modes of Overt and Covert Institutionalization: Theoretical Interpretation and Empirical Examples

The starting point of the argument is that the diversity of Member States' interests together with the primary formal institutions create the necessity for consensus which very often is not reached. Instead, a deadlock situation emerges in the main political arena, the Council: a 'joint-decision trap' (Scharpf 1988). This is a formal decision-making setting where the consensus or unanimous vote of all the representatives of the sub-units of a polity are needed to bring about a decision. As a consequence the decision-making process tends to stall. At the same time there are no exit options open for leaving the polity either. The necessity for consensus in the Community derives from the fact that the formal institutions of the polity have been constructed in such a way as to preserve the diversity of Member States which wish to safeguard their sovereignty. In other words, the founding Member States established a decentralized and fragmented polity that gives individual members the power of veto but does not have a strong central power for coordinating its various decision-making bodies: actors and institutions are linked by increasingly complex rules in the legislating process. This aspect of institutional development may well be accounted for by the claim that the new European institutional arrangements were negotiated with regard to their likely distributional impacts (Knight 1992; 1995). The specific institutional impacts at stake here are decision-making competences and sovereignty, which the European supranational institutions would have taken over had they been granted significant and well-defined powers, a step which Member States were reluctant to take. Hence the founding Member States deliberately created an institutional structure whose central decision-making powers lie with an intergovernmental body, the Council of Ministers, whose Parliament is relatively weak, and whose decision-making process is contingent on the simultaneous agreement of several institutions, making it a rather unwieldy and cumbersome process. However, by establishing such a complex and fragmented decision-making structure the founding members inadvertently created a power vacuum into which some actors moved, applying strategies of overt and covert institutionalization to overcome the frequent decision-making deadlocks; in particular in our case, these were an entrepreneurial Commission and the European Court of Justice (ECJ). Another related source of overt and covert institutionalization results from the lack of specific detailed rules in the original Treaty about how to deal with all kinds of future contingencies. Instead, often as a result of a compromise between conflicting interests, the rules of the Treaty of Rome and all subsequent treaties provide latitude in the application of rules and competences which has to be interpreted when applied to a new context. These possibilities may be exploited by entrepreneurial actors in order to achieve their goals.

The various overt and covert modes of deepening institutionalization deployed in the light of these possibilities can be best explained by a variety of theoretical viewpoints: institutions whose rules and basic goals are defined constitute the starting point of the analysis. The first mode of deepening institutionalization—the straightforward modification through interpretation and bargained change of existing rules which had been established to maintain the existing distribution of competencies, in other words consensus rule (Knight 1992)—may be accounted for by theories which describe the exploitation of existing formal institutions by organizational entrepreneurs (North 1995) or by skilled social actors (Fligstein and Stone Sweet, this volume). Thus the specification of vague primary rules may bring about a change. Similarly the theory describing the development of dyadic and triadic governance based on third-party dispute resolution accounts for the generation and modification of institutional rules (Stone Sweet 1999). Further, principal-agent theory or the modified trustee scheme of independent non-majoritarian institutions (Majone 1998) explicates how agents or trustees—the Commission or the ECJ—gain latitude if the contending principals—the Member States—have created ambiguous rules which are open to interpretation (Marks, Hooghe, and Blank 1996; see also Sandholtz and Stone Sweet 1998). Straightforward institutionalist change through negotiated agreements has been extensively theorized in bargaining theory, explicating how gridlock is overcome by forming compromises, striking package deals, or paying compensation. The second path of overt institutionalization, deploying soft instruments of information and monitoring as well as mobilization and network building, and the emergence of social conventions, is described by the theory of regulation through publication (Majone 1995) and network theory (Mayntz 1993), and the theory of the spontaneous emergence of institutions (Calvert and Johnson 1998), respectively. The third covert mode of institutionalization—committing actors and concealing decision-making making processes as well as recontextualizing—may be explained by sociological organization theory, which points out that decision-making processes are frequently as much concerned with creating actors' commitment as they are with rationally weighing the costs and benefits of specific decisions, and how, by isolating decisions from the wider political decision-making process, policy changes may be brought about (Brunsson 1989). Finally, the practice of re-labelling issues has been discussed in policy analysis as a mode of enhancing their chances of acceptance in the political arena (Windhoff-Héritier 1987; Riker 1996).

3. Overt and Formal Modes of Changing Rules

3.1. The formal interpretation of rules

Treaties are negotiated in interstate bargaining processes in which each state government has the power of veto over the content of the agreement. This is an invitation to ambiguity on points of contention 'to allow each participating government to claim success in representing national interests' (Marks, Hooghe, and Blank 1996: 354). As a consequence, once primary rules are enacted, they often do not clearly delineate the assignment of powers and responsibilities for all categories of future issues and situations (Calvert and Johnson 1998). This is one reason why existing rules need to be clarified and interpreted (Shapiro, in this volume). They are thereby modified and as such become the guidelines for subsequent action. The process of rule generation and alteration has also been conceived of as the emergence of governance through dyadic and then triadic governance with third-party dispute resolution (TDR) (Stone Sweet 1999; Stone Sweet and Caporaso 1998b). It may come about as a result of mutual agreement and delegation of authority to a third party, or on a compulsory basis through jurisdiction. The conflicts around a rule are adjudicated and the rules of adjudication discussed and elaborated in such a way as to develop a normative structure which subsequently guides conflict solution. 'TDR generates a discourse about how people ought to behave. Because rules, reasoning about rules, and the adaptation of rules to specific social needs constitute the core of this discourse . . . precedent follows naturally. Precedent helps to legitimize TDR by simultaneously acknowledging rule-making behavior, while constraining that same behavior with a rule: that like cases shall be settled likewise' (Stone Sweet 1999: 157). At the end of this process 'we find ourselves in a rather different world' (Stone Sweet 1999: 158). Vague primary rules will also be exploited, applied and interpreted by entrepreneurial actors in ways that best fit their own particular agendas, with all actors seeking to enhance their respective spheres of activities. By investing in the acquisition of knowledge and the coordination of skills, they gradually learn how to wield more power in policy-making and in so doing gradually alter institutions and may produce results which differ from these intended by the designers of the formal institutional structure (Fligstein 1997a; North 1995).

In the European context, with its complex and interlinked decision-making structure, it has been the Commission and the European Court of Justice in particular which, by means of clarification and adjudication, have specified interpretable formal rules and mediated between conflicting actors to overcome policy stalling. The Court acts as arbiter in decisional conflicts, interpreting and specifying rules which then serve as reference points for future decision-making (Stone Sweet and Brunell 1998a). Thus, the ECJ has constantly defined and redefined such concepts as 'market control' and 'market share' in interpreting statutes, regulations, and derogation clauses, thereby significantly contributing to the creation of a regional European integrated market (Egan 1998; Shapiro 1968). The Commission has also struggled to determine exactly what constitutes an 'equivalent to a quantitative trade barrier', the latter being prohibited under the Treaty of Rome (Art. 30). One of the most important policy consequences of overt institutional change through rule interpretation by the Commission and the Court has been the dominance of negative integration over positive integration (Scharpf 1999). Negative integration, or market-creating measures, have relied on judicial law-making and Commission decisions based on the competition principle which is embedded in the Treaty of Rome, by-passing the Council, such as under Art. 90,3. By contrast, positive integration, or market-correcting policies, have to rely on the consensual capacity of the Council, and more and more on the European Parliament, which have to overcome considerable hurdles. These are particularly great when it comes to highly politically visible, redistributive issues. Thus, close observation of market integration has become the overarching principle of European policy-making as a result of non-majoritarian decisions—for example, judicial law-making and Commission decisions. This policy has been extended 'without much political attention, through interventions of the European Commission against infringements of Treaty obligations, and through the decisions and preliminary rulings of the European Court of Justice' (Scharpf 1999: 51). The doctrines of 'direct effect' and 'supremacy' have brought about the 'constitutionalization of competition law' (Scharpf 1999: 54).

3.2. Formal change through bargaining

Existing institutional rules are constantly being adjusted to meet the requirements of new circumstances, not just by judicial interpretation but also through direct renegotiation. These new political bargaining processes are largely conducted with regard to their distributional effects. However, the process of deliberation and the exchange of views which accompany it may produce new information and may alter the participants' basic preferences (Calvert and Johnson 1998:17). At least such deliberation is helpful in establishing a common understanding of what is at stake (Knight and Johnson 1994), but most likely, even after deliberation, 'people will continue to disagree in good faith about the common good, and about the issues of policy, justice and right' (Waldron 1996: 2189, quoted in Calvert and Johnson 1998:17). Conflicting interests regarding the 'right' interpretation of a rule will remain, with each participant seeking to achieve solutions to his or her own advantage. However, throughout the process, arguments which are accepted by the majority are those which will influence future rule interpretations (Calvert and Johnson 1998). They become principles that legitimize policy decisions and 'are likely to remain acceptable, and thus to remain influential in policy making, tomorrow' (Calvert and Johnson 1998: 31). As such they are used by politicians and courts as a means of supporting their position in resolving the interpretation of a rule.

While deliberation may clarify the order of preferences of the actors involved and the nature of the conflict at stake, as well as create 'legitimate' arguments which can be used as a resource, divergent interests nevertheless still have to be accommodated if deadlock is to be avoided. This may be achieved by arriving at package deals or issue-linkages: measures from which the losers of the contested, proposed policy stand to gain are added to the 'focus issue' in order to win the opponent over. Losers may also be offered compensation in return for their support. Another way of settling conflicts is to pass only framework solutions, which leaves all parties free to shape the respective policy in more detail as they choose. The Commission frequently acts as broker and prepares such deals and solutions. It surveys all ongoing policy developments and is engaged in multiple negotiation arenas. With its intimate knowledge of the complicated institutional rules, it is able to exploit this information and seize opportunities to act in overcoming decisional deadlocks.

A recent example of how a redistributional conflict was resolved and a policy impasse avoided in an institutional context requiring unanimous decision-making is the compromise struck in the reform of the regional funds policy. Reform of the regional aid package was long overdue. In particular, the prospect of the central and eastern European countries joining the EU put pressure on the Commission to speed up reform. Many parts of the present Union which currently receive regional aid, intended for the poorest areas, will lose it before the enlargement takes place. Individual Member States have naturally sought to retain their share of EU structural funds. The conflict has been resolved by letting Member States deal with potentially difficult questions: by invoking the subsidiarity principle, the unpleasant decision as to which regions were to be denied aid has been passed over to national governments. The former Objective 1 regions—regions whose development is considered to be 'lagging behind' the EU average—also receive 'transitional support' over the next five years. The 'phase-out' assistance which will be made available in progressively diminishing amounts is designed to soften the blow (*European Voice* 2000).

A case of institutional competences being renegotiated when threatened by impending deadlock could recently be observed in the Commission and the European Parliament. Under the Amsterdam Treaty the Parliament has to confirm the new composition of the Commission in its entirety. During its hearings of the new commissioners, the Parliament disapproved of individual candidates. It then secured a promise from the President of the Commission that, in return for Parliamentary support for the entire team, the President would in future dismiss individual commissioners who no longer enjoyed the support of the Parliament (*Süddeutsche Zeitung* 1999a). Thus, the European Parliament gained de facto the right of a vote of confidence *vis-à-vis* individual commissioners (*Süddeutsche Zeitung* 1999c).

The first two modes of explicit formal change of the primary institutional rules of the Community are well known and constitute the central focus of political science research on Europe. This is not the case for the two remaining modes: the overt, informal soft strategies and the more covert ways of changing existing rules.

4. Overt Change through Informal Strategies and Patterns

The second basic mode of overcoming policy-making gridlocks by developing informal overt and covert institutions is the establishment of soft institutions or informal rules. The existing formal institutions are thereby modified and a decisional impasse may be circumvented. The introduction of soft rules may take the shape of an explicit intentional strategy, such as information/shaming/monitoring and network building, or a spontaneous, decentralized co-ordination (Demsetz 1988).

4.1. Exchange of information, naming and shaming, monitoring

The purpose of the exchange of information is to prepare the first stage of a Community policy. Initially Member States provide only mutual information, which is followed by binding regulatory measures. 'Naming and shaming' is used after Member States have provided information about their activities in the context of monitoring. It implies the attempt to change the behaviour of regulatees by exposing their behaviour if sanctioning tools are not readily available for the regulator, as is often the case in Europe.

The recent Amsterdam Treaty chose the first path in the initial stages of a common labour market policy. A number of Member States, such as Britain and Germany, opposed the introduction of explicit European competences to create employment, while France, Italy, and some other Member States were in favour. The way round the deadlock was the introduction of unemployment policy as a soft programme with each country reporting annually on the development of its employment figures, the measures taken to reduce unemployment, and the mode of monitoring the development; sharing experience in the field of fighting unemployment was also promoted. Another example of the Commission using this soft method of introducing a new policy is in telecommunications and research and technology policy. The attempt to establish a European policy had met with the resistance of Member-State governments. Hence the Commission sought new means: it introduced business round tables to facilitate regular exchanges of information and opinions and offered research funds which could be used on a voluntary basis to push national governments' policy in a new direction. In the end it succeeded in establishing a European telecommunications and research and technology policy.

In order to compensate for its lack of formal powers for ensuring that Member States comply with Community policy, such as in regional policy and environmental policy, the Commission frequently attempts to gain control of implementation by publicizing implementation details. Member States have to provide information about the activities they have undertaken with regional funds money; and in the case of environmental policy, they have to publish emission data on water and air quality. The Commission highlights this by publishing this information as performance tables in order to shame governments into compliance. It also organizes campaigns to inform citizens about their rights *vis-à-vis* national administrations under Community legislation, such as by guaranteeing access to information on the environment held by national administrations. It thereby gains information on the quality of implementation of Community legislation. These routine measures have subsequently been formalized by the Access to Information Directive in environmental policy.

4.2. Network building and mobilization

Network building and mobilization may be used by the Commission by empowering domestic actors, such as ministries and interest groups and large firms, to differing degrees. Cleavages in the domestic political arenas are exploited and alliances formed with different actors in order to build support for a specific European policy measure when faced with an impending deadlock. The strategies of network building and mobilization used by the Commission may be illustrated by the example of anti-poverty policy (Bauer 1999). The Commission employed a variety of methods to circumvent the gridlock in the Council which was preventing the programme from being continued and extended. Ignoring the situation in the Council, the Commission proceeded to set up a separate programme to combat poverty and social exclusion. Applications were invited. In a very short time the Commission received more than 2,000 bids, a sizeable number of which were from precisely those countries whose governments were most opposed to the programme— Germany and Britain—and quickly initiated 86 demonstration programmes. An entire network of actors with a stake in the poverty programme was created. To strengthen the network the Commission mobilized non-governmental organizations on an International Day to Eliminate Poverty and raised support for European competences to fight poverty. Britain, supported by Germany and Denmark, went to the Court of Justice claiming that the Commission was spending money 'illegally' and without authorization. The Court of Justice ruled that 'Contrary to what the Commission has argued, the purpose of the projects . . . was not to prepare future Community action or launch pilot projects. Rather, it is clear from the activities envisaged, the aims pursued and persons benefited that they were intended to continue the initiatives of the Poverty 3 Programme, at a time when it was obvious that the Council was not going to adopt the Poverty 4 proposal, which sought to continue and extend Community action to combat social exclusion' (ECJ 1998*a*).

The Commission also engages in network building in order to build up an informal capacity in implementation. By establishing links with sub-national public and private actors, as mentioned above, it seeks to obtain information on implementation performance such as in environmental policy where subnational actors are explicitly solicited to supply information to the Commission regarding implementation practices (Héritier, Knill, and Mingers 1996).

4.3. Spontaneous coordination

The other type of informal rules emerges at a decentralized level and spontaneously as social conventions. Here, strategic uncertainty about others' preferences promotes behaviour that resolves a collective action dilemma. It makes sense to shape the other actors' perceptions of one's preferences and to give signals that one is willing to cooperate and to trust. These signals enable the like-minded to locate others who are trustworthy, who in turn can build up a reputation for responding cooperatively to trust (Bates 1988). Because actors prefer coordination as opposed to non-coordination as one of the co-operative outcomes, they will use whatever salient information they have—focal point—in order to achieve it (Schelling 1963). In time more actors will follow suit, and a social convention is established which provides information about the future actions of others (Knight 1995).

A well known example of the decentralized development of such a social convention which enables the policy process to move on is the rule of diffuse reciprocity in the Council of Ministers. It is an informal mechanism which ensures that the interests of one Member State are not blatantly disregarded when conflicts are settled, because every country is aware that on some future occasion it may be the one in the minority. The Committee of Permanent Representatives (COREPER), for example, has developed a peer-consciousness that is oriented towards the notion of fairness and maintains a focus on future concessions (Héritier 1997). An institutionalized preference for cooperation has emerged. There is a belief that all participants will profit in the long term, since offending one another's interests in an outspoken way would make future retributions likely (Schmidt 1995). And since Member States are highly likely to stay together under the common roof of the European Union, they are well advised to establish a fair balance between all the actors concerned.

5. Covert Institutionalization

Finally, there is a more covert mode of playing with the formal institutional rules in order to bring about change which is more indirect in the sense that conflictual issues are not fully revealed with all their implications. One mode is to commit actors at an early stage; another mode is to shape policy behind closed doors in such a way as to make it difficult for those subsequently responsible for formal decision-making to unravel the decisions reached. And finally, in order to avoid deadlock decisions are re-labelled and fitted into a new context of policy-making so as to win the support of decision-makers. As a representative of the Commission put it at a European Community Studies

Association meeting in Seattle in 1997, 'We all know that agricultural policy needs to be reformed. But it is so much more difficult to achieve this by putting it explicitly on the agenda'. These more indirect, indeed devious, modes of overcoming deadlock by institutionalization are well described by sociological organization theory (see for instance Brunsson 1989), which analyzes how organizations seek to deal with conflicting expectations in their environment by committing actors to a decision in principle where they are not fully aware of the implications and potential conflicts. In terms of participatory scope, the organizational leaders also seek to avoid stalling by isolating a larger number of actors from the decision-making process. Complex decisions are wrapped up 'behind closed doors' in such a way that they are difficult to unravel at a later stage when more actors are allowed to participate in the decision-making. The strategy of re-labelling or redefining issues, such as to link them up to other, popular, issues, has been elaborated in policy analysis (Windhoff-Héritier 1987).

5.1. Committing actors

Organization theory draws attention to the fact that decision-making is not only about choice but also about commitment. Decisions may be made primarily to secure the support of actors and to create motivation and expectations which encourage participants to pledge themselves to a specific action. Once the commitment of the actors is secured, the organizational action can be mobilized. The prime intention here is to reduce the uncertainty about actors' behaviour rather than the uncertainty about the content and consequences of alternatives. 'Preferences are adapted . . . motivation and expectation attaching to a specific action are promoted' (Brunsson 1989: 179).

We are quite often faced with this unofficial 'under-cover' mode of institutional development in a deadlock-prone polity such as the European Union. An example where the introduction of a new institutional rule unavoidably triggered further extensive institutional changes of which the actors were initially unaware was the decision to establish monetary union, which has been termed a Trojan horse in European policy-making. It exerts pressure on all involved to introduce, in addition, a common monetary policy and fiscal policy, together with the deregulation of financial markets. In other words, there are long-term policy implications and spillover effects which were not the explicit objectives of all the actors who explicitly acquiesced to the initial decision at the Maastricht conference. As Germany's former chancellor Kohl put it, monetary union is synonymous with the rise of Europe and is an auxiliary device—*Notaggregat*—for necessary European reforms (*Süddeutsche Zeitung* 1999*b*).

A further example of a precise and extensive institutional commitment being created without the actors involved being fully aware of what they committed themselves to is the 1982 Framework Directive on Industrial Installations. Although this directive initiated the Commission's important change in strategy from a quality-oriented to an emission-based policy, the decision-making process proved surprisingly unproblematic. The measure was adopted after only a year of negotiations: a very short period by EU standards. One reason for this was that the directive itself did not lay down special emission limits for pollutants, but was restricted to general procedural provisions for licensing industrial plants. The absence of statutory limits at the time of the negotiations possibly led some countries to misjudge the full consequences of the provisions. 'We were astounded ourselves at how quickly the thing was dealt with. We'd never expected that it [the directive] would be adopted in less than a year. For me there's only one explanation: the member states didn't realize at the time what they were signing' (Interview with the EU Commission, DG XI, September 1993, in Héritier, Knill, and Mingers 1996: 180).

5.2. Secluded decision-making processes

Conflictual demands that are likely to end up in a decisional stalemate in open debate are often hived off into special organization units which sit down and hammer out decisions with the benefit of advice from experts. As a consequence, once such decisions have been reached it is difficult to undo them at a later stage when the political debate is again opened up to a wider range of participants. This mode of under-cover institutional change is quite often the case in highly contested areas such as, most recently, the attempt to harmonize the taxation of capital income, where a specific working group was instituted for the purpose of producing proposals which could accommodate the objections of Britain and Luxembourg, or in complex technological fields of decision-making such as the Volatile Organic Compound Directive in environmental policy. By establishing specific policy working groups and networks in such questions, state executives give the Commission latitude to formulate very precise regulations. Here the Commission functions as a 'hub of numerous highly specialized policy networks of technical experts designing detailed regulations' (Marks, Hooghe, and Blank 1996: 355).

5.3. Re-labelling and restructuring a choice situation

By linking an issue with another issue which enjoys wide support, or by relabelling it, its prospects of being accepted in the political arena may be improved, because new and compelling aspects are highlighted (Windhoff-Héritier 1987). A related strategy is to include alternatives into a choice situation in such a way that even the opponents of a measure are compelled by the structure of the situation to support it . Actors' choices on the issue are altered. 'And this is what *heresthetics* is about: structuring the world so you can win. For a person who expects to lose on some decision, the fundamental *heresthetical* device is to divide the majority with a new alternative, one the person prefers to the alternative previously expected to win' (Riker 1996:9).

Again, the Commission's poverty programme provides an example of re-labelling and re-contextualizing. By re-introducing the programme in the context of the European Social Fund as the Employment-INTEGRA Initiative, and concentrating on the integration of migrants, refugees, the homeless, lone parents, and ex-prisoners into the labour market, the programme was able to build on a new supportive coalition. The Commission thus shifted the focus from 'more "traditional" labour market integration strategies', which are the preserve of the Member States, to the integration of marginal groups. In the end, the Commission succeeded in having a new Article 137(2) TEC (ex118(2)) incorporated into the Amsterdam Treaty: 'The Council, acting in accordance with the co-decision procedure may adopt measures designed to encourage co-operation between member states through initiatives aimed at improving knowledge, developing exchanges of information and best practices, promoting innovative approaches and evaluation of experiences in order to combat social exclusion' (Bauer 1999: 12–13).

Another case of re-contextualizing is the attempt by the Commission to present a labour contractual issue as a health and safety issue to be decided under qualified majority voting (QMV). By linking contractual rights to health and safety issues, which are decided according to the qualified majority rule of Art. 118a, it sought to outwit the British government which was vetoing the working-time measure. The British did not implement the directive and brought an action in the ECJ challenging its legal basis under QMV, arguing that the regulation of working time should not be linked to social—health and safety—issues. In 1996, the Court ruled that the directive had been adopted correctly on the basis of Art. 118a and called for a broad interpretation of the words 'working environment', 'safety', and 'health', using the definition of the World Health Organisation (Héritier 1999).

6. Consequences and Contradictions

It has been argued that the consensual decision rules and the heterogeneity of Member-State actors tend to lead to stalemate in decision-making. This deadlock situation is overcome by an overt and covert deepening of institutionalization. Three modes of overt and covert institutionalization have been distinguished here: the explicit and straightforward specifying and modification of existing formal rules by adjudication and negotiations; the formation of new informal soft rules and strategies; and the more indirect and covert methods of circumventing deadlock by committing actors in advance to decisions which have far-reaching consequences, by concealing delicate issues in secluded circles, and by fitting issues into a new policy context where their chances of being accepted are greater. Thus the primary institutions established in the 1950s have produced situations which have had consequences which none of the actors involved, who sought to influence the original institutional structures in line with their own interests, were able to foresee. Rather, the original formal structures have been creatively and strate-gically exploited to achieve rule innovation. Also, many elements of the struc-ture now in place in the EC/EU, including much that is expressed in formal law, originated from outside the formal legislative process in informal processes, and was eventually incorporated into it (Sandholtz and Stone Sweet 1998).

Of course, the rules of any polity which open up repertoires of acceptable actions rather than determine behaviour are used creatively. However, I contend that, given the diversity of its members and their inability to agree on the direction in which the polity should develop, this constitutes a *structural* feature of the European Union. The changes that have evolved along different paths have different implications for the European polity as such. The bargaining-oriented escape routes—seeking compensation, the use of issue-linkage and package deals—are chosen with the full knowledge of those con-cerned, and indeed, they normally provide means of overcoming an imminent decision-making gridlock under conditions of lesser diversity than those which currently exist in the European polity. They constitute a normal means of oiling the wheels of democratic decision-making processes under conditions of diversity. The same holds true for the type of soft strategy which seeks to increase the transparency of European policy-making by facilitating mutual control on the basis of a well-balanced representation of diverse inter-ests and building supportive networks which are structurally unbiased. By contrast, a candidate for reform would be covert modes of institutionalization which involve an element of stealth or surprise for those involved, in the sense that they are inadvertently brought into situations where they are forced to pursue a route of action that they did not want to embark on in the first place. For unlike the first two modes of overt institutionalization, the covert mode of policy-making constitutes a way of circumventing deadlock which contradicts two important principles of institutions: that they are known and accepted by all the parties concerned, and are based on shared expectations about appro-priate behaviour. Instead, this type of overt and covert institutionalization is surreptitious by nature and remains a grey area of unofficial short-cuts; it thrives on and seeks to exploit uncertainty, and is concealed from general pub-lic scrutiny.

Finally, the question arises as to whether overt and covert institutionaliza-tion occurs under any conditions, or whether there are instances in which this type of escape route is not chosen and does not take place. Such conditions do indeed exist. The first is, of course, when there is no deadlock situation in the first place and Member States agree to take specific policy steps to enlarge the scope of European activities. This condition arises in a situation where all stand to win from cooperation and, as a consequence, there is wide domestic support for the proposed policy. What happens more frequently, however, is that Member States agree *not* to take policy steps, and pull out of a specific policy area altogether, because some players would suffer a loss from the decision. This tends to be the case when a redistributional issue is at stake and important domestic alliances within Member States oppose the proposed decision. The outspoken refusal to adopt a European policy may also be the result of Member States' governments learning from the experience of overt and covert institutionalization and explicitly seeking to prevent policy expansion in a specific area, such as was done by exempting the Third Pillar—cooperation in matters of justice and police—from the jurisdiction of the ECJ. De-institutionalization, as it were, may occur in the form of offering single Member States possibilities for opting out, or by deciding to end a programme at the European level altogether, thus leaving activities to individual Member States. The possibility of opting out is illustrated by the example of social policy (Rhodes 1995). New institutional avenues were sought and found under the Social Protocol in the Maastricht negotiations: opting out and twin-track policy-making. Since it seemed highly likely that Britain would be prepared to block changes to the Treaty through its use of the veto, an escape route to circumvent the deadlock emerged 'through the most unusual and unpredictable of compromises' (Lange 1992: 249). The other eleven Member States signed a separate protocol that allows them to use EC 'institutions, procedures and mechanisms' to formulate and implement social policies on which they agree. In order to accommodate the diverse views, they went outside the Treaty: that is, provisions passed under the Social Protocol did not require enactment by Britain, which has an opt-out option. As far as active social policy-making was concerned, therefore, the looming deadlock was avoided by the creation of a twin-track institutional process. Monetary union and the Schengen Agreement on the abolition of border controls are further examples where not all Member States formally adopt a new policy, but some remain outside it instead.

The other form is where European policy measures are brought to an end altogether. Thus, in the case of European anti-poverty policy, Member States decided at one point not to pursue the anti-poverty programme. As we have seen, however, the Commission ignored this intention and sought to continue the programme by other means. Another example is in the area of social insurance, where the Court decided on the 'portability' of insurance rights of migrant workers within the Community. Recently Member States have sought to overturn the Court's ruling on coordination in portability. They have unanimously agreed to decisions that allow Member States to restrict the granting of benefits rights after proper notification, which in turn is subject to the unanimous approval of Member States. So far there has been an informal agreement to allow such self-exemptions (Leibfried and Pierson 1995: 64). It may well be that with a range of new members joining the Community and diversity deepening even further, this reverse route of opting out and unanimous refraining from widening the scope of European policy-making becomes more frequent.

4

Institutionalizing Promiscuity: Commission-Interest Group Relations in the European Union

SONIA MAZEY AND JEREMY RICHARDSON

1. Introduction: Predicting Promiscuity and Institutionalization

Our study is concerned with two key actors present in all advanced policy making systems—bureaucracies and interest groups—although we recognise that the EU policy process involves many other key actors, such as national governments, who may at times be more powerful. Without entering the debate over whether national governments or supranational institutions dominate the EU policy process, we simply note that the EU is now a maturing system for the making of public policy at the European level. As such, its public policy outputs over the past decades now amount to a critical mass of public policy similar to all advanced industrial states, in terms of both quantity and scope. In a sense, the EU policy process is now as much about building on past policies as it is about creating completely new ones. It is to be expected, therefore, that it now exhibits the kind of regularized and institutionalized system of relations between the state bureaucracy and interest groups that we see in all western European states.

Thus, our central thesis is that once the EC/EU began to develop into a significant venue or arena for public policy making in Europe, and for whatever reasons, a certain trajectory of institutionalized interaction between the EC/EU bureaucracy—in this case the Commission and interest groups—was likely. We base this prediction on three theoretical assumptions concerning the class of actors under study. First, we assume that *bureaucracies have a tendency to construct stable and manageable relationships with interest groups in each policy area as a means of securing some kind of 'negotiated order' or stable environment*. Second,

We wish to acknowledge the cooperation of many Commission and interest group officials who agreed to be interviewed, and we are especially grateful to Mark Rhinard for his research assistance on this project. We would also like to thank Rachel Cichowski, and Neil Fligstein for comments on an earlier draft. Jeremy Richardson wishes to acknowledge the support of the Nuffield Foundation.

interest groups generally exhibit a preference for state bureaucracies as a venue for informing themselves about and influencing public policy. Third, *interest groups will seek to exploit new opportunity structures or venues as a means of maximizing their capacity to shape public policy to their own advantage.* We are suggesting that different types of actors have associated behavioural patterns, or at least exhibit *procedural ambitions* (Richardson and Jordan 1979) which condition and structure their behaviour in the real world. Moreover, as many of these procedural ambitions are deeply embedded in the political cultures of the majority of the 15 Member States, it should be no surprise to see what we have elsewhere described as a 'European policy style' emerging over time (Mazey and Richardson 1995: 337–59).

Most of what we have to say in this chapter is focused on the Commission, as we see it as the main EU level organization able to facilitate demands for the expansion of cross-border exchange (Stone Sweet and Sandholtz 1998: 2–26). In being an enthusiastic supplier of policy initiatives which facilitate further cross-border exchange, the Commission is merely acting as a 'purposeful opportunist' (Klein and O'Higgins 1985; Cram 1994). In acting strategically to facilitate further transnational exchange, the Commission has recognised the utility of interest groups as sources of (1) information, (2) support, and (3) legitimacy. Like all state bureaucracies, it has recognized that the more institutionalized the consultation with interest groups becomes, so the risks of policy or political disasters is reduced. By seating the appropriate stakeholders at the appropriate seats, bureaucrats can reduce the risk of opposition elsewhere, in other venues. By emphasising collective decision-making, they can also avoid blame for future policy disasters or fiascos (Henderson 1977).

Interest groups, of course, are usually willing participants in this process of institutionalized intermediation between themselves and the Commission. By participating they too reduce risk. Indeed, simply *knowing* what is going on may be just as important to an adaptive interest organization as trying to *influence* what is going on. In that sense, participation in the institutions of intermediation is perfectly rational even if no policy pay-off for the interest group results. However, the increasing technical content of EU policy, and the 'unpacking' of big policy issues such as tax harmonization into more manageable, low-salience, technical issues, increases the incentive for groups to form policy partnerships with bureaucrats in—preferably—closed policy-making structures. This process facilitates continuous trade-offs in a system of 'mutual exchange' (Jordan and Richardson 1982). For mutual exchange to take place over time, new organizations and institutions need to be created. Thus, for example, groups and bureaucracies have a mutual interest in trying to form stable policy communities and policy networks if they can, even though this can be very difficult when so many actors can claim stakeholder status. Similarly, actors have an incentive to construct new organizations which facilitate intermediation over time.

The problem in trying to create stable organizations and institutions, however, is that, as the EU policy process is so obviously a multi-venue system, the incentives to 'venue shop' (Baumgartner and Jones 1991) are quite high. The history of the institutionalization of Commission-interest group relations presents a paradox, therefore. On the one hand, it is quite clear that the Commission has engaged in strategic action (see Stone Sweet, Fligstein, and Sandholtz, this volume) in trying to create institutions and organizations in which groups can participate. On the other, there are many unintended consequences resulting from the promiscuity of both Commission officials and groups and the venue shopping by groups. The move towards institutionalized European governance is, in some respects, still an *experiment* in finding the forms and methods which serve the interests of different participants in the process (Stone Sweet, Fligstein, and Sandholtz, this volume) and in constructing stable institutions. Even though it is difficult to be certain of the final outcome of the expanding interest group system at the EU level, however, the process has a very long history of institution building. Our guess is that institutionalized intermediation is becoming embedded and, therefore, structures future action. Moreover, it is unlikely to be reversed, even if very powerful actors, such as Member States, wished to do so. Similarly, the substantive rules and organizations that are in place act as some kind of ratchet. Thus, the Commission's suggestion, in 1999, that some of its powers in the competition field should be delegated to the Member States met with very strong opposition from business groups.

2. Replicating the Past: the Logic of Promiscuity

It is a truism that there is nothing new under the sun. The formation of the European Coal and Steel Community (ECSC) is no exception. Most institutional innovations bear some relation to past experience and borrow from it. In the early years of the Community, the High Authority—the executive of the ECSC—began to exhibit familiar bureaucratic features, namely, functional specialization and expansion (Downs 1967). The trend between 1945 and 1955, notwithstanding Monnet's ambitions to the contrary, was to create a more traditionally organized bureaucracy. As a result, members of the High Authority involved in policy-making began the first stages of a long process of institutionalizing the cross-cutting relationships with organized interests and national administrations (Mazey 1992). A degree of path dependency seems evident. What was barely visible in those very early years has now become a central feature of the EU policy style, namely, the 'increasingly dense networks of transnational actors comprised of people who are representatives of Member State governments, firms, lobbying organizations and members of the European Union organizations . . .' (Stone Sweet, Fligstein, and Sandholtz, this volume; see also Mazey and Richardson 1995: 337–59).

2.1. Interest groups: incentives, fashions, and learning

In essence the predictions made by Ernst Haas in 1958 have come true (Haas 1958). There is now a dense and mature *European* interest group system (Coen 1997; Green Cowles 1997; Greenwood 1997; Coen 1998; Bartle 1999; Greenwood, Strangward, and Stanich 1999). As Sidjanski (1970: 402) noted, some of the groups were formed at the same time as the European institutions were created. Many others were created only when it became clear that the European regulations emanating from these new institutions would directly affect a wide range of societal interests. As Fligstein and Stone Sweet hypothesize in this volume, 'the founding of new lobbying groups will be provoked by increases in transnational exchange and in the production of legislation'. However, they also note, correctly, that actors who do not engage in transnational exchange will also go to EU organizations in order to destabilize national rules or procedures which they do not like (Stone Sweet and Sandholtz 1998). As the Fligstein and Stone Sweet data show, the rate of formation of European associations in Brussels has been quite low, at 1.5 a year over time, but it has exhibited 'spurts', starting with a flurry at the formation of the EC, with peaks and troughs thereafter, and with a considerable increase following the passage of the SEA (Fligstein and Stone Sweet, this volume; Mazey and Richardson 1993*b*: 5–6). The incentive structure for the formation of Euro-level lobbying is twofold. First, European regulations could have an adverse effect on interests. Second, the shaping of new European regulations was also an *opportunity* to be exploited to the disadvantage of others unaware of the importance of the new venue or less able or willing to mobilize the necessary resources. Rules of the game—informal and formal—distribute costs and benefits between interests unevenly. If one set of interests can 'rig' the rules in its favour, it can secure all sorts of direct benefits. Thus, as Cichowski notes in this volume, women were adept in influencing the EU agenda-setting process. Once the European regulatory state (Majone 1996*a*) began to emerge, the incentive structure for EU lobbying was in place.

Once one set of groups begins to exploit incentive and opportunity structures at the European level, others are bound to follow; they cannot afford to be left out, whatever the cost. Hence, the formation of a European-level interest system has exhibited elements of both competition and fashion. In practice, business groups were generally the earliest to recognize the benefits of participating in European level policy-making and, therefore, to devote the necessary, and increasing amounts of, resources required to create win situations in the Euro-policy game. Literally, business organizations had the greatest *interest* in the early years of the EC. Their opponents inevitably followed business groups to Brussels. The new venue could not be left exclusively to business interests. As Kirchner (1977: 28) found from his study of trade-union lobbying in the European Community, European trade union-interest group organizations emerged because of a perceived threat from already organized business groups. He notes that there were also positive incentives for trade unions, as well as for firms and their associations. Thus, one reason for increased trade-union mobilization at the European level was that they could 'promote, at the European level, the interests which become increasingly difficult to promote at the national level' (Kirchner 1980*a*: 132). Reflecting neo-functionalist theory, his broad conclusion was that there was a linkage between the extent to which Community policies exist in a given sector and the degree of cooperation and integration reached by European interest groups in that sector (Kirchner 1980*b*: 115). Deciding which comes first—the creation of European regulation or the creation of European-level interest intermediation—is a difficult empirical question. Kirchner seems to imply that European policy precedes interest-group formations. For our part, we merely note that one would need to know much more about the specific origins of European legislation and the nature of the advocacy coalitions behind it before drawing any firm conclusions from the available quantitative data. Thus, as so much lobbying in Brussels is not via Euro-associations or necessarily via established Brussels offices (see below), trying to correlate formation of Euro-level groups with legislative output in an attempt to decide which comes first would be risky.

The fact is that by 1992 the Commission estimated that there were 3,000 special interest groups in Brussels with up to 10,000 employees working in the lobbying sector (CEC 1992: 4). It is difficult to gauge how reliable this information is or, indeed, how active in the *lobbying* process all of these groups and individuals are. Aspinwall and Greenwood (1998: 2) consider the Commission's figure to be something of an overestimate. Undoubtedly, many Euro-groups will be small-scale operations: mere 'listening posts' whose function is to simply gather information on funding opportunities or new EU-level policy initiatives. However, it is also possible to argue that the true size of the Brussels-level lobbying industry could actually be *higher* than the Commission's estimate, if the census were to include all of those individuals who visit Brussels in order to lobby but who are not based in Brussels. Our guess is that the number of people who fly into Brussels on a regular basis, but who are not based in Brussels, runs into many thousands. For example, one interviewee, who worked for one of the major broadcasting organizations, reported to us that he has to visit Brussels at least once every two weeks in order to lobby Commission officials on behalf of his organization. This was in addition to the permanent office that his organization maintained in Brussels. This is quite typical of most Euro-level groups. They have a core Brussels staff but draw in much larger numbers of personnel as and when required. The more technical European public policy becomes, the greater the need for even those organizations which do have Brussels offices to draw in experts on an ad hoc basis, as technical expertise is such a crucial lobbying asset. This, no doubt, explains why there are no fewer than 22 flights a day from London to Brussels as, ant-like, British interest groups—and government officials—beat a path to the EU organizations in Brussels.

The most *European* of the interest organizations are, of course, the European associations. These are associations created at the European level who purport to represent a European-wide—often beyond the European Union—constituency to European-level policy-makers. In a sense, the Commission as an opportunity structure admits to an institutional bias by stating its preference for consulting Euro-associations. In theory, Euro-associations present a potential organizational pillar for corporatism. They aggregate national interests into a *European* interest and might significantly reduce the transaction costs for Commissions bureaucrats. Alan Butt Philip (1985: 1) estimated that there were approximately 500 such associations in 1985; but this figure had risen to nearer 700 by 1996 (CEC 1996*b*). By February 2000, the Secretary General's list of non-profit making interest groups included some 800 groups, divided into eleven categories as follows:[1]

- regions, towns, rural life;
- trade unions and employers federations;
- political interests;
- consumer organizations;
- animal welfare, nature, and environmental organizations;
- conservation and development;
- welfare and social interests;
- religion;
- human rights;
- small and medium-sized enterprises;
- miscellaneous.

Data on the formation of Euro-associations collected by Greenwood, Strangward, and Stanich (1999: 129) show that two-thirds of their sample of Euro-associations were formed before 1980. Our hypothesis is that the rate of formation of new Euro-associations will in future be quite slow. Most significant interests in Europe have by now formed a Euro-association, no doubt partly reflecting the fact that there are few areas of public policy still unaffected by European legislation of various types. The existence of a Liaison Committee of Podiatrists of the European Union suggests that there are few interests yet to be organized at the Euro-level! In any case, Euro-associations are often thought to be rather sluggish policy actors, due to the complex and slow process of consensus building within many of them. Also, they are often said to be under-resourced, especially in terms of the technical expertise which is often the currency of influence. Greenwood, Strangward, and Stanich (1999: 130) however, suggest that Euro-associations are rather better resourced than conventional wisdom suggests. They report that 'over half (56%—230) of all Euro groups have at least 3 employees'. While no doubt true, this leaves 44 per cent with fewer than three employees: hardly an indicator of a robust pillar on which the Commission, or European Parliament, could build a stable and manageable system of interest group intermediation. In practice, it is probably unusual to find examples of Commission officials relying solely on Euro-associations in the consultation process. Our own interviews suggest that

---

[1] http://europa.eu.int/comm/secretariat_general/sgc/lobbies/

officials habitually go directly to the source of technical expertise on which the Euro-associations themselves usually draw. Even though 'consult the Euro-associations' is certainly a 'rule' which the Commission follows, there are other, more important, informal rules such as ensuring that proposals are technically robust and that all of the stakeholders have been mobilized. For example, one Commission official confided that he had found it necessary to make direct contact with people who work in the markets and had, therefore, set up a 'Market Practitioners' Group'. He wanted to contact people 'whose bread and butter it was to work in the markets, who might come across the problems we identified in their day-to-day practices'. He admitted that this caused 'a lot of bad blood with the federations because we end up by-passing them'.[2]

Whatever the Commission might wish, however, the individual members of Euro-associations, such as national associations and individual firms, increasingly spread their lobbying resources in a risk-avoidance strategy. Like other organizations, interest groups have a learning capacity and can act strategically. Also, as Cichowski notes in this volume, *individual* strategic action can be important. Brussels might be a policy-making maze, but groups learn their way round it. They cannot be corralled into working exclusively via Euro-groups, even if the Commission wished it. For example, there appears to be a proliferation of ad hoc coalitions focusing on single-issue politics (Coen 1997; Pjinenberg 1998 and definitely an increase in the direct Euro lobbying by firms (Coen 1997; 1998). The more complex the multi-venue Euro-policy game becomes, the greater the need for flexibility and manoeuvrability by interest groups if they are to create policy win situations. Concentrating resources on one type of—federal or confederal—organ of representation is a very risky strategy and likely to fail. Creating ad hoc coalitions, often between groups that might oppose each other on different issues, is a sensible strategy, particularly when multiple opportunity structures, each having a different institutional bias, present themselves. Rational action demands direct lobbying in multiple venues, not a reliance on bodies which have cumbersome consensus-building processes. The problem for the Commission and for the Euro-associations is that direct lobbying is not conducive to the creation of the type of associations on which a corporatist or neo-corporatist system could be built. Promiscuity, rather than monogamy, is more rational interest-group behaviour. However, promiscuity can be difficult to institutionalize effectively.

2.2. The Commission's organizational needs: information, support, and legitimacy

The demand by groups for participation in the European-level policy process has been matched by the Commission's willingness to supply and institutionalize it, and is consistent with the demand/supply theory of 'supranational

---

[2] Interview DG XV, 9 July 1999.

governance' (Stone Sweet and Sandholtz 1998). As we have argued elsewhere (Mazey and Richardson 1997*a*: 180), the Commission is a broker at the centre of a complex and varied network of relationships and can act as a *'bourse'*—or, sometimes, garbage can—where vital information and knowledge can be gained and where 'frame reflection' between competing interests can take place (Schön and Rein 1994). Thus, although the EU policy process is decidedly 'messy'—multi-level and multi-arena—all policy proposals invariably have to pass through the Commission gateway and are subject to detailed *processing* in the Commission venue. Moreover, much of the 'stuff' of European integration is about technical detail—standards, parameters, procedural rules, and so on—which can be handled effectively only in a bureaucratic/technical setting. It is routine, and increasingly routinized, day-to-day policy-making of the type familiar in national policy settings. Most debates are not about high politics, or what Peterson (1995: 72) terms 'history-making decisions', and do not prompt life and death battles between Member States. Periodically, the Union goes through what may appear to be history-making phases—the 1986 Single European Act (SEA) and the 1992 Treaty on European Union (TEU) being obvious examples. However, the process of European integration in between these 'big bang' policy occasions is more about politics at the margins than about changing the shape and direction of European integration as a whole. Increasingly, EU policy-making is a continuous process of building on, refining, and extending *existing* policies. This facilitates the emergence of institutionalized relationships between bureaucrats and groups. Encounters are not always one-off; 'business' is continuing. For example, policy areas, such as the environment, agriculture, and telecoms, have been constructed at the European level for a very long time now—sometimes irrespective of the treaties. Therefore, there are incentives for the Commission to invent structures—organizations—that facilitate long-term interaction, and to create rules—institutions—which condition actor behaviour. Each player has an incentive to invest resources in participating when there are prospects of a continuing relationship. Also, interest groups often focus on detail— one group's nectar being another group's poison. In consequence, the Commission is a magnet for groups as this is where much of the detail is decided. This is not to say that groups are not concerned with history-making events or that these events do not shape subsequent lobbying strategies via changes in institutional arrangements (see Mazey and Richardson 1997*b*). Nor is it to suggest that groups do not lobby national governments or that national governments are not concerned with details. Although both are the case, our focus here is on the institutionalization of that 'chunk' of European space: Commission/group intermediation.

As a maturing bureaucracy, the Commission is both a receptive institution to interest groups and adept at using group intermediation strategically in the policy change process. Thus, most EU interest groups are 'pressing' against an open door. Indeed, some groups in the NGO sector are now being courted by the Commission to participate in the legislative process to the extent that they are finding it difficult to meet the 'demand pull' from the many Directorates-General (DGs) who seek their participation. They are 'pressured lobbyists'. Thus, the Commission has been a 'purposeful opportunist' not only in terms of policy expansion. It has also been opportunistic in creating new institutions as a means of locking in a wide variety of interests into the *ongoing* process of Europeanization. It has been the strategic actor in constructing constellations of stakeholders concerned with each of the Commission's policy sectors. We later outline the wide range of institutional forms which this innovation has taken, but before doing so it is important to stress that each innovation is linked to a broad *organizational culture* which has become embedded in most parts of the Commission. This culture is clearly outlined in the 1992 Communication issued by the Commission, *An Open and Structured Dialogue between the Commission and Interest Groups* (CEC 1992), and further developed in later Commission publications subsequent to the Cardiff European Council of 15–16 June 1998. The latter stressed the need to bring the Union nearer to its citizens by making it more transparent and more understandable. In practice this has meant an even greater emphasis on interest group accommodation by the Commission. In its December 1992 Communication, the Commission had argued that it 'has always been an institution open to outside input. The Commission believes this process [i.e. group consultation] to be fundamental to the development of its policies'. The document went on to acknowledge that it was in the Commission's own interest to maintain open access 'since interest groups can provide the services with technical information and constructive advice' (CEC 1992: 1).

More recently, the Commission has created a website devoted to its relations with interest groups reflecting its 'wish to create a single site reserved for the working tools that enable officials to promote the participation of socio-economic circles and the representatives of civil society in the legislative process'.[3] The *functional logic* of consultation is at the fore of these statements, as is the determination to further extend the consultative process. Here, we see the re-creation at the EC/EU level of what Heisler and Kvavik (1974: 48) long ago saw as the dominant style of national policy making in Western Europe. They saw the 'European polity' as exhibiting the following characteristics: 'a decision structure characterized by continuous regularised access for economically, politically, ethnically and/or subculturally based groups to the highest levels of the political system, i.e. decision-making sub-system'. Many years later, characterizing the EC as shifting towards 'bureaucratic politics', Peters (1992: 18) suggested that ' . . . given the decentralised structure of policymaking in Europe, with multiple actors at the European level and even more at the national level, it should not be surprising if policies were the product of loosely organized and flexible policy communities'. The Commission's 'procedural ambition' to seek out and institutionalize interests is absolutely clear. In practice, this procedural ambition is itself a recipe for promiscuity in terms of relations between the Commission

---

[3] http://europa.eu.int/comm/sg/sgc/lobbies/en/index_htm#top)

and interest groups. The more the Commission stresses openness and consultation, the more new groups will come to Brussels. The more groups there are in Brussels, the more groups will want to come to Brussels. Thus, as Heinz *et al.* (1993) noted in the US, lobbying begets more lobbying; attempts to reduce uncertainty by lobbying create more uncertainty, which in turn begets more lobbying. Once created, however, promiscuity has to be 'managed' if the system is to work. This means that consultation has to be institutionalized.

3. Institutionalizing Promiscuity

What form does this institutionalization take? There appear to be two principal forms, not necessarily in order of importance.

(1) *Evolution of some formal, but more often, informal, behavioural rules, codes and norms.*
(2) *Formation of structures/sites/venues where intermediation can take place at various stages of the policy process.*

3.1 Rules, codes, and norms

One particularly good indicator of the scope and density of the Euro-level interest groups system is that the Commission and the Parliament have identified lobbying, for some years now, as a 'problem'. Both organizations have, therefore, conducted investigations into the nature of interest groups and their activities. Possible legal regulation of lobbying has, therefore, been an important agenda item for both organizations (for a comprehensive review, see Greenwood 1997: 80–100; Preston 1998: 222–32). In practice, the usual difficulties have arisen and it would be wrong to suggest that even a basic, legally-based regulatory system has emerged. However, some very basic written rules, in the form of guidelines and voluntary codes of practice exist. In reality, these are supplementary to some rather important informal, but unwritten, rules and norms which facilitate exchange among individuals, and create opportunities for collective action (Stone Sweet, Fligstein, and Sandholtz, this volume). We discuss written and unwritten rules in turn. For the most part, the rules—or institutions—with which we are concerned relate to procedures that need to be followed in making substantive rules.

3.2. Formal written rules and codes

As Greenwood (1997: 96) demonstrates, attempts to formulate agreed formal written rules governing lobbying have not had a happy history. For example, it took the European Parliament some seven years to agree finally in 1996, a set of rules governing lobbying. Moreover, different EU institutions face different problems posed by interest groups and have differing strategic motivations in constructing norms and rules. Thus, whilst the Parliament has considered a more restrictive approach to lobbying, the Commission, as we have suggested earlier, has been greatly concerned to maintain its culture of open consultations with as wide a constituency of groups as might emerge or, indeed, can be mobilized. If anything, the Commission's strategic objective seems to be to expand the range and diversity of groups consulted. On the other hand, the Parliament has been attacked for corrupt relations with groups and has sought to clean up its image. In a sense, institutionalizing relations with groups has been dysfunctional to the legitimacy of the Parliament yet functional to the legitimacy of the Commission. At least until recently, the Commission was less under attack for its corruption than for its 'nannying' policy style and capacity for policy errors. Thus, the imperatives for legally regulating relations with groups were quite different for the two institutions. Above all, the Commission—the sole focus of our study—needs to demonstrate two things. First, it must try to ensure that its proposals are technically robust and workable in the 15 different and dense 'policy hinterlands' of the Member States (Mazey 1998). Second, it must strengthen its legitimacy as an institution and for each of its policy proposals. To pursue an *exclusive* rather than an inclusive policy towards interest groups would not be conducive to either objective. Consulting as many stakeholders as possible is rational in terms of gaining the best information and knowledge. It is also a good way of avoiding the dangers of asymmetric information supplied by lobbyists (for a discussion of lobbying and asymmetric information, see Potters and van Winden 1992). The need for a more balanced institutionalization of interest group intermediation is reflected in the Commission's encouragement of NGOs. Thus, in 1997 it adopted a communication *Promoting the Role of Voluntary Organizations and Foundations in Europe* (CEC 1997a). This document recognized that NGOs needed to be consulted more widely and systematically. The increasing institutionalization of NGO-Commission relations is also reflected in the considerable financial support the former receive from the Commission. For example, approximately 2.65 million ECU has been set aside for funding environmental NGOs for the period 1998–2001.[4] Similarly, one Unit (F/2) of DG V (Employment, Industrial Relations and Social Affairs) provided 5 million ECU for NGOs in 1997. The Commission recognises that relying on producer groups for advice, however technical and accurate it might be, is a risky business in terms of legitimacy. Even if the broadening of consultations produces no new, or usable, information, it does strengthen the Commission's position in interinstitutional battles. Sometimes the receipt of information can be as important as the information itself. Thus, as Potters and van Winden (1992: 286) suggest, '. . . it need not be the *content* of the message as such that transmits information, but merely the *fact* that a message has been received'. For example when the Environment Council failed to adopt a Common Position on a text from the Council in December 1998, the Commission responsible complained that the delay was unnecessary as 'industry had been consulted all along'.[5] The

---

[4] See OJ L 354 of 30 December 1997.
[5] see http://europa.eu.int/comm/dg11/press/bio99108-1.htm.

Commission's approach to the formal regulation of lobbying, has, therefore, been extremely cautious and has been designed to discourage extreme forms of abuse. The Commission has sought to achieve this objective by merely specifying some minimum standards of behaviour and the use of voluntary codes. It has been strongly opposed to 'licensing' of groups. Nothing has been done which would deter groups from approaching the Commission or participating in its policy-making processes. The Commission is promiscuous and intends to remain so! The process of institutionalization demands that the Commission should be a user-friendly organization so far as interest groups are concerned.

The Commission has included guidance on how to deal with interest groups in its staff regulations with which all officers are issued. Currently, a code of conduct is being discussed with staff representatives. The draft of March 1999 had a brief section on dealing with interest groups and is anodyne in the extreme. Basically, the Commission is determined to preserve open access for interest groups. Thus it '. . . plans to preserve the open relationship with special interest groups ensuring them equal treatment'.[6] The 'Minimum Requirements for a Code of Conduct between the Commission and Special Interest Groups', which appeared as an Annex to the 1992 Communication discussed above, is indeed minimal in terms of the constraints it imposes upon groups. For example, it states that 'special interest groups should behave at all times in accordance with the highest possible professional standards. Honesty and competence in all dealings with the Commission are specifically viewed as being of great importance'. Almost the only significant 'rule' is that 'special interest should neither employ, nor seek to employ, officials who are working for the Commission. Nor should they offer any form of inducement to Commission officials in order to obtain information or privileged treatment'. The two voluntary codes of conduct, produced by two associations of Brussels lobbying firms, are similarly anodyne.

The most revealing statement from the Commission itself is to the effect that everyone knows what the rules of decent behaviour are. In the introduction to the 'minimum standards' document, the Commission observes that it 'would like the special interest to adhere to the rules of conduct that both parties have followed for many years'. The informal rules are such that everyone in Brussels knows how to behave in town by now: a good example of institutionalization. As Stone Sweet, Fligstein, and Sandholtz note in this volume, rules not only facilitate exchange, they also define how an actor expresses and pursues an interest and they specify the limits of action. The sanction behind the rules of the game is, of course, the threat of exclusion. The Commission generally decides who is in and who is out, apart from those cases—possibly an increasing number—where certain groups are specified in legislation as having to be consulted. The informal rules of the game simply reflect the functional logic of interest-group intermediation. As they are informal and unwritten, however, there can be no definitive list.. Moreover, as the system matures, the list of 'rules' is almost certain to be extended.

---

[6] http://europa.eu.int/comm/sg/sgc/lobbies/en/approche/

One of the few systematic attempts to make explicit what the best lobbyists already knew was made by a senior Commission official, Robert Hull (1993). We have extended his list somewhat, although our distillation of the rules of the game is very similar. The unwritten rules can be understood in terms of effective participation in EU policy-making. The following informal rules and norms appear to be essential if an interest is going to be recognized as an effective partner by the Commission. These informal rules and norms—or institutions—might be thought to be recommended tactics rather than the rules of the game themselves. However, we believe that it is difficult to make this distinction in practice. Thus, over time, certain tactics of influence appear to work. These become embedded—possibly even hegemonic—as norms. Once generally accepted as prescriptions for successful action, they take on the form of rules—institutions—which all must follow. This does not mean that they can never change, of course. Shifts in the balance of power between organizations—and, no doubt, other perturbations—can destabilize existing norms and rules.

- Commit the necessary resources in order to participate. This means, above all, an ability to deliver expertise quickly and in a readily usable form for the Commission.
- Be prepared to participate in policy framing, especially in the very early stages of policy formulation when problems are being identified and options are being searched. This often means being as interested in seminars, workshops, conferences, and observatories as in more structured 'consultation' in the later stages of the process.
- Maintain close professional links with Commission officials at all levels, across a wide range of DGs and across a broad spectrum of nationalities.
- Present rational/technical arguments based on reliable data.
- View European policy as an opportunity, not a threat.
- Formulate European, not national or particularistic, solutions.
- Understand the problems and perspectives of other stakeholders with whom the Commission has to deal: other interest groups, the European Parliament and the European Court of Justice, national governments, and other international bodies—for example, the World Trade Organization and the World Health Organization.
- Be willing to work with other stakeholders, including interests who are usually opponents, either in ad hoc interest group coalitions or in special venues constructed by the Commission to solve policy problems.
- Be cooperative, positive and trustworthy: building up trust is a long-term investment.
- Participate in the whole race: the policy process often never terminates.
- Do not gloat when you succeed!

No doubt other rules are important—and our list refers only to influencing the Commission—but this list reflects the type of behavioural norms and cultural values that national bureaucracies have traditionally encouraged in

Western European states. Some of these rules reflect an institutional bias, of course. The requirement to adopt a European perspective, for example, is a good example of the general observation that, in conditions of asymmetric lobbying, the characteristics of the interest group are as important in influencing policy-makers as the content of the messages the interest groups convey (see Potters and van Winden 1992). Thus, observing informal rules and codes helps define who an actor is (Stone Sweet, Fligstein, and Sandholtz, this volume, p. xx). The regularized contacts which Heisler and Kvavik (1974) saw as characteristic of a 'European polity' were underpinned by a cultural attachment in many Western European states to consensual and trustful policy-making. Similarly, 'problem solving via consensus' seems to be a cultural value embedded in the Commission too, even if it is less fashionable in some Member States today. Again, groups need to recognize this 'rule'.

Complex policy processes cannot rely solely on norms, however, if effective public policy is to emerge. Norms are crucial but cannot structure participation sufficiently for the system to produce effective policy outputs. Participation has to be *organized* via other institutional processes. It is to the cascade of structures and processes of intermediation that we now turn.

3.3. Structures or organizations of intermediation

In its general overview of interest groups, the Commission stated that its relations with groups needed to be placed on a 'slightly more formalised footing'.[7] Thus, it outlined two basic procedures for taking account of the opinion of interest groups: formal procedures such as the creation of advisory committees and groups of experts, and informal, ad hoc procedures. Both types of consultation tend to be routinely used. The more formalized nature of committees is, naturally, reflected in procedural rules. Thus,

When the Commission opts for dialogue by putting in place a committee, it lays down the rules of this formal consultation (mission, composition, appointment and terms of reference) in the decision creating the advisory committee. The selection criteria focus in particular on the degree of representativeness of the group to be consulted, with an eye to a fair balance of the different interests involved. In other words, besides the economic sectors in question, more general interests such as the trade unions, consumers and environmentalists are also represented.[8]

As van Schendelen (1998: xiii) argues, the 'committee method' characterizes the EU policy process. He estimates that there are 'probably 1,000 committees, accounting for at least 50,000 representatives from the Member States, divided more or less equally between the public and the private (profit and non-profit) sectors' (van Schendelen 1998: 5). In terms of our particular focus, however, it is important to note that this includes all types of committees, including Comitology Committees. The latter usually comprise national officials, though interest-group representatives do sometimes appear as members. Even

---

[7] http://222.europa.eu.int/comm/sg/sgc/lobbies/en/approche/apercu_en.htm   [8] Ibid.

so, a large proportion of the total number of committees are Commission committees, which contain a high proportion of interest-group representatives. The underlying philosophy is that policy change needs to be preceded by stakeholder participation in order for the Commission to produce what it calls 'balanced proposals'.

An important part of this process is the provision of information concerning the early stages of policy development. Here, the Commission has the advantage of having one of the main tasks of governance—policy formulation—without the political and electoral risks of a conventional government. The *political* costs of being increasingly open in the early stages of the policy process are relatively low, unlike for elected governments. Indeed, the political benefits of such widespread consultation to the Commission are quite high in terms of constructing a supportive constituency of interest groups (Downs 1967). Being a user-friendly and open institution is functional to the Commission's legitimacy within the system as a whole. Thus, there has been a discernible increase in the number of Green Papers since 1990. Prior to that date the Commission appears to have published only four Green Papers, whereas in the following eight years approximately 50 were published. The function of Green Papers is to set out the Commission's ideas, to present possible measures, and to 'lay the foundations for a framework in which interest groups can present their viewpoints'.[9] In reality, Green Papers, though significant, are less important than other means of policy 'kite flying' by the Commission. For example, its Annual Work Programme and publications in the *Official Journal* are important ways of indicating the direction of future policy development. The Internet is an increasingly important source of information on EC/EU policy initiatives, which has opened up the market for advance intelligence considerably. Getting information to interest groups is relatively easy. Interest groups are voracious as well as promiscuous. The more difficult task is to construct a European policy process that can both utilize the expertise of groups and mobilize a degree of consensus in favour of policy change. For each proposal, an advocacy coalition needs to be constructed if the proposal is to wend its way through the institutional maze that characterizes the EC/EU. Insofar as advocacy coalitions can be constructed, whether for a specific initiative or, better still, over a long period of time (Sabatier 1998)—they can be regarded as another form of institutionalization. As Héritier notes in this volume, the Commission is very active in network building. The multiple venue structure of the EC/EU can decouple policy debates. For example, as one Commission official put it to us in an unattributable interview, 'normally the Parliament is less expert than the Commission and we have to fight the whole f . . . g thing from first principles'. Thus, stable advocacy coalitions can assist the Commission greatly by *linking* the main EC/EU institutions, as advocacy coalitions can be effective carriers of ideas and frames across different venues (Dudley and Richardson 1998).

[9] http://222.europa.eu.int/comm/sg/sgc/lobbies/en/approche/apercu_en.htm.

Here, we see the importance of multi-venue policy making to the Commission as well as to interest groups. The Commission has an acute sense of, for example, the role and power of national governments in the EU policy process. Also, increasingly, it is highly conscious of the European Parliament's powers. Thus, it needs to guard against a single focus on institutionalizing interest groups as it knows that they are only one set of stakeholders. However, as we suggest, interest groups are key players, with other types of stakeholder, in the advocacy coalitions which carry proposals through the EU quagmire. It is no accident that many of the consultative structures formed by the Commission are multi-actor institutions, including representatives of the Member States. The underlying philosophy is to mobilize as broad a constituency of stakeholders as possible, as this will help carry policies forward.

While reliable and systematic data are not available—even within the Commission—on all the Commission's consultative structures and processes, there is sufficient evidence for us to be able to suggest some general features of the processes of institutionalization in terms of structures of intermediation. It is, however, vitally important to note that there is no standard pattern, in terms of specific institutional forms, across the DGs or even within DGs. Nor is any one 'division' of a DG necessarily consistent in its use of institutional forms over time. The specificity of consultation rules is not very great. The rule is 'consult', not consult in a particular way. Hence, innovation and experimentation in terms of processes and structures is the norm. It is tempting to classify forms of institutionalization in terms of a 'procedural teleology' (Rhinard 1999). For example, the Commission's procedural ambition is often achieved via four stages of policy making, as follows:

Stage 1: *Initiating dialogue and debate*: a wake-up call for stakeholders. Typically, this involves the publication of a Green Paper or other communications.
Stage 2: *Mapping opinions, frames, and interests*: deciding who matters. Typically this involves bringing together the many stakeholders in a forum or conference.
Stage 3: *Insider processing*: frame reflection. Typically, this involves the creation of a smaller group advisory committee or high-level group, for the detailed processing of issues.
Stage 4: *Formal proposals*: a new policy cycle begins and other venues become involved. Typically, this involves the Commission in continued close dialogue with the key stakeholders as the inter-institutional battle develops.

In practice, however, this neat pattern is not always followed. For example, the setting-up of an insider group may *precede* the holding of a much larger conference or forum. This may happen when previous policy exercises have already identified 'who matters'. This sometimes exclusive group—effectively a small policy community—might well be involved in the pre-Green Paper or 'communication' stage, with a large conference being organized later in order to bring on board a wider range of stakeholders. Moreover, the teleology follows a legislative timetable whereas many of the forms of institutionalization are permanent structures which meet irrespective of specific legislative actions: they are ongoing institutionalized sites of trust formation and frame reflection which can be used for discussing legislative initiatives if need be. The Commission is now replete with permanent forums and high-level groups which continue to meet irrespective of legislative initiatives. Their existence reflects our earlier suggestion that the EC/EU policy system is rather mature and that much business is *ongoing*.

Although still not necessarily as robust as one would wish, a more useful characteristic of institutionalization might be to distinguish between rather open and 'thin' institutional sites, such as very large conferences, forums, seminars, and so on, whose actors often have rather weak inter-relationships, or none at all, and the more restricted 'thick' institutional sites where only the key players, however defined, are present and have a more intense and regular inter-relationship. The existence of these two rather different procedural types (see also Héritier in this volume for a discussion of 'soft' or 'informal' institutions) reflects the functional needs of the Commission: namely, it must demonstrate an open and accessible policy-making style, yet it needs to produce practicable and technically sound proposals at the end of the day. The more open structures—loose organizations—facilitate legitimization and the identification of key players and 'sticking points'. They are concerned with generalized consultation. The more restrictive structures—dense organizations—facilitate the detailed technical negotiation resulting in practical proposals within the wider parameters established by the more amorphous group. They are concerned with the drafting of specific rules or proposals, and often subsequent implementation. Officials also draw on the legitimacy conferred by the wider gatherings. As one interviewer put it, the larger gatherings 'allow us to whistle-test our ideas'. If our analysis is correct, then this helps explain why the policy process does not always follow a neat pattern of starting with a large gathering and ending up with a smaller committee. Legitimization can be required at different stages of the policy process, not just at the beginning. Moreover, it can take different forms. Whatever the truth of the matter, our central thesis is that there has been a proliferation of both thick and thin institutional sites for interest-group intermediation.

In any one year there are likely to be hundreds, if not thousands, of examples of institutionalized intermediation. Below, we give some illustrations from across a range of DGs.

We turn, first, to the very open and fluid forms of intermediation: what we term 'thin institutionalizational sites'.

3.4. 'Thin' institutions: whistle testing

Almost invariably, once a draft proposal is ready, whether in the form of a Green Paper or other 'Communication', the Commission sets up a gathering of the relevant stakeholders. Access is extremely open at this stage. Such large gatherings may also *precede* the formulation of a Green Paper or other

'Communication' in an even more fluid policy-formulation process at which problems and opportunities are identified.

DG III (Industry) is typical of other DGs in that it hosts a myriad of information-gathering and proposal-vetting conferences, symposiums and so forth. For example, it hosted the Petro-Chemical East-West Co-operation Conference in December 1998 and a European Standardisation Conference in 1999.

DG IV (Competition) organized four seminars in May 1999 to discuss the relevance of EU competition rules for sport, as a means of assisting the Commission in formulating proposals for safeguarding existing sporting structures.

In October 1997 it organized a public hearing for industry and other interested parties on a Green Paper on Application of Community Competition Rules to Vertical Restraints.

DG V (Employment, Industrial Relations and Social Affairs) held a European Social Fund (ESF) Congress in May 1998 to review progress, share ideas, and discuss the future policy framework of the ESF.

DG VII (Transport) published a 'discussion paper' in 1998 on sea ports and maritime infrastructure to be followed by a conference in 1999. This was intended to develop a 'Europe-wide debate' on the issues with a view to improving existing policies and identifying areas where new initiatives might be taken.

DG XI (Environment, Nuclear Safety and Civil Protection) organized a conference, in conjunction with the European Parliament, in 1997 on Environment and Employment, which involved more than 300 participants from a wide range of sectors.

DG XII (Telecommunications, Information Markets, and Exploitation of Research) organized a Business Round Table on Global Communications in June 1998 as a means of launching its Global Business Dialogue. Also in 1998 it held a Forum on Telecommunications Deregulation, in part to 'identify future challenges thrown up by liberalisation . . .'. Over 170 stakeholders were invited.

3.5. 'Thick' institutional sites: problem solving

Some of the institutions listed above are very large gatherings of stakeholders—not solely interest groups. When they involve 100–200 stakeholders and sometimes more, they cannot be effective problem-solving venues. They are often, however, crucial in mapping the practical and political contexts in which later detailed decisions take place. Stakeholders bring to these large gatherings competing frames—for example, polluters and environmentalists—and these frames must eventually be subject to a detailed process of 'frame reflection' (Schön and Rein 1994) if a consensus is to emerge. If no consensus emerges, then venue shopping by 'defeated' stakeholders is very likely. Thus, as another interviewee put it to us 'they [groups] fight battles until the last possible moment . . . at certain points [they] switch their lobbying from the Commission over to the ministry or [European] Parliament'.[10]

It is no surprise, therefore, to see the Commission setting up a large number of 'thick' institutional sites that bring together, in a more intense process of interaction and *bargaining*, the interests that really do matter. These are groups, and other stakeholders, who have a central and vital *interest* in the policy problem and who may also have potential veto elsewhere in the system. Institutions for processing technical detail are a functional necessity. As one interviewee revealed, they focus on 'more operational questions . . . a more technical component'.[11] They meet much more regularly, participants know each other much better, and detailed bargaining can take place in private. Again, we list some typical examples. Our list concentrates on examples of structures which are relatively long-lived or permanent, as longevity is perhaps a good indicator of the thickening of institutions and some kind of 'lock-in' processes at work. However, the Commission has a very large number of advisory committees at any one time—as suggested earlier, probably over 1,000—often concerned with specific legislative initiatives. These committees comprise the relevant 'policy communities' for each policy problem and are quite different from the 'thin' institutions, such as large conferences, described above.

DG IV (Competition) set up, in 1995, the 'Multi-modal Group'—antitrust unit—to examine how the Commission's policy on multi-modal transport price fixing could be best implemented. The objective is to create a more efficient and cost effective European inland transportation system. It is a small committee, consisting mainly of experts from private companies.

DG V (Employment, Industrial Relations and Social Affairs) set up a High Level Group on the Economic and Social Implications of Industrial Change in January 1998. The group consists of former ministers and business leaders and was set up in response to a request by the Cardiff European Council. The DG also hosts a large number of permanent committees: for example, in 1998 it reformed the Sectoral Dialogue Committees as part of the social dialogue process. Each sectoral committee consists of representatives of both sides of industry.

DG XI (Environment, Nuclear Safety and Civil Protection) provides a now classic example of a committee set up to process a specific policy problem, namely, the emissions from motor vehicles. It instituted the Auto-Oil Programme—so-called Auto-Oil I—in 1992. The programme lasted for four years and led to Directives on cars, heavy-duty vehicles, fuels, inspection and maintenance. It has been followed by a second programme—the so-called Auto-Oil II Programme—and exhibits a very high degree of 'thickening'. The Programme constitutes a partnership between the European Commission and the automobile and oil industries and has the aim of identifying the most cost-effective way of meeting desired future air quality in the EU. What is

[10] Interview DG XIII, 8 July 1999.   [11] Interview DG XIII, 8 July 1999.

significant, is that whereas Auto-Oil I was largely confined to the Commission and the two industries, Auto-Oil II has been modified to extend the stake-holder dialogue beyond the vehicle manufacturing and refining industries, to Member States, NGOs and other experts. Moreover, seven Working Groups of experts, with strong interest-group representation have also been created. If ever there was a European-level policy community, this is it! A much smaller, but similar exercise was conducted in producing the Ozone Position Paper. This emerged from the 'Ad-Hoc Working Group on Ozone Directive and Reduction Strategy Development', which consisted of experts from Member States, NGOs, industry, the World Health Organization, and the European Economic Area (EEA).

DG XII (Science, Research and Development) established the Industrial R&D Advisory Committee (IRDAC) to advise the Commission on strategic issues relating to the shaping and implementation of Community policy in the field of research and technological development. It consists of 24 members, 19 of whom are senior industrialists.

DG XIII (Telecommunications, Information Markets and Exploitation of Research) set up a High Level Group on Benchmarking in May 1998, in order to help the Commission fix priorities for benchmarking and to cooperate with the Commission in interpreting the results with a European-wide impact. The former Chairman of Ericsson chairs the Group. There is also a European Digital Video Broadcasting Group (EDVBG), not formally a DG XIII Committee, but on which DG XIII is represented. This plays a key role in policy development.

DG XV (Internal Market and Financial Services) set up a Business Test Panel in September 1998 with the aim of improving the assessment of the potential costs and administrative consequences for business of implementing new legislation by consulting business in the Member States before proposals are made. The Panel consists of business interests. The DG also has an Expert Group on Banking Charges, set up in 1997. The Group consists of experts drawn from banking and payments systems, enterprises, and consumer organizations. In 1998 the DG also announced that it was setting up a High Level consultation mechanism to ensure that market practitioners and users were able to make a full contribution to policy formulation in the financial services area.

DG XVII (Energy) set up an Energy Consultative Committee in 1998 which the Commission consults when Community legislation in this field is being considered. The Committee consists of 31 members representing the energy industries, unions, consumers, and environmental organizations.

DG XXII (Education, Training and Youth) created a Study Group on Education and Training in 1995, consisting of 25 high-level experts selected from a variety of concerned constituencies—companies, trade unions, schools, vocational training bodies, adult education, and universities.

DG XXIII (Enterprise, Policy, Distributive Trades, Tourism and Co-operatives) set up a Business Environment Simplification Task Force (BEST) in 1997 to tackle the issues of enhancing Europe's competitiveness and growth. The Task Force is made up of entrepreneurs, public administrators, and academic experts. In 1998 it also set up a High Level Group on Tourism and Employment, consisting of 18 tourism entrepreneurs and experts.

Our distinction between thin and thick institutionalizational sites is, of course, somewhat arbitrary. Commission officials might not see a clear distinction, as the use of different organizational forms is part of a continuous process of learning and mobilizing. However, there appears to be a significant qualitative and quantitative difference between an institutional structure which, say, brings together 300 diverse participants in a one-off conference, and something like the Auto-Oil Programme, where participation is much more restricted and regular meetings take place between the selected actors over several years and where detailed *bargaining* over specific policy proposals takes place. Thus, the primary characteristic of a thick institutional structure for interest intermediation is continuity of interactions over a period of time in order to hammer out agreed specific policy proposals and rules for governing the policy area in question.

4. Conclusions: A Seamless or Disjointed Process of Institutionalization?

The fact that one can see both thick and thin structures should not disguise the fact that, from the Commission's perspective, consultation is a rather seamless and long-term process. As one interviewee in telecoms told us, 'we have our style—a *process* of consultation—not just single consultations, but we consult often on [these] documents in order to judge people's views and gauge how far people's views have changed during the process. This has worked very well and has been used over a period of ten years'.[12] Interestingly, he was emphasizing the dual role of institutionalized consultation: the discovery of views and the changing of views. Thus, consultation is often about mutual learning. The same official stressed the role of continuous consultation in the process of policy change: 'you have to consult often in order to advance the cause and make progress'. This interviewee captures a common response from a range of DGs, namely, that the process of consultation itself shapes actors' preferences over time. Institutionalized structures are also preference-formation sites. The act of joint problem solving changes perceptions of what the problem is, the range of options available, and actors' understanding of what is possible and desirable to achieve.

Hence, as we suggested earlier, institutionalization is not just about immediate problem-solving, even though it is crucial to that process. It is also about the building of long-term trust and understanding which can facilitate both future problem identification and problem solving and sets the parameters of

---

[12] Interview DG XIII, 8 July 1999.

reasonable behaviour. It is a central aspect of collective decision-making over time and is embedded. The creation of trust between actors is a necessary prerequisite for problem-solving by consensus—one of the Commission's key objectives. The construction of institutions and organizations of various types to facilitate learning and compromise between competing frames or across competing belief systems is *especially* important in the EC/EU. The EC/EU system is characterized by multiple cultures, languages, and policy traditions and varied national agendas. Such factors as industrial structure can also generate rather different policy frames which then have to be resolved at the European level (Dudley and Richardson 1999). The potential for conflict is great and there is, therefore, a considerable functional need to search for sufficient areas of agreement for workable policies to emerge. For what Sabatier (1988: 156) terms 'policy orientated learning across belief systems' to take place there needs to be a forum—'organization' in the terminology of this volume—'which is a) prestigious enough to force professions from different coalitions to participate and b) dominated by professional norms'. As Sabatier suggests, the purpose of these structures

is to force debate among professionals from different belief systems to which their points of view must be aired by peers. Under such conditions, a desire for professional credibility and the norms of scientific debate will lead to a serious analysis of methodological assumptions, to the gradual elimination of the more improbable causal assertions and invalid data and thus probably to a greater convergence of views over time concerning the nature of the problem and the consequences of various policy alternatives.

A typical example of this frame reflection or accommodation of different belief systems is provided by one interviewer who found that, initially, opposing interests were full of distrust for each other: 'at the outset, the relations between banks and users, particularly consumers, were rather bad. I remember one bank saying "if I have to be in the same group as consumers, then I don't come! I will not speak to them." This is in 1990 when the two groups were completely separated. Today, we organize joint meetings of these groups and there is no longer any problem between on one side of the table bank representatives and the other side consumer representatives and the users'.[13] The advantage the Commission has over other institutional venues is that it is seen as an honest broker. It is in an especially good position to create and manage structures of intermediation and frame reflection.

An added reason for the continued institutionalization of interest intermediation is that the Commission's general policy style (Cram and Richardson 2001) is changing in ways that further reinforce institutionalization. The old Pavlovian reaction to policy problems—'let's draft a Directive'—is changing in favour of other policy instruments. Thus, as one official observed to us, 'there is a growing awareness that we might get better results by not using legislation but instead using peer group pressure non-legislatively'.[14] Here we see the

---

[13] Interview DG XV, 8 July 1999.   [14] Interview DG XV, 9 July 1999.

notion of a collective approach emerging via the construction of Euro-level policy communities. The same official revealed the existence of a clear incentive structure for interest groups to participate in the process of institutionalization. Thus, 'the national federations have to be much more on the ball at the very early stages of policy making. Because some of our solutions are not legislative and are non-regulatory, if you're not in very early on you lose out very quickly and very easily in the process of policy making'. Again, we see the process of institutionalization is continuing on its set trajectory.

In conclusion, what might be the result of the institutionalization of interest group intermediation? Clearly, the incentives for both Commission officials and interest groups to continue to develop permanent structures are very considerable. As we suggested earlier, there is logic of participation and institutionalization. However, as we also noted, there is also a logic of promiscuity when interest groups operate in a fundamentally multi-venue policy system. The combinations of the huge numbers of groups and the great variety of belief systems and public policy positions in the 15 Member States is always going to make procedural ambitions for stability and predictability difficult to achieve, even within a single venue such as the Commission. Thus, although the Commission has made considerable efforts to improve its internal coordination, each DG remains, essentially, a separate venue for interest-group intermediations. As Cram (1994) has emphasized, the Commission is essentially a multi-organization. Our account has emphasized the continuous process of institutionalization of Commission-group relations that has occurred. More and more groups participate in more and more institutions of intermediation. However, we do not suggest that these institutions are necessarily stable or, indeed, neutral. All institutions have a bias and create winners and losers. Openness does not guarantee equity. The central paradox is that institutionalization and promiscuity go hand in hand. In a sense, institutionalization is an attempt to constrain promiscuity. The fact that there are so many other different venues for lobbying outside the Commission is likely to leave the institutional structures in what elsewhere we term the 'hollow core of the EU' (Mazey and Richardson 2001) part of an inherently *disjointed* EC/EU policy process. Deals done at one institutional site can get undone at another. At best, therefore, we might see a process of serial institutionalization in each EC/EU venue, leaving problematic the ambition for joined-up governance in the European Union.

5

The Institutionalization of European Administrative Space

MARTIN SHAPIRO

A CHAPTER on the administrative law of the European Union (EU) is central to a volume on the *Institutionalization of European Space*. Formal legal rules as announced and enforced by courts are not the only kind of institutionalization, but they are the prototypic kind.

Administrative law is a set of rules prescribing the proper rule-making behaviour for administrative agencies; that is, administrative law is a key set of procedures.

In Western political spaces we can expect to find a key form of institutional change—legal change—largely controlled by skilled actors called lawyers employing mimetic techniques: that is, producing changes that are incremental adjustments in existing traditions of law, in either their own or very closely culturally related legal spaces. EU administrative law is a set of rules that partially defines the deliberative processes by which EU legal rules are made and largely determines the degree of knowledge of, and participation in, those processes available to citizens.

In the Western administrative law tradition there are two basic dynamics, dialectics, tensions, or paradoxes continuously at play. The first of these is the tension between rule and discretion. As polities encounter new circumstances, they are prone to grant political executives discretion to deal with those circumstances. Yet even as the discretion is granted the urge to bring that discretion under rules is felt. Administrative law is an endless game of catch-up in which previously granted discretions are brought under rules, even as new discretions are granted. The second dynamic pits expertise against democracy. Administration is a doing. The doing of something should be assigned to those who best know how to do it. It follows that public administration is done legitimately only by those who possess expertise. Administration is governing. In a democracy the people must govern. It follows that administration is legitimately done by the people, not by a special set of experts.

An appreciation of these long-term dynamics of administrative law is particularly important in approaching the administrative law of the EU because that law is in its earliest stages of development and is as yet nine-tenths potential and one-tenth reality. In its initial phase the European Community essentially was a treaty-based attempt at a customs union distinguished by a peculiarly elaborate set of transnational organs designed to police it. The principal decisions of the European Court of Justice (ECJ) were bent on establishing the supremacy of EC over Member State law and the legal compulsion of the freedom of movement of economic resources across national boundaries provided for in the treaties.

With the increasing perfection of the common market as a free trade and investment zone, the EU then entered a phase in which it enacted by statutory law—that is, regulations and directives enacted by the Commission-Council—a great deal of government regulation of business enterprise. This second phase of EU legal development has now been roughly completed. Although regulatory law is constantly being amended, the crucial problem for the Union is now not making new regulatory law but implementing the regulatory statutes it has enacted. Administrative law is the law that prescribes the behaviour of the administrative organs that implement regulatory law.

It is important to understand that this implementation behaviour itself has strong law-making components. First, in order for a government administrator to determine whether a business enterprise is or is not in compliance with the regulatory statutes, the administrator must interpret the statutory law. Such *interpretation* of law necessarily involves a certain amount of making of law. Second, many regulatory statutes explicitly delegate to implementing agencies the power to make supplementary law to fill in the details of the statutes sufficiently that they can be implemented effectively. Thus, administrative law not only prescribes how administrative agencies shall make highly particularized decisions but how they shall make laws.

There is almost no administrative law in the treaties themselves. Thus, such law must be created either by statute or by the case law of the courts of the EU There is no administrative code. There is also no separate system of administrative courts. The administrative law of the EU is mostly in the case law of the courts of the EU Where law is generated case-by-case by a set of transnational courts of general jurisdiction with serious legitimacy problems, such institutional change is likely to be dominated by skilled actors employing mimetic techniques. Such courts are hardly likely to invent brand new things. Instead, typically they will depend on cycles of institutionalization in which court decisions hinting at rules invite litigators to file new cases pushing those hints into more concrete and demanding forms followed by further court decisions and so on. The obvious thing to do is to scan all of the law of all of the Member States, picking up whatever rules seem to work and enjoy fairly high levels of interstate consensus. Given the particular historical circumstances, however, there is one more obvious thing to do: borrow from, or at least take cautionary lessons from, the US. But this tactic is far more obvious to EU judges than to the lay readers of this volume, so some further explanation is needed.

1. The American Experience

The administrative law of the US underwent an enormous transformation from about the mid-1960s to the 1980s, both in doctrine and in the level of judicial intrusiveness into administrative affairs. This institutional change occurred largely through case law confirmed and supported by the language of new Congressional statutes (Stewart 1975; Shapiro 1988). In their typical fashion the courts did not openly admit that they were changing the law. Most of the judicial change occurred through judicial *interpretation* of the Administrative Procedures Act (APA) which had been enacted in 1946 and whose key provisions never have been amended. From that unchanging language the courts generated a host of new demands on the agencies and a new position for themselves as *partners* of the agencies in administrative decision-making. Congressional confirmation came not through amendment of the APA to reflect the new case law but only indirectly through Congressional echoes of the new case law in new procedural provisions that Congress wrote into new statutes.

Earlier we noted the tensions between rule and discretion and between technocratic and democratic administration. The New Deal temporarily had overcome these tensions. From the late 1930s until well into the 1960s, New Deal judges paid extreme deference to expert administrative discretion, trusting to political executives chosen by a democratically elected President to supervise the technocrats adequately. As the New Deal consensus waned so did this judicial deference to administrative expertise.

As the New Deal waned, a democratic political theory of pluralism replaced that of majoritarian democracy in the US. A government decision was democratically legitimate if it were the result of a process to which all relevant groups had equal access. A correct decision was one that 'satisficed' all of the participating groups, that is, one that gave each group as much of what it wanted as possible given the desires of all the other groups. It was from this now dominant political theory that, beginning in the 1960s, the courts generated a new administrative law whose watch words were 'transparency' and 'participation'. Groups could not participate equally unless governmental decision-making was fully transparent to them all. Full participation by all groups was one of the methods of achieving complete transparency. Thus transparency and participation were mutually reinforcing democratic values from which administrative law norms were generated.

This pluralist theory and its administrative law derivatives provided channels of expression for the extremely strong reaction against technocracy that followed World War II. Science and technology had brought allied victory but in the form of atomic weaponry that threatened to destroy mankind. Technical experts, of whom the physicist had become the model, no longer were seen as standing above and beyond the political fray but instead as another interest group with its own, very expensive, demands made on and through the political process. This anti-technology sentiment could be seen not only in the fear of nuclear war and denunciation of the military-industrial complex but in the environmental and consumer movements.

Yet environmentalism and consumerism demanded a new round of government regulation of technologically advanced businesses. Only technocrats could generate and implement this new regulation, but they could not be trusted to do so in ways that truly benefited the *demos*. One answer was the new administrative law. Technocracy is essentially specialized, esoteric knowledge translated into political advantage. If the technocrats were required to make everything that they knew known to everyone else, that advantage would be reduced. And if the technocrats were forced to give a seat at the decision-making table to everyone else, alternative and rival centres of expertise to check the technocrats would be generated. Moreover, a set of laymen, namely, the judges, could be set to supervise the technocrats on behalf of the general public. Judges are indeed expert, but only in law. By education, judges were fundamentally ignorant of all those technologies that armed and narrowed the perspectives of the technocrats. By office, judges had the power to intervene against technocratics. The judge was the lay person armed: the true democrat.[1] By inventing and enforcing an administrative law of transparency and participation, judges could counter the interests of technicians and bring expert discretion under rules. In the 1960s and 1970s, the US went through a huge change in institutionalization, that is, in administrative law, because renewed distrust in technocracy blossomed at the same time as a new round of government regulation of high-tech business. Under the umbrella of pluralist political theory and its values of transparency and participation, the judges became hyperactive in the subjugation of expert discretion to rules and the control of lay persons—themselves—over experts.

Transparency, participation, and generally anti-technocratic themes have been endemic to European politics as they have to American in the post-World War II period, and they become particularly active and politically relevant to the Union for certain special reasons. The very indirectness, peculiarity, and complexity of Union decision-making processes acutely raises the problem of transparency. Even more important in bringing actual political clout to Union transparency, participation, and pluralist concerns are the differences between Union and Member State regulatory decision-making processes. American regulation has always been rather legalistic and adversarial. European regulation typically has been highly corporatist. Government regulators and business managers meet in closed and confidential sessions and collaboratively work out regulatory compliance arrangements. When regulation moves from national capitals to Brussels, some degree of opening and distancing takes place. So long as the corporate regulated were insiders to regulation they did not worry about transparency and participation. But as corporate managers begin to feel a little less intimately connected to regulators, the charms of transparency and participation grow.

---

[1] Europeans must recall that American judges are elected or politically appointed not members of a career civil service.

Specifically for Union administrative law, all this means not only that generalized European anti-technocratic sentiment generally presses for pluralist transparency and participation changes in administrative law but also that there are particular persons with particular money to hire particular lawyers to bring particular lawsuits designed to persuade particular judges to produce a new administrative case law of the Union which will guarantee those now less on the inside what they now need: transparency and participation. Thus it can be anticipated that European case law to some degree will go down the route travelled earlier by the American case law. Just as in the 1960s and 1970s American concerns for transparency and participation intersected a new round of environmental, health, safety, and consumer regulation and produced a new administrative law, so now European concerns for Union transparency and participation intersect the round of new regulation that occurs when Union regulation must be invented to replace national regulation. So a new, or rather an initial, Union administrative law should emerge favouring transparency and participation.

One final American-European comparison is relevant. New case law emerges in part because litigants press for it, but also in part because judges want to give it. American judges are part of a general, all-purpose federal judiciary headed by a Supreme Court that is both an administrative court and a constitutional court. To US federal judges, second guessing an expert bureaucracy and striking down an administrative act is not such a big deal, not when they are part of a court system that, from time to time, strikes down whole statutes. Judicial activism in administrative review comes fairly easily to courts that are active in constitutional review. Constitutional judicial review, which once appeared to be almost exclusive to English-speaking federal states, is now common in Europe (Stone Sweet 2000). Unlike most of its Member States, the Union does not have separate administrative courts. Although the Court of First Instance to some degree specializes in administrative law matters, it hears some other matters as well, and the Court of Justice handles the full range of litigation. The ECJ has been quite active in making *constitutional* law. It would not be a big step out of character for it to be activist in the field of administrative law as well.

It might well be argued that the US and the EU situations are similar but time-staged: that we may expect the same results from the same causes in Europe that occurred in the US, but a couple of decades later. No mimetic techniques necessarily would be involved, but only a parallel response to the perceived needs for transparency and participation. On the other hand, given the time staging, it might be argued that to the extent that EU administrative law is moving in US directions, the innovations are the result of deliberate borrowings from the US by EU judges and litigators. Like many American observers, Europeans have viewed the American transformation as having gone too far in injecting the judiciary into administrative matters. In the eyes of many Europeans the trick is to go a little way but not too far down the American path.

So much for the windup. But what is actually happening? Have the ECJ and the Court of First Instance actually begun to make a new administrative law? Are they likely to make more? Are they institutionalizing transparency and participation in the administrative sector of European political space? The answers to these questions is 'yes'.

2. Giving Reasons

The only relatively specific administrative law provision of the treaties is the requirement of Article 253—formerly 190—that Union organs give reasons for their acts including their rule-making acts. In the terms of this volume, the giving-reasons requirement is a procedure or rule specifying how other rules should be made. In conventional legal terms it is an administrative-law rule in that it specifies how administrative agencies must act in making their decisions. It is a constitutional rule in the sense that it is found in the treaties that constitute the Union's constitution rather than in a statute enacted by the Council.

The giving-reasons requirement is a good example of the breadth of law-making discretion vested in courts that are authorized to do constitutional interpretation. At one extreme of interpretation a giving-reasons requirement is a purely pro-forma, purely procedural rule in the narrowest sense of the word 'procedure'. It says to the administrator: 'you may make any rule you please in any way you please so long as along with the rule you issue a piece of paper with the word "reason" at the top and any set of words you want further down the page.' A court that interprets a giving-reasons provision in this way merely checks whether such a piece of paper did indeed accompany the administrative rule being challenged.

Such an interpretation is a plausible one in terms of the intentions of the authors of the text and/or its purported purposes. Even the bare requirement of giving reasons—any reasons—serves as a mild restraint on administrative discretion. An administrator who is required to give reasons is unlikely to act as arbitrarily and capriciously as one who does not have to give any reasons at all. Out of considerations of sheer self-respect and preservation of the appearance of professional competence, administrators are unlikely to offer reasons that are sheer gibberish or to take decisions the only reasons for which would be sheer gibberish. The reasons given need not be the real reasons the decision was taken, but decisions are unlikely to be made for which no respectable reasons can be offered. The giving-reasons requirement so interpreted grants maximum discretion to administrators but imposes some slight real restraint on that discretion.

Such an interpretation is, however, inherently unstable in terms of both the politics of litigation and the autopoetic dynamics of legal discourse. Legal discourse makes fundamental claims to rationality or reasonableness or making sense at least to those trained in the discourse. If an agency were to respond to a giving-reasons requirement with a page titled 'reasons' followed by the first two pages of *Moby Dick* or the Oxford dictionary, how could judges stick to the most narrow interpretation of the giving-reasons requirement? How could they say: 'we have checked off the procedural box "reasons supplied" because the "reasons" page is there; we don't really care what it says on that page'. Once the court begins to read the page, however, and to say 'we check off the box "reasons supplied" because the "reasons" page is there and what is printed on that page does indeed constitute reasons', where is the stopping point? If the form of the language on the page is reason giving but the reasons given by the administrator are clearly silly or flagrantly unjust? 'We did it because our parents wanted us to.' 'We did it because our astrologer advised it.' 'We did it because it was the cheapest thing to do even though there was no chance it would work.' Once a court demands that the reasons given make at least minimal sense, it is difficult for the court to stop there. For litigators will immediately take the next step of seeking to show that the reasons given are bad or trivial or mistaken reasons; and surely a giving reasons requirement cannot be satisfied by the offering of obviously wrong reasons. The EU, like most administrative law systems, recognizes that agencies will be judicially reversed for 'manifest error' (Nehl 1999: 145). The only way for the litigator to demonstrate that the reasons offered in defence of an administratively constructed rule are wrong is to offer other reasons counter to the reasons given. Inevitably the judge will be confronted with a reasons conflict: 'some reasons in favour of the rule, some against it'. There is a strong dynamic running from 'there must be some reasons that make some sense' to 'there must be good reasons' to 'there must be better reasons for the rule than against it'. Somewhere along that path, of course, the judge has begun to substitute his or her own policy judgements for those of the administrative agency required to give reasons. Almost inevitably a giving-reasons requirement turns into a reasonableness requirement. Courts start with the procedural requirement that an agency do something, give reasons. They tend to end up with a substantive requirement that the agency decision be reasonable.

There are stopping points along the path. A familiar technique of administrative judicial review is for a court to reject only those agency rules that no reasonable person could accept. A court may say it will treat the giving-reasons requirement as met so long as the agency can offer any reason for it that some reasonable person would accept no matter how heavy the weight of reasons on the other side and no matter whether the judge himself finds the reason given acceptable. When adopting such a rule, typically judges say that it is adopted so as to avoid substituting judicial policy discretion for agency discretion. No matter how defensible such a rule is, however, in terms of court-agency relations or of democracy it nonetheless runs against both common and legal sense. For it says that a judge will sometimes award victory to the side with less good reasons than the losing side has offered. Thus, not only is the absolute minimalist judicial interpretation of the giving-reasons requirement inherently unstable, but so is the next step of judicial deference to an agency so long as it can offer any sensible reasons at all.

Initially the ECJ did not adopt the absolutely minimalist position, at least formally. Instead it early announced the following formula:

'[It] is sufficient . . . to set out, in a concise but clear and relevant manner, the principal issues of law and of fact upon which [such action] is based and which are necessary in order that the reasoning which has led the Commission to its Decision may be understood. . . . Article 190 . . . seeks to give an opportunity to the parties of defending their rights, [and] to the Court of exercising its supervisory function . . . (*Germany v. Commission*, ECJ 1963*b*)

Such a formula is quite demanding in the extent to which it requires rather full-scale explanation from EU organs. It deliberately stops very far short, however, of a judicial demand that the agency have better reasons for what it has done than its challengers can offer against what it has done.

The early cases show a clear pattern (Shapiro 1992). Where, usually through staff carelessness, no reasons at all are offered, the challenger of an agency action on giving reasons grounds may win although even in such situations the Court will search hard for some excuse to find otherwise. Yet litigating lawyers rather consistently attached giving reasons claims to their other claims in challenges to agencies. And their claims took a particularly American form. In the 1960s and 1970s American drive toward transparency and participation, American courts had invented the so-called 'dialogue' requirement. In rule-making proceedings the agency was required to respond to each and every point raised by each and every interested party. The American courts had built up this requirement out of two provisions of the Administrative Procedures Act, one requiring the agencies to give notice of proposed rules and receive public comments on them, the other that the agencies publish a 'concise, general statement of basis and purpose' along with the completed rule. This latter was the American form of a giving reasons requirement. EU litigators would claim that, even where an EU organ, usually the Commission, had given some reasons, it failed the giving-reasons test because it had failed to respond to some particular objection to the proposed rule that had been raised by an outside party when it was considering the proposed rule.

EU lawyers often made this claim and just as often lost. It is possible that the lawyers were simply shotgunning, making every possible claim they could think of. If you are litigating against an agency decision it is easy to throw in a giving-reasons claim along with whatever other claims you are making. It is also possible that the ECJ was consistently rejecting these claims out of inherent caution. It is far more likely, however, that both lawyers and judges were benefiting from American experience. The EU lawyers were making the claim just as American lawyers did, by pawing through all the past communications between regulating agencies and the regulated enterprises searching for any point raised by the regulated that hadn't been met by the regulator. The US Courts of Appeal had encouraged this strategy. In the process they had immensely increased transparency and participation. An exhaustive dialogue was created between regulator and regulated and even those private groups not regulated themselves but favouring the regulation of others. This dialogue, however, was not only exhaustive but exhausting, adding considerably to the time and staff costs of the regulating agencies and to litigation costs and delays. The EU lawyers could learn from their American counterparts. The EU judges could see just how much pushing giving reasons up to dialogue could add to the time and staff costs of new law-making in a new legal system that needed a lot of new rules and was characterized by a very sluggish law-making process. The ECJ could also see how deeply a dialogue requirement, which appeared on its face to be purely procedural, actually projected American courts into administrative policy-making. For once courts begin to demand that agencies giver a counter reason for each reason offered by an opposing party, extremely strong pressure necessarily arises for courts to decide between the rival reasonings. The American experience was very dramatic and very well-known in European legal circles. It seems to me that the ECJ's consistent refusal to accept the litigators' invitation to move toward a dialogue requirement was greatly informed by the American experience.

As one tracks the ECJ cases over time, however, one sees not only the constant reiteration of the Court's rather demanding giving-reasons formula but an increasing tendency on the part of the Court to devote part of its opinion to stating the reasons the agency has given and demonstrating at least summarily and sometimes at length that they are good reasons. Lawyers sometimes speak of the 'negative pregnant'. What if a court begins to say, 'We have examined the reasons the agency gave, and they are good. So we find the agency has met the giving reasons requirement'. Isn't it also saying, 'If we found the reasons offered not good, we would find the agency not to have met the giving reasons requirement?' When the ECJ began to actually discuss the substance of the reasons given, hadn't it crossed the Rubicon? If so, it had not crossed simply because the US courts had crossed earlier and swept on to Rome. Indeed, the American experience may well have slowed its advance. But given that the EU courts were subject to the same outburst of new regulation and the same anti-technocratic pushes toward transparency and participation that American courts had experienced earlier, weren't they likely to move in the same direction?

In 1991 they did. In civil law systems where *stare decisis* is formally eschewed, it is rarely possible to say that a court has reversed a long line of precedents because technically there is no line of precedents to reverse. Remember, however, that the ECJ more or less follows the model of the French Council of State, which does operate a case-law system. In the ECJ there are a number of advocates-general who rank as judges. They make a presentation to the deciding judges which analyzes the law, including the past case law of the Court, and recommends an outcome to the case at hand. The Advocate-General's opinion is published along with that of the Court. These opinions are frequently cited in academic writing and subsequent cases. In the 1991 giving reasons case (*TUM*, ECJ 1991*a*), the Advocate-General admitted that in a long line of previous decisions the Court had paid extreme deference to the reasons given by the Commission and other EU organs but argued that the Court ought to break with that line of precedents and engage in a far more searching examination of the reasons offered by the government in support of its actions. The Advocate-General then argued that if the Court were to do so in the case before it, it would find for the complainant against the government on the grounds that the giving-reasons requirement had not been met. The government in fact had given reasons, so it was quite clear that what the Advocate-General had in mind was that the reasons given were inadequate. The ECJ engaged in an extended analysis of the reasons given and decided the case against the government on the grounds that the giving-reasons requirement had not been met. That is about as close as any court on the continent is ever likely to come to formally reversing its—supposedly non-existent—precedents. In the same year, the Court of First Instance, using a different set of legal categories, issued a parallel decision (*La Cinq*, CFI 1992*b*).

So the bridge has most definitely been crossed, but the American experience remains a cautionary tale. In a series of decisions on seemingly minor and highly technical matters, the Union courts have put additional teeth in the reasons requirement. They have held that the courts themselves may raise giving reasons issues even if the parties challenging EU actions have not. Older case law tended to treat the giving reasons requirement as merely procedural in the sense that the 'harmless error' rule might apply. Commission action in which reasons had not been supplied were not judicially annulled if the failure to give reasons did not actually harm the parties, reduce the court's capacity to review the action, or distort the outcome. In recent cases the Union courts treat the failure to give reasons as automatically resulting in a judicial annulment of the action taken. Litigators have learned to make comprehensive giving-reasons claims (Nehl 1999:146–7).

Following the ECJ's shift in direction, the Court of First Instance (CFI) moved strongly, injecting extra lift into the giving-reasons requirement by combining it with duty of care (see below) and manifest error doctrine. In *Automec Srl II* the CFI (1992*a*) said that if the agency failed to give detailed reasons the court could not perform its review function of determining whether the Commission had met its duty of care. Then in *Asia Motor France II* the CFI (1994) speaks both of 'insufficient reasons' and 'whether the reasoning is "well founded"'. It engages in a detailed analysis of the factual case made by the Commission. It then annuls the Commission decision, and it is not actually clear whether the annulment rests on 'manifest error' or failure to give good enough reasons. Indeed, the conflation of the two shifts giving reasons far from the procedural end and toward the substantive end of its range. For if the CFI is indeed rejecting the reasons given because they contain manifest error, it is doing substantive review of the reasons, not just checking that some reasons have been offered. Subsequently the CFI has not offered this doctrinal combination again, but it does now frequently engage in detailed analysis of the reasons given (Nehl 1999: 145).

This shift toward substance is almost inevitable in terms of both the internal dynamics of administrative law and the characteristics of the CFI. Here path dependency is at work to a degree. It is hard for any court to treat a textual giving-reasons requirement as purely procedural, that is, treating it as satisfied no matter how mistaken or disingenuous the reasons offered by the agency so long as they offer some. Moreover, the CFI was created in large part because certain kinds of cases, particularly in competition law matters, require the taking of a good deal of evidence, and the ECJ was essentially an appeals court unprepared to hear extended new factual evidence. The CFI was deliberately set up as a 'trial court', that is, a court designed to hear evidence to supplement the EU's appeals court, the ECJ. If a court is set up that is supposed to be comfortable dealing with facts, then it will deal with facts. And the more a court deals with facts the more it will be pushed toward substantive review. Where technical regulation is involved, a court which doesn't know the facts, or must rely on the factual record compiled by the agency, can fault the agency for not using the right procedures but can hardly say that the agency's decision was substantively wrong. For substantive rightness or wrongness will depend almost entirely on the facts. Where a court has its own independent access to facts, it is in a position to say that the agency was wrong. Thus it is hardly surprising that a Union court specifically established in order to deal more extensively with facts than the ECJ will push further into substantive judicial review than the ECJ.

In the *SIDE* and *Sytraval I* decisions the CFI (1995*b*, *c*) has now employed giving reasons very much in the American style, approaching 'partnership' with the Commission. It engaged in its own extensive re-analysis of the facts before concluding that the Commission's reasons for a discretionary decision were not good enough. Here giving reasons has grown from a purely formal procedural requirement—you may do what you want so long as you append a reasons-giving statement to your decision—to a quasi-substantive one—you may do what you want only if you can give persuasive reasons in the light of the facts and the law for what you have done. 'Giving reasons' verges on 'reasonableness'. Of course, we can also expect the typical American pattern in which when the judges disagree seriously enough with the agencies they will speak the language of *Sytraval*, and, when they don't they will speak of judicial deference to agency fact finding.

3. Right of Defence

Administrative agencies do some work that looks like that of criminal investigators, prosecutors, and judges combined. Where an agency engages in such a set of activities, it is almost inevitable that a right of the accused to present some kind of case in his own defence will be raised. Such an institution is too well established in criminal procedures to be ignored in their administrative neighbours. Such a right of administrative defence, however, no matter what its origins, imports a certain amount of transparency and participation into administrative processes. It becomes one of the building blocks of an institutionalization of pluralism.

The initial treaties of the European Communities do not specify a right of defence. Council statutes authorized the Commission to investigate, prosecute, judge, and levy penalties against anti-competitive behaviour. The statute did not mention a right to defence. The Community courts rather quickly created such a right by case law. Such a right existed in both the criminal and the administrative law of all the Member States. Even the earliest cases arose not because the Commission as judge had refused to hear the defendants' case at all but only because it had done something to improperly hamper that defence, such as refusing to hand over a confidential document in its possession that might have aided the defence case. It is in this mode that the right to defence is a transparency as well as a participation claim.

Once established in competition law this right of defence tends to float free and become a general, abstract right in all areas of administrative implementation. This movement is largely a product of the internal dynamics of law itself. The right to defence is first invoked where a criminal penalty like administrative sanction is invoked for violation of a legal rule. Some statutes provide for a government benefit that will be withheld from particular private entities for misconduct. There is still hearing in which the agency alleges and then judges misconduct. If the 'defendant' is found 'guilty', it isn't 'fined'. But it still may have to pay back a lot of money to the government that it would have kept if found not guilty. Isn't such a beneficiary entitled to a right of defence? What about a statute that provides a benefit but only to those who meet certain qualifications? The implementing agency denies or demands repayment of the benefit to X because it finds that X is not qualified. X is losing money because the agency has made a finding adverse to him. Isn't X entitled to defend against that adverse finding? This has been the course of development by EU litigators and courts so that the right to defence, including both the right to be heard and the right to access to documents in the hands of the government necessary to building a defence, has spread (Nehl 1999: 39–101).

Precisely because it is a right to defence analogized from criminal law rather than a right to be heard or to participate in government decision- or policy-making processes, the right of defence is very far from a full-scale institutionalization of pluralist transparency and participation. The right to defence in EC administrative law was first limited to those directly sanctioned or denied a benefit. It did not extend to others who would be indirectly adversely affected by a government decision, such as the competitor of two firms whose merger the Commission found did not violate competition rules. Gradually, and sometimes aided by new Council statutes, the right of defence has been extended to many such indirectly affected parties, but generally only to those who can show a distinct and particular injury. The right is not generally enjoyed by consumers or environmentalists who claim that a particular government decision adversely affects the buying public or the breathers of air.

Almost certainly with US experience in mind, the EU courts have been extremely leery of proclaiming 'third party' right of defence, that is, the right to documents and the right to be heard of parties who merely want the law to be implemented in a certain way rather than suffering a distinct and palpable injury.

'Third party' right of defence raises all the issues that 'standing' raises in all administrative law systems. The more numerous those who have the right to be heard in administrative proceedings, the longer and more costly those proceedings will be. The more people who can trigger court intervention by claiming they did not receive an adequate hearing from administrators, the more court intervention in administrative decision-making there will be. The fewer people can claim a right of defence, the less pluralist transparency and participation there will be. The general environment has constrained the ECJ not to be too activist in creating a right to defence. Yet right-of-defence claims by litigators and right-of-defence doctrines by courts are part of the dynamic of building up a broader EU administrative law of transparency and participation.

4. Duty of Care

We have just seen that the 'right of defence' is difficult to extend to third parties themselves not directly adversely affected by an administrative decision because of its origin in an analogy to the right of defence in criminal proceedings. On the other hand, the giving-reasons requirement easily floats free of such party considerations because the Court bases it not only on the parties' need to be able to determine whether they have been legally mistreated but also on the Court's need to be able to do effective judicial review. In the cases to be considered below, the ECJ tends to brigade duty of care with giving reasons and the 'right of the person concerned to make his views known', a phrasing that moves as far away as it can from the criminal procedure origins of the right of defence. Obviously if an EU organ has a duty of care, that is a duty to administer carefully and diligently, it owes that duty to everyone in the Union, not just 'defendants'. The agency owes the duty to give reasons not only to the 'defendant' but to the ECJ. Thus, phrasing the right of defence as it does and running it together with a duty of care and a duty to give reasons tends to erode the distinctions between third parties and those directly affected, and to allow both to raise broad, judicially cognizable objections to administrative decisions.

We have already noted that, given the paucity of treaty provisions and the absence of a Council-enacted administrative code, the ECJ has announced that it is operating under general principles of administrative law. In two 1991 cases it announced that, among those principles, was one that required that where a Union organ exercised discretion it must act with 'necessary care' or to 'examine carefully . . . all the relevant aspects' of the matter (*Nolle I*, ECJ

1991c; *TUM*, ECJ 1991a). While there are technical quibbles about the actual grounds of the holding in the first case, effectively in both cases the Commission loses for failure to be careful enough, and in both the Court combines this failure with failure to give good enough reasons; obviously, if you have failed to be careful enough, you can't give good enough reasons, and your failure to give good enough reasons is one indication that you have not been careful enough. The CFI quickly picked up the duty of care doctrine (*Nolle II*, CFI 1995a).

How much care is enough care? In *Nolle I* the ECJ explicitly rejects a synoptic dialogue requirement. The Commission is not required to consider every point raised to it. It must only take 'essential factors' into account. But by *TUM* the Court is speaking of a 'duty . . . to examine . . . all the relevant aspects of the individual case' (ECJ 1991a: para. 14).

The CFI has been moving this doctrinal initiative even further. In *Automec Srl II* it speaks of 'requisite care, seriousness and diligence' (CFI 1992a: para. 36). This case involves competition proceedings. Then in the *SIDE* and *Sytraval I* cases duty of care floats over into state aid cases, near neighbours both procedurally and substantively to the competition cases.

5. The Dialogue Requirement

If institutionalized, the so-called dialogue requirement is one of the most severe restraints on administrative action. It is a product of interests and values both internal and external to law. It begins in the right of defence in quasi-criminal administrative proceedings, which we have already examined. The government must say to the 'accused' in advance enough so that the accused can prepare something to say back as a 'defence' at the trial. If we then add a pluralist democratic theory, a democratic decision is one in which each interested group has had its say.

The government must give sufficient notice of what it has in mind to allow outsiders to comment meaningfully. But it does little good for even on-notice outside groups to comment relevantly to government unless government really listens to their comments. The only way a reviewing court can insure that administrators have listened is to require them to respond to the comments they receive. The dialogue requirement is then a duty of government to say enough to private groups to enable them to comment effectively and then a duty of government to respond to their comments to prove that the commentating groups have really been heard. Dialogue assures both transparency and participation.

The dialogue requirement has a number of other consequences. It gets a lot of facts on the record and so allows courts to do more substantive review. It provides an incentive to private parties to act strategically by raising as many and as amorphous issues and allegations as possible, in the hope that government cannot, or will have to take a long time to, reply to them all. And it sets the stage for making impossibly synoptic demands on administration. It is only one step from saying 'you must respond to all points raised by interested parties' to 'you must respond to all points that might have been raised', that is, 'you the agency must show that you have made not a defensible or reasonable but a perfect decision'.

The dialogue requirement is the ultimate in the 'Americanization' of administrative law and one of the principal roots of the incredibly cumbersome and time-consuming administrative policy-making process that is a frequent cause of complaint in the US. It cannot be proven by quotations from the cases, but there can be no doubt that one of the reasons that litigators kept proposing and the European courts repeatedly and explicitly rejected a dialogue requirement— *La Cinq, SIDE, Sytraval I,* and *Matra* (ECJ 1993)—was European knowledge of the American experience. Yet if the values of pluralist transparency and participation are at the forefront, dialogue is awfully appealing. The European trick would be some compromise in which courts somehow required enough dialogue to get transparency and participation without getting the long delay resulting from strategic behaviour. Indeed, the US Supreme Court had attempted something of the sort in the famous *Vermont Yankee* decision (US Supreme Court 1978) in which the justices accepted the 'transformation' in administrative law wrought by the courts of appeal but tried to persuade them not to comb through the whole administrative record and insist that the administrators respond to every last nit raised for picking by every last litigator.

In the *Sytraval* case, by combining reasons, care, and manifest error standards with a fine-tooth judicial re-examination of the administrative record, the CFI appeared to come close to accepting litigators' invitations to declare a full-scale dialogue requirement. The Pandora's box opened by the ECJ in *Nolle I* and *TUM* (Nehl 1999:133; Swarze 1994) appeared to burst forth. In *Automec Srl II, Asia Motor France II* (CFI 1994), *SIDE,* and *Sytraval,* the CFI speaks of the duty of the Commission to investigate *relevant* facts and give *sufficient* reasons. It goes so far as to say that in particular instances the Commission would be 'obligated to give a reasoned answer to each of the objections raised . . . by an outside complainant' (*Sytraval I,* CFI 1995c: paras 62, 69). 'The Commission's obligation to state reasons for its decisions may in certain circumstances require an exchange of views and arguments with the complainant . . .' (para. 78). There is even a move toward the ultimate synopticism. The Commission has an 'obligation to examine objections which the complainant would certainly have raised' if the complainant had known what the Commission knew (para. 66).

The ECJ then responded in a very *Vermont Yankee* kind of way (*Sytraval II,* ECJ 1998b). That is, it expressed great unease with the prospect that the CFI would do what the US courts of appeal had done but in the process it actually accepted much of the transformation. In the particular set of procedures at issue, the ECJ denied that a complainant, that is, someone seeking to get the Commission to initiate a proceeding against someone else, had a formal right to be heard at the stage of initial Commission decision-making about whether to initiate a proceeding. The ECJ rejected specifically the term 'dialogue'. It also specifically rejected the CFI move to synopticism, that is, any requirement that the Commission consider points that the complainant would have raised if it had known enough to do so. The ECJ also sought to impede tendencies to conflate procedural and substantive review by chiding the CFI for failing to fully distinguish between giving reasons and manifest-error review.

But the opinion of the ECJ shows clear signs of having been cobbled together from conflicting views on the Court, some of which approve the basic stance of the CFI. The CFI formula—'to conduct an exchange of views and arguments with the complainants'—is at one point in the ECJ's opinion said to have no legal basis (ECJ 1995: para. 58). But then the Court says that such a Commission obligation 'cannot be founded *solely*' on the giving reasons provision of the Treaties (para. 59, emphasis added). And then it goes on to speak of the Commission's obligation to 'sound administration' and 'diligent and impartial examination of the complaint which may make it necessary for it to examine matters not expressly raised by the complainant' (para. 62). Thus the ECJ itself seems to be combining giving reasons and duty of care to move, as the CFI does, toward synopticism. The ultimate holding of the ECJ is to support the CFI annulment of the Commission decision. The ECJ does so on giving-reasons grounds because the Commission has failed to respond to a particular point raised by the complainant which the Court characterizes as 'not secondary'.

So what is the upshot of *Sytraval II*? Like *Vermont Yankee*, it expresses a mood of a higher court that a lower court has gone too far. Like *Vermont Yankee* it imposes no firm doctrinal barrier to the lower court continuing to do what it has been doing. Specifically, it rejects a formal dialogue. But whether under giving reasons or duty of care—or, more likely, the two together—the Commission is declared to be under an obligation to respond to all 'not secondary' points either raised or not raised by the complainant and to engage in an actual exchange of views when that is necessary to adequately considering all 'not-secondary' points. It would be a foolish Commission indeed which on the basis of *Sytraval II* refused to prepare a record that showed that it had listened carefully to, and responded seriously to, all relevant points made to it including points that might or might not subsequently be considered 'not secondary' by a court.

In the final analysis, the ECJ supports transparency and participation about as much as the CFI does, allows the CFI to continue along the line of institutionalization it has been pursuing, but warns litigators that the courts will be eager to punish strategic behaviour on their part, that is, the raising of clouds of flimsy arguments and allegations in their complaints. Dialogue, but not the American babelogue, is required.

The CFI immediately responded to *Sytraval II* in a long series of cases mostly involving Commission levying of fines for competition violations. The CFI's opinions repeatedly announce the requirement that the Commission give detailed reasons while explicitly rejecting a requirement that the Commission respond to all points raised. In most of the cases it lets the Commission off while essentially warning it to do better in the future. It seeks to achieve quasi-dialogue and quasi-synopticism short of the American extreme by adopting and repeating a rhetorical formula that insists that Commission reasons-giving must be judged by the Court case by case in the context of the specific circumstances, the content of the administrative measure being taken, the non-*ex-post* reasons relied upon, and the interests of the party subject to the Commission decision. While the Commission need not respond to all arguments, it must set out all facts and legal considerations having 'decisive importance' in the context of the decision (see, for example, *Gruber*, CFI 1999*e*; *Cascades*, CFI 1999*c*; *Buchmann*, CFI 1999*b*; *ITT Promedia*, CFI 1999*f*). The CFI struck down one Council refusal to make documents available based on a mere formulaic invocation of public security (*Svenska Journalist forbundet*, CFI 1999*g*). More important is a cluster of CFI decisions striking down Commission decisions that, in the judges' view, had not provided sufficiently detailed economic analysis (*ENS and Others*, CFI 1999*d*; *British Airways and Others and British Midland Airways*, CFI 1999*a*).

6. Conclusion

Hans Peter Nehl (1999), in his excellent book on EC administrative law, argues that the EU courts are concerned with efficient administration and the protection of individuals rather than pluralist democracy. He comes to this conclusion largely because he gives the duty of care rather than the giving-reasons requirement pride of place in his story of the transformation of EU administrative law. As he notes, however, care and reasons march together in the jurisprudence of the EU, some sort of dialogue requirement lurks, and the courts show a tendency toward substantive judicial review. Whatever the ultimate value priorities of particular judges, what is happening is an institutionalization, that is, the construction of a set of enforced rules—procedures—that compel transparency of administrative action, access of non-governmental groups to administrative decision-making processes, and judicial, that is, lay, checks on technocratic decision-making.

In terms of democratic versus technocratic government, this institutionalization is a two-edged sword. It reduces the discretion of government bureaucracies by exposing their decisions to outside scrutiny, but, in the realm of regulation of modern economies, it shifts politics in the direction of a highly technical discourse of reasons-giving in which technocrats are advantaged. More generally, it advantages all those with the resources to contend at the level of technical discourse over those who simply have preferences about ultimate outcomes. In the contexts of other concerns expressed in this volume, the institutionalization of administrative space described here moves in the direction of coercing the Commission to open its 'thick' proceedings to all and of reducing opportunities for 'covert' policy-making. This institutionalization is itself overt, but amounts to low-visibility, incremental policy-making by the judiciary. Precisely because it is judicial policy-making it is constrained by the legal culture norms within which these judges operate, particularly the complex norms of precedent which both constrain and facilitate judicial policy-making. The CFI and the ECJ were not required, either by legal culture or political necessity, to go where they did, but comparisons with the US suggest that like causes have like effects. Tensions between technocratic administrative regulation and pluralist democracy lead to demands for the institutionalization of participation and transparency norms that judges are well situated, and under heavy pressure, to satisfy. But judges have considerable discretion to satisfy them more or less. For any political system, the extent to which judicially enforced giving-reasons or duty-of-administrative-care rules are mere facades or actual institutionalizations of administrative behaviour is a difficult empirical question, the answer to which may vary not only polity by polity but among the various administrative organizations within a given polity.

Nearly all of the institutionalization we have been examining applies specifically in realms of administrative quasi-adjudication or particularized decision-making, that is, to situations where the Commission must decide how a particular regulated party or how a particular person seeking a favourable decision from the Commission shall be treated. The EU has now entered a period in which the comitology process and the independent agencies (Joerges and Vos 1999; Dehousse 1997)—both nominally under Commission control—the national administrations implementing Union legislation, and the Commission itself are producing not only a great many particular decisions about particular individuals or business entities but also a great many rules and regulations that apply generally rather than only to a particular individual. These rules and regulations fill in the details of the legislation enacted by the Council, such as how many parts per million of a certain chemical are allowed in smoke-stack emissions, or what gas can be used as a coolant in refrigerators. The major open question of institutionalization is how much of the administrative law developed for dealing with administrative adjudications will now be transferred to administrative rule-making.

Most of the recent transparency and participation institutionalization we have been looking at occurs in a peculiar intermediate realm. Where administration is 'prosecuting', there are obvious 'rule of law' reasons for maximizing transparency and participation for the defendant and few reasons for doing so for 'third parties'. Where X is requesting the administration to 'prosecute' Y because Y's behaviour is illegal *and* harms X, X is not exactly a mere third party. Where Z is asking the administration to make a rule favouring him but equally applicable to everyone, Z is a third party, but everyone is a third party. Or, if you believe in democratic pluralism, Z and everyone else are first parties. Much of the new case law involves X asking administration to act against Y because Y is hurting X. What we have been seeing is a greater and greater tendency to see X not as a third party but as an interested party entitled to transparency and participation. It hardly needs to be spelled out that such complainant parties serve as a bridge between the rights of defence we might confer on defendants and rights we might confer on any group that had an interest in a particular administratively made public policy. The question is obviously: will the EU courts go on with the process of transferring transparency and participation institutionalization from particular administrative 'defendants', to 'complainants', to interest groups? One's prediction about this question depends in part on how much force is to be assigned to the autonomous dynamics of law, in part on how one assesses the strength of pluralist democratic ideology in Europe, and in part on how one evaluates the other patterns of institutionalization depicted in this volume. At the very minimum it might be argued that a polity which exhibits so much *Angst* about the democratic deficit, and so much difficulty in overcoming that problem by changes in legislative organs and electoral mechanisms, is likely to move in the direction of judicial, that is, low-visibility, incremental, democratic institutionalization of the administrative process in general and specifically in administrative rule—law—making.

6

Judicial Rulemaking and the Institutionalization of European Union Sex Equality Policy

RACHEL A. CICHOWSKI

IN the late 1950s, moved by a hope for peace and economic prosperity in Europe, six governments constructed the foundations of an unprecedented form of supranational governance: the European Community. Heads of governments came together around the negotiating table to begin developing the rules and organizations that would govern what was largely an international economic agreement. Women were but a distant presence at this table and women's rights were not on the agenda. Today, in the year 2000, this same supranational space, the European Union (EU), possesses an ever-expanding women's rights policy: from equal treatment in employment to maternity leave. Further, national executives are no longer alone in this space. Instead, public interest groups and individuals—from legal consultancy firms to women activists—and EU organizations such as the European Court of Justice (ECJ) are active in pressuring for and determining European policy outcomes. This consequence was unimaginable for the creators of the Treaty of Rome and this path was largely paved by the rulemaking of a court.[1]

This chapter examines the impact of the European Court of Justice on the institutional evolution of EU sex equality policy. In 1957, national governments provided that under the Treaty of Rome men and women would receive equal pay for equal work—Art. 119 EEC,[2] now Art. 141—a provision that protected businesses from unfair competition. Today this same provision bestows a positive right on individuals throughout the Member States, a judicially enforceable right that remains the backbone of an ever-expanding European

---

[1] The ECJ's rulings are now widely recognized as having far reaching consequences: most famously, having transformed the Treaty of Rome into a quasi-supranational constitution through its constitutional doctrine of 'supremacy' (*Costa*, ECJ 1964) and 'direct effect' (*Van Gend en Loos*, ECJ 1963a) (see Lenaerts 1990; Mancini 1989; Weiler 1981; 1991).

[2] An amended version of this provision is now Art. 141 under the Treaty of Amsterdam (ToA). As this historical analysis focuses on a period prior to the ToA and also largely prior to amendments, I will refer to the provision as 'Art. 119'.

social-justice policy. Over time, strategic action on the part of litigants and their lawyers and the ECJ's judicial rulemaking capacity—the Court's authoritative interpretation of EU rules[3]—has constructed a supranational space where women can not only demand the right to equal pay but can also receive protection as pregnant workers. This dynamic process is the focus of my analysis.

The study involves three basic mechanisms of institutional evolution. First, I examine the process by which self-interested private litigants and their lawyers are able to activate the EU legal system. The Art. 177 procedure, now Art. 234,[4] provides such an opportunity, as it allows national individuals to invoke EU law before national courts. Second, I examine the Court's authoritative interpretation of Art. 119. In particular, the analysis focuses on how Art. 119 became directly effective in national legal systems. Finally, I examine the feedback effects of this judicial rulemaking. How has the litigation environment been changed? What have been the EU and national-level policy consequences? In particular, this latter point is traced through the development of EU pregnancy and maternity rights.

1 Theoretical Perspectives and Analytic Framework

This analysis contributes to a growing body of research examining the Court's role in integration processes (for example, Cichowski 1998; Mattli and Slaughter 1998; Stone Sweet and Brunell 1998a; Stone Sweet and Caporaso 1998a). While this research has developed a strong theoretical basis for its assumptions, specific policy-sector empirical research is still needed. Furthermore, in the area of EU sex equality policy, there is an extensive body of legal scholarship on equal pay litigation (for example, Ellis 1998; Hoskyns 1996; Kenney 1992; 1996; Mazey 1998; Prechal and Burrows 1990). My analysis extends these findings by placing the evolution of sex equality in a larger institutional analysis. What are the consequences of the litigation for national and EU policy and how does this affect the larger process of integration? My analysis does not adopt a normative framework to evaluate whether sex equality policy is currently effective in the EU. While others have addressed this important question (for example, Elman 1996), I focus on the process in which formal rules were created to define this policy area.

---

[3] I use the term 'judicial rulemaking' to refer to the Court's authoritative interpretation of the Treaty and secondary legislation which results in the clarification of EU laws. It is well documented elsewhere (for example, Alter 1998; de la Mare 1999; Mancini 1989), that these interpretations can significantly alter the original measure in a way that changes what is lawful and unlawful behaviour for individuals and public and private bodies operating under EU law. For example, when the Court interprets Art. 119 in a way that now brings maternity pay under the purview of the equal pay principle, this creates a new rule (see *Gillespie*, ECJ 1996a, and discussion of the case later in the chapter). The behaviour of public and private bodies must reflect this new rule. And if it does not, individuals now have the ability to claim recourse before national courts.

[4] Art. 177 is now Art. 234 under the ToA. Again, this analysis will consistently refer to the procedure by the prior numbering as this applies to the period covered in this study.

Generally, institutionalization in this policy area evolves over time as a product of a dynamic relationship between institutions (the Treaty and secondary legislation), organizations (the ECJ) and actors (litigants and their lawyers) (Stone Sweet, Fligstein, and Sandholtz, this volume, p. xx). For the purposes of this analysis, I adopt the generally agreed distinctions between these three entities (see North 1990; Hall and Taylor 1996). Institutions constitute the macro level. They are complexes of rule systems that pattern and prescribe human interaction. Organizations make up the meso level and they are more or less formally constituted spaces occupied by groups of individuals pursuing collective purposes. Finally, the micro level consists of individual action.

The studies in this volume adopt varying approaches to understand how the interaction between institutions, organizations, and actors lead to institutional change or evolution. This chapter understands institutionalization as a process of rule construction that is endogenous to existing governance structures (March and Olsen 1989). That is, the Court's judicial rulemaking capacity operates within the institutional framework of the Treaty, yet the Court's jurisprudence can subsequently alter these institutions. This approach is not unfamiliar to scholars of judicial rulemaking (Shapiro 1988; Stone Sweet 2000). Furthermore, it is similar to other chapters in this volume that examine the institutionalization of a mode or technique of governance in the EU (for example Héritier; Le Galès; Mazey and Richardson; Shapiro).

How can we measure institutionalization? Institutionalization in the sex equality area begins by looking at the transformation of Art. 119. First, I examine how the provision has changed in precision and whether it has become more binding and enforceable. As European rules become more precise and non-compliance is met with greater enforceable penalties, we can expect the policy area to become more institutionalized at the EU level (Stone Sweet, Fligstein, and Sandholtz, this volume, p. xx; Stone Sweet and Sandholtz 1998). Second, institutionalization can be measured in terms of whether the scope of the provision has changed. As the purview of the provision expands, we can expect a greater number of actions to be formally governed by EU law. As we move across this continuum of precision, enforceability, and scope, we find institutionalization at the EU level taking place. Institutional evolution had distinct policy consequences both in national legal systems and at the European level. This analysis suggests an explanation for these dynamics. The chapter is organized as follows.

In the first part, I examine the necessary conditions for institutional evolution. First, Art. 119's inclusion in the Treaty. I highlight the origins of the provision and the logic for its placement in the Treaty. In particular, I focus on the role of national governments and the set of dual rights implied by the provision. Second, institutionalization relied on the direct effect of Art. 119. The Court's *Defrenne II* decision (ECJ 1976) transformed a distant Treaty provision into a provision conferring rights on individuals that were directly enforceable in national legal systems. In this analysis, I examine how the rights discourse around Art. 119 evolved. Who supported and who opposed this shift to a rights-based reading of Art. 119? Lawyers, the advocate general, the Commission, and Member States were all involved in this transformation. All parties, especially national governments, did not necessarily welcome the outcome. Finally, this transformation is linked to the general development of sex equality secondary legislation.

In the second part, I examine the specific consequences this rights discourse had on the development of maternity and pregnancy rights in the EU. Art. 119 did not include provisions on pregnancy, nor did it govern maternity leave; rather, it provided for equal pay for equal work. How did this equal pay principle evolve into a distinct set of rights protecting pregnant workers and requiring national governments to alter their laws regulating maternity benefits? I look to the sources and consequences of the case law in this area. First, I study how the Court's jurisprudence expanded the Community's equality principle to include a set of rights protecting pregnant workers. The final section will focus on the policy consequences of this case law: the Court's jurisprudence was integral to development and implementation of the Pregnancy Directive and there have been significant national policy changes to secure compliance.

2. Institutionalization of Art. 119

Art. 119 of the Treaty of Rome provided the legal basis for EU sex equality law. Essential to the evolution of the policy sector was, first, a decision by Member State governments to include the provision in the Treaty of Rome, and second, strategic action on the part of a private litigant and her lawyer to activate the ECJ, which subsequently transformed Art. 119 into an enforceable rights provision. Together these two factors activated a dynamic of litigation that ultimately brought the creation of a complex set of rules governing sex equality in Europe.

2.1 Origins of Art. 119

Art. 119 provided that Member States ensure and maintain the principle that women and men receive equal pay for equal work.[5] Member States were required to implement the principle by the end of the first stage of the Common Market, 31 December 1962. It was the French delegation which originally

---

[5] Full Text of Art. 119 from the Treaty of Rome:

'Each member state shall during the first stage ensure and subsequently maintain the application of the principle that men and women should receive equal pay for equal work.

For the purpose of the Art. 'pay' means the ordinary basic or minimum wage or salary and any other consideration, whether in cash or in kind, which the worker receives, directly or indirectly, in respect of his employment from his employer.

Equal Pay without discrimination based on sex means:

a) that pay for the same work at piece rates shall be calculated on the basis of the same unit of measurement; b) that pay for work at time rates shall be the same for the same job.'

demanded that an equal pay provision be included in the EC Treaty, the 1957 Treaty of Rome. France was the only country to possess equal pay laws at the time, and French employers saw this as a potential barrier to fair and equal competition between Member States. The role of activist women can be traced back to this initial policy stage of getting the issue on the agenda, for the existence of this French law was a result of political activism among French women in the 1940s (Hoskyns 1996). However, the intention of Community architects was not based in a concern for equality between the sexes.

Scholars observe that Member State agreement to the equal pay provision was founded in an attempt to 'placate the French' rather than a serious commitment to provide for equal pay in national markets (Warner 1984: 143). In fact, implementation of such a measure at the time would have resulted in considerable costs and restructuring of the labour market. In the original six Member States, women constituted almost 30 per cent of the waged workforce. And equal pay varied widely; four countries had some provision, while Belgium and the Netherlands lacked any legislation. Dutch pay disparities were in the order of 40 per cent, with many sectors of the economy relying on low-paid female labour. Not surprising, Treaty debates were characterized by Dutch resistance to the idea of equal pay (Collins 1975).

These varying national positions also reflected an overarching conception of the relationship between social protection and the functioning of the Common Market. In particular, there were two opposing logics that underpinned Treaty negotiations in 1957. The French believed a 'harmonization' of social costs was necessary in order to provide a fair playing field for businesses across the Community once barriers to the free movement of goods and persons were removed. French businesses were rightly concerned that mandated national social legislation, such as equal pay and longer paid holidays, would increase the costs of production in France and thus put French industry at a comparative disadvantage with other Member States. On the other hand, German negotiators were sceptical of the need to equalize social costs by way of Treaty provisions. They believed that 'harmonization' of social costs would be an inevitable consequence once the Common Market was established. The position taken by Germany stemmed from a more general commitment to low levels of government interference in the area of wages and prices (see Ellis 1998: Ch. 2).

These opposing traditions led to the Treaty's minimal social provisions. The French delegation persuaded the other Member States to accept a very specific provision on equal pay (Art. 119) and a similarly narrow provision regarding paid holidays (Art. 119a). These negotiations remained strictly focused on fair competition, with the principle originally appearing in the portion of the Treaty dealing with competition distortion. However, both provisions were ultimately shifted—though the text remained unchanged—to social provisions as an attempt to develop at least some harmonization of social costs within the Treaty (Hoskyns 1996: 57). Stated generally, Art. 119 was inserted into the Treaty for economic reasons, but was placed in the position of having social consequences. Its inclusion laid down a precise legal obligation on Member States, yet at the same time it also embodied a general social ideal or instrument—at least indirectly—to harmonize social policy. The policy consequences of this Treaty provision were not foreseen.

2.2. The transformation of Art. 119

Until the late 1960s, Member State governments all but ignored Art. 119. Not one national government had undertaken domestic policy changes to implement this equal pay principle. However, Art. 119 was far from dead, as it was soon to gain life as a result of the strategic action and activism of a Belgian lawyer. Elaine Vogel-Polsky, who specialized in social and labour law, regarded Art. 119 as a stepping stone to expanding women's labour rights (Hoskyns 1996). Through a series of cases involving Gabrielle Defrenne, a flight attendant with the Belgian national airline, Sabena, Vogel-Polsky was able to work with the European Court of Justice to expand the scope of the Article and to begin to provide real situations in which Art. 119 was applicable. The Court's *Defrenne* judgements (ECJ 1971; 1976; 1978), in particular the second case, were critical in transforming Art. 119 by establishing its direct effect, and in doing so provided Community citizens with individual rights enforceable under EU law.

The conditions that gave rise to these cases are as follows. Until 1966, Sabena's male flight stewards earned higher wages, were allowed to retire 15 years later, and were entitled to a special pension plan, all benefits that their female counterparts failed to receive. Job responsibilities of stewards and stewardesses were identical. Defrenne challenged these inequalities. The *Defrenne I* case questioned whether Sabena's pension system contravened the principle of non-discrimination embodied in Art. 119. The Court ruled against Defrenne stating that under EU law the Sabena pension did not constitute direct or indirect payment. However, Advocate General M. Dutheillet de Lamothe raised a critical point not addressed by the Court: did Art. 119 provide individuals with direct legal rights that were enforceable in national courts? In his opinion it did:

Although the difficulties of application encountered by certain countries were great and although in particular a conference of Member States extended until 31 December 1964 the period initially laid down, it appears to me certain that at least from this date Article 119 created subjective rights which the workers of the Member States can invoke and respect for which national courts must ensure. (ECJ 1971: 456)

Five years later the Court would agree.

The direct effect of Art. 119 was central to the *Defrenne II* case. Similar to the first case, Defrenne's claim was dismissed first by the Belgian *Tribunal du Travail*, was appealed before the *Court du Travail*, and finally reached the ECJ by way of Art. 177. This case involved the issue of wage inequalities. Vogel-Polsky persisted with the question of direct effect. In order to resolve this

dispute, the Belgian Court referred two questions. First, does Art. 119 introduce the principle of equal pay directly into the national law of Member
States, and if so from what date? Second, has Art. 119 become directly applicable in the internal law of Member States by virtue of the Treaty's adoption or
is national legislation alone competent in the matter? The consequences of an
affirmative answer were legendary.

The Court expanded the scope and purpose of Art. 119 by stating that the
principle was creative of both enforceable rights in national courts, regardless
of national implementing legislation, and that the scope requires further
clarification and development. In its reasoning, the Court emphasizes what it
sees as the dual function of Art. 119:

First, in the light of the different stages of the development of social legislation in the
various Member States, the aim of Article 119 is to avoid a situation in which undertak-
ings established in States which have actually implemented the principle of equal pay
suffer a competitive disadvantage in intra-Community competition . . . Secondly, this
provision forms part of the social objectives of the Community, which is not merely an
economic union, but is at the same time intended, by common action, to ensure social
progress and seek the constant improvement of the living and working conditions of
their peoples . . . This double aim, which is at once economic and social, shows that the
principle of equal pay forms part of the foundations of the Community. (ECJ 1976: 470)

The argument of Advocate General (AG) Trabucchi stated quite clearly that he
believed Art. 119 was not only an enforceable right, but a fundamental
Community right: 'In view of this it seems to me that the prohibition of all
discrimination based on sex (particularly on the subject of pay) protects a right
which must be regarded as fundamental in the Community legal order as it is
elsewhere' (ECJ 1976: 483).[6]

Not all parties participating in this case concurred with this expansive reading of the Treaty. The governments of both the United Kingdom and of the
Irish Republic exercised their right to submit a written brief, or 'observation',
stating how they believed the Court should decide the case. In their opinion,
Art. 119 did not confer rights on individuals, citing the potential 'cost of the
operation' if the Court was to find the principle directly effective, especially
retroactively. Furthermore, their arguments were similar in stating that Art.
119 merely implies a commitment to a constitutional principle, but can be
effective only when implemented via national legislation (ECJ 1976: 460). The
Commission's observation urged the Court to answer the question of direct
effect in the affirmative, yet stated this effect was limited to the relationship
between individuals and the state, and did not impose obligations on private
employers (ECJ 1976: 462). The Court's authoritative interpretation of the
Treaty developed otherwise.

Not only did the Court's ruling lay down that Art. 119 was directly enforceable in national courts, regardless of national implementing legislation; it also

---

[6] AG Trabucchi's opinion would be realized in the Court's subsequent *Defrenne III* judgement (ECJ
1978). I discuss this later in the paper.

suggested who would be protected and obligated by this right. In its judgement, the Court stated:

The principle that men and women should receive equal pay, which is laid down by Article 119, may be relied on before the national courts. These courts have a duty to ensure the protection of the rights which that provision vests in individuals, in particular in the case of those forms of discrimination which have their origin in legislative provisions or collective labour agreements, as well as where men and women receive unequal pay for equal work which is carried out in the same establishment or service, whether public or private. (ECJ 1976: 475)

Beyond the Commission's argument for 'vertical' direct effect, that is, in relationships involving the state and the individual, the Court's ruling also established the 'horizontal' direct effect of Art. 119: granting enforceable rights in contracts between individuals. Art. 119 was no longer a distant obligation on Member State governments. Following the Court's interpretation of the Treaty, individuals, national courts, and public and private bodies were all bound into a tighter web of legal obligation.

2.3. The expansion to secondary legislation

The Court's judicial rulemaking in the *Defrenne II* judgment enabled Art. 119 to become the site for an expansive rights discourse. Art. 119 would become the driving force behind EC sex equality legislation in the 1970s and 1980s. Scholars describe the impact of the Court's jurisprudence as having, 'opened the way for women within the Commission's own bureaucracy to push for stronger policy' (Hoskyns 1996: 74). The repercussions of these landmark judicial decisions continue today as lawyers, national equality agencies, and women organizations throughout Europe see the European Court of Justice as an access point to influence policy making (Docksey 1998). Art. 119 opened the door to further policy expansion.

Three pieces of EC legislation were passed between 1975–9 which clarified the goals set out in Art. 119. They were the Equal Pay Directive, the Equal Treatment of Work Directive, and the Equal Treatment in Social Security Directive.[7] These policies were heavily influenced by a comprehensive study carried out in 1968 on the status of women's employment in the Member States. The author was a French sociologist, Evelyne Sullerot, who had pioneered academic studies on women's work in Europe (Hoskyns 1996). However, the policy debates surrounding the Equal Pay Directive remained similar to the original discussions of Art. 119 as it remained primarily conceptualized as an employment issue. Yet, within these negotiations, there was continual pressure and call to expand the scope of this EC policy area. This pressure and the effect it had on the other two equality Directives is depicted in the following account of the policy debate:

---

[7] Council Directives 75/117/EEC, 76/207/EEC, and 79/7/EEC.

During the course of the equal pay negotiations there were constant reminders from Sullerot, the Commission and in the end even the Court, that this was not a sufficient policy to tackle women's inequality. It needed to be expanded. The next two Directives, while remaining within the employment field, went much wider and began to raise issues such as child care and dependency, which crossed the public/private divide and were therefore more controversial. (Hoskyns 1996: 93)

Due to both the decision-making procedures at this time and the protected nature of these policy decisions, these Directives were all adopted under unanimity voting and provided general rather than specific policy prescriptions. In particular, the Equal Treatment Directive failed to bring clarity between issues of discrimination and general equality. The Directive states that 'no discrimination whatsoever on grounds of sex' will be allowed under EU law. Scholars have observed that this general 'whatsoever' expression has given ample opportunity to both litigants and the Court to expand the Directive's scope (Ellis 1998). This includes one Court decision that found protection for transsexuals against dismissal within the scope of Community law (ECJ 1996*b*). Furthermore, the Directive failed to clearly provide a definition for the concept at the heart of the legislation, namely, how is indirect discrimination embodied in general equality? This ambiguity would later be at the centre of a series of cases heard before the ECJ (see ECJ 1986).

Art. 119 and these three Directives together provided the basis for European sex equality law. The Council subsequently added only two Directives to this policy area in the 1980s,[8] both of which are largely symbolic. In the 1990s, we have seen the addition of six more equality Directives. Three Directives introduce new areas of EU equality law: parental leave,[9] pregnancy[10] and burden of proof in discrimination cases.[11] One of the remaining three amends EU rules on equality in social security[12] while the other two extend the parental leave framework agreement and the burden of proof Directive to the UK, as a result of the Agreement on Social Policy formally being included in the Treaty of Amsterdam.[13] In terms of secondary legislation, the Commission has made a valiant effort. At a recent conference 'Equality is the Future', the then President of the Commission, Jacques Santer, stated:

---

[8] Council Directives 86/378/EEC and 86/613/EEC. While this later Directive might suggest special rights regarding pregnant workers—see Directive description in the References—the Directive merely required Member States to 'examine' their national systems for protecting self-employed pregnant workers (Art. 8).

[9] Council Directive 96/34/EC is a framework agreement on parental leave concluded by Union des Industries de la Communauté (UNICE), Centre Européen de l'Entreprise Publique (CEEP), and the European Trade Union Confederation (ETUC), three main cross-industry organizations. After previous unsuccessful attempts by the Commission, this framework directive finally came to fruition in 1996.

[10] Council Directive 92/85/EEC.

[11] Council Directive 97/80/EC.

[12] Council Directive 96/97/EC amends Council Directive 86/378/EEC in order to adapt the provisions which were affected by the *Barber* case-law. The Court's judgment in *Barber* (ECJ 1990*a*) automatically invalidated parts of the Directive. For a complete list of associated cases see the text of Directive 96/97/EC.

[13] Council Directives 97/75/EC and 98/52/EC. The Agreement on Social Policy was previously relegated to an annex of the Treaty of European Union in order to accommodate the British government's insistence on its opt-out position on further EU social protection.

the Commission will maintain a strong and omnipresent policy in terms of equal opportunities. 'Equality is the Future' is not only a necessity and an obligation for us all, it is also a fundamental ambition to which the Commission is fully committed and which it seeks to pursue. (CEC 1998: 4)

As the number of adopted pieces of legislation would suggest, the Member States have been less ambitious in terms of adopting new directives or regulations in the area.[14] Generally, Art. 119 and the Equal Pay, Equal Treatment, and Equal Treatment in Social Security Directives remain the backbone of EU equality litigation. Of the Art. 177 cases involving sex equality laws from 1970 to mid-1998, in 98 per cent—125 out of a total 127—litigants are invoking one or more of these four EU rules.[15]

The legislative development of EU sex equality policy has arguably been a slow process. The varying national positions on this policy area have provided road blocks along the way. Furthermore, the generalities in principles and tensions between economic and social interests have led to varying implementation and thinly developed EU legislation. However, the evolution of this policy area has also been characterized by successful strategic action on the part of lawyers and trade union and equality unit activists to take advantage of opportunities embedded in these EU rules; and the result has been the expansion of sex equality rules. The Court is willing to solve these conflicts and the path of institutionalization is pushed forward. As the following analysis demonstrates and as others have documented, when EU sex equality legislative advancements were at a standstill in the late 1980s and early 1990s, the ECJ actively expanded the scope of this policy area (see Stone Sweet and Caporaso 1998a).

3. The Path of Institutional Evolution: From Equal Pay to Pregnancy Rights

The institutionalization of Art. 119 had consequences not only for secondary legislation in the 1970s and 1980s, but also for the litigating environment. The institutional path was paved. Individuals were provided with a new arsenal to demand rights under EU law before national courts. In this second part, I examine how the litigation in turn pushes for further institutionalization in the field of EU sex equality policy. Have the rules governing EU gender equality become more precise, binding, and enforceable? Furthermore, how has the scope been expanded? As earlier argued, this path of

---

[14] Further, in terms of Treaty amendments in the 1990s, the Treaty of Amsterdam (ToA) presents a slightly bolder move on behalf of Member States. With the full inclusion of the Agreement on Social Policy and enabling provisions such as Art. 6a, which suggests greater protection from discrimination based on a host of factors from sex to sexual orientation, the ToA may bid well for future legislative innovations. See Craig and de Búrca (1998: Ch. 19) and More (1999) for implications of the ToA on EU equality policy.

[15] This data was compiled utilizing the *European Court Reports* (ECJ, various years) and general preliminary reference data from a larger set (Stone Sweet and Brunell 1999).

institutional evolution began with the self-interested activation of the EU legal system by private litigants. This activated the Court's judicial rulemaking function—authoritative interpretation of Art. 119—and in doing so transformed Art. 119 into a judicially enforceable rights provision. The final, and perhaps most important, stage of this process of institutionalization is the feedback effects of this strategic action and rulemaking. How have they changed the litigating environment, and what are the policy consequences of these changes? How have they affected the intergovernmental or supranational nature of this policy sector? Furthermore, who are the main actors fueling this evolution?

3.1. Effects on litigation

The following case law analysis focuses on the sources and consequences of the Court's case law on pregnancy and maternity issues. It is an important policy area that our scholarship currently fails to examine in terms of its origins in judicial rulemaking and the subsequent consequences on both national and EU policy. Art. 119 did not mention maternity leave or pregnancy rights. It laid down a principle regarding 'pay'. How did it come to be that women all over Europe were able to demand their rights as pregnant workers by invoking a right to equal treatment that is embodied in Art. 119? These demands did not go unheard. Instead, they resonated loudly, first through ECJ rulings that often required costly national policy change, and second, in the form of Community legislation. This is the process of institutional evolution I will explain.

3.1.1. The legal basis for pregnancy and maternity litigation
This litigation has primarily grown out of rights claimed under Art. 119 and the Equal Treatment Directive, 76/207/EEC. The majority of these cases focus on women who have experienced discrimination in terms of either access to or dismissal from employment on the basis of pregnancy. As the Equal Treatment Directive is on its face more relevant to these rights arguments, it lays out 'the principle of equal treatment for men and women in regards to access to employment, including promotion, and to vocational training and as regards to general working conditions . . .' Why is Art. 119 continually invoked in this litigation?[16] The answer becomes evident from the *Defrenne* decisions. Advocate-General Trabucchi's arguments in the *Defrenne II* judgment, which drew largely from the Court's earlier 1970 ruling in *Internationale Handesgesellschaft* (ECJ 1970), emphasized the relationship between Art. 119 and this general principle of equal treatment:

---

[16] Furthermore, the Equal Treatment Directive does mention protection for pregnant workers in Art. 2. However, this is to prevent a Member State's special protection for pregnant workers from being challenged under EU equality law, rather than placing any obligation on a Member State to provide such provisions.

If the principle of equal treatment were to apply only to pay in the strict sense of the word or to absolutely identical work, the practical effect of Article 119 would be rather small. This gives the Member States and the Community institutions enormous scope in taking action to put into effect the principle of non-discrimination laid down in Article 119 without having to rely on its direct applicability. (ECJ 1976: 491)

The Court would later adopt a similar stance in legal argumentation for the *Defrenne III* ruling:

The Court has repeatedly stated that respect for fundamental personal human rights is one of the general principles of Community law, the observance of which it has a duty to ensure. There can be no doubt that the elimination of discrimination based on sex forms part of those fundamental rights. (ECJ 1978: 1365)

As these passages illustrate, the Court's jurisprudence has found this general principle of equal treatment in Art. 119 and today it is formally included in the Treaty of Amsterdam.[17] Litigants and their lawyers are acting strategically by invoking this right as they provide the Court with a powerful tool to decide the case. General principles, in theory, do not have the ability to override Treaty provisions, yet they have enabled the ECJ to justify a 'liberal interpretation of what might otherwise seem to be a narrow rule' (Ellis 1998: 181). As for the equal treatment principle, the ECJ has utilized it to dismantle both discriminatory administrative decisions and to justify broad interpretations of EC secondary legislation (Ellis 1998). Art. 119 is invoked for this purpose.

3.1.2. Judicial rule-making and the evolution of maternity and pregnancy rights

The rights of pregnant workers under Community law were first considered by the Court in *Dekker* (ECJ 1990*b*). The case was brought before the ECJ by a Dutch court in 1988. Mrs Dekker applied for a job with a Dutch company, VJV, and after an interview was found to be the most qualified for the job. She was three-months pregnant at the time and while the hiring committee recommended employment, VJV management decided not to employ Mrs Dekker because its insurer would not cover the necessary maternity pay. Mrs Dekker instigated legal proceedings against VJV, claiming that she had been discriminated against on the basis of her sex. The case was referred to the ECJ for a preliminary ruling on the protection of Mrs Dekker under Art. 119 and Directive 76/207/EEC (Equal Treatment).

In this 1990 ruling, the Court found that discrimination in employment opportunities on the ground of pregnancy can constitute direct sex discrimination, contrary to the Equal Treatment Directive. Scholars observe that the ruling in effect created new European rules by providing explicit protection of pregnant workers under EU law and also created a new interpretation of sex equality for women, emphasizing disadvantage to women rather than comparable treatment with men (McGlynn 1996: 238; Bamforth 1993: 877). Later

---

[17] See Craig and de Búrca (1998: Ch. 19) and Ellis (1998: Ch. 3) for an in-depth discussion of the principle of equal treatment.

that same day, the Court made a similar ruling in a case originating from Danish courts, the *Hertz* case (ECJ 1990*c*), concluding that the dismissal of a pregnant employee also amounts to discrimination under EU law. Together these two rulings established protection under EU law against the dismissal of or the refusal to employ pregnant workers.[18]

This question of protection against dismissal was further raised in a case originating from Germany in 1992. *Habermann-Beltermann v. Arbeiterwohlfahrt* (ECJ 1994*a*) concerned the dismissal of a pregnant woman who had been employed on an indefinite contract to work at night, despite the national law that forbad night work by pregnant women. The Court decided the case by emphasizing that the national law affected only a limited duration, in contrast to the unlimited nature of the contract, and found that dismissal under these circumstances was contrary to the Equal Treatment directive. While this clearly represented an expansion in protection of pregnant women, it also defined the limitation of this protection:

The termination of a contract without a fixed term on account of the woman's pregnancy . . . cannot be justified on the ground that a statutory prohibition, imposed because of pregnancy, temporarily prevents the employee from performing night-time work. (ECJ 1994*a*: 1677)

This ruling begs the question of what protection is provided in EU law for pregnant women with *fixed*-term employment. The question presents an ambiguity that may be the subject of future litigation.

A closer look at these ECJ rulings reveals many unanswered questions regarding pregnancy, maternity, and discrimination. In particular, when is pregnancy to be regarded as the determining factor in discriminatory treatment? In a now pivotal case in the development of EU equality law, the British House of Lords referred a set of questions in the *Webb* case (ECJ 1994*b*) to the ECJ asking for clarification. Ms Webb, a pregnant woman, had her indefinite employment contract terminated when her employer found out that she would be absent from work during the same period as another pregnant employee whom she was hired to replace. The House of Lords decided that while Ms Webb had no rights under UK law, she might under Community law (Directive 76/207/EEC) and so asked for a preliminary ruling. The ECJ framed the problem thus:

The national court is uncertain whether it was unlawful to dismiss Mrs Webb on the grounds of pregnancy or whether greater weight should be attached to the reasons for which she was recruited. (ECJ 1994*b*: para. 14)

---

[18] Advocate-General Damon in his joint opinion for *Dekker* and *Hertz* stresses that the principles involved in the two cases require the Court to decide what place maternity holds in European society. Prior to these rulings, protection for pregnant workers remained an unelaborated right in the Equal Treatment Directive. Art. 2(3) of the Directive states: 'This Directive shall be without prejudice to provisions concerning the protection of women, particularly as regards to pregnancy and maternity' (ECJ 1990*a*).

The Court reaffirmed its early ruling in *Dekker* and found that 'dismissal of a pregnant worker on account of pregnancy constitutes direct discrimination on grounds of sex' (para.19). The Court continues to argue that the need for special protection of pregnant workers is embodied in the Equal Treatment Directive and also in the Pregnancy Directive, which had not come into force yet when the case arose: 'the Community legislature provided . . . for special protection to be given to women, by prohibiting dismissal during the period from the beginning of their pregnancy to the end of their maternity leave' (para. 21). Therefore, the Court concludes, 'greater weight' cannot be attached to the reasons for recruitment. The defendant's argument of hardship is viewed not as the reason for dismissal, but as justification for the discriminatory treatment. Under Community law, once direct discrimination is established, it cannot be justified (Boch 1996).

Scholars have both lauded and criticized the Court's decision in *Webb*. The ruling clearly emphasized and expanded the Community's goal of protecting pregnant workers from discriminatory action, despite the harmful costs inflicted on employers and Member State governments.[19] Yet the ruling also highlights a significant area of equality law that needs further clarification. The relationship between Art. 5 of the Equal Treatment Directive and the Pregnancy Directive remain speculative (Ellis 1998). In both the *Webb* and *Hertz* decisions, the Court implied that the Equal Treatment Directive leaves unanswered the question whether pregnant women in fixed term employment are protected. While the Pregnancy Directive is not explicit about unlimited coverage, the Court in the *Larsson* decision (ECJ 1997a) concludes that Art. 10 of the Directive in fact offers such blanket protection. Interestingly enough, in this case originating from Danish courts, the Court found that the dismissal of a woman due to pregnancy-related illness was in fact lawful under the Equal Treatment Directive—again, the facts of the case were prior to implementation of the Pregnancy Directive—when the dismissal took place after the end of her maternity leave. The Court's clarification of the Pregnancy Directive and the extension of protection came as a side remark stating that had the Directive been in force the Court would have found the action unlawful.[20]

This remark clearly foreshadowed the Court's *Brown* ruling (ECJ 1998c), a case referred from the British House of Lords. Mrs Brown was absent from work for over six months during her pregnancy for pregnancy-related reasons. All employees at Rentokil Ltd, her employer, were governed by the policy that absences of six months due to sickness justified dismissal. Accordingly, Mrs Brown was dismissed. The Court held, in an explicit reversal of the *Larsson*

---

[19] The *Webb* decision helped form the foundation for settlement claims involving pregnant women discharged from the British armed forces. After the dismissal of more than 5,000 women during 1978–90, British courts began awarding settlements in the figures of £33,000–£173,000 per claimant. See Stone Sweet and Caporaso (1998a).

[20] The Court remarked: 'It is clear from the objective of Article 10 that absence during the protected period, other than for reasons unconnected with the employee's condition, can no longer be taken into account as grounds for subsequent dismissal' (ECJ 1997a: para. 25).

decision, that it was contrary to the Equal Treatment Directive to dismiss a woman for pregnancy-related illnesses during her pregnancy.[21] Scholars have rightly argued that this reversal has done little to clarify EU rules in this area, as it contradicted its earlier interpretation of the Equal Treatment Directive (Ellis 1999).[22] However, one could argue that at least the Court has brought past interpretations of EU equality laws—in particular, the Equal Treatment Directive—into conformity with the new norms governing European maternity and pregnancy rights, as established through the Court's expansive reading of the Pregnancy Directive. Furthermore, we are able to see how the Court actively brings national law into conformity with these new rules, even after these appeal cases were previously turned down by numerous national courts (McGlynn 1996).

The final set of cases I will discuss demonstrate the Court's further expansion of pregnancy rights in areas other than dismissal and refusal to hire. In particular, these cases involve the clarification of employment rights of pregnant workers. Again, the facts involved in the first case were prior to implementation of the Pregnancy Directive, and thus rely on the rights provided for pregnant workers under the Equal Treatment Directive and also Art. 119. Yet both of these cases provide an example of the Court's 'parallel' legislating, which in effect provided more stringent requirements than the Directive.

In the *Gillespie* case, the Court was referred a set of questions regarding the applicability of Community law to levels of maternity pay (ECJ 1996a). The referral came by way of a Northern Ireland appeals court after the case of 17 plaintiffs had been dismissed by the lower industrial tribunal. The plaintiffs had all been on maternity leave from their employment in various offices of the Northern Ireland Health Services during a period in which a proposed back-pay increase was to be given. The maternity leave avaliable to Health Service employees consists of a percentage of their given wage. The plaintiffs instigated proceedings on the grounds that they had suffered sex discrimination because they did not receive the full benefit of the back-dated pay rise due to the fact that they were receiving a reduced amount of their wage while on maternity leave. The Court ruled in favour of the plaintiffs and its judgment further clarified how national maternity policies must be interpreted in light of Art. 119 and the Equal Pay Directive.

[21] As in the *Larsson* case, the facts of this case arose before the Pregnancy Directive came into force and so the Equal Treatment Directive was the only instrument available to the litigants.

[22] In particular, the Court's adherence to the rule that where the discriminatory treatment is based on the fact of pregnancy, since only women can become pregnant, this must amount to discrimination based on sex. The *Brown* decision takes this a step further by arguing that pregnancy-related illness is inseparable from the fact of pregnancy and therefore similar treatment as a result of this condition is also discrimination on grounds of sex. Mainly, this is problematic because it again reduces pregnancy to the status of illness; as well, this reliance on illness rather than absence as the cause for dismissal removes the employer's interests from the situation. The European Parliament when reviewing the Council's amendments to the Pregnancy Directive proposal also echoed concerns with the link between pregnancy and sickness. This later logic could dilute the complexity of the situation and thus impede the Court from its job in balancing all the interests in the dispute at hand. See Ellis (1999) for a further discussion.

The second case involves the protection of employee rights regarding assessment and evaluation while absent on maternity leave. It is worth mentioning that while the facts of the *Thibault* case (ECJ 1998*d*) took place after the implementation of the Pregnancy Directive, the only instrument which can be relied upon where unfavourable treatment takes a form other than dismissal or refusal to employ is still the Equal Treatment Directive (Ellis 1999). The case arose when Mrs Thibault registered a complaint with the Labour Tribunal in Paris against her employer for failing to perform her annual performance evaluation, which is linked to a minimum 2 per cent pay rise and promotion, due to the fact she did not fulfill the requisite six months attendance within the evaluation year. Mrs Thibault was on maternity and pregnancy-related leave for seven months of this time and she argued that her employer's failure to assess her performance based on absences related to maternity leave was discriminatory. Despite the observation submitted by the UK government stating that the employer's action did not constitute sex discrimination under EU law, the Court expanded the rights under the Equal Treatment Directive by concluding that it was unlawfully discriminatory to deny a woman the right to possible promotion because of her absence on maternity leave.

The final two cases represent the Court's first opportunity to rule on the Pregnancy Directive. The Directive will be discussed in further detail below. In *Boyle* (ECJ 1998*e*), six female employees of the British Equal Opportunities Commission[23] applied to the industrial tribunal, Manchester, for a declaration that certain conditions of their maternity leave was unenforceable in so far as it discriminated against female employees and was thus contrary to Art. 119 of the Treaty and to Council Directives 75/117/EEC, 76/207/EEC, and 92/85/EEC. While the Court re-emphasized the provisions in the Pregnancy Directive which afforded national government discretion in determining when maternity leave commences, it found that a contract prohibiting a woman from taking sick leave during maternity leave without returning to work first was contrary to the Directive. Again, UK laws were the subject of litigation.

In the month following the *Boyle* ruling, the Court gave its second decision involving the Pregnancy Directive in the *Pedersen* case (ECJ 1998*f*). By way of a Danish Commerce Court, the four plaintiffs challenged a national law which stated that women who were unfit for work for a reason connected with the pregnancy before the three-month period preceding the birth date were not entitled to full pay. Three women were declared unfit to work while one was only partially unfit to work during this period, and thus their employer ceased to pay them. The four women claimed this law was contrary to the rights given pregnant workers under Art. 119 and Directives 75/117/EEC, 76/207/EEC, and 92/85/EEC. The Court ruled in favour of the plaintiffs, finding that Danish legislation did not aim to protect women's conditions, but rather favoured the

[23] It is worth mentioning that the Equal Opportunities Commission (EOC) is the UK governmental administrative unit that has supported litigants in a significant number of British preliminary reference cases. Ultimately, the EOC's litigation strategy has brought into question and altered British equality laws (see Alter and Vargas 2000).

interests of the employer. This case represented the first time the Court was asked to interpret the rules governing the duties of employers regarding adjusting the workplace to the needs of pregnant workers. The Pregnancy Directive (Arts 4 and 5) requires an employer to introduce temporary adjustments to working conditions and hours in response to risk assessment of the pregnant workers' situation. The Danish employer failed to provide other opportunities to these women. The Court gave breadth to the Directive by defining the scope of this right.

Together the *Boyle* and *Pedersen* rulings represent an extension of the concept of maternity benefits under EU law. The Court has argued that under certain conditions women have the right to receive maternity benefits before maternity leave. Furthermore, scholars have emphasized the importance of the Court's interpretation of Arts 4 and 5 of the Pregnancy Directive in that it imposed duties on the employers, and in doing so the Court recognizes that pregnancy and maternity may require re-organization of the work place (Caracciolo di Torella 1999).

Overall, the case law in this analysis reveals that the Court does not hesitate to shift the control over maternity and pregnancy away from national competence even when a decision is costly to Member State governments. Furthermore, this is consistent with what we know about the larger body Art. 177 litigation involving EU sex equality laws. When we look at the Commission and Member State policy positions as stated in their observations in the cases, we find the Commission is much more likely to predict or reflect the final ECJ preliminary ruling (see Table 6.1). The Commission's success rate is 88 per cent, whereas the United Kingdom's rate was much lower at 57 per cent. Similarly, German preferences predict ECJ judicial decisions only 50 per cent of the time. These ruling do not go unheard. Looking at national court compliance with these rulings, we find that in 89 per cent of the cases the ruling is applied to the case at hand (see Table 6.2). The Court is not systematically constrained by national governments. Likewise, this litigation has clarified and expanded maternity and pregnancy rights under EU law. The rules have become more precise, binding, and enforceable.

3.2. The effects on supranational and national policy

Pregnancy and maternity rights have become an integral part of EU sex equality law. Strategic action by private litigants and the judicial rulemaking function of the Court has led to the institutionalization of these rights at the European level. What began as a principle governing equal pay has evolved to include a set of rights governing pregnant workers. Through the process of litigation, EU sex equality law has become more binding and precise, and it has expanded in scope. Furthermore, this pregnancy and maternity litigation has had distinct legislative policy consequences at both the EU level and the national level. I will discuss these in turn. First, I will demonstrate how particular rulings influenced the construction of EU secondary legislation, in particular the Pregnancy

Table 6.1. Member State government observations and judicial outcomes pursuant to Art. 177 references in sex equality cases, 1970–93

	Successful	Unsuccessful	Total
Belgium	3	4	7
Denmark	11	3	14
France	7	2	9
Germany	12	12	24
Ireland	4	4	8
Italy	6	3	9
Netherlands	12	16	28
United Kingdom	35	26	61
The European Commission	84	12	96
TOTAL	174	82	256

Note: Observations were coded as 'successful' when their argument agreed with the subsequent ECJ ruling, and 'unsuccessful' when their argument disagreed with the ECJ ruling.

Source: Data compiled from Stone Sweet and Brunell (1999) and ECJ (various years, 1970–93).

Table 6.2. National Court compliance with preliminary rulings in the field of sex equality, 1970–92

	Complied	Desisted	Non-compliance	Total
Germany	7	1	0	8
Netherlands	8	0	1	9
United Kingdom	9	1	0	10
TOTAL	24	2	1	27

Note: The total number is 27 out of a possible 59 cases from 1970–92. The numbers are low as the ECJ's database relies on the voluntary action of national courts to forward their decisions to the ECJ for documentation.

Sources: Nykios (1999) and data compiled from national court cases provided by the European Court of Justice's Research and Documentation Centre.

Directive and the resulting national government positions in the development of this Directive. Furthermore, I will highlight the national impact of subsequent rulings that amended the Directive and in effect, changed lowest common denominator decisions made in the Council. Finally, I examine the state of national compliance with the Directive and identify potential conflicts that may be the source of future litigation.

3.2.1. Supranational consequences: the construction of EU policy
The Pregnancy Directive of 1992 was born out of litigation.[24] In particular, legal scholarship suggests that Art. 10 of the Directive 'codifies and amplifies the European Court's decision forbidding discrimination on account of

[24] Council Directive 92/85/EEC.

pregnancy in the *Dekker* case' (Ellis 1993: 66; see also Hoskyns 1996; McGlynn 1996; Mancini and O'Leary 1999). It is important to emphasize, however, it was the Court that defined and constructed these rights in *Dekker*, while national governments, the UK in particular, stymied the legislative process that would later develop these rights in the Pregnancy Directive. The political processes that inflicted the passage of this Directive, in particular the production of lowest common denominator outcomes, ultimately led to legislation that went little further than the general rights of protection introduced by the Court's earlier rulings. Subsequently, as the previous section of this chapter demonstrated, potential conflicts remained and this led to more litigation seeking a clarification of women's and employers' rights in the this area of EU law.[25]

The text of the Directive is based on Art. 118a—now Art. 138—of the Treaty, which governs policy on the health and safety of workers. Directives adopted under this Article permit the Council to act in the field of qualified majority voting. While the principle of majority voting suggests the potential for passage of legislation that not all Member States agree to, the legislative history of the Pregnancy Directive illustrates why this is not necessarily true in practice.

The text proposed by the Equality Unit in Directorate General V (Employment, Industrial Relations and Social Affairs) was 'far-reaching' (Ellis 1993: 63). This original proposal provided for 16 weeks of paid maternity leave, replacement services for self-employed women, paternity leave, and a reversal of the burden of proof in cases arising out of these rights. However, the final proposal adopted by the Commission in September 1990 was considerably weaker; it reduced the minimum leave to 14 weeks and omitted references to paternity leave and replacement services. Furthermore, the burden of proof issue was removed and instead Member States were instructed to review their legal rules in this area (CEC 1990). The proposal elicited varying reactions. The UK government protested that the Directive was too far-reaching. In particular, the British Employment Secretary, Michael Howard, at the Social Affairs Council in June 1991 argued that only the aspects of the draft concerning issues regarding exposure to harmful substances fell under Art. 118, and thus only this portion should be governed by majority vote, with all other aspects utilizing unanimity. The Commission threatened to withdraw the proposal for fear of fragmentation. Ultimately, a common position was arrived at in December 1991.

However, both the United Kingdom and Italy abstained from this position, the latter on the grounds that the proposal was now too thin to be effective.[26] The proposal experienced considerable 'last-minute political horse trading' between the more stringent amendments proposed by the European Parliament and the UK's reluctance to accept such expensive changes (Ellis 1993: 65). Finally, on 19 October 1992 the Directive was passed, with abstentions from both the UK and Italy, in a form that largely reflected the minimalist ambitions of the UK. Furthermore, while the UK abstained from the

[25] The *Boyle* (ECJ 1998*e*) and *Pedersen* (ECJ 1998*f*) cases are examples of this.
[26] Unanimity was necessary at this point under EEC Art. 149(1) because the Council was amending the Commission's proposal, yet unanimity does not preclude abstentions under Art. 148(3).

vote, it was not able to prevent the Directive's adoption. In codifying the Court's *Dekker* decision, the Council's adoption of the Pregnancy Directive gave pregnant women greater legitimacy and protection under EU law. Yet ultimately the Directive did little to clarify the complexity of rules that the Court had begun to create forbidding discrimination based on pregnancy or involving maternity rights. Both before and after national transpositions of the Directive, the Court continued to expand EU rules in this area. These rulings had distinct implications for national policy.

3.2.2. National consequences: compliance and policy change

The Pregnancy Directive—hereafter referred to as the Directive—however minimalist, did introduce changes in national legislation governing pregnancy and maternity rights. Furthermore, the Directive may suggest a set of rights that come in conflict with the national laws in some Member States and also could be interpreted as conflicting with existing EU laws (CEC 1999). The three main areas of potential conflict surround the issues of night work, maternity leave pay, and general discrimination protection.

Generally, all Member State governments provided some protection for pregnant workers before the adoption of the Directive. In Italy, the Netherlands, and France protection was higher than required, whereas in other Member States, primarily Sweden and Portugal, implementation of the Directive had the effect of increasing the health and safety protection and the employment rights of pregnant workers. In the UK, qualifying periods of maternity leave were reduced. Ireland experienced considerable improvements, in particular the possibility of 'health and safety' leave if a woman's work could not be altered in order to avoid an identified risk to the pregnancy. Finally, paid time off for ante-natal exams was introduced in Belgium, Austria, Denmark, Ireland, and Finland (CEC 1999).

National governments have generally implemented the Directive without too much national legislative change. Exceptions include Ireland, which has experienced significant national reaction to this new set of rights. The 1995 Annual Report of the Irish Employment Equality Agency states there were 1,747 queries involving the Maternity and Adoptive Leave Legislation, which implemented the Pregnancy Directive. The Irish Government was asked to change a policy area that was deeply embedded in existing employment structures (CEC 1997b: 41). Implementation of the Directive by the Spanish government has also received attention. Legal experts have observed that its transposition has been 'far from sufficient', particularly in the area of protecting workers from health risks (CEC 1997b: 43–4). The Commission instigated Art. 169 proceedings against Luxembourg for failure to transpose the Directive, but has since terminated the action.[27]

This general picture of national compliance would be misleading without examining the provisions that remain contentious in national politics. The

---

[27] Case C-409/97 *Commission v. Luxembourg*, dismissed.

issue of night work is one such conflict. Art. 7 of the Directive states that Member States shall ensure that workers are 'not obliged to perform night work during their pregnancy and for a period following childbirth'. Pregnant workers are provided special treatment by not being required to work at night. As a result of national government opposition, this Article fails to solve the real issue at the heart of night work, that is, balancing non-discrimination with a concern for the health and safety of workers. It has been the subject of national government contention since 1991, when the ECJ ruled that a French provision which banned night work by women, when no such ban existed for men, was contrary to the Equal Treatment Directive (*Stoekel*, ECJ 1991*b*). The ruling led to subsequent infringement proceedings against Belgium, Greece, Italy, Portugal, and France. These proceedings culminated in two judgments in 1997 involving France and Italy.[28] Many national transpositions of the Pregnancy Directive go further than required, and ban pregnant women and women who have just given birth from working at night. The Commission has since initiated infringement proceedings on this point with Austria, Italy, Luxembourg, and the UK; and German provisions are currently under scrutiny for possible infringement (CEC 1999). National governments have resisted having the issue of night work dealt with at the Community level. This resistance was voiced in the debates surrounding the adoption of the Directive (Ellis 1993: 65). However, over time, we can also see how the Court has shifted this issue to the European level despite this continual opposition. This is evidenced through the infringement proceedings and Art. 177 rulings on the subject.

A similar dynamic has occurred over the issue of maternity pay, which had been a major concern of the UK throughout negotiations of the Directive (see Ellis 1993: 63–5). This would later be at the heart of the *Gillespie* case, discussed above. Far more than the individual back-pay amounts allotted to the plaintiffs, the ruling had a more general financial impact on UK maternity pay policies. Almost two years after the transposition of the Pregnancy Directive into national law, this 1996 ruling created the very maternity pay requirements, which the UK government was careful to remove from the Directive. The Court concluded that neither Art. 119 nor the Equal Pay Directive lays down a criterion to determine the amount of pay required, however EU law does guarantee a minimum level: 'The amount payable could not be so low as to undermine the purpose of maternity leave, namely the protection of women before and after giving birth' (ECJ 1996*a*: para. 20).

Prior to this ruling, the UK's statutory maternity pay system was calculated on the basis of length of employment and weekly hours worked prior to commencement of the maternity leave, and was figured in terms of relevant statutory sick pay. In practice, the UK laws left some pregnant workers in a position of receiving no maternity pay during their leave. Those numerous part-time employees who do not earn more than the national insurance threshold do not qualify for UK statutory sick pay. Therefore, they do not qualify for maternity

---

[28] ECJ (1997*b, c*). The Commission has since initiated Art. 171 proceedings against both of these countries for failing to implement these 1997 rulings.

pay. Maternity leave without any pay may induce an employee to return earlier to work, and thus undermine the real 'purpose' in the 14-week leave period . The UK's lowest common denominator position, as embodied in the Directive, was ultimately shifted upwards by the Court.

The final national-level conflict involves the Directive's general discrimination protection, in particular its prohibition of dismissal from employment. As earlier mentioned, the Directive in effect codified the Court's decision in *Dekker* and it has subsequently been amended through the Court's *Hertz*, *Habermann*, and *Webb* rulings. However, not all Member States have duly recognized or enforced this prohibition on discrimination. As earlier noted, Spanish legal experts were less than enthusiastic at the government's transposition of the Directive and cited a general lack of knowledge among national judges and lawyers regarding the protection it provided (CEC 1997*b*). However, a ruling from the Spanish Constitutional Court (SCC) would begin to change this. In a case concerning the dismissal of a pregnant women, the SCC arrived on 23 July 1996 at an important shift in the burden of proof applied in these cases. This was particularly significant, as the burden-of-proof clause had been removed from an earlier version of the Pregnancy Directive due to national government opposition. It was now up to the employer to prove that the real cause of dismissal was unrelated to discrimination on grounds of sex. Furthermore, the SCC based its ruling on the above-mentioned ECJ judgements, as clarifying the Pregnancy Directive. This ruling led to subsequent lower-court decisions; interestingly enough, no reference to EU law is made in these latter cases.[29] These judgements are significant because we are able to see how the acceptance or enforcement of EU law by national judges in effect forced compliance where the national government action had failed to do so.

4. Conclusions: Litigation, Mobilization, and Governance

The EU today governs what has historically been a protected national legal domain, social policy, of which pregnancy and maternity rights are an integral part. The analysis demonstrates that the creators of the Treaty did not foresee this process of institutional change and that the policy implications have not all been welcomed by Member State governments. Despite the belief of certain scholars, the relative power of national governments cannot explain the expansive logic that characterizes the Court's jurisprudence (for example, Garrett 1995; Garrett, Kelemen, and Schulz 1998; Garrett and Weingast 1993; Moravcsik 1995).

Institutional evolution in this policy area began with the self-interested activation of the EU legal system by a Belgian stewardess and her lawyer. This led to the European Court of Justice transforming Art. 119, a Treaty provision

[29] For example Tribunal Superior de Justicia of Malaga, judgement of 1 February 1996 and Tribunal Superior de Justicia of Pais Vasco, judgement of 19 March 1996.

governing equal pay and fair competition, into a positive right enforceable in national courts. Transformation into a positive right conferred on individuals the opportunity to bring claims before national courts, and the provision no longer simply placed duties on Member State governments. The consequences have required national governments to construct or change national policies to protect these rights. Positive integration has ensued, as the Court's judicial rulemaking provided the framework and the necessity—given the opportunity, litigants were able to claim that national practices were in conflict with their EU rights—to develop a common European policy on sex equality.

This chapter has focused on the mechanisms of institutionalization. The evolution of governance resulted from a dynamic interaction between actors (legal activists and their litigants, national judges), organizations (the ECJ, the Commission) and institutions (Art. 119, Treaty of Rome, and subsequent equality secondary legislation). Through process tracing and case-law analysis I am able to demonstrate how this institutionalization had distinct policy consequences at both the national and the supranational levels. I would like to conclude by suggesting a set of broader lessons for scholars concerned with newly evolving political spaces.

First, beyond substantive policy creation, the Court's rulings can have significant consequences on social power relations.[30] The jurisprudence of the Court has shifted the distribution of gains away from the business community, which benefited from a Treaty provision protecting its right to fair competition. Art. 119 has become a social-justice provision which empowers women in the EU policy arena and in their national legal systems. The door has been opened to those who have historically been excluded from EU decision-making—not surprising in light of the economic goals of the single market. It also provides a new arena for individuals who have exhausted domestic legal routes to challenge or participate in contentious national debates. Women activists, as lawyers, labour union activists, and Commission staff, have become integral components in the process of European integration. Put simply, altering the institutions in a given policy arena can change who has access to that policy space. This can simultaneously empower new actors and disempower others. This consequence is not always intended or foreseen by the creators of the game; and the feedback effects can have a significant impact on the original institutions structuring the game (Pierson 1993).

Second, these Court rulings do not just float in space. Instead, the extent to which they create new rules or policies, they may impact the emergence of new social spaces.[31] Individuals reorient their activities as a result of new opportunity structures, and over time the space, so to speak, is filled in.[32] In

---

[30] More generally, legal mobilization scholars have observed this possible effect of court rulings (see for example, McCann 1994; Scheingold 1974).

[31] This argument is consistent with American policy scholarship that examines the link between public policies (or rules) and politics (for example, Lowi (1964) and Wilson (1979). In particular, a body of research derived from this tradition argues that policies (beyond substantive policy change) can have a direct impact on the creation of new spaces that promote discussion and citizen

the early 1970s, armed with a distance Treaty provision, Art 119, national legal activists, such as Vogel-Polsky, shifted their litigation strategies to include the European Court of Justice. In the 1980s, legal experts operating within national equality agencies, such as the British Equal Opportunities Commission, began utilizing European laws to force national legislative change (see Kenney 1992; Alter and Vargas 2000).

Throughout the 1980s and 1990s, an expanding net of EU rules provided by ECJ precedent and secondary legislation, gave national activists the basis and instruments to push for greater discussion and inclusion of women's rights in EU policies. During this period, these activists have become increasingly present at the supranational level, through their work within research centers (Centre for Research on European Women); umbrella organizations (European Women's Lobby); Commission-sponsored networks, such as the National Legal Experts Group on Equal Treatment; and consultancy firms, such as Engender—to name just a few. Now, in the year 2000, over 40 years since the Treaty of Rome came into force, these individuals have become permanent policy actors in Brussels. The Commission depends on and solicits their technical knowledge, both in the development of legislative proposals and to ensure national compliance.[33] Furthermore, the European Court of Justice, as demonstrated in this study, has developed a sex equality jurisprudence that was activated by and depended on individuals and their lawyers. This mobilization, as realized in the form of legal argumentation, technical expertise, and a constant transnational exchange of information, over time becomes embedded in the fabric of the Union. Individual mobilization becomes institutionalized into a formally constituted public, or European, interest. The space is not only occupied by an evolving set of institutions—EU rules—but it is characterized by an equally dense network of actors operating in Brussels.

In light of this evolving dynamic among actors, organizations, and institutions, it is not surprising that today the EU regulates national pregnancy and maternity policies despite a continual national government opposition to this expansion. Certain rights are established and through the actions of individuals and organizations these rights are expanded in a direction that leads those governed by these rules down a path that becomes increasingly hard to change (see Pierson 1996). The judicial rulemaking of the Court has expanded institutions that over time have empowered new actors and created new social spaces. In consequence, a more formal, precise, and binding set of institutions has been constructed. The deepening of European integration does not only hinge on a series of intergovernmental choices, but has evolved from the accumulation of strategic activism operating above and below the state.

inclusion in policy processes (for example, Schneider and Ingram 1997; see Ingram 2000 for a full discussion of this literature).

[32] Social movement scholars have begun to observe this general trend at both the transnational and international level (see Keck and Sikkink 1998; Marks and McAdam 1998; Tarrow 1998).

[33] Based on interview with legal adviser to the Equality Unit in DG V of the Commission, April 1999, Brussels, Belgium.

7

Est Maître Des Lieux Celui Qui Les Organise: How Rules Change When National and European Policy Domains Collide

PATRICK LE GALÈS

THERE is more than one path to the institutionalization of European space. In their introductory chapter to this volume, Alec Stone Sweet, Neil Fligstein, and Wayne Sandholtz note: 'As jurisdiction has moved from the national to the EU level, complex, often unintended, linkages and tensions between modes of supranational and national governance have developed. The myriad processes through which these tensions are revealed, exploited, exacerbated, or resolved are today at the core of European politics' (p. xx). Several chapters in this book—for example, those by Fligstein and Stone Sweet, Richardson and Mazey, Shapiro, and Turnbull and Sandholtz—seek to explain the institutionalization of supranational sites of governance. My purpose here is to examine the dynamic interaction between rules systems at two different levels, concentrating on how conflicts between French and European institutions have emerged and have been resolved (see also Cichowski, this volume), in two policy domains: state aids to firms and regional development. In both cases, national policy had long remained more or less immune from the impact of European rules and the work of EU organizations. In the late 1980s, the two rules systems started increasingly to interact, which led to their transformation.

In the case I examine here, the central mechanism for institutionalization of European governance—and for the Europeanization of French modes of governance—has been endogenous rule innovation through conflict over, and interpretation of, the meaning of European rules. In a first stage of the process, Commission officials and French administrators disagree about the nature, scope, and application of EU rules governing state aids and regional development. In a second stage, these conflicts are resolved, which then establishes the context for the next rounds of negotiation, and tensions, between the two levels. This process, which links rule systems, interpretation, threats, and the manipulation of resources on both sides, leads to the gradual clarification and hardening of the relevant rules; it thus constitutes dynamic institutionalization. Generally, European officials have had the upper hand, successfully imposing their interpretation of EU rules on the French government in each round. Once fixed, these rules are taken for granted by all of the relevant actors, while conditioning subsequent national resistance and contestation. New rules are typically legitimized by political summits between political elites and the Commission, with the French government's opposition or support usually decisive.

The chapter is divided into three parts. The first provides a summary overview of the development of EU competition policy and its intersections with state aids. The second focuses on state aids in two sectors, which are analyzed against the backdrop of the development of European competition law. The third part discusses my findings in light of this volume's priorities.

1. Turning the Screw : How Competition Rules Became More Binding

Competition policy is a major element of the European regulatory state (Majone 1996b), and a symbol of market driven Europeanization (Cini and McGowan 1998). In the 1980s, partly inspired by the American example, it became a cornerstone of the institutionalization of the EU. The elaboration of a regulatory framework for mergers and acquisitions constitutes a well publicized part of it (Allen 1995; Dumez et Jeunemaître 1991). By contrast, state aids to firms—one element of competition policy—is usually judged to have had only marginal effect, if any.

This section briefly recounts how the Commission sought to expand and then institutionalize rules governing state aids. It then concentrates on contradictions between state aids and regional policies, the resolution of which led to more precise rules.

1.1. State aid: *'parent pauvre'* of competition policy?

Public subsidies, or 'state aids', to firms has been part of the basic toolkit of industrial and regional policies of most central, regional, and local governments for a very long time. To adequately describe all the means and instruments used by public authorities to support firms is far beyond the scope of this chapter, but these include: grants, tax breaks, and investment; and the provision of land, services, and equipment to firms willing to locate in areas in the periphery, or to cities in crisis.

Economic development through industrial policy, and the maintenance of social and territorial cohesion, have been staple functions of European states.

By contrast, the Rome Treaty (Arts 92–4) declares that state aids that create distortions to or undermine fair competition are in principle not compatible with the making and completion of the single market. Although the question of state aids is raised specifically by the Treaty, ambiguities were also obvious (Cross 1996). First, there is no clear definition of 'state aids', while governments have evolved myriad modes of subsidizing industry and investment. Second, the Treaties provide for exceptions to the rules, the case of regional development being just one of these. Third, state aids are so densely rooted within nation state-policies, so 'institutionalized', in our terminology, that obtaining a detailed comprehensive, and thus comparable, account of them has proved a daunting task for the Commission officials. In any case, both the amount of any subsidy and the technical details governing its provision are sometimes buried in a small article within a major law. Last, most Member States support the Commission's drive towards the control and the limitation of state aids, if mainly for the other Member States. National ministries of finances typically favour reducing state aids. However, governments, for political reasons, are often reluctant to see the Commission imposing precise constraints on their provision.

The Commission, interpreting the Treaty, recognizes exceptions to the general prohibition of state aids, in relation to underdeveloped regions, small and medium size firms, certain labour market practices, and for policies concerning environmental protection, research and development, and the restructuring of firms (Evans 1997). Further, the Court of Justice has recognized that these and other exceptions reflect the general interest of Member State governments, although the general interest is limited by European law (Allen 1995). There is therefore a large grey area in the implementation of the rules concerning state aids. For the first decades of the EU, that grey area was not policed, to the benefit of the Member States. In the 1970s, most governments avoided the rigours of competition rules as applied to state aids policies. The Commission used its powers cautiously, and national political interests remained central in the taking of decisions and the negotiation of exceptions.

1.2. The Commission hardens the rules

A simple account of the institutionalization of state aids over time would tell the following story. In the 1980s, the decision to push for the completion of the Single Market, coupled with the neo-liberal turn in economic policy in Western Europe, delegitimized extensive state interventions in industry (Jobert 1994). The result was a large increase in conflict between EU law and national regimes, with contradictions emerging both inside the Commission and between the Commission and the Member States. The Directorate-General of competition (DG IV), energized by Commissioners Andriessen, Sutherland, Brittan, and van Miert, began to assert the Commission's competence to develop and implement existing rules. It became more active in defining regulatory frameworks and managed, in a small number of highly visible cases, to constrain Member States. Following several supportive rulings of the European Court of Justice, the Commission started to reject certain aids, and to demand a defence of others (Cini and McGowan 1998). By the 1990s, the Commission's work had become quasi-systematic; hence the explosion of cases in DG IV. By 1998, reforms had formally enhanced the powers of DG IV to monitor and police violations, and had clarified the procedures through which Member States could invoke exceptions provided they conformed with the Treaty.

In the 1980s, most governments believed that exceptions to the state aids rules would be the norm, and that such exceptions would be achieved through political negotiation. Mrs Margaret Thatcher, Britain's Prime Minister, was able to mobilize substantial subsidies for the Nissan investment in Sunderland; Italian policy towards the Mezzogiorno was not contested; and France, through nationalization and privatization, was still able to give substantial public subsidies to both successful and failing national champions (Cohen 1989). Even when the Commission began to elaborate more precise rules, few could foresee the dynamics of institutionalization in the field.

For the period 1989–94, the Commission estimated state aids to industry at about 40–45 billion euros a year. Such subsidies have since declined to 35–37 billion euros. Belgium, Italy, and Germany after reunification are the largest providers of state aids to industry, whereas the UK is the smallest. France is in a medium position. State aid with a regional dimension represents about half of these subsidies, mainly to Italy's *Mezzogiorno* and Germany's new *Länder*, but also to Ireland and the UK, if to a more limited extent (Rouam 1998). Annual EU reports of competition policy reveal the long-term task undertaken by the Commission: to limit, gradually but as much as possible, subsidies that distort competition. Member States are required to notify in advance to the Commission changes to state aids to firms. In principle, if a given set of aids is considered by DG IV to be incompatible with the common market, states may be asked by the Commission to abolish them or firms may be required to repay them.

According to the competition policy reports, the number of registered cases examined by the Commission rose in the 1980s from 100–200 a year to 534 in 1990 and to 803 in 1995, and has hovered between 650 and 700 ever since. The number of decisions adopted by the Commission increased from 181 in 1985 to 619 in 1995, levelling off at around 500 a year thereafter. Decisions include detailed investigations in a number of contentious files—about 10 per cent—and the interdiction of aids—2 per cent of cases. In addition, simply registering a case can trigger a range of important reactions from governments anxious to settle the conflict before it turns litigious. Germany and Italy consistently rate first for the number of difficult cases, whereas the UK is subject to far fewer. France has a small number of such cases, but these tend to be high-profile cases involving large financial stakes.

The more the Commission has intervened, the more formal, precise, and binding the rules have become, not least because the legitimacy of the Commission's work is constantly contested, both by the pro-competition groups suspicious of the alleged political biases of Commission interventionism and by national administrators that resent and oppose detailed investigations into their practices. Nonetheless, once rules had hardened sufficiently, new possibilities were opened for actors to make use of them. In consequence, DG IV has become far more powerful, a position enhanced by its relative insulation from other parts of the EU bureaucracy and its centralized decisionmaking procedures.

1.3. State aids rules vs regional policy

States aids rules fall under a market perfection logic, whereas regional policy is about social cohesion or market correction. Arts 92.2 (b and c) and 92.3 of the EEC Treaty—now Arts 87 and 88—list exceptions related to regional policy. Some of these relate to general objectives of economic and social cohesion, which are invoked in Arts 3 J and 130 A-E of the Treaty (Rouam 1998). Clearly, supporting the poorest regions within Member States is part of the larger set of 'cohesion' goals of the European Union. This objective, which was also at the heart of Delors agenda (Ross 1995), was reaffirmed in the Maastricht and Amsterdam treaty revisions. Although an imprecise and contested concept, social cohesion led DG XVI (Regional Policy) to accept more state aids to attract firms to impoverished regions. Thus, while state aids were generally being restricted, European regional policy legitimizes and renders acceptable some amount of public aid to firms; hence its growing importance to the question.

Despite the emphasis on social cohesion and convergence, the completion of the Single Market remained the overarching goal for policy elites. Yet the deepening of market-building creates or reinforces social and spatial inequalities. If pushed to its limits, the competing logics of state aid and competition policy will generate contradictions. Governments have sought to legitimize public aids to firms under the heading of regional policy and the general interest, both national and European, in order to prevent the further decline of a region. The UK used the argument to support Korean investment in Wales in the early 1980s; and Germany invoked it with regard to aid to the eastern *Länder* (Thielemann 1999). There exists a long-standing, and similar, line of argument in France and Italy.

Inevitably, the conflict between policy to limit state aids on the one hand, and, on the other, the dynamics of social cohesion and structural funds which fuelled and legitimized state aids to firms became more apparent. Building upon its success under the strong leadership of Commissioner van Miert in the 1990s, DG IV developed a strategy to impose its rules and norms on DG XVI and then back on the Member States. The story of this successful extension of DG IV rules and norms to other policy domains—and not only to DG XVI—cannot be told here (but see Wishlade 1998). In the end, most state aids to firms falling within the purview of 'regional policy' has to be approved by DG IV. Further, DG IV heavily participated in the revised New

Regional Aid Guidelines[1] of March 1998, which extended the domain of more precise and authoritative rules for the new round of structural funds for the period 2000–6.

These new sets of rules decrease the amount of state aids, despite social-cohesion priorities. Established on the basis of competition reports, specific rules take into account the geographic concentration of state aids to industry, in parallel with the geographic concentration of structural funds, and the importance of employment criteria, in line with the priorities given to the problem of unemployment which emerged at the Amsterdam summit. Last but not least, for our purposes, the Commission now insists on coherence between the European regime of state aids and national and local aids, with each country obtaining a quota.

The long march of DG IV to establish a more precise and authoritative regulatory framework concerning state aids therefore took an important step in 1998. The new guidelines, which have the force of secondary legislation, explain in detail how DG IV will exercise its discretion, how it will interpret the Treaty, and what procedures bind Member States. The Commission will set the parameters for Member States and will possess a reinforced capacity to obtain relevant information and to enforce compliance if necessary.

In our terminology, the rules have become, first, more authoritative. The dynamics of decisions undertaken by DG IV, supported by the European Court of Justice when it has proved necessary, demonstrate clearly the Commission's political commitment to tightening the rules and to standing up to governments, including the more powerful. Second, the rules have become more formalized and precise. The limits of state aids to industry are not only now supposed to take into account all categories of state aids—from environment to research and development—but are calculated with respect to subsidies given by all levels of government. This result is non-trivial since over the years the Commission has had to untangle myriad modes of giving—and hiding—aids by Member States.

The Commission was able to set simpler, clearer, and more general rules on matters of controversy, such as the maximum amount of aid acceptable, how aid is to be measured, and the relationship between the various geographic zones, each of which possesses its own regime. In the process, DG IV increased its power and legitimacy in monitoring and enforcing the implementation of the rules.

This institutionalization of state aids engendered conflict with national administrations. The following section examines the processes through which national rules changed in interaction with the Commission, focusing on the French case.

---

[1] JOCE N.C74 10/03/98.

2. European Competition Rules vs French Regional and Industrial Policy

During the second part of the 1980s, France turned towards a more market-oriented organization of the economy (Cohen 1989; Boyer 1997). In terms of industrial policy, France turned from a Colbertist tradition to more diversified forms of support to industry (Cohen 1992; Hancké 1999; Lévy 1999; Le Galès 1994; 2000). The state's relationship with big business, however, did not disappear, including in the banking and finance sectors, which experienced extensive privatization (V. Schmidt 1996). Although the French state appeared to conform to European rules concerning fiscal and monetary policy, it kept alive the tradition of heavy support for industry when deemed necessary in the general interest. Classic French *dirigisme* was reframed in terms of regional policy and support to small and middle size firms. The completion of the Single Market made it more difficult for the state to maintain its aid to industries, although some dominant organizations, in particular the Ministry of Finance, had long argued that state aids to industry ought to be scaled down. But, following various economic shocks and crises, public interventions invariably took place. These themes were central in the political debate in the 1990s, and in particular during the debate to ratify the Maastricht Treaty.

This section first describes the basis for increasing conflict between France and the Commission. It then focuses on two cases. The first, *'plan textile'* is a case of state aid to an industrial sector in crisis which went ahead despite EU warning. The second case is about state aid to cities in crisis.

2.1. State aid to rescue firms: *plan textile* in contravention of EU Rules

Until 1988, the French government took little notice of the European regulatory framework concerning state aids. In this area, European rules and national rules simply did not interact, at least not in a legal manner. They evolved in parallel and the occasional tension was resolved through intense negotiation.

From the French point of view, the shocking revelation that DG IV was becoming serious about enforcing hard rules took place in 1988 and 1990, when DG IV ordered the automobile firm Renault—a symbol of successful nationalized industry—to repay public loans of over 100 million euros. More was to come, notably when British Airways asked the Commission to prevent aid to Air France—some 3 billion euros between 1993 and 1997—and when the Commission set limits on state support to France Telecoms. On several other occasions, in the textile, chemical, steel, and computer industries, DG IV made it clear that the environment had changed, requesting information, investigating, and threatening to claim repayment. Within the Ministry of Industry and the government agency charged with European policy, European rules started to be noticed, learned, and negotiated or obeyed (Lequesne 1993). Government officials began to play within these rules, and through ongoing negotiations with the Commission even managed to secure positive outcomes in several contentious cases.

Yet DG IV did not prohibit all forms of state aid, despite what a strict inter-pretation of the rules might have implied. Its approach was gradual. Where DG IV did allow aids, it preferred to consider them as one-shot but last-shot measures. At the same time, a wider range of aids came under the supervision of the organization, and this supervision became ever more systematic. Further, the Commission successfully litigated a conflict concerning French aids to a failing business before the Court of Justice in 1990—the Boussac Judgment. As M. Smith (1998*b*) writes: 'the Court's . . . judgement gave the Commission authority to suspend the application of an aid granted without prior notification in accordance with article 93 (3). The Boussac procedure made it possible for the Commission to demand full information on the case within one month and, in the absence of full compliance, to declare the aid incompatible with the common market on the basis of the information at its disposal.'

2.2. Learning European rules

It is 1995 and a set of cases brought by the Commission against France is pend-ing, including the government's attempt to save Air France, a leading insur-ance company which received about 3.5 billion euros, and a bank, Crédit Lyonnais, which received more than 15 billion euros of state aids, from total collapse. The Prime Minister's office prepares a list of reports listing the main contentious issues and summing up the evolution of discussions between the government and the Commission. In one of these internal documents, the fol-lowing paradox is underlined. On the one hand, the relationship with DG IV has improved, due to the departure of Leon Brittan—the symbol in France of Anglo-Saxon economic neo-liberalism—and the willingness of France to fol-low European procedures. On the other hand, the number and scope of conflicts between the government and the Commission has risen. 'Une amélioration générale de la position française dans un environnement insti-tutionnel qui se durcit', the report succinctly puts it. The conclusion is quite clear: DG IV is moving to increase the precision and bindingness of European law in the sector. The French government considers this development is a mis-take and a further constraint in a global economy where competitors do not face equivalent restrictions. France should therefore contest the hardening of these rules, and strengthen its expertise in negotiating the increasing number of contentious cases.

The political stakes are high too during this time. A presidential election is about to take place; administrative and political elites are divided about the strategy to adopt towards the Commission's increasing pressure; and within the right-wing governments of Balladur—1993–5—and Juppé—1995–7—an important political faction known as *les souverainistes,* which emerged in opposition to the Maastricht Treaty, favours more open conflict with the Commission. Administrative elites, some of whom are themselves *souverainistes,* are under increasing pressure to respond to Brussel's queries reinforcing the perception that they are losing power.

2.3. The *plan textile*: the Commission teaches the French administration a lesson

The post-World War II story of French textiles is one of the continuous decline of a once powerful economic sector, an industry located predominantly in the north and north east of France, and therefore also suffering from the massive decline in the steel industry. Since the 1970s, the Ministry of Industry has initiated a series of financial schemes to encourage the reorganization and modernization of the sector. Although the state has provided substantial public finance support for the textile industry since that time, the number of jobs decreased from over 600,000 in 1981 to 300,000 in 1998.

In 1995, Franck Borotra, the Minister of Industry under the Juppé government of 1995–97, generated a plan to support small and medium enterprises in the textile sector with some 80 million euros of state money going to 550 firms. The minister, an old-style Gaullist, a powerful local *notable,* and part of the *souverainiste* group, was keen to use the state for direct economic intervention to support French firms. The *Plan Borotra* was a reaction to the competitive currency devaluations of other European countries—Italy's in particular—that occurred in the early 1990s, and the Commission's failure to respond effectively. The plan was seen as a rather typical initiative to defend industrial interests against competitors who had obtained unfair advantage.

Parliament adopted the main provisions in April 1996—law 96–314, Art. 99. The law's aim was to encourage failing firms to sign contracts, at the meso level of firms representation, with the state to reduce working times, in exchange for special reductions in social security costs per employee. Branch agreements were signed in those textile sectors in May and June 1996, and the scheme went into effect. Firms pledged to maintain 35,000 jobs and to recruit 7,000 young workers.

When the government's own agency in charge of European affairs warned it that the Commission was likely to react, it was told to stop supporting 'foreign bourgeois law', that is, European law. Other groups of civil servants, by contrast, were rather fed up with DG IV supervision and queries. They felt that DG IV did not have the requisite legitimacy to prevent the French state from following its own standard policies, that French interests trumped European ones, and that dealing with European law could await subsequent negotiations. Thus, Minister Borotra chose not to take European rules as the authoritative context for his ministry's decision-making. The *plan textile* went ahead without Brussels being notified.

In May 1997, the Commission attacked the scheme: it considered the reduction of social security contributions to be 'an illegal state aid' under Art. 92.[2] In its letter of notification, the Commission complained that the scheme was implemented without having been communicated to DG IV. The Commission then required the French government to stop the scheme and to recover the aid from the affected firms. In his letter, Commissioner van Miert stressed that national sectorial state aid was forbidden under Treaty law.

In the early 1990s, according to EU officials, French-DG IV relations were characterized by intense negotiation and conflict, and after 1993 the French side chose not to communicate with Brussels on a regular basis. Legal conflicts between France and the Commission accumulated as the decade wore on, including over the Crédit Lyonnais and Air France cases. When queries related to DG IV's investigation of the *plan textile* arrived in Paris, the administration ignored them. But this time DG IV decided to use the case as an opportunity to make its point, and to establish the legitimacy of European rules and its own authority. Supported by other Member States, the Commission ordered France to abolish *plan textile* and to recover aid already paid; but France refused. Negotiation and compromise thus pre-empted, the Commission and the French government went to court.

The French government presented the court with two arguments. First, because the scheme was financially neutral for firms, it did not constitute illegal state aids. Second, the government, using data drawn from existing programmes, argued that the new scheme was less attractive for firms than many other legal schemes, and thus competition was not being distorted. France was particularly upset by the fact that DG IV had contested statistics and empirical evidence which had been provided by the French administration about the potential productivity gains for firms. The French assumed that DG IV had not understood, or could not understand, the details of the scheme, which linked the reduction of working time for employees, job creation, and state subsidies. A further, if implicit argument, had it that the scheme, because it provided for a reduction of social security costs and created jobs, was social policy, which should not come under the purview of competition law. In any case, the scheme raised costs for firms

In Spring 1997, a new Socialist government was elected whose policy was to comply with EU rules generally, but to negotiate on the margins of very important issues. The bank Crédit Lyonnais was still on the verge of bankruptcy, and efforts to save it were being watched carefully by officials at DG IV. The government did not want this highly complex and important problem to be spoiled by bickering over other minor issues. Outside the Ministry of Industry, few were ready to fight for a declining old-style industrial sector, and certainly

[2] This section is based on interviews with French and Commission officials, Arrêt de la Cour Européenne de justice, 5 octobre 1999, Affaires C-251/97, République française contre Commission des Communautés Européennes ayant pour objet l'annulation de la décision 97/811/CE de la commission, du 9 avril 1997 concernant les aides accordées par la France aux secteurs du textile, de l'habillement, du cuir et de la chaussure (JO, L 334: 25). See also the Advocate-General's summary, 26/11/1998.

not the Ministry of Finance, the prime minister, or the prime minister's office for European policies. The latter, indeed, argued for strict compliance with European rules, and the prime minister decided to give in. During the subsequent meeting between DG IV officials and the ministers, the Commission made it clear that the only compromise it would accept would be to delay the repayment of aids already allocated. It also used the opportunity to explain its interpretation of the rules, and to discuss how DG IV intended to work in the future. In the end, the French government accepted the DG IV's conditions, with the Commission agreeing to extend the timetable for repayment.

The EJC decision of 5 October 1999 condemned France and required the full recovery of state aids, thus preventing any escape for the French government. The Court decision attracted some limited coverage from the business press. The government was not portrayed in favourable terms and the Court decision seemed reasonable. The former Industry minister Borotra, who started the whole process, was outraged by the lack of reaction. He wrote an article in the main business newspaper (*Les Echos* 1999) in which he launched a vicious attack on Europe. He blamed the cowardice of the government in front of what he called 'une commission totalement discréditée'. According to him, and by contrast to the heroic Gaullist period, the French state had surrendered to enemies, had lost sight of the general interest of the nation, had not even kept its word to firms. But times had changed, and the article engendered only a polite silence.

2.4. Region policy and state aids

Another set of tensions developed around the relationship of French regional and urban policy to the Commission's rules for state aids. French regional policy, run by *Délégation à l'Aménagement du Territoire et à l'Action Régionale* (DATAR), an agency attached to the prime minister, and *Délégation interministérielle à la ville* (DIV), which helps to coordinate urban policy for the Ministry of cities, has long been an important tool of state building and legitimization.

Among the instruments at its disposal, DATAR could grant tax exemptions and state aids to investment projects in selected areas. The first European guidelines for regional aids, issued in 1971, proposed the crucial distinction between central 'regions' and 'peripheric regions', with state aids considered justified for the latter. The guidelines defined legitimate state aid to peripheries as those funds and policies designed to encourage economic development through the promotion of investment and job creation in one specifically defined geographic zone. In the 1970s, the legality of DATAR aid to industries in assisted regions was presumed. With the development of EU competition law and the DG IV's organizational capacities to monitor and enforce that law, French regional aids became an issue.

By the early 1990s, the negotiation of structural funds and the designation of assisted areas had led to divergence and contradictions. European criteria used to designate areas eligible for assistance did not correspond well to DATAR's criteria, a problem made more acute for French officials since they were typically under strong pressure from local mayors to be included in development schemes. Negotiation between DG XVI and DATAR officials were difficult and often very technical. The French viewed the European regime as legitimate in principle but believed that its rules must, in practice, yield to French priorities, since the French state alone was in charge of '*l'aménagement du territoire*'. In fact, the French government remained firmly in charge until the mid-1990s.

2.5. Cases: '*Loi Pasqua*' and the new urban policy

Minister Charles Pasqua is a character in French politics, a conservative Gaullist who became the leading figure to oppose the Maastricht Treaty in 1991. In 1993, after the right-wing landslide, he became a heavyweight in the Balladur government, and the closest political ally of the prime minister—against Chirac—during the 1995 presidential election campaign. During his tenure as minister of the interior, Pasqua developed a strong rhetoric of national unity against outsiders, including the forces of Europe and globalization. In addition, he revived the classic Gaullist tradition that views itself as opposed to 'traitors' who have weakened French sovereignty and independence.

The now famous *Loi Pasqua d' Aménagement du Territoire* of February 1995 sought to re-establish the authority and legitimacy of the state and its representatives and its role in ensuring the economic development of the French territory. The law included a whole range of subsidies to firms in rural areas, measures largely hidden in a long and very technical law, and left uncommunicated to the Commission. Politically, the project was celebrated as a reaffirmation of state authority within markets, particularly those dominated by outsiders—Anglo-Saxons—and *vis-à-vis* Europe. The Commission noticed, but chose to turn a blind eye at that time.

A second project, on urban development, emerged a year later, with a the *Pacte de relance pour la ville* of 1996. The idea was to organize the economic development of urban neighbourhoods in crisis through state aid to firms and the creation of enterprise zones in a number of cities. The French state, the rhetoric went, could not accept the decline of its *banlieues*—outer areas—and that, in contrast to the US, the state would intervene forcefully to prevent further decline. Although the Commission was not informed officially, informal contacts took place between French officials and DG IV; the latter expressed doubts about such a scheme, which the government ignored. The administration remained dominated by a powerful body of civil servants who resented the growing ability of the Commission to impose its rules; the new policy offered an opportunity to re-establish the primacy of national administration over DG IV and DG XVI. Relations were at their lowest ebb.

The situation was, in fact, more complex. First, although the French government did not notify the Commission, the new laws did not breach, obviously and immediately, state aid rules. In both cases, initial stages of implementing the schemes would be acceptable, but later stages, which would go beyond the limits and zones defined by the Commission, would not be compatible with EU rules. Second, the Commission understood that the political stakes in France were very high. DG IV decided not to delve deeply into the *loi Pasqua*, and instead opened amicable negotiations on urban policy; in fact, the Commission was simply waiting until after the presidential election had taken place, preferring not to become involved in very complex partisan wrangling. Third, the urban and regional dimension made things even more complicated. When regions or cities are facing harsh economic and social difficulties, it is rather difficult to argue that, according to EU criteria, some areas are allowed a certain level of support while others are not. By contrast, it is easy for anti-European politicians to blame the Commission. 'Wait and see' was therefore the motto of the day.

In the event, Commissioner van Miert asked for clarification, and made it clear that the Commission would accept the argument according to which neighbourhoods in crisis were to be eligible for extra state aid. At a time when issues of urban policy were quickly gaining salience within the Commission, DG IV chose not to interpret state aid rules rigidly. However, it used that opportunity to further define the rules. DG IV specified that special schemes bringing an exceptional amount of state aid to urban neighbourhoods in crisis, besides cases covered by Objectives 1 and 2 of the structural funds, were to be considered legitimate, provided limits were set. DG IV and the French government then negotiated an overall limit of 1 per cent of the population covered by the scheme. In doing so, DG IV accepted the argument that the national state could not abandon urban areas in crisis, even if aids offered did not exactly fit criteria defined by European rules. In exchange, DG IV made it clear it would not accept any breach of the rule according to which advanced notification of any change to the regime of state aid was obligatory.

Last but not least, the Commission set an overall limit to state aids which it also used in negotiations with other countries. The Commission used statistical indicators to trigger financial aids to poorer areas at the regional level, thus masking the most severe cases of urban deprivation.[3] By contrast, the French programme *'Pacte de relance pour la ville'* identified assisted areas at the micro level, neighbourhood, or municipality. The Commission accepted the argument and set new guidelines for deprived urban areas[4] within the limit of state aids. It became stricter on the overall limit and became more flexible of the details of the implementation.[5]

[3] In technical terms, the Commission uses indicators such as GDP per capita and unemployment rate at the NUTS II and III level. But some of the most deprived areas are within rich regions—Ile de France in France, for instance, or London—and therefore cannot get funds

[4] OJ C 215, 25/7/1996.

[5] In other, more technical, words, 'Deprived urban areas are defined as areas which have a population of between 10,000 and 30,000, belong to a city with at least 100,000 inhabitants, and have significantly worse statistics than both the national average and the city to which they belong . . . The maximum aid intensity is 26% net grant equivalent of the investment or ECU 10,000 per job created' (S. Simon 1999: 28).

Once a new government was elected 18 months later, it appeared that the relevant agency had not supervised the scheme's implementation. No one could estimate, with any precision, the impact of the scheme. As usual in the French political system—given the impact of the *cumul des mandats*, or multiple office-holders—mayors lobbied the government. More than once the government capitulated, designating new areas eligible for the urban policy scheme. When ministers are cross-pressured by the intense pressure and lobbying of a powerful MP-Mayor-political leader on one side, and the—only potential—consequences of breaching technical European criteria on an other, the former tends to win out. At the end of the day, the scheme covered far more than 1 per cent of the population: about 1.6 per cent. Worse, firms excluded from the scheme began to appeal to French courts but also to the European Commission on the grounds that the policy violated competition rules.

In 1997, the new Jospin government appointed the leader of the Greens, Dominique Voynet, as Minister of *Aménagement du Territoire and Environnement*. She was quickly shocked by furious letters from Commissioner van Miert demanding details about state aids to some marginal firm in the periphery. Her Ministry was surprised by the scolding tone of the letter. As one civil servant put it: 'Il lui écrit comme un ministre écrit à un préfet, même pas, comme à un chef de service. C'est pourtant un ministre de la République.'

In his letter sent in the autumn of 1997, Commissioner van Miert starkly reminded the minister of past agreements with her predecessors, and breaches of rules negotiated and agreed upon, and indicated that the Commission was ready to take immediate action. He gave the minister two weeks to respond to a series of questions concerning the scheme. DG IV had clearly heard enough of this 'territorial' argument of the French government. Rather, he asked the new government to assess its regional and urban policies in light of newly clarified EU rules (see section 1).

Largely pro-European, both the minister and the prime minister's office did not want to fight the DG IV just after they had come into office, and just as the prime minister was defending his employment agenda in EU forums. The minister therefore urged her administration to respond to all the queries and to demonstrate goodwill and cooperation towards DG IV. That message did not go down well with most of her civil servants, who had grown used to avoiding DG IV and to ignoring its queries. But this time they had lost. Within a few weeks, EU competition policy became real: civil servants were required to master its intricacies and to assess their own work in light of probable responses of DG IV. Until this moment, EU rules had been treated as both distant and irrelevant.

I now assess these cases as processes of institutionalization.

3. Conflicts over the Meaning of the Rule to Permit Institutional Change

These vignettes are part of a larger story of what has happened as a result of increasing interaction between the European and the French political spaces in the domain of state aid and regional policy. The following section attempts to identify the more generic elements of these processes as they relate to what the introduction to this volume calls 'endogenous' institutional change. In such instances, conflict over the meaning of rules leads to clarification through interpretation and the authoritative decision-making of EU organizations.

In both cases, at different points in time, large sections of the French administration were ignorant and/or dismissive of European rules. Within a few years, a large body of European rules came to be taken for granted by national actors; national modes of governance had seriously changed. Tensions between France and the Commission nonetheless remained, and new rounds of conflict opened. There is a particular dynamic to this kind of European institutionalization. At any given point in time, the institutional environment is both partly known and accepted, and partly unknown and contested. The process through which clarification and acceptance occurs works through stages, or round by round. After rules have been fixed in a previous round, a new round of resistance emerges; yet, this time, the institutional context for these new disputes has been decisively shaped by rules of the game produced by previous rounds—in particular, the resolution of conflicts—which are now more or less taken for granted by all the actors. How do the contested elements come to be fixed as new institutional arrangements?

Two different processes emerge in this chapter, both of which are related to the collision of European with national spaces. In both cases—and these are only part of a more general story—DG IV officials and the Commissioner have had the upper hand. European officials have been generally better positioned and better able to interpret 'the rules of the games' than their French counterparts, and to make these interpretations stick. EU officials have behaved as clever, strategic actors, lying low during major national elections but acting aggressively at other times. Commission officials also used the ECJ for their own purposes, and the Court responded in supportive ways.

The process of fixing rules is therefore the result of skilled, strategic action in the face of conflict and uncertainty, through the manipulation of various resources.

In the first part of this chapter, I noted that Leon Brittan and Karel van Miert worked intensively to strengthen the regulatory framework of competition policy as a whole. Within that field, DG IV's mandate has gradually gained an enhanced status, by being increasingly insulated from outside political pressure (M. Smith 1998*b*). France did not anticipate these changes and was ill-prepared to respond to the new environment in which conflicts were to be played out.

None of this could have been easily predicted at the beginning of the process. After all, France was a powerful Member State whose support for the completion of the Single Market was essential. Further, the nation's industrial and regional policies were highly institutionalized and long-standing. One might have expected a robust inertia to protect state and regional aids in the defence of alleged national interests. But the Commission was able to use the Single Market logic, pressure from other Member States, the Court, and the hostility of those transnational private firms injured by these policies to motivate and legitimize its new aggressive posture. At the same time, France was struggling to find a way between privatization and the retention of a nationalized public sector, given globalization and the demands of markets. The French state was therefore quite divided between (1) those pressing for decreasing state aids and market-friendly solutions, (2) those seeking to retain only selective aids on a case-by-case basis, and (3) those supporting the classic 'French' interventionist, industrial-policy view which envisages a substantial amount of state aids, decided independently of Brussels. These divides typically cut across left-right cleavages.

The tensions between these three views, and between the coalitions of interests associated with them, were exacerbated by two other factors: the long and uncertain debate surrounding the ratification of the Maastricht Treaty, which revealed the strength of the *souverainistes* favouring a Europe of nation states and strict limits on the development of supranational governance; and the economic downturn of the early 1990s, which hit some leading French firms hard and raised the question of their survival. Unstable political times since 1988—a new government every two years, each with a very different political orientation—only increased the fragility of the French position in negotiating with Brussels.

Conflicts between France and the Commission over state aids, regional policy, and competition law emerged as a part of a bigger set of processes associated with the completion of the Single Market. How these conflicts were ultimately resolved must also be understood in light of these bigger processes. The post-SEA era clearly raised the stakes, creating conflicts of interests between firms and states, and straining existing institutional arrangements. The literature on competition policy makes the link between the increased Europeanization—or globalization—of economic competition and increased attention brought to unfair competition issues, state aids in particular (for example, Cini and McGowan 1998). But these dynamics accelerated when combined with the more neo-liberal turn of the Commission. In Peter Hall's (1992) terms, we can identify the crucial elements of what is, in fact, a paradigm shift. For the more market-friendly fringe of the Commission, fair competition was a more important and legitimate goal than was social cohesion or other values. Commissioners such as Leon Brittan did not hide their deep antipathy towards classic state aids. Conflicts related to the interpretation of EU rules are not simply formal or legalistic, but deeply political.

In this regard, the Renault case of 1988 was quite central, since the Commission was able to force Renault, still part of the public sector, to repay aid to the French state, its main shareholder. Winning that symbolic case signalled the end of national capacities to neutralize DG IV with political pressure. It took DG IV and its commissioners a considerable amount of energy to resist political pressure—including that of Delors himself—and to defeat what was considered to be a considerable distortion to competition—and probably the last remnant of old-style socialism. In such cases, conflict over the scope and meaning of rules are surrogates for deeper political and ideological conflict.

In the first part of the 1990s, French administrators first began to take European rules into account in their own decision-making. Rules that were once sites of conflict—prior notification of, or prior negotiation with, DG IV—became the accepted basis of further interaction and conflict. By 1995, the French had accepted the legitimacy of the DG IV regulatory framework, and thereafter played by most of these rules. And they worked to develop enough expertise to challenge the further hardening of the rules—precision and authority in terms of state aids. In that year, the French government, defending an interpretation once made by the Italians, argued that state aid rules had to be analysed in relation to the overall competitiveness of the economy. In other words, Member States should not naively tie their hands and prohibit support to firms, including important European firms, when their economic competitors were not similarly constrained. Despite these changes, France never wavered in its view that state aids represented a legitimate instrument for the furtherance of the general and national interest, rather than simply a discrete problem that competition law could resolve.

French officials welcomed the arrival of Commissioner van Miert, once a socialist. They expected him to take more seriously public interest and competitiveness arguments in his understanding of the broader logic of competition rules. But they made a strategic mistake. The *plan textile* did not serve to assemble the kind of coalition of diverse interests which might have successfully challenged DG IV, but crudely revealed parochial motivations. In that instance, the defeat of the French government was complete and humiliating. That round ended with the government promising to comply with various rules and procedures. The Socialist government that came into power in 1997 did not want the fight these battles all over again. In order to preserve its leverage on what were seen as far more important cases—for example, Crédit Lyonnais and Air France—the government capitulated completely to DG IV. In subsequent conflicts, DG IV officials were thereby advantaged, and could in effect bully French officials into compliance.

Each French decision to contest EU rules is shaped by political priorities. The conflicts in the mid-1990s were structured by right-wing political pressure. By contrast, the new Jospin government, which included the Green minister, accepted, in one go, a series of rules which administrators had contested over the previous five years. Within a few months, the government acted to legitimize the Commission, and EU rules, at the expense of delegitimizing certain national practices. Since 1997, the new DG IV regulatory framework has been largely accepted by most of the relevant actors, and has been actively implemented by the administration. Europeanization of national political spaces is, again, a political process.

4. Conclusion

This chapter has focused on how a new mode of governance is institutionalized through a series of iterated conflicts over the meaning of rules which had been organized in contradiction with one another. European organizations have been far more effective in expanding the domain of the rule structures they manage than French officials have been in protecting national rules and practices. Despite conscious, purposeful resistance on the part of some key actors operating within the domestic administrative spaces, over time actors and organizations have learned how to use a new set of rules. This change, which took place over only a decade, is quite impressive. It provides evidence in support of more general claims made in this book. Although some commentators still see state aids policy as a dog which barks but does not bite (McGowan 2000), the evidence in this chapter rather points to slow, but decisive, institutionalization.

This chapter's response to questions about how institutions are formed and changed over time does not comfort those who argue that the construction of specific modes of supranational governance was unavoidable, or predetermined. It rather points to the complex and deeply political nature of Europeanization, which binds together, gradually, a set of diverse but increasingly interrelated processes. The exact sequence of events, and the exact constellation of actors, interests, and other factors, will not be repeated. But some of the shared features of the processes I have described may indeed be of a much more general nature; and, if so, I have identified some of the mechanisms favouring Europeanization and the continuing institutionalization of European governance.

Finally, the outcomes traced here are unlikely to be rolled back. The way the Commission works and interacts with Member States has changed as rules have been clarified. More precise rules leave fewer and fewer loopholes for national officials to exploit for their own purposes, and now provide a relatively stable framework which is unlikely to be seriously challenged, even when some Member States attempt to do so. In any case, in the areas under examination here, the result has been more precise and more legally binding rules that have radically enhanced the capacity of the EU's organizations to monitor compliance, and to enforce penalties for non-compliance.

8

Where do Rules Come From? The Creation of the European Central Bank

KATHLEEN R. MCNAMARA

B Y creating the first supranational central bank in modern history, the European Union (EU) has embarked on a great experiment in governance. The European Central Bank (ECB) formulates monetary policy for the participating European states, and its currency, the Euro, will physically replace national monies by 2002. Yet the deepening institutionalization of a truly European policy arena, although perhaps uniquely visible in the ECB case, is not itself unique: the chapters in this volume reveal the myriad ways in which positive integration, or the construction of common policies and rules, has evolved in the EU, resulting in 'the emergence and institutionalization of European space' (Stone Sweet, Fligstein, and Sandholtz, this volume p.xx). Despite these real-world developments, our theories regarding these processes remain nascent at best. Attention to organizational and institutional dynamics is now reviving, however, and the increasing integration and institution building of the European Union provides an excellent opportunity to examine the relative merits of our theoretical tools while deepening our understanding of European integration.

To accomplish these goals, this chapter seeks to tease out some initial hypotheses regarding the origins of the ECB's organizational rules. I start from the premise that the creation and evolution of organizations—groups of actors, relatively formally constituted—and institutions—the rule systems or norms which govern behaviour—can be understood subject to three general logics of explanation. The first has its roots in power politics, and argues that organizations and institutions directly reflect the distribution of material power and have no independent effects on outcomes since they are themselves endogenous to political relations. The second is a functional-efficiency or rational-institutions argument, where organizations and institutions arise as efficient solutions to specific collective-action or other technical-policy problems. Finally, a third view associated with sociological perspectives stresses the impact of broader social institutions on the construction of specific organizations. This perspective argues that organizations are in large part a function of the norms of the larger institutional setting within which they are embedded, and argues that organizations and institutions cannot be explained solely in terms of pure power or functional efficiency calculations.

I provide a preliminary evaluation of these different explanations by investigating the creation and evolution of rules governing the organizational form and policy content of the ECB, arguing that the sociological institutionalist perspective offers an important yet often overlooked logic of action. I demonstrate that the rules of the ECB reflect a pre-existing and very well developed set of informal rules, or a normative structure, which governed monetary interactions in advance of the Maastricht Treaty. This structure was grounded in a network of policy-makers who regularly met in the Committee of Central Bank Governors to coordinate monetary policy, which provided a crucial medium for the development of these norms and their eventual expression in the design of the ECB. This perspective allows us to understand why the ECB, a new organization, actually may produce more continuity in European policy-making than generally assumed. My emphasis on social dynamics also indicates why the ECB is likely to be difficult to dismantle despite the manifold tensions that it engenders, while showing how continual and incremental changes can coexist within more persistent institutional structures. Although this chapter represents a 'plausibility probe', not a conclusive test of these explanations, it should underline the importance of the social and cultural institutional setting in the creation and operation of European organizations.

1. Explaining Institutional Creation

This section provides an overview of the basic arguments offered by three theoretical traditions concerning institutionalization and why organizations arise and what they do, and teases out some specific predictions from each about the likely evolution of the ECB. It should be evident that I am most interested in making broad-brush, not nuanced, distinctions among the theoretical approaches: within each set of theories there are many more subtle arguments.

Power politics, or realism, has long been the dominant mode of analysis of political life among states (Waltz 1954; 1979). In this view, the condition of anarchy—that is, the lack of a central authority governing the international system of states—or, for some theorists, human nature, drives states to be very concerned about their security and relative position *vis-à-vis* other states. Sovereignty is to be guarded jealously, and states are wary of any commitments which will bind them far into the future. In this view, institutions will directly reflect the balance of power among states in their design, and will have no independent causal effects beyond what could be predicted by examining the underlying power politics (Mearsheimer 1994/95). Thus, in the context of the ECB, we would expect a supranational central bank to be structured to reflect the interests of the state or states with the preponderate material power, and for the ECB to evolve in ways that assist the dominant state(s) in carrying out their goals.

A separate set of arguments arises from economic liberalism (Keohane 1984). In this view, relations among states are driven to a large extent by the need to find functional solutions to overcome collective action problems and other such challenges. Market failures and information problems inevitably create problems for interactions across borders, creating a 'demand for international regimes' or institutional arrangements to solve problems. Institutions arise to fulfil the demands for solutions to policy problems; in this view, they adapt relatively efficiently to the rational, technically based needs of actors.

The final approach is centred on the premise that relations among states are social in nature, and that the political and economic dynamics of these relations are greatly affected by larger cultural frameworks or structures (Scott and Meyer 1994). Without an understanding of these structures, sociological institutionalists argue, we cannot understand peoples' choices and preferences (Powell and DiMaggio 1991). Institutions, understood to mean shared rules or normative structures and the social networks which support them, channel the range of action of individuals by defining the possible. Institutions thus are central to relations among states because they diffuse the standards, norms, and structures which constitute political life. In this perspective, organizations' tendency towards 'chronic reproduction' in form and legitimization in terms of prevailing norms may drive creation and change, rather than rational adaptation to functional problems or pure power politics (Jepperson 1991). Change in these structures is always possible, as structures are seen as both enabling and constraining actors, but emphasis tends to be on continuity and stability of institutions and organizations (Sewell 1992).

Figure 8.1 summarizes these three separate perspectives in terms of their general hypotheses on the creation and evolution of organizational rules.

The issues of institutional creation and evolution are complex and poorly understood, making definitive predictions from each theoretical school and thus tests of these competing explanations extremely difficult. Indeed, each explanation carries some weight in the ECB case, and these logics ultimately should be theorized as interacting, not separate (McNamara 2001a). But given the preliminary nature of these investigations, in both empirical and theoretical terms, examining these different explanations in turn is useful for demonstrating the particular strengths and weaknesses of each, and for highlighting what is new about the social institutions approach and what it can tell us about the likely future of European integration.

	Organizational creation	*Organizational evolution*
Power politics	Only weak supranational organizations, window dressing for power politics	Evolution will reflect shifts in underlying power distribution
Economic functionality	Organization is welfare enhancing and effectively addresses economic problems; expert technical concensus on design	Policy problem-solving dynamics; rational adaptation
Social institutions	Design must fit pre-existing normative structures; legitimacy in terms of expert knowledge will dominate	Unique organizational culture will arise; professional networks key

Fig. 8.1. General hypotheses about organizational rules

2. The Creation of the ECB

Given the fact of the Maastricht negotiations on Economic and Monetary Union, what determined the ECB's form and policy content? My goal in this chapter is not to explain the factors producing monetary union and the single currency *per se*, but rather to ask about the rules governing the single currency.[1] This latter question is as important as the former. The rules regarding the design of the central bank, the criteria for membership, and the operational rules of the ECB are critical to policy outcomes in the EU. These three types of rules—ECB design, membership, and operations—help define the nature of governance in this emerging area of European institutionalization. The following section therefore teases out hypotheses regarding these three sets of organizational rules from the power-politics and economic-functionality approaches, before taking a more detailed look at the construction of the ECB as predicated on prior social institutions.

2.1. Institutions as mirrors for power

The power-politics approach would generally lead us to expect that the states would evaluate the ECB in terms of their sovereign interests, traditionally defined. In an anarchic world where one's allies can readily turn into one's enemies, states should avoid binding agreements which might require the ceding

[1] EMU is generally regarded as the product of most European leaders' desire to lock in peaceful relations among their historically warring states (Sandholtz 1993; Baum 1996), and German reunification in 1989 is widely viewed as a crucial spur to the Maastricht Treaty (Sandholtz 1993: 31; Cameron 1998: 16; but see Moravcsik 1998: 428, 437–38).

of significant control over important aspects of governance. International institutions are unlikely to be well developed, nor do they have any profound causal effects on politics among states. Where they are created, they are likely to reflect the desire for retaining or extending control on the part of the most powerful states in lieu of the pursuit of efficiency or other goals. In the EU case, this would mean that the ECB should reflect the interests, narrowly specified, of the most powerful nations.

The realist emphasis on keeping the central functions of the state close at hand makes the very creation of a supranational organization whose rules direct it to set interest rates and formulate monetary policy seem improbable. A more nuanced realist theory might argue that the ECB was in the national interest of states whose own national banks were severely under-performing, such that the costs of surrendering autonomy were outweighed by the benefits of replacing them. However, this would then predict that Germany, the most economically powerful EU state in GDP terms, should be opposed to the creation of an ECB, as it replaces a wildly successful domestic institution, the Bundesbank, which has been a central component of post-war governance in Germany. France, the UK, and Italy, the next three most economically important and, in terms of the France and the UK, militarily more powerful EU states, might present a better case for the replacement of their national institutions with a supranational bank, as they have all suffered from poor monetary management at one time or another (Goodman 1992).

Yet the German government, in the form of Chancellor Helmut Kohl with critical participation of his foreign minister Hans-Dietrich Genscher, was a central partner with French President François Mitterrand and his finance minister Edouard Balladur in supporting the design of EMU (Dyson and Featherstone 1999: 3). There is little doubt that German leadership drove the movement towards a single currency as at crucial points along the way. Kohl was the skilful ring-master pulling along the sceptics and smoothing the way forward. Italian officials also welcomed the goal of EMU. It is only the UK that fits the realist predictions, consistently trying to move the negotiations away from the creation of a supranational institution towards an EMU with a very different set of rules, a market-based currency regime where national autonomy would not be compromised (Gros and Thygesen 1998: 414–18.)

Another way of approaching the ECB through the logic of power politics would be to ask whether the specific design of the ECB reflects the concerns of the most powerful states. If indeed the powerful states agree to the creation of an ECB, they should emphasize in its design the retention of control over policy authority and all important decisions. Delegation should be minimal, and occur only when the most powerful state can be quite sure of the alignment of the agent's interests with its own. The power politics approach would predict that the ECB would be designed so that Germany could exercise control over the form and content of policies, with France, Britain, and Italy attempting to ensure some measure of oversight as well. Here the evidence is more mixed and more interesting. It is difficult to argue that states retained sovereign control over the new supranational central bank. The European leaders agreed on a design for the ECB which ultimately made it the most independent central bank in the world, with no formal avenues for political control by the national governments, and its mandate allows for little flexibility in its policies. The Treaty begins its delineation of the organization of the European System of Central Banks by professing the independence of the ECB and prohibiting it from seeking or taking any directions from 'Community institutions or bodies, from any government of a Member State or from any other body' (European Communities 1992: 31). The ECB is further directed to make price stability its 'primary objective'; and, to reinforce this mission, the Treaty places limits on the amount the ECB can finance national budget deficits and prohibits it from either providing credit to national governments or paying off their debts. One member of the European Commission and the President of the European Council can participate, but not vote, in the meetings of the Governing Council. Responsibility for exchange rate agreements and revaluations is kept under the purview of the Council of Ministers in Stage III. These two aspects could dilute somewhat the independence of the ECB, although only to a very small degree. Overall, the design of the ECB is clearly in support of political independence, which is hard to square with a traditional power-politics approach.

A more plausible argument would be that German power is being projected on to the whole of Europe by the creation of a supranational central bank which is actually the Bundesbank writ large. Indeed, the ECB resembles the Bundesbank more closely than any of the other European banks (Alesina and Grilli 1992). It would be logical to assume from this that Germany held the upper hand in the negotiations and used either carrots or sticks to force agreement from its EU partners on the institutional design. The historical record indicates that the EU states believed that a deal on EMU was possible only if the design reflected German preferences (Dyson and Featherstone 1999: 306–69). The dynamics within the German camp were such that the German government, which was very pro-EMU, decided early on to bind the anti-EMU Bundesbank into the negotiations, which allowed it to set the agenda on the design of the institution and rules for entry into EMU (Heisenberg 1998). Strategically, the partner EU states understood that this would probably be the only way to move EMU forward and there was little dissent on the contours of the ECB's design. This is congruent with a view of Germany as a powerful negotiating presence which used rule-making strategically. However, anomalies in the organization of the ECB remain. Although the rules for entry were ostensibly very strict, following the longstanding German commitment to economic convergence in advance of monetary union, they were written and executed in ways which allowed for the European leaders to make their own, politically driven judgements on who should enter EMU. This presents a mixed picture, therefore, where the German preference for financial and monetary sobriety was embodied in law, but the element of decision-making control over membership in EMU at the highest political level was maintained in the Treaty language, which ultimately favoured a more lax interpretation of the Treaty.

In sum, the power-politics approach does not fully explain the decisions about organizational design taken at Maastricht. It is difficult to square the establishment of the ECB with the view that powerful states will try to maximize their sovereignty over important levers of governance, blocking efforts to set up meaningful, binding international institutions. The modeling of the ECB along the lines of the Bundesbank, and the fact that the convergence criteria were made subject, ultimately, to a political decision regarding entry, not automaticity, might suggest power factors coming into play. However, the eventual 'broad EMU', which included almost all the EU Member States—even those which did not meet the criteria—suggests that the ECB still represented an unlikely outcome for a Germany power argument.

2.2. Institution as functional imperative

If the establishment of a strongly independent supranational institution does not make sense in power-politics terms, perhaps there were important functional problems besetting the European economy which could be solved only through the establishment of a new central bank and a single currency. A large body of literature stresses the creation of institutions in response to a policy problem or as a way to increase efficiency by providing information or other goods (Keohane 1984).[2] This has often been the argument put forth by European Commission officials for the creation of EMU and the ECB, most prominently elaborated in the EU's document *One Market, One Money* (Emerson and Gros 1992). Below, I present the arguments and their predictions for the design of the ECB, comment on their logical persuasiveness, and discuss the evidence for the political importance of these efficiency concerns for the move to EMU.

One important and overarching rationale for EMU has been that a single European market cannot fully function without a single European currency. A single currency immediately transforms the economic landscape, making prices transparent across borders, allowing for more efficient resource allocation, and strengthening the performance of the economy. The Commission report states emphatically that 'Indeed, only a single currency allows the full potential benefits of a single market to be achieved' (Emerson and Gros 1992: 20). The underlying assumption is that *without* a single currency, exchange rate uncertainty and variability depress economic activity, as actors cannot effectively judge exchange rate risk. However, there is surprisingly little empirical evidence or academic agreement on whether exchange rate uncertainty and currency transaction costs hinder trade flows (Dixit 1989; Chowdhury 1993; Bini-Smaghi 1991; Gagnon 1993). The world's closest trading partners,

[2] Some rational choice institutionalists have turned to principle-agent theory as a way to move from a narrowly conceived focus on whether institutions matter to a more fruitful discussion of variations in their design and function (Pollack 1997; Keohane and Martin 1999).

such as the US and Canada, have not shared a single currency, yet have seen their trade and investment flows increase dramatically. This makes the functional logic of the ECB seem less imperative than at first glance. A second functional argument commonly made is that the single currency would eliminate the transaction costs of changing currencies for businesses and travellers. The most optimistic scenario, tallied by the Commission, was that the transaction costs would be reduced by only half of one per cent of total EU GDP (Emerson and Gros 1992: 21). The costs of giving up the exchange rate as a policy instrument are quite substantial, and it is far from clear empirically that the relatively small benefits of increased transparency and reduced transaction costs outweigh those costs.

An alternative line of argumentation used by proponents of EMU is that it provided an opportunity for an optimally designed central bank to replace those already existing in the national settings. The ECB, from this perspective, would be more efficient because it would be designed as a highly independent bank which would thus have credibility in the eyes of financial market participants who might have price stability as their primary concern. Indeed, the ECB's rules prescribe such a high degree of central bank independence. However, it again is not clear why the country with the most lauded central bank, Germany, was one of the strongest supporters of the ECB. Neither is the actual optimality of central bank independence as clear as is assumed in the policy discussions on this subject (Berman and McNamara 1999; Posen 1993). In the years leading to EMU, inflation fell to historic lows in the majority of the EU states, which again casts doubt on the functional imperative of a more credible central bank.

There are other problems with the economic-efficiency argument when we consider the empirical record. For example, one important aspect of the institutional creation of the ECB, the criteria for entry into the single currency, did not reflect prevailing wisdom about the most effective way to ensure that the central bank would fulfil its economic mandate. The convergence criteria for entry into EMU, agreed to in the Treaty on European Union signed in Maastricht, set a series of rigorous goals in the area of inflation, budget deficits, and public debt that states were advised to be approaching, if not actually meeting, before they can join EMU. The criteria also include language indicating that the Member State's currency should be within the normal fluctuation bands of the exchange rate mechanism of the European Monetary System. What is striking about the criteria is the lack of agreement on technical grounds of their necessity in producing a viable monetary union, that is, in their functional necessity.

Economic theorizing has traditionally argued that monetary unions work best when they constitute what the literature calls an 'optimal currency area' (Mundell 1961; Kenen 1969). These areas are characterized by the free movement of the factors of production workers and capital, such that adjustments to economic shocks can be made internally, within the monetary union, without the need for external exchange-rate changes. Some degree of fiscal federalism—

the pooling of resources and the transfer of funds to areas needing temporary assistance due to downturns in their economies—is prescribed as a way to smooth the functioning of a currency area, as is done in all national economies (De Grauwe 1996; Eichengreen 1992). Yet none of the functionally relevant issues is addressed in the rules of the convergence criteria for entry to EMU, nor was a fiscal-coordinating function or federal structure included as a counterpart to the ECB. While it makes intuitive sense that similar economies will have an easier time pooling their monetary policies, it is not technically necessary that they have low rates of budget deficits or public debt or inflation. It is arguably more important to ease the functioning of a monetary union that they have similar inflation rates than that they are low. Economically, the importance of fiscal rectitude for the functioning of EMU is still much debated; instead, the optimal currency area literature recommends microeconomic reforms such as labour market flexibility and the creation of partner supranational institutions such as a monetary union-wide automatic fiscal stabilizing system. Yet the rules governing the design of EMU do not reflect these more functionally important issues.

2.3. Institutional environment and social structures

The third perspective on the institutional creation of the ECB looks to the role of the broader social environment in shaping organizational form. How did the pre-existing institutional setting structure the ECB's design, mandate, and operation? Instead of power politics or technical functionality being the central determinant of the form and content of the ECB, this approach focuses on the importance of wider cultural and ideational patterns of relationships. As the editors note in their introduction to this volume, most sociologically oriented institutionalists 'focus their analyses on dense and fully articulated social structures already in place' (Stone Sweet, Fligstein, Sandholtz, this volume, p. xx). What is the empirical evidence for viewing monetary policy as a highly institutionalized policy arena long before the ECB began operation? I argue that there was indeed a very well developed and widely shared set of informal rules, or a normative structure, governing monetary interactions in advance of the Maastricht Treaty, and it was the need to legitimize the new central bank in terms of these broader norms which formed the basis for the ECB's laws and shaped its evolution. This broader institutional environment was grounded in a network of central bankers who regularly met in the Committee of Central Bank Governors to coordinate monetary policy, which provided a crucial medium for the development of these norms and their eventual expression in the design of the ECB. The following section develops each of these points while linking these dynamics to the outcomes of the ECB's organizational design and evolution.

2.3.1. Normative structures
Despite its novelty as a new supranational central bank, the ECB rests on a rich institutional foundation, that is, a complex of rules and procedures governing

monetary politics. The organizational expression of this institution was the European Monetary System's (EMS) fixed exchange-rate regime that for almost two decades coordinated currency values among the European states (Gros and Thygesen 1998; Giovazzi and Giovanni 1989). After a very shaky start, the EMS had by the mid-1980s achieved a high level of exchange-rate stability. The formal rules of the EMS exchange-rate system were fairly straightforward, and its organizational presence was extremely limited. A grid of bilateral currency parities was established by the central bank governors, and it was left to the national banks to carry out the policies needed to stay within the agreed guidelines. There were lines of credit established among the national central banks; but even though the formal rules allowed states to draw on them relatively early to ease adjustment costs, the norm was quickly established that they were only to be used as a last resort (McNamara 1998). In practice, the strong and stable German mark quickly emerged as the anchor currency of the EMS exchange rate regime to which the other currencies had to adjust.

More important than the limited formal organizational rules were the informal normative rules that underpinned exchange rate stability (Sandholtz 1993a; McNamara 1998; 1999). A normative consensus developed across the majority of the European governments beginning in the mid-1970s and solidifying in the 1980s. This shared belief system elevated the pursuit of low inflation over growth or employment goals and replaced the Keynesian policy ideas of political elites, ultimately contributing to a downward convergence in inflation rates across Europe. The construction of this social consensus allowed for the redefinition of state interests in European cooperation, underpinned stability in the EMS, and induced political leaders to accept the domestic policy adjustments needed to stay within the system, despite ongoing distributional asymmetries. Though this monetarist-influenced consensus was by no means unwavering or monolithic, it represented a clear break with the divergent economic policy paths and diverse priorities of Keynesianism as practised by the European states during the early post-war Bretton Woods era.

The consensus can be more broadly characterized as resting on two interrelated norms or social institutions. The first, more specific, norm was the elevation of price stability as an absolute good, in contrast to using monetary policy actively in an attempt to increase growth or employment. This was evidenced in the statements and actions of monetary-policy officials. The second was a broader commitment to government non-intervention in the economy, and the placement of economics above, and separate from, politics. This is evidenced in the organizational form that the precursor to the ECB took, that is, a small elite group of central bankers, without linkages to other political actors or institutional spaces in the EU. These two pre-existing norms set the structure for the later ECB by defining what was considered a legitimate organizational design in the area of monetary policy.

The logic of the price-stability norm was as follows. First, expansionary monetary policies used in the hope of stimulating demand and employment will instead produce inflation and inflationary expectations and are thus counterproductive. In this view, such policies will also prompt financial markets to drive down the exchange rate, further worsening inflation and creating balance-of-payments problems. Second, high and varying rates of inflation are incompatible with growth and employment, in contrast to the assumptions of the Phillips Curve, which posits an inverse relationship between inflation and unemployment. Instead, the dominant view in the EU monetary-policy community was that inflation creates uncertainty over future price levels, high nominal interest rates, and falling financial asset values, all of which dampen business and spending activity, producing low levels of economic growth. Thus, growth and employment can come about only if inflation and inflationary expectations are brought under strict control. The larger implication is that this is best achieved by governments committing themselves *not* to intervene in the economy with expansionary policies, but instead to abjure short-term activism and set macroeconomic policy in a medium-term frame to contain inflation. This norm can be empirically demonstrated in the statements, public and private, of policy actors and their policy actions (McNamara 1998: Ch. 6). The larger norm that follows from this price stability framework is a norm of government non-intervention in the economy, or the separation of economic policy from politics.

2.3.2. Professional networks

These monetary policy norms were developed in an informal organizational setting in interactions among the EU central bankers who had responsibility for managing exchange rates. The organizational expression of this normative structure is quite revealing for the later design of the ECB. The central monetary organization prior to the ECB was the Committee of Central Bank Governors (CCBG), which was a loosely organized group, created so as to be operationally and legally separate from other EU institutions and out of the reach of the other economic policy-makers. In essence, the organizational form expressed the norm of prioritizing economics over politics by seeking the removal of monetary policy-making from the pull and haul of political life. It also reinforced the beliefs outlined above by providing a forum for dissemination across the 'organizational field' or network of actors concerned with monetary policy (DiMaggio and Powell 1983; Fligstein 1991).

The CCBG was created in 1964 to facilitate exchange-rate management among the European states in the wake of a series of currency crises under the Bretton Woods international monetary regime. The Committee was to have a primarily consultative and informational role, as envisioned by the EU Council of Ministers, and was 'a very intimate association', being made up of the six Member States of the European Economic Community (EEC) (Andrews 1999: 5).[3] The Committee did not have much in the way of its own bureaucratic resources, and in fact for most of its existence held its short monthly meetings at the Bank of International Settlements, in Basle, Switzerland, not

---

[3] Drawing on unique primary research, Andrews (1999) offers a detailed assessment of the history of the Committee.

in Brussels (Andrews 1999: 8). This was not by chance but by choice, as it meant that the central bankers themselves could keep a tight rein on the nature of their interactions among each other, and with other political bodies, national and European.[4]

Crisis marginally pushed forward the organizational presence of the CCBG. Waves of currency attacks in the Bretton Woods system of the late 1960s and early 1970s prompted more cooperation, particularly the systematization of lines of credit between the European central banks and increased coordination within the Committee, as did the decision in Hague in 1969 of the European political leaders to make monetary union a goal of the Community. The estab-lishment of the first solely European exchange-rate regime—the 'Snake'—in 1971 brought about a period of flux in the CCBG, extending through the cre-ation of the Snake's more successful successor, the EMS. Andrews (1999) argues that the CCBG developed over the 30 years preceding EMU from mod-est beginnings to a more developed organizational presence by the late 1980s. Surveying the historical development of the CCBG, he notes a continued effort to put distance between the central bankers and the rest of the European institutions and a resistance to a centralization of authority within the Committee itself or to any bureaucratization beyond a very limited secretariat based in Basle. As per the Maastricht Treaty, the CCBG became the European Monetary Institute on 1 January 1994 and moved to Frankfurt to prepare for its transformation into the European Central Bank. In doing so, it was trans-formed from a body with a very limited number of personnel—the CCBG had two staffers in 1965, seven in 1989, and 30 in 1993—to today's ECB which, although tiny by EU standards—about 930 at the start of 2001—is now expanding rapidly.[5]

The second organization influencing the path of monetary policy in the EU was the Monetary Committee, a broader organization encompassing all the national central bank governors as well as the members of the ministerial-level Council of Economic and Finance Ministers (ECOFIN). The Monetary Committee, in contrast to the CCBG which never had treaty status, was estab-lished with the Treaty of Rome. Meeting monthly, it was the forum for broader discussion of economic policy-making. However, because of its large number of participants and much broader purview, it seems to have never developed the important coordinating functions of the central banking group.

The CCBG played an important role in the further development of the mon-etary-policy institutions. It providing the medium within which the shared beliefs could be formulated and solidified. It facilitated policy emulation and gave a platform for those in the national governments who viewed Germany's stability-oriented policies as an example that the Community should follow. Gradually the national central bankers developed a close rapport and their

---

[4] See Heritier (this volume) for a systematic analysis of the various formal and informal channels of institutionalization in the EU.

[5] Figures on the CCBG are from Andrews (1999: 24); the ECB figures are from personal commu-nication with ECB personnel.

organizational interactions supported efforts at policy coordination and the choice of national strategies towards a German stability model in the 1980s. As one central banker commented in a private interview in 1993, 'The atmosphere in the Committee of Central Bank Governors is very professional; people do not come to meetings with distinctive national positions, but instead we all share a very common agreement on the correctness of a monetary policy model very close to that of Germany.'

Thus, by the start of the Maastricht negotiations, monetary policy had already taken up an important institutional residence in the European political space. That is, it had evolved into a 'complex of rules and procedures that governs a given set of human interactions' (Stone Sweet, Fligstein, Sandholtz, this volume, p. xx), despite the lack of formal and legally binding rules and a relatively limited set of organizational resources. The evolution occurred in part because the intensive and frequent interactions of central bankers had the effect of diffusing policy models and encouraging a shared vision of monetary policy goals and instruments.[6] This professional interaction occurred within the club-like atmosphere of a small community of central bankers, and had the characteristics more of a loose collective or network, with a very limited formal supranational presence and minimal bureaucratic resources. The central bankers continued efforts to make themselves organizationally independent from the political and bureaucratic powers of the Community. Indeed, the legal basis for much of the organizational arrangements in the monetary area was 'official' but not Treaty-based, and operated outside the normal Community jurisdiction.

These prior normative structures are evident in the Maastricht Treaty's rules in three areas: the ECB's design as a politically independent body modelled on the Bundesbank; the membership criteria for entry into the ECB; and the operational rules of price stability. I discuss each one in turn.

First, as discussed above, the design of the ECB embodied the view that monetary policy should be kept separate from political authority, which is congruent both with the prevailing ideas of economic functionality and with the prior institutional history of the monetary policy arena. The ECB's personnel and oversight procedures are designed to keep external political pressures to a minimum to best ensure that price stability will be credibly maintained. One member of the European Commission and the President of the European Council can participate, but not vote, in the meetings of the Governing Council. However, responsibility for exchange-rate agreements and revaluations is kept under the purview of the Council of Ministers in Stage III, which could dilute somewhat the independence of the ECB. The ECB is required to come before the European Parliament to present its annual report, yet the Parliament is prohibited from influencing the ECB; it can only ask questions and comment. The ECB's laws cannot be changed except by treaty revision with the unanimous consent of the EU Member States, which has the

---

[6] Interviews, European Community officials from DG II and the Committee of Central Bank Governors, Brussels, October 1991 and May 1994; see also Thygesen (1979: 205–24).

effect of further insulating it from political interference beyond what is required in a national setting. Internally, this autonomy is preserved as well in personnel and other operational matters, as the ECB is not legally considered part of the EU institutional system and thus sets its own personnel policies and other procedures.[7]

The second key set of ECB rules was the criteria for entry and continued membership in EMU. As has been noted above, the convergence criteria for entry into EMU spelled out a series of targets for the EU Member States: downward inflation and interest rate convergence; nominal exchange rate stability; fiscal convergence around a budget-GDP ratio of 3 per cent and a debt-GDP ratio of 60 per cent, or at least a substantial movement towards these goals. The most pivotal criteria were the last two dealing with the fiscal issues. While the eleven Member States entering into EMU met most of the conditions most of the time, structural reforms were often overshadowed by one-off measures and revenue-raising programmes (McNamara 2001b). The fiscal criteria survive as targets in the guise of the 'Stability and Growth Pact' which governs continued membership in the EMU. While these rules are subject to exceptions should the political leaders decide that a country is suffering from particularly difficult economic or political hardships, as in the case of the convergence criteria in the run-up to EMU they have taken on a great deal of importance as focal points for the financial markets and political debates about fiscal policy (Mosely 1999).

As argued in the previous section, the convergence criteria are not functionally logical in the sense that they do not focus on those things, such as factor mobility and the development of a federal fiscal structure, which could analytically be shown to be important for monetary union. Instead, they encapsulate the broader convention wisdom, championed by the German Bundesbank, to keep EMU to the most financially 'sound' Member States. The emphasis on low inflation, low government deficits, and low public debt is in keeping with the norms of price stability and the idea of an economic rubric removed from politics. The criteria clearly served a strategic purpose for Germany, keeping the Bundesbank on board; it would not have been accepted by the other Member States if it did not resonate with a broader and pre-existing set of norms already institutionalized in European political life.

The rules regarding membership criteria give us a good example of how change and dynamism continue even under conditions of strong institutionalization. In implementing the convergence criteria, the heads of state have found themselves between two opposing norms. That is, the history of EU integration has stressed inclusiveness, as programmes have been configured to ensure participation by all Member States. The fact that so few of the states actually met the exact numbers meant that the criteria would have to be decided on by the heads of state, as was directed in the Maastricht rules. As the issue of who to let in became more subjective, the broader institutional setting

---

[7] Interviews, Frankfurt (1998).

became more relevant, and the norm of inclusiveness bumped up against the economic-policy norms about financial sobriety. This example suggests the importance of examining the institutional setting more broadly to understand outcomes when there is a potential for overlapping or clashing norms (Sandholtz 1999) or gaps and tensions in institutional arenas (Smith, this volume). It also demonstrates that the multiple overlapping institutions governing social and political life will produce change as they come into conflict and mediate previous institutional arrangements (Sewell 1992).

Finally, there is a strong relationship between the operational rules of Maastricht—the third design element of concern—and the economic policy norms of the ECB's institutional setting. The Treaty formalizes and makes more precise and authoritative the price-stability norm in the statute of the ECB and the European System of Central Banks (ESCB) within which the ECB is embedded. The 'primary objective' of the ECB is to 'maintain price stability' (Art. 105), reflecting the prior consensus. However, as with the membership criteria, there may be conflict with other overlapping policy structures. The Treaty goes on to say that 'Without prejudice to the objective of price stability, the ESCB shall support the general economic policies of the Community as laid down in Article 2'. Art. 2 catalogues a series of goals of balanced social and economic development without harm to the environment, respecting social cohesion, and so on. The emphasis on price stability has been the sole stated goal of the ECB so far, however, as the ECB's President, Wim Duisenberg, has preached the virtues of anti-inflationary policies. While many of the European central banks have had price stability as a central goal of monetary policy, they have all included growth and unemployment as explicit goals as well, even in the case of the Bundesbank. Thus, the legal mandates of Maastricht, and their current interpretation by the ECB's personnel, are examples of how the ECB's organizational rules rest on a broad normative consensus, while leaving a small opening for challenges and the potential for change.

3. Conclusions

This chapter has offered a preliminary investigation into the sources of the organizational rules of the European Central Bank. I have argued for attention to a sociological approach, where organizations are seen to be reflections of their broader institutional environment while encompassing the potential for change. Instead of being understood solely as the result of efficiency or power-politics calculations, the ECB's rule structures should also be seen as a product of the need for policies to be legitimized in terms of existing normative structures. It is certain that the timing of the decision to move ahead with EMU, as well as its overall *raison d'être* as a political project to lock in peace and stability, should be attributed to other sources and exogenous factors that lie outside the particular institutional setting I have described. But a strong case can be made that the organizational form and policy content of the ECB reflect the

normative structures within which it is embedded. The prior institutional setting of the EU, with a well-developed network of central bankers and a set of
widely held norms stabilizing interactions over monetary policies, can be
linked to the concrete decisions made about the rules of the ECB. The ECB
thus represents much more policy continuity than the startling creation of a
new formal organizational presence might indicate.

What can the creation of rules in the ECB tell us about its likely evolution
and about the process of institutionalization in the EU more generally? As
Sewell (1992: 19) argues, normative structures tend to be reproduced over time,
yet 'their reproduction is never automatic. Structures are at risk, at least to some
extent, in all the social encounters they shape' in part because structures are
'multiple and intersecting'. Tensions arose along the path to the ECB, for example in the strict guidelines for membership in the single currency conflicting
with the norms of political inclusively which drive the EU more generally.

Two important and related challenges face the ECB; and the unfolding of
norms governing these challenges will shape the central bank's evolution over
the next decades. The first challenge concerns how the ECB will develop
dynamic relationships with other organizations in the EU. The rules laid down
in Maastricht stress autonomy and independence, without providing rules to
govern the ECB's relationship to the other economic actors in the EU, particularly the national economic and finance ministers. While a clear monetary policy mandate is provided in the Treaty, the need for more flexibility may
become apparent as linkages begin to form between the ECB and other salient
political actors. The second challenge is related to the first. The ECB, while
fitting the logic of legitimacy within the organizational field of monetary politics, does not necessarily meet the standards of legitimacy in the sense of democratic accountability and transparency to the European citizenry as a whole. As
a concrete, formal organization, it now must evolve in terms of its relationships
with other organizational actors such as the European Parliament so as to meet
the expectations of democratic legitimacy within the EU political landscape.
Shapiro (this volume) highlights the critical tension between rules and discretion, and between administration and expertise, at work in the arena of EU
administrative law. The monetary arena is remarkably similar in its sources of
potential change to its institutional norms and organizational form.

My argument here has been that the logic of social institutions must be
factored in so as to fully explain the path of monetary governance in the ECB.
European institutionalization is likely to evolve in ways that make sense based
on standards of appropriateness, or normative rules, as much as it will be a
function of economic efficiency or power politics. Of course, judging *a priori*
what these new organizational relationships and, perhaps, new institutional
structures will be is very difficult. But the sociological institutionalist approach
does tell us where to look, and what we should expect, in terms of the evolution of European integration. For the ECB, the stakes are very high, and understanding the sources of its rules and design may help the great experiment that
is EMU to succeed.

9

The Quest for Coherence: Institutional Dilemmas of External Action from Maastricht to Amsterdam

MICHAEL E. SMITH

IMPROVING the effectiveness and coherence of the European Union's (EU) external capabilities was a key motivation behind the Maastricht Treaty on European Union (TEU). By formally linking the European Community's (EC) capabilities in trade and other external economic affairs to those of the second pillar—the Common Foreign and Security Policy (CFSP)—and to a lesser extent the third pillar—cooperation in Justice and Home Affairs (JHA)—the TEU represented an important step toward realizing this goal. In particular, the Treaty established a single institutional framework to govern all of the EU's policies, internal and external. This new architecture was expected to provide greater discipline over the two methods with which Europe's external relations had long been conducted: the supranational Community method on the one hand and the intergovernmental methods of European Political Cooperation for foreign and security policy, and the Trevi and Schengen frameworks for JHA on the other.

However, while the single institutional framework seemed to resolve certain institutional questions about the conduct of the EU's external relations, it also raised a number of other problems once Maastricht came into force in November 1993. It is now generally accepted that Maastricht's provisions concerning external relations and, more importantly, the EU's record in this area reveal a number of limitations. These difficulties have received a great deal of attention from those charged with managing the EU's external affairs, have persistently attempted to improve the EU's provisions in this area. As a result, some of these institutional problems were addressed with temporary mechanisms, others were resolved with the Amsterdam Treaty on European Union during 1995–97, and still others remain in place. In other words, Maastricht set the stage for a new set of debates among key EU actors about institutionalization, involving both the consolidation of a new policy domain—the CFSP—and the linkage of that domain to the EU's broader system of governance through a more ambitious principle: coherence.

These actor perceptions about institutional performance and change prompt two major questions that I address in this chapter. First, what kinds of institutional problems resulted from Maastricht's provisions on external relations? Second, to what extent, and how, have these problems been resolved? To answer these questions, in the rest of this chapter I first map out the EU's institutional space in the policy domains most directly concerned with external relations. I then show how these mechanisms created new problems, and thus pressures for institutional change, once the Treaty came into effect. These problems are defined primarily in terms of institutional gaps and contradictions across the EU's external policy domains. Finally, I explain how the EU has attempted to resolve these problems through two sets of institutional reforms, one informal and the other formal.

1. Maastricht and External Relations: The Institutionalization of Coherence

There is little mystery about why the TEU attempted to enhance the EU's external capabilities, and why it references 'coherence' in this domain. Debates about these matters, and about the relationship between the EC and European Political Cooperation (EPC) in particular, were clearly influenced by an extraordinary series of events surrounding the Maastricht negotiations. After more than 15 years of informal, and very limited, policy coordination between the EC and EPC, the two policy domains had been linked and legalized in treaty form with the Single European Act (SEA) in 1986. Although EPC's performance improved after the SEA (Regelsberger 1988; Lodge 1989), only two years after the Act came into effect it was confronted with an unprecedented set of challenges: the fall of the Berlin Wall, the unification of Germany, democratic change in the former Soviet bloc, the Persian Gulf War, and the first signs of disintegration in the Soviet Union and Yugoslavia. Most EC states clearly felt their external capabilities needed improvement to cope with such problems, if only because of their potential to disrupt other important goals such as the single European market and monetary union. Uncertainty about the willingness of the US to play a leading role in the post-cold war era provided an additional motivation. Finally, crisis response in general had been a particular deficiency of EPC (Praag 1982; Edwards 1984; 1992; Hill 1992; Wood 1993), and the lack of a coordinated European policy toward these problems was felt among most EC Member States. These considerations weighed heavily during the intergovernmental conference on political union that helped produce the TEU (Corbett 1992; Laursen and Vanhoonacker 1992; Baum 1995/96; de Schoutheete de Tervarent 1997).

As a result, and to counterbalance the compartmentalization of the EU's external relations that had been established by EPC, the principle of coherence appears throughout the Maastricht Treaty. Under Arts A and C, the EU is charged with ensuring the coherence of its actions, in particular ensuring 'the consistency of its external activities as a whole in the context of its external relations, security, economic, and development policies' (Art. C). Title V (Arts J.1 and J.8) also mentions the concept as a guiding principle behind the CFSP. The fact that the TEU established a single institutional framework covering all three pillars of the EU's activities further demonstrates the importance of coherence in European integration (Curtin 1993).

Despite these various references to what seems to be a fundamental principle in the EU, coherence has not received a great deal of attention (Neuwahl 1994; Krenzler and Schneider 1997; Tietje 1997).[1] However, it should also be noted that the concept of coherence as mentioned in the TEU is not entirely new; it continues a trend that had been developing for some time in the EC's external affairs (M. Smith 1998b: 319–21; see also Lak 1989; Coignez 1992). In fact, an entire body of legal arguments and other decision-making principles, such as mixed agreements and dualist case law, emerged to enhance what I call the 'damage-limitation' function of EPC and to improve the general institutional linkages between EPC and the EC, particularly when EPC wished to use EC competencies for its own ends. In addition, becoming a 'cohesive force in international relations' was an explicit incentive behind the inclusion of EPC as Title III of the Single European Act (Art. 30.2(d)). Maastricht merely attempted to clarify and reinforce this trend. In a sense, then, the CFSP represented the next stage in a transition from EPC's primary focus on a damage-limiting objective—ensuring that Member State foreign policies did not adversely affect the Community—to positive integration—equipping the EU with the means to act coherently in world politics. This major change in emphasis—coherence across external policy domains or organizational fields—required a qualitative shift in institutional design.

Since Maastricht, to what extent does the principle of coherence actually play a role in the way the EU governs its external activities? Four caveats will inform my consideration of this question. First, this chapter focuses on what Tietje (1997: 211) has called 'horizontal coherence', or the extent to which the various foreign affairs activities of the EU are logically connected or mutually reinforcing. 'Vertical coherence', or the extent to which the foreign policy activities of individual EU states actually mesh with those of the Union, is another matter. In general, horizontal coherence means that the EU should be able to pursue its foreign policy goals despite the use of different institutional mechanisms and policy tools. These goals involve those codified by Maastricht

---

[1] In fact, the term itself is not used consistently in various translations of the TEU. As Tietje (1997: 211–12) points out, the English translation favours 'consistency', or the absence of contradictions, while most continental languages use the term 'coherence', meaning positive connections). For Tietje, coherence is evidently the favoured term for most EU states and it clearly sets a higher standard for the EU's policies. Thus, I use the term here.

and specific objectives set down by the European Council, particularly the June 1992 Lisbon summit (Council of Ministers 1992).

Second, although it is clear that the creation of the EU and its external capabilities was originally motivated by the changes in its external context noted above, most of the post-Maastricht institutional changes discussed in this chapter have been influenced by internal dynamics. As there are no major distributional issues surrounding the specific question of coherence, contests about institutions are mostly legal or ideological in nature. The central, macro-level—rule-system—battle is about the constitutional structure of the EU and the right of EU states to preserve their own foreign policy autonomy within that structure. Moreover, by attempting to create a closer link between the EC and the EU's other external capabilities, the drafters of the TEU unwittingly created potential tensions, inconsistencies, and gaps between the rules governing these domains at both the meso—organizational—and micro—individual—levels. Such problems provided openings for governments and EU policy-makers to work at cross-purposes with each other. The fact that the EU was also *legally* required to present a coherent front on the international stage provided an additional motivation to improve the working relationships among the EU's external activities. These issues would have to be resolved once the TEU entered into its implementation phase.

Third, I assume that the primary actors are representatives of EU governments acting within the European Council and Council of Ministers, and of EC organizations—chiefly the Commission, but with supporting roles for the European Parliament (EP) and European Court of Justice (ECJ). In other words, this is largely a story about elites, as the problems and debates examined in this chapter do not have the same capacity to draw in domestic actors and interest groups as do other EC policy domains (on this point, see Mazey and Richardson, this volume). In general, I assume that governments attempt to balance their inherent desire for foreign policy autonomy against the external goals of the EU, and that EC actors like the Commission are generally 'pro-integrationist'. However, it must also be recognized that governments and the Commission are not monolithic; they have conflicting goals and their officials compete with each other to pursue those goals. Still, for my level of abstraction, where the chief conflict is between those who seek more 'Europe' and those who seek less, it is reasonable to suppose that the Commission's goals are uniform and that EU governments of any type have strong reasons for keeping all EC organizations at bay in certain aspects of foreign affairs.

Fourth and finally, it is beyond the scope of a single chapter to analyze all EU policy areas that affect external relations; instead, they may be categorized according to their basic institutional structures:

1. External policy domains where supranational EC organizations—chiefly the Commission and the Court—and procedures—qualified majority voting (QMV)—dominate. Here economic concerns, the driving force behind

European integration, are paramount. The EC's trade, aid, and development policies—or 'external relations'—generally fall under this heading.

2. Domains that involve interaction between EC organizations and intergovernmental forums—chiefly the European Council and Council of Ministers, or 'Council of the EU'—and procedures, and where economic concerns coexist with other goals, such as political stability. This domain includes regional or political dialogues, the CFSP, and perhaps certain areas that overlap with JHA concerns, such cooperation to combat drugs and terrorism outside the EU.

3. Domains where intergovernmental forums and procedures clearly dominate, such as security and defence, which can also involve the Western European Union (WEU). In these areas economic concerns are usually subordinated to the goals of 'high politics', if cooperation can be achieved at all.

EU external policies are conditioned according to these three institutional categories, which differ from the EU's three *pillars*. Some of them privilege EU Member States, while others privilege supranational EC organizations. The Commission, for example, enjoys the exclusive right to initiate policies and negotiate agreements on behalf of the EU in domains that fall under the external-relations competencies of the Community, such as trade. In other areas, such as the CFSP and JHA, it shares these rights with EU Member States. Similarly, the Council of Ministers and the Commission must ensure the coherence of the Union's external policies, thus giving these bodies—one an intergovernmental forum, the other a supranational organization—a joint role in this responsibility. Equally important here is the fact that the ECJ is *excluded* under the TEU (Art. L) from exercising its jurisdiction over the activities of the second and third pillars. Thus we cannot rely on Court decisions to determine how coherence has fared as a general principle; we must look to decisions and policies.

In addition to the way they affect normal policy-making, each of the categories also conditions institutional change within its respective sphere. In areas where the EC dominates, institutions are more or less self-sustaining. Here, the Commission's activities related to policy initiation and implementation inevitably produce new rules, and even new competencies, whether as a by-product of implementation—that is, through secondary legislation—or otherwise. These rules then condition later initiatives. This 'spill-over' is well-known and has occurred in other external policy areas such as environmental policy (Sbragia 1998) and the extra-territorial application of competition policy (Damro 1999). In areas where intergovernmentalism is the rule, most institutional changes, even the most unassuming, often require tense discussions or bargains among EU governments or their representatives (for related examples, see the chapters by Turnbull and Sandholtz on JHA and McNamara on EMU in this volume). Areas of mixed competency are the most problematic, as some EU Member States have opposed Commission involvement, or required the Commission to justify its involvement, in such areas or have blocked the use of EC procedures or resources for external political activities.

In fact, we can break down these TEU external policy categories in terms of their institutional provisions, the actors and stakes involved, and the types of external behavior—that is, foreign policy tools—each one has the capability to produce (Fig. 9.1):

These categories are not discrete, of course; in fact, it is their tendency to interfere with each other that generates many of the institutional problems examined in this chapter. Still, they establish an initial set of reference points with which we can assess institutional performance.

	EC/supranational competencies	Mixed competencies	Intergovernmental competencies
Dominant focus of policy domain	Economic issues	Political issues	Security and defence
Examples	Trade, aid, development	Dialogues, CFSP, certain aspects of JHA	CFSP/WEU
Decision rule	QMV is allowed	QMV is allowed under special circumstances	Concensus only
Agenda-setting and implementation	Commission	States/Commission	Primarily states
Policy resources	Primarliy EC	EC/states	Primarily states
Legally binding ?	Yes	Depends	Depends
ECJ involved ?	Yes	Very limited role	Highly unlikely

Fig. 9.1. Governance of the EU's external relations

2. Institutional Performance

Given the way Maastricht organized the EU's external capabilities, how did the system perform once it was implemented? More accurately, how did *perceptions* of performance among EU elites, defined mainly in terms of coherence, create pressures for further institutionalization? To answer this question, we can examine the EU's record of external policies towards a region or problem that have involved more than one type of the three decision-making competencies described above—EC-dominant, mixed competency, and intergovernmental-ism-dominant—*and* that have produced conflicts between EC organizations and EU governments. These areas include EU activity in the Balkans, perhaps the EU's most important challenge; EU activity regarding arms control or non-pro-liferation, such as the control of dual-use goods and the EU's involvement in the Korean Peninsula Energy Development Organization; and various actions toward South Africa, Russia, central-eastern Europe, and the Middle East.

More specifically, it is possible to break down institutional incoherence into several areas that have affected policy performance in the view of several observers (Regelsberger and Wessels 1996; Ginsberg 1997; M. Smith 1998*a*); these problems help create a demand for new rules and procedures. In the rest of this section, I analyze the relationship between institutional change and actor perceptions of the TEU's performance by focusing on several sets of institutional problems. Again, I am not attempting to evaluate all of the EU's external policies, only those which have raised serious institutional problems—chiefly due to clashes between the first two pillars of the EU—in terms of policy performance and coherence.[2]

2.1. Decision-making rules

Perhaps the most common complaint about incoherence between the pillars in terms of external relations involves the fact that decision-making rules have not been applied uniformly where competencies overlap. Recall that the CFSP is expressed through two primary instruments, *common positions* and *joint actions*, which take the place of normal EC legal instruments (under Art. 189). However, in the first place, qualified majority voting for CFSP joint actions, and JHA joint actions as well, has not been utilized. The rules for QMV are so convoluted that it has been nearly impossible to apply them quickly, consistently, and efficiently. In fact, Maastricht set up a series of up to five veto points where EU Member States have an opportunity to prevent themselves from being outvoted on a particular CFSP decision. Blocking the use of QMV has been done primarily for ideological reasons: the fear that one QMV vote on any CFSP action, no matter how trivial, would set a precedent leading to the 'contamination' of the second pillar with supranationalism. These fears are somewhat justified; lower-level CFSP officials have tended to draft policy texts with the understanding that legal precedents are being set, even where EC treaty articles do not apply.

Second, when there is a conflict between policies requiring CFSP and EC decisions, particularly the use of economic sanctions, the procedures of the CFSP have tended to dominate. Art. 228a was supposed to clarify the legal conflict between Art. 113—the common commercial policy, which allows QMV—and the CFSP; however, CFSP's intergovernmental procedures—that is, unanimity—have prevailed.[3] Some CFSP and JHA[4] decisions have even undermined the EC's

---

[2] The analysis that follows is based in part on confidential interviews conducted by the author with officials from the Commission, Council of the EU, COREPER, European Parliament, and the permanent mission of the US to the EU.

[3] Art. 228a was established to govern the way economic—under Art. 113—and financial—under Art. 73.1—sanctions could be applied against non-EU states after years of confusion about whether EPC was allowed to impose such sanctions. Under Art. 228a, such sanctions can be imposed only by reference to a competence provision of the EC, which allows QMV, or under a CFSP common position or joint action, which stresses unanimity.

[4] For example, JHA ministers, using their own procedures, have attempted to require a clause to be inserted into all future EU agreements with third countries, even those handled by the EC, like the Lomé Convention, allowing the EU to deport illegal immigrants back to the state from which they entered the EU, even if that was not their state of origin.

own competencies, thus contaminating the EC with intergovernmentalism, a development that led to many Commission complaints during the preparatory stages of Amsterdam.

Third, Art. 116, which obliged Member States to adhere to common positions, decided by QMV, in international economic organizations, was conspicuously omitted by the TEU. This article was not often invoked before the TEU removed it, but it did impose a certain discipline on Member States to coordinate their actions with those of the EC in external economic affairs. Commission officials argue that the absence of Art. 116 has led to 'a marked change in climate. More and more often the opinion is expressed that the complicated rules of the CFSP regarding settlement on a common position [Art. J.2] replace Art. 116' (da Fonseca-Wollheim 1996: 2). Since these rules require unanimity rather than QMV, it has become more difficult to arrange compromises in such matters. This is additional evidence of the way some rules of the intergovernmental pillars have apparently undermined the EC's own supranational procedures.

2.2. External representation and policy implementation

In addition, external representation and implementation have created problems of coordination in areas where the EC—and thus the Commission—does not enjoy exclusive competency. The CFSP is vague on the division of labour between the two main actors charged with representation and implementation: the EU presidency and the Commission. Within this pillar, arrangements for their respective roles have generally been worked out on a case-by-case basis, which can create delays at best and confusion at worst. Depending on the issue at hand, representation can be handled by the Commission; the EU presidency; the 'tandem' formula, also known as the 'bicephalous Presidency'; the 'Troika' formula; or the designation of special representatives on an ad hoc basis. In some cases, such as the 'Stability Pact' with central and eastern Europe, the tandem formula worked very well; in others, such as Bosnia, confusion ensued about who was speaking for the EU, and with what authority. Where policies cross pillars, disputes arose over the division of labour among Commissioners—particularly Brittan for trade and van den Broek for the CFSP—even in areas where the Commission dominates, such as trade.

A more serious problem regarding representation and implementation involves relations not among Commissioners but between Commission representatives and those of EU Member States. As with fear of precedent-setting over decision-making, some EU states have preferred to keep the Commission at arm's length when dealing with cross-pillar or CFSP/JHA matters. This is especially true when military or defence issues are involved; recall how EU states reproached external-relations Commissioner van den Broek in 1996 when he suggested that EU states may have to maintain their forces in the Balkans even after the US withdrew its own troops. Thus, although the Commission enjoys the *de jure* right to speak on these matters, and thus link them to EC affairs, the *de facto* practice has been for such decisions to be left up to intergovernmental bodies like the European Council and Council of Ministers.

2.3. Financing the EU's external relations

Institutional mechanisms regarding financial resources for external actions also opened up a series of problems after Maastricht. The EU was built on a rule that some areas of external actions would be funded by the EC budget, and others, such as the CFSP and JHA, by contributions from Member States. The CFSP/JHA pillars began operating under a rule that the 'operational' side of their respective joint actions would be funded by national contributions, unless decided otherwise, while 'administrative' expenditure would be drawn from the EC budget. In practice, the arrangements for providing operational funds from national contributions became subject to logistical problems and domestic difficulties in EU Member States. The EU's administration of Mostar in the former Yugoslavia revealed how difficult it would be to fund the CFSP's operations through national means. Nearly a year after the initial Council decision of 8 November 1993 to support the operation in part with national contributions, only three EU Member States—Ireland, Greece, and Denmark— had contributed to it (Hagleitner 1995: 6; Court of Auditors of the European Communities 1996).

Additional problems arose over the basic distinction between administrative and operational expenditures under Arts 199, J.11, and K.13 of the TEU. Simply defining what constitutes operational expenditure has been a most difficult issue under the new arrangements. The TEU (Art. J.5) provides that the EU presidency shall be responsible for implementing *joint actions*, but also that the Commission (Art. 205) implements the *budget*, so several Member States suggested that QMV be used (under Art. 205) to implement the later financing stages of the joint actions in the former Yugoslavia that had been decided unanimously. This led to protracted debates over 'joint action imple- mentation' by the EU presidency, and 'budgetary implementation' by the Commission. Britain adamantly refused to use QMV procedures in this area, and every phase of the EU's actions in the Balkans—Mostar and otherwise— required a tedious repetition of the consensual decision-making process at the highest levels, when normal disbursements of EC funds could have been made with QMV decisions.

2.4. The EU and the WEU

The fact that Maastricht (Art. J.7) mentions the WEU as a potential defence arm for the EU was considered a major breakthrough as military affairs were treated as taboo subjects under EPC. However, the TEU did not clarify the prac- tical relationship between the EU and the WEU, which led to inane procedural debates over how the EU could 'avail itself'—in the words of the TEU—of the

WEU in order to implement its decisions. Also, the fact that after 1995 one-third of the EU—Austria, Denmark, Finland, Ireland, and Sweden—did not enjoy full membership of the WEU complicated decision-making. As a result, the CFSP has had very little to do with the WEU in operational terms. By the start of the Amsterdam negotiations, only one very minor Art. J.4(2) joint action, which provides for WEU participation, had been decided: a Council decision of 27 June 1996 to have the WEU prepare contingency plans to support the possible emergency evacuation of EU nationals from third countries if necessary.[5] Later, during the Kosovo crisis, the WEU decided in May 1997 to send a 'Multinational Advisory Police Element' (MAPE) to Albania, consisting of 94 officers from 23 WEU nations. Although this was not a CFSP-related joint action, MAPE was supported by EU funds under the Poland and Hungary Assistance for Economic Restructuring programme amounting to 4.8 million ECU during 1998–9. Thus, from the perspective of both EU actions and WEU actions, cooperation between the two bodies has been far less frequent than proposed in the TEU.

Also complicating matters in this area is another potential 'hard core' EU on defence issues: the 'Eurocorps', a small—60,000 troops—land force that became operational on 30 November 1995. This unit, supported by contributions from France, Germany, Spain, Belgium, and Luxembourg, is loosely linked to the WEU and the two forces began joint exercises, 'Cilsex', in December 1995. Although these activities may have much symbolic importance for European integration, they still do not live up to the hopes of the TEU's architects that the WEU would significantly enhance the EU's external policies. Rather than find a pragmatic way for the WEU and CFSP to take joint actions, the EU seemed to be paralyzed by the larger issue of fully merging the EU and the WEU. Moreover, since NATO rapidly transformed itself into a convenient, effective substitute for EU military actions, particularly in the Balkans, the EU's most problematic area, there was no longer any operational incentive for the EU to quickly resolve its institutional problems in this area.

2.5. Democratic oversight

Finally, to the extent that the EU's external relations are supposed to involve democratic oversight by the EP—which is more a legitimacy issue than a capability issue—some problems of coherence have emerged. The EP is directly involved in some external policy domains—the EC—only consulted in others, and largely ignored in yet others. Indeed, the democratic deficit is one of the primary deficiencies of the CFSP, and the EU in general, according to some observers (Stavridis 1997). The dominance of the CFSP/EU by the European Council makes it difficult for Euro-enthusiasts to claim that the EU is becoming more transparent and open. Although members of the European Council are elected in their respective states, this body is not a Community institution,

[5] WEU support of the EU's administration of Mostar was not an official CFSP joint action made at the request of the EU under Art. J.4(2).

has a dubious legal identity, meets in secret, and does not publish its deliberations. In addition, since Maastricht the EP has consistently complained about being ignored by the Council of Ministers (Grunert 1997). The EP wants consultation to take place before policies are decided; the Council often prefers to provide information *post hoc*. The EP has also threatened to use its leverage over the CFSP budget if its views were not taken into consideration (European Parliament 1994*a*), and has continually pushed for institutional changes on these issues.

Also, not all external agreements have been submitted to the EP for consideration;[6] the Council seems to decide at whim which agreements should be presented to the EP, and at what stage in their development. As Regelsberger and Wessels (1996: 42) observe, the CFSP is also far-removed from most national political elites. These are serious problems, and there is clearly a lack of openness and accountability in the EU's intergovernmental pillars, but it cannot be said that this legitimacy problem has adversely affected the EU's institutional performance in external relations in any significant way. Yet it repeatedly figures in debates about the institutional architecture of Europe, which repeatedly stress democracy, so we must be sensitive to it.

2.6. Institutional gaps

Beyond the problems raised by existing provisions in the TEU, coherence has been hindered by at least three other fundamental issues that were not fully addressed at Maastricht.

First, since the EU lacks legal personality, it is difficult to conclude international agreements or join international organizations where the Community, which enjoys legal personality under Art. 210, is not a signatory (Cheyne 1994; Sack 1995; Wessel 1997). This is especially problematic for the EU's membership of international organizations when competencies appear to cross pillars.[7] The problem of legal personality similarly complicates the manner by which the EU—or CFSP/JHA—once it finally decides on a negotiator, attempts to implement a policy by way of an agreement with non-EU states or other actors. For example, the EU could not participate in the Korean Peninsula Energy Development Organization (KEDO) as a board member despite its initial financial contribution of 5 million ECU, and EU legal officials are continually telling CFSP diplomats that they lack the legal authority to make a particular agreement on behalf of the EU. Similarly, the principle of exclusivity, which means that EU states are not permitted to join international

---

[6] The Interim Agreement with Russia is perhaps the most notable example.

[7] This has been a problem even within the EC's exclusive sphere of competence, like trade matters. For example, a debate opened up about whether the Commission, representing the EC, or individual Member States should sign the General Agreement on Trade and Services (GATS) and the Trade-Related Intellectual Property Rights (TRIPS) as part of GATT's Uruguay Round of trade negotiations. The ECJ ruled on 15 November 1994 that the Commission alone should sign GATT—now WTO—provisions due to its exclusive authority over trade in goods under Art. 113 of the TEU, but that it shared this competency with Member States in the GATS and TRIPS agreements. Therefore, EU Member States as well as the Commission could sign those agreements.

organizations where the EC has exclusive competence, had to be clarified in terms of cross-pillar issues. This point was raised during a heated debate when Britain and France wanted to sit on the board of KEDO while the EU, through the CFSP, was pursing that goal as well. In the end, the parties agreed to have the EC, by virtue of its Euratom competencies, represent the EU on KEDO's board.

Second, the Maastricht Treaty says little about how to ensure compliance with CFSP/JHA decisions or other external intergovernmental actions, so there is no way to evaluate or punish defections. TEU confers this responsibility on the Council of Ministers, and since they decide such matters by consensus, no one state is likely to criticize another. Compliance after the fact has not been much of a problem since few CFSP actions have required it. Although the Commission is fully associated with all aspects of the CFSP and must ensure coherence, in this domain it clearly does not enjoy the extremely important monitoring and enforcement role it actively plays in the EC (Art. 155). As we have seen, one of the most visible examples is the EU's administration of Mostar, where most EU Member States did not make their financial contributions to the operation in a timely fashion. This greatly contributed to debates over the CFSP budgetary process (see below). Similarly, the Commission chooses its battles carefully and has not emerged as a major enforcer of compliance. For example, it was decidedly reluctant to invoke Arts 34, 35, or 192 of the Euratom Treaty to halt French nuclear tests in the Pacific for fear of a backlash,[8] and did not attempt to censure Greece for its unilateral actions regarding the former Yugoslav Republic of Macedonia. A related problem is a temptation for EU states to pursue their interests unilaterally or in other forums like the UN Security Council, NATO, or 'Contact Groups'. Again, there is no independent way for the EU to discipline its Member States for these apparent transgressions.

Third, the ECJ is effectively excluded from second and third pillar issues, so there is no independent dispute-resolution procedure in these domains. As noted above, under Art. L the ECJ may not exercise any jurisdiction over the CFSP and JHA pillars. This may not seem to be an issue for the EU, because its Member States seem to assume that disputes cannot arise from decisions made by consensus. Even when they are dissatisfied when the foreign policy actions of other EU states conflict with common EU policies, EU governments tend not to criticize too loudly for fear of inviting future criticisms in the event their own foreign policies fail to conform to those of the EU. Thus they would be unlikely to take each other to Court over such matters, even if they enjoyed the right to do so. However, Art. M provides that nothing in the TEU shall affect the Treaties amending the EC, except for certain stated provisions to that effect. In other words, CFSP/JHA activities cannot be used

---

[8] In brief, these articles require EC states to provide the Commission with information about nuclear testing, to allow Commission officials to access test sites, to obtain a Commission opinion prior to conducting particularly dangerous experiments, and to support provisions of the Euratom Treaty in general.

or allowed to modify Community competencies. This means that the ECJ 'can and must police the borderline between the Community pillar and the CFSP' (and JHA) (Eaton 1994: 221). Yet the ECJ had made no major rulings in this area during the time period under consideration, so we can conclude that its jurisdiction over these questions is more of a conceptual issue rather than a practical one.

3. Institutional Reforms

In this section I analyze how institutional inconsistencies or gaps have been resolved after Maastricht was implemented. In other words, to the extent that solutions to the problems of incoherence discussed above have now become standard operating procedures for conducting the EU's external relations, we can say that they have been institutionalized. As with the Maastricht negotiations, this reform process has been encouraged in part by exogenous factors, such as American pressures to play a greater role in global affairs or the need to improve the EU's representation or negotiating positions in certain international forums. One major exogenous incentive is the need to clarify the relationship between the EU's emerging capabilities in security/defence policy and those of other functionally-related institutions, namely NATO and the WEU. Yet these pressures have always been part of the EU's internal debate about external coherence, and they did not necessarily increase in any dramatic fashion since 1991—especially compared with the events surrounding the Maastricht Treaty. Moreover, they explain only the general incentives for greater institutional coherence, not the specific choices made by the EU. Thus, most of changes discussed in this section are better explained by endogenous processes, most of which involve the ongoing, macro-level ideological debate in the EU between supranational and intergovernmental visions, or rule-systems, of external policy-making.

One part of this internal debate involves *policy effectiveness*, which involves defending the example of supranational EC procedures as the most efficient and legitimate means for achieving common European goals. In other words, the EC has a powerful mimetic effect on other pillars and the relationships between them; it is the most important frame of reference, at least in terms of effectiveness, in debates about institutional change. Arguments over this question are fuelled by evaluations of policy successes and failures, both of which have occurred during the period under consideration. As I noted above, here the Commission enjoys a privileged role—though not an exclusive one—by virtue of its policy implementation function, which often requires it to establish new procedures to accomplish its tasks. Another part of its power derives from its role in evaluating policy outcomes, and it has often attempted to make its case for greater institutional coherence, particularly during the preparatory stages of Amsterdam, by emphasizing implementation problems rather than invoking the virtues of supranationalism.

However, another part of the debate involves *policy appropriateness*, and this aspect of the institutional reform debate is far more subtle and complex. Two major strands of argument can be discerned here. One is that even though EC procedures may be more effective, foreign and security policy are still special domains where Member States enjoy the dominant role and should maintain the maximum freedom of manoeuvre. Control over this aspect of policy is still considered a defining characteristic of a state, and EU governments feel they would be acting irresponsibly were they to surrender this right to supranational EC actors. The result is a constant bargaining process between governments and EC organizations about the appropriate boundaries of their respective domains. A second strand of argument derives from simple disagreements about what the rules actually mean, particularly concerning the division of labour across the external relations functions. This area of disagreement is about the legalities of certain behaviours within respective spheres of competence, and, not surprisingly, those who know the rules best, particularly the EC's much larger and complex body of rules, often have the upper hand in this argument.

Within these grand, macro-level debates over institutional change, which by their nature are the most difficult to resolve, we can also find more common, parochial contests that have produced some reforms. These conflicts have occurred at both the micro-level and the meso-level. In general, micro-level activity often involves problems such as turf battles among Commissioners whose portfolios involve external relations; meso-level activity involves delineating the proper roles for the various EC organizations, policy domains, and intergovernmental forums involved in EU foreign actions. In the rest of this section, I first examine the informal mechanisms of institutional change, such as unwritten rules, then turn to a more formal expression of the EU's institutional reforms of the TEU: the Amsterdam Treaty (for a similar distinction between types of institutional mechanisms, see Héritier, this volume).

3.1. Informal mechanisms

Given the great sensitivity among several EU Member States about the supranational governance of external relations through formal mechanisms, and given the inherently unpredictable nature of foreign affairs, there is a strong inherent tendency in this area toward informal, flexible procedures whose obligations are less demanding, and also not justiciable. This tendency dates back to the formative years of EPC, which relied on a host of unwritten rules or 'gentlemen's agreements' about appropriate behaviour in this domain and its overall relationship to the EC's own more formal rules (Nuttall 1992; Smith 1998*a*: 316–24). The EU has continued this tradition by using a number of informal procedures, many developed under EPC, to fill in the gaps between the TEU's external relations competencies. These procedures apply to both decision-making and the implementation of external policies.

For example, in the sphere of decision-making, the EU has had to devise several ways to contend with long-standing prejudices among some EU states against linkages between the EC and the CFSP in general and the application of QMV procedures in particular. A number of compromises have emerged; these are used to guide later decisions. For example, the first 'dualist' EC/CFSP act, a policy to control the EU's exports of dual-use goods, required much debate among EU officials, particularly those in the legal services; but it was resolved on terms acceptable to both sides of the supranational-intergovernmental divide.[9] More importantly, this exercise then encouraged the establishment of 'model common positions' to help avoid time-consuming legal debates over EC/CFSP decision-making.[10] These models can be used as templates for future decisions. Also, casting combined EC/CFSP agreements as 'administrative' in nature has also helped to reduce disagreements about the application of decision-making rules to joint EC/CFSP decisions. Finally, rather than relying on QMV in the CFSP, EU states have occasionally refrained from forcing a vote—that is, 'refrained from insisting on unanimity', in the words of Declaration No. 27 on voting in the CFSP, TEU—during four relatively uncontroversial CFSP implementation decisions.[11] Although this type of decision-making is probably not what the architects of the TEU had in mind, CFSP officials have temporarily managed to find a middle ground between strict intergovernmentalism through unanimity and the use of supranational QMV procedures.

The controversies over decision-making have also had negative repercussions regarding the initiation and implementation of second pillar, or cross-pillar, actions. Rather than wasting its resources and inviting disputes by initiating numerous CFSP actions, the Commission has tended to pursue a strategy of embedding foreign policy issues in broader sets of EU agreements or policies, such as 'Association Agreements' with states outside of the European land mass, 'Europe Agreements' with applicants to the EU from central and eastern Europe, and 'Partnership and Cooperation Agreements' with Russia and other former Soviet states.[12] These agreements are in fact institutionalized frameworks to help achieve coherence among the EU's policies toward important areas of interest. The Commission has occasionally attempted to instigate actions which involve the CFSP alone, but it is understandably far more

---

[9] The compromise involved using a CFSP joint action (94/942/CFSP) to establish the *content* of the policy—that is, lists of affected products and technologies—and an EC regulation (3381/94/EEC) to *implement* it.

[10] See the 'Mode d'emploi concernant les positions communes définies sur la base de l'Article J.2 de Traité sur l'Union Européenne', internal Council document 5194/95 of 6 March 1995.

[11] These were: financial sanctions against Bosnia-Herzegovina, the prohibition against making payments under contracts caught by the embargo against Haiti, some minor disbursement decisions concerning Mostar, and the EU's anti-personnel mine-clearing directive.

[12] These 'all-inclusive' agreements, however, have raised other problems. First, since they involve competencies that cross pillars, they must usually be negotiated by Commission officials and an official from a Member State, usually the holder of the EU presidency. Second, assuming this 'tandem' approach results in an agreement, certain aspects of such agreements—that is, those involving the second and third pillars—must then be ratified by individual EU states, a long and complicated process which delays the full implementation of the agreement.

successful when engineering long-term, cross-pillar strategies towards other states and regions—an approach which has been formally institutionalized since Amsterdam (see below). And the Commission is fully aware of the power of precedent-setting; it has been quietly trying to develop a 'critical mass' of precedents and experience outside of normal EC affairs to serve as a foundation for future foreign policies. This is especially crucial when economic instruments besides aid and joint-action financing are involved—that is, sanctions or association agreements—since they affect the internal market and the external economic relations of the EU and must involve the Commission. Involvement in security- or defence-related external policies has been far more problematic, and even discouraged by some EU states, although the Commission played a role in the Nuclear Non-Proliferation Treaty renewal conference and the EU's initiative on de-mining war-torn areas.[13]

Beyond these measures, policy coordination was improved, and turf battles were reduced, among Commissioners over foreign policy in areas where external activities overlap, such as central and eastern Europe and South Africa, after President Santer institutionalized regular *'relex group'*—for *relations extérieures*—meetings of the six Commissioners who have external relations portfolios, plus himself. These are supported by regular meetings of Commission planning staff, meetings of cabinet officials, particularly the *chefs de cabinet*, involved in the CFSP, and monthly meetings of the directors-general of the major external relations directorates, where the DGs coordinate political and economic affairs in between the Commissioners' meetings. The results have been generally positive.

It should be noted, however, that when turf battles over foreign policy occur within the Commission, Commissioners whose external portfolios involve a core policy area of the EC, such as trade, tend to win out over the others, such as the CFSP and human rights. Part of the reason for this is institutional: there is naturally an inherent bias in the Commission towards protecting its economic functions, and Commissioners defer to those who oversee those functions. And part of the reason for this is political: Commissioners who handle economically-oriented policy areas simply have more resources to use when bargaining over policy. Still, these efforts toward internal coordination have been especially helpful in promoting cooperation between DG I for external economic relations and DG VIII for development before the latest Commission reorganization, both of which are linked to the CFSP, and which did not always share information with each other under EPC.

---

[13] It should also be kept in mind that the Commission was preoccupied with a number of internal changes to help its implementation of external policies, such as creating DG IA to accommodate the CFSP and related policies. These changes represented the most extensive reorganization of the Commission's responsibilities in foreign affairs in the entire history of the organization. They were not all successful, and the Commission had to scale back some of them in the first few years of the implementation of the TEU (Allen and Smith 1994; Nuttall 1995). Yet reforms have continued; for example, the Commission's main external competencies have been reorganized into development/humanitarian aid, enlargement, trade, and external-relations spheres. Also, the new Commissioner for external relations, Chris Patten, is now attempting to streamline the EU foreign-aid delivery process.

These efforts to coordinate external policy at the individual level within the Commission have been duplicated at the organizational level. Much preparatory activity for EC policies takes place in the Committee of Permanent Representatives (COREPER) working groups; when the TEU came into effect all relevant EC and EPC working groups were merged to help end the compartmentalization of these policy areas. In addition, the EU has established a few 'tri-pillar' working groups—EC/CFSP/JHA—for certain countries and regions, such as the US. The role of COREPER in the preparation of all General Affairs Council meetings was also enhanced, although there is still some confusion about the division of labour between COREPER and the long-standing Political Committee that prepares CFSP decisions for foreign ministers. However, to overcome that difficulty, each permanent representation to the EU has established a 'CFSP counsellor': in an important precedent, these officials now prepare all matters relating to the use of economic sanctions.

In the area of financing external policies, after months of debate an informal agreement was reached in June 1994 to use a GNP scale as a general rule to determine national CFSP contributions (*European Report* 1994: 3). Even then, given the problems raised by Mostar noted above, EU states increasingly looked to the EC budget for CFSP funds, making Commission and EP involvement certain. Until then, lack of policy guidelines meant that petty ideological disputes over funding often held up actions; even something as uncontroversial as the EU's election-monitoring mission to Russia led to internal wrangling over how to pay for buses to transport the monitors. Once again, it took months before a temporarily acceptable procedure was worked out (Hagleitner 1995; Monar 1997*a*, *b*). Against the wishes of their partners, France and Britain supported financing the CFSP's operational expenditure under the *Council*'s line in the budget, to be used at the Member States' discretion. Naturally the EP was adamantly opposed to this idea; instead, it adopted a resolution in 1994 to establish a CFSP operational line (line III-B-8) within the *Commission* budget, which includes money for actions previously decided in Council and a 'general CFSP reserve fund' (see European Parliament 1994*b*). Transfers of funds would still be approved by the EP. In an important victory for the Parliament, this was the solution adopted, and the Commission and the EP have more discretion over the disbursement of CFSP operational funds than ever before.

While this temporary solution was being worked out, EU states engaged in creative financing by raiding operational funds from the EC budget, such as monies for development or cooperation. For example, the Council of the EU charged the costs of supporting Belgian 'Blue Berets' in Somalia to the EC Development Fund Budget, a clear case of EC support for a military operation. The excuse was that the EC was not able to spend its Somali aid due to unrest there, so EC officials argued that 'military assistance to the civilian power' in Somalia was a proper charge to the EC development budget (Keatinge 1997). Disbursing these EC funds for CFSP-related actions also raised legal questions, since the EP has the right to participate in the EC's budgetary process (Art. 209) and the right to approve all non-compulsory expenditure (Art. 203), such as the CFSP (European Parliament 1994*a*).

One final informal rule involves the problem of legal personality. As we have seen, since the EU/CFSP lacks legal personality, it is difficult to conclude international agreements or join international organizations where the Community is not a signatory. Since it lacks legal personality, the EU has tended to rely on somewhat convoluted 'mixed agreements', which provide for both EC representation and representation by individual EU states, or 'administrative agreements' that refer to both CFSP and EC competencies. These formulae perform a dual function in the EU: they help prevent tedious debates about decision-making rules and they help overcome the EU's own lack of legal personality. In other cases, the EU relies on 'memorandums of understanding' negotiated on its own, mainly for CFSP activities, which are not always binding under international law.[14] Although all of these agreements are difficult to negotiate, nearly impossible for the EP to oversee, and raise unresolved questions about their enforcement, they do represent a pragmatic and creative way to circumvent the legal personality problem. Without such informal mechanisms, the EU would be extremely limited in its capacity to implement its second and third pillars. The EU's legal officials were partially responsible for devising these solutions, and they reflect the continued importance of common understandings about the rule of law in explaining the dynamics of European integration.

3.2. Formal mechanisms

In this section I examine and evaluate a number of formal mechanisms codified by the Treaty of Amsterdam, which prioritized the institutional reform of the EU's external capabilities. In their official contributions to the 1996–7 intergovernmental conference, most EU states and organizations admitted to serious disappointments with the EU's external relations in general and the CFSP in particular. The Commission (CEC 1995; 1996*a*) and the European Parliament (1995) were the most critical of these difficulties, while even the official Council report on the functioning of the TEU (Council of Ministers 1995) also referred to the disappointment of some Member States with the performance of the CFSP. As with the original TEU, coherence is preserved (Arts 1 and 3) as a key principle governing the EU's policy domain. In addition, the new Treaty (Art. 17) fully incorporates the so-called 'Petersberg Tasks'—humanitarian and rescue tasks, peacekeeping tasks, and tasks of combat forces in crisis management, including peace-making—as foreign policy objectives of the EU, and it provides a new CFSP policy tool to help improve coherence: common strategies (Arts 12, 13).

---

[14] For example, the despatch of European observers during the cease-fire between Slovenia and Croatia and the EU's administration of Mostar relied on such memorandums of understanding. For more this issue, see Lopandic (1995).

Beyond these general provisions, Amsterdam made key reforms in three other areas of foreign policy: decision-making, implementation, and financing.

First, the issue of decision-making was addressed at Amsterdam, but the new provisions (Arts 17 and 23) do not go as far as extending real QMV procedures to security or defence cooperation, as some, such as Commissioner van den Broek (*Economist* 1997: 59–60) suggested. Instead, unanimity remains the rule here, and the Amsterdam Treaty attempted to accommodate both pro- and anti-defence factions in the EU by following the new doctrine of 'flexibility' in such matters, effectively opening the door to two classes of membership in the CFSP—WEU members and non-WEU members—although all states, even non-WEU members, are entitled to participate in all activities in this pillar. EU states are permitted to abstain from any CFSP actions, although they must 'accept that the decision commits the Union' and must 'refrain from any action likely to conflict with or impede Union action based on that decision and the other Member States shall respect its position' (Art. 23.1). However, if such abstaining members represent more than one-third of the votes weighted in Council, the decision will not be adopted.

In non-defence-related areas, if enough members decide to go ahead with a CFSP decision, the Council can act *automatically* by QMV under two circumstances, that is, without an additional consensus decision to apply QMV as under Maastricht: (1) when adopting joint actions, common positions, or taking any other decision on the basis of a common strategy; and (2) when adopting any decision implementing a joint action or a common position. However, as under the TEU, there is still a powerful escape clause that may paralyze the EU: if a member of the Council declares that 'for important and stated reasons of national policy, it intends to oppose the adoption of a decision to be taken by qualified majority, a vote shall not be taken' (Art. 23.2). The Council may, acting by QMV, request that the matter be referred to the European Council for decision by unanimity, but this action requires at least 62 votes in favour, cast by at least ten members. As usual, none of these provisions applies to decisions having military or defence implications, which must be taken by consensus.

Second, Amsterdam also modifies the issues of policy implementation and external representation. As under Maastricht, the new treaty (Art. 18) provides for the presidency, associated with the Commission, to represent the EU in CFSP affairs. However, Amsterdam provides that the presidency 'shall be assisted by the Secretary-General of the Council who shall exercise the function of High Representative for the common foreign and security policy' (Art. 18.3). He will also have responsibility for the new 'CFSP Policy Planning and Early Warning Unit' housed in the Council and linked to the Commission and WEU. This provision for a new high official provoked much debate, but at least Amsterdam did not reflect the French proposal to establish a new grand political official to speak for the CFSP. Instead, the High Representative is a more modest solution, clearly subordinate to the presidency. A new CFSP representative—Spain's Javier Solana, former secretary-general of NATO—was not formally appointed until mid-1999. There was some concern that whoever held the position would be only a figurehead, but the choice of someone like Solana, a high-profile, respected, competent diplomat and administrator, is helping to allay those fears. The choice was also made with remarkably little discord, especially compared with the embarrassing debacle over choosing the first head of the European Central Bank and the headaches over appointing an entirely new Commission after the EP forced the resignation of Santer's team. Solana also seems willing and able both to raise the profile of the CFSP and to oversee a merger of the EU/WEU very soon (*Financial Times* 1999: 2). Finally, the Council may, whenever it deems it necessary, appoint yet another special representative with a—temporary—mandate to handle particular policy issues. Whether these new officials will aid or impair the EU's external policy coherence remains to be seen.

Third, given the budgetary problems of the CFSP/JHA over the past several years, the Amsterdam Treaty also outlines specific provisions in the area of CFSP financing (Art. 28) and JHA financing (Art. 41). Under these articles, both CFSP/JHA administrative expenditure and operational expenditures are to be charged to the budget of the EC, under its normal procedures, which inevitably involve the Commission and the European Parliament. There are, as usual, key exceptions to these procedures for expenditures arising from operations having military or defence implications and cases where the Council, acting unanimously, decides otherwise. In keeping with the new doctrine of 'flexibility', EC Member States who formally abstain from military or defence actions according to the above provisions are not required to finance such actions.

After years of debate, the Amsterdam Treaty also includes a unique inter-institutional agreement between the EP, the Council, and the Commission concerning CFSP financing. The new CFSP budgetary procedure is described in detail in this agreement, and it includes sections regarding the funding of various types of external actions. Considering the haphazard nature of CFSP funding since 1993, and disagreements among EU Member States regarding this issue, this agreement could be a great step forward and go a long way to improving the budgetary process. Amsterdam also mentions greater co-operation in armaments production (Art. 17.1), although there are no more specific provisions toward this end. However, since Amsterdam the CFSP has enjoyed a major budget increase, for the first time since it was established in 1993. The CFSP budget had languished in the range of 20–25 million Euro, but the post-Amsterdam budgets provide for an increase in the range of 40–60 million Euro. This increase, the choice of Solana, and the potential for related institutional changes, such as merging with the WEU, at the next inter-governmental conference suggest that the EU is still committed to making the coherence of its external relations a reality.

To summarize, the EU has managed to use a number of institutional devices in creative ways to enhance its pursuit of coherence. As many institutional conflicts have occurred within the EU at the micro and meso levels, so too have many solutions been found at these levels. These actors tend to rely upon pragmatic and inconspicuous, even clandestine, mechanisms to help improve policy performance, continuing a trend established by EPC. Larger, more complex institutional questions, such as the fundamental battle between supranational and intergovernmental visions of integration, have been addressed at the macro level in terms of treaty reform and intergovernmental bargaining. This occurred most dramatically with the doctrine of flexibility, which was the price the EU had to pay to accommodate the persistent divergence of views concerning a European security and defence identity (ESDI). However, even in this sensitive area EU governments are re-thinking their positions regarding institutional reform, thanks in part to the Kosovo crisis and NATO's forceful, though controversial, response to it. This can be seen in the Franco-British agreement at St Malo in 1998 to pursue an ESDI and in the Cologne and Helsinki European Councils of 1999, which produced blueprints for a European rapid-reaction force and for EU armaments cooperation.

All three logics of individual action discussed in this volume—rational choice, appropriateness, and social skill—have motivated various solutions. For example, regularly using EC funds for the CFSP is seen as a rational way to solve the problem of delays when EU states have failed to make their own contributions. Allowing the EP to have some oversight over these funds reflects acceptance of the Parliament's appropriate—that is, legal and legitimate—role in approving the EC budget. And certain new arrangements such as CFSP counsellors and tri-pillar working groups attest to the social skill and creativity of those most closely involved with the EU's external affairs. Moreover, it should be kept in mind that EU actors themselves may respond to one logic of action over another. Some individuals, such as those representing the United Kingdom, are motivated to find pragmatic solutions to recognized problems; others, such as those representing France, are driven by a grander vision of the EU's proper place in the world. And still others, such as Commission officials, are required to satisfy all three logics: as the chief policy initiators and administrators—rational logic; as guardians of the EU's treaties and rules—appropriateness logic; and as the primary locus of the EU's institutional memory and its evolving operating procedures—social skill.

One final point concerns the question of whether these reforms, and the principle of external coherence itself, are likely to persist or instead will be rolled back because they are ultimately unworkable. The experience of the EU in general and of its external relations capacities in particular suggests that the former outcome—reproduction and incremental adaptation—will be the case. EU external relations rest on a fairly solid foundation of Community provisions and the experience of EPC and, to a lesser extent perhaps, of Trevi and Schengen. In other words, the logics of rationality and appropriateness are becoming even more salient in the pursuit of coherence: new rules in this area must be respectful of both the functional record of EC/EPC rules and of the legitimacy those rules have earned based on that record. Moreover, the informal working methods and the formal Amsterdam improvements, particularly in terms of decision-making, funding, and external representation, seem to provide a feasible balance between institutional stability—to promote coherence—and flexibility—to allow a variety of responses and participants. These new provisions also demonstrate the continuing ability of EU actors to exploit institutional gaps and contradictions with new mechanisms. In other words, these institutions are increasingly self-sustaining. As with the Maastricht Treaty, however, the real test will come during implementation: when the EU attempts to achieve its formidable goal of true security and defence cooperation under the new doctrine of flexibility, particularly after the next series of enlargements.

4. Conclusion

Ten years have passed since European integration reached a new stage with the negotiations that produced the Treaty on European Union and its ambitions concerning foreign affairs. During that time, the EU has faced a number of severe challenges in that domain. Some of these challenges have fallen under the direct authority of the EC, such as the conclusion of the Uruguay Round of trade negotiations, while others have not, such as problems in the Balkans and the former Soviet Union. This chapter has argued that the institutionalization of EU external-relations competencies in terms of coherence is helping the EU forge more uniform methods and solutions for dealing with such problems.

Yet when we consider the powerful political and economic forces that have shaped the outcomes of these issues, it may seem that the EU's internal debates about the institutional arrangements for dealing with these problems have been self-indulgent. Indeed, institutional debates are partly a symptom of more fundamental problems: uncertainty about the need for an EU common security and defence policy, a lack of political will, divergent interests, and honest disagreements over policy. But to the extent that these issues are in fact defined in terms of institutions, and, more importantly, to the extent that institutional ideas and mechanisms increasingly condition these debates and conceptions of interests, they deserve our attention. Moreover, EU states and EC organizations are never content to let these problems lie; since the EU is a work in progress, there are constant pressures for reform and improvisation. In fact, questions about institutional design have become part of the regular political discourse at the EU and domestic levels about Europe's purpose, values, and identity.

Nowhere is this more relevant than with the idea of making the EU into a significant international actor. Ambitions in this area date back to the founding of the EC, and mechanisms to achieve those ambitions have been painstakingly pursued on the parallel tracks of the EC's external policies and those of EPC/CFSP and to a lesser extent, JHA. Since Maastricht, these tracks have moved ever closer together. As we have seen, and as under EPC, exogenous events such as enlargements and periodic intergovernmental conferences have acted as 'institutional moments' during which EC states reconsidered the ends and means of their external relations. External crises such as the Soviet invasion of Afghanistan, the Falklands Islands War, the Gulf War, the break-up of Yugoslavia, and the Kosovo crisis have also led EU states to engage in institutional debates. And changes in other important institutions, such as the WEU and NATO, have required corresponding changes in the EU's own institutions for political cooperation.

However, institutional change has also been influenced by endogenous factors, such as policy problems—paying for Mostar; policy successes—the Stability Pact; internal contradictions concerning working procedures; imitation of established EC rules; and the turnover of officials through institutions like the EU presidency. The more common of these institutional reform mechanisms in the international relations literature—hegemonic leadership or *quid pro quo* bargaining—played a very limited role in this analysis. While EU states did bargain over the broad structure of the Union, such as linking EMU with progress on political cooperation during the Maastricht negotiations, most innovation took place within the system—at this, at the micro and meso levels—according to its own logic of appropriate rules and behaviours. This logic is largely based on a simple, fundamental principle: do not attempt to codify working procedures until they have proved their necessity and usefulness to those who must implement them. This fact also points to the creative ability, or social skill, of EU governments and EC organizations to work out the practical details of normal policy-making in the face of contradictions or omissions in the treaties.

Finally, and most encouragingly, there is still no thought of going back to pre-World War II times of naked competition and conflict among Western European states. Coherent common policies are still difficult, but a return to the opposite end of the spectrum—wholly self-interested, short-sighted, unilateral approaches to foreign policy problems—is unthinkable. The EU has fundamentally changed the way its Member States define, pursue, and institutionalize their interests. And in the face of challenges to those interests, EU Member States tend to respond by strengthening institutions, not by weakening them. This alone give reason for hope that the EU will find its way in foreign policy, but since change here always occurs incrementally, we must be patient as well.

10

Policing and Immigration: The Creation of New Policy Spaces

PENELOPE TURNBULL AND WAYNE SANDHOLTZ

BECAUSE the Treaty of Rome is silent on issues of migration and policing, their emergence as policy spaces in the European Union offers a clear instance of institutional innovation. The outcome of this innovation was the Third Pillar of the European Union, on Justice and Home Affairs (JHA). This chapter, like those by McNamara and Smith (this volume), accounts for the institutionalization of new policy competences and arenas for governance. We primarily address the early phases of institutionalization, when new rules and practices emerge. Because policing and immigration are still relatively new additions to the institutional structure of the EU, we cannot yet say much about the later stages of institutionalization, when actors fully adapt to the new structures, and when rules and practices acquire a stable, taken-for-granted quality. We do, however, report some evidence in the conclusion that actors are beginning to reorient their activities in JHA and offer propositions regarding the potential for future institutionalization in these arenas.

With the 1991 Treaty on European Union (TEU), migration and policing were formally intertwined in the Third Pillar. The TEU thus imposed a significant degree of centralization and codification on hitherto separate domains. In fact, with the implementation of the TEU, most of the pre-existing organizations created by the Member States were disbanded. This dramatically simplified the institutional landscape and intensified the impact of entangling the two policy areas. The 1996Amsterdam Treaty then unwound the two domains, restoring the general separation that had previously prevailed, but with a completely different institutional structure. The EU had created new policy spaces in immigration and policing.

Our analysis of the migration and law enforcement domains deploys, and highlights the importance of, several of the arguments developed in the framing essay (Stone Sweet, Fligstein, and Sandholtz, this volume). To begin with, we depict the emergence of JHA as a process of institutional innovation. At the outset, no policy domain at the EU level embraced either migration or policing. We are thus interested in the process by which a new institutional space was invented. In addition, we argue that three of the mechanisms of institutional change proposed in the introduction played a role in the construction of the Third Pillar. First, migration and policing achieved a place on the agenda in part as a result of the endogenous development of the European Community, in particular, the Single Market. The removal of national barriers to the movement of goods and people within the EC implicated other public policy domains. That is, if border controls were removed within the EC, how would states control the flow of migrants and transnational crime? Equally important, if internal borders disappeared, the external frontier became crucial for regulating migration into EC states and for keeping transnational criminal activity outside.

Second, the creation of JHA responded to a dramatic change in the EC's external environment, namely, the end of the cold war and the liberation of the countries of central and eastern Europe from Soviet rule. The collapse of the Iron Curtain unleashed a flood of immigrants from the east, and seemed to open the way for criminal organizations from the east to move into the EC. Though a number of EC countries regarded these possibilities with concern, for Germany they created a domestic political crisis. Chancellor Helmut Kohl saw common EC policies on migration and policing as a solution to the potentially damaging political conflicts he faced at home.

Third, the creation of the Third Pillar involved skilled social action and considerable reframing. Helmut Kohl played the role of policy entrepreneur, pushing migration and policing on to the agenda for the 1991 Intergovernmental Conference (IGC). The reframing that occurred is not traceable to a single actor or group, but rather occurred gradually and simultaneously in multiple European governments. The reframing involved two crucial linkages, one that tied policing to immigration and another that tied both issues to the completion of the Single Market through the 1992 project and the Schengen Agreement.

Our analysis also shares with the introductory chapter conceptualizations of the logic action and of institutional context. We assume that actors seek to maximize the attainment of their values and objectives, and that they do so by matching ends to means. However, we also assume that institutional context shapes the way actors conceive of both their goals and the available methods for achieving them. Institutions do this not just by providing norms of appropriate behaviour, but also by diffusing cognitive constructs, or frames, of how the world works and what kinds of action are possible. Thus we expect pre-existing institutions to structure the way in which actors frame both problems—by tying them to current institutional categories—and solutions—by defining ranges of action that are both appropriate and feasible. The empirical account confirms these expectations. The institutionalized forms and cognitive frames already in place shaped the definition of migration and policing problems in terms of the central project of the EC, that is, the Single Market, and offered institutional structures into which JHA would be inserted.

In the following section we briefly describe the institutional landscape in policing and migration in Europe prior to the Treaty on European Union. We then assess the major internal and external changes—the Single Market and the collapse of the Iron Curtain, respectively—that provoked the move toward institutionalizing police and migration cooperation at the EU level. We devote particular attention to the domestic crisis in Germany. Finally, we analyze how the Third Pillar of the TEU borrowed from existing institutions.

1. The Institutional Backdrop Before 1991

Migration and policing began as two separate policy domains in Europe, each following its own path of development in the 1970s and 1980s. In both cases, cooperation among states took the form of largely ad hoc arrangements outside the framework of the EC. Within the two broad domains of migration and policing, cooperation was fragmented across policy sub-sectors[1] and across institutional levels—practitioners to ministers.[2] Furthermore, the most highly regarded and successful cooperation was that which occurred on a bilateral basis, often with respect to a specific problem.[3] The multiple forums that brought Member States together to cooperate on these issues were thus seen primarily as 'facilitators' for the continuation of good bilateral relations rather than as mechanisms to further the institutionalization of multilateral cooperation in the EC.[4]

Cooperation among west European states in the areas of policing and immigration developed slowly and piecemeal throughout the post-war period, generally on a bilateral basis at first. Multilateral cooperation began as a reaction to events that seemed to challenge groups of states collectively, or as a response to perceived failures of existing organizations; the European Secretariat of Interpol was, for instance, a reaction to the shortcomings of the broader international police organization. Trevi was organized to promote collective responses to the terrorist threat in western Europe. The Trevi group provided the foundations for subsequent justice and home-affairs cooperation. It consisted of interior ministers at the top level, senior officials with a co-ordinating role, and working groups made up of civil servants and police practitioners. The group had no permanent secretariat and generally operated behind a shroud of secrecy.

---

[1] Thus, for example, within the policing sector, drug trafficking, organized crime, and terrorism were largely dealt with by a variety of separate organizations with little or no coordination occurring between them.

[2] Past research on European police cooperation by the Centre for the Study of Public Order in Leicester, UK, utilized an analytical framework which classified cooperation into micro-, meso-, and macro-level arrangements. This broadly paralleled the existence of organizations and procedures which bring together local forces, middle-ranking officers, and national ministers respectively.

[3] Interviews in Brussels, London, the Hague, Bonn, Wiesbaden, and Frankfurt with senior government and EU officials, and police and immigration practitioners, 1995–7.

[4] The Trevi organization is a good case in point as it brought together all Member States to discuss issues of terrorism and, later, crime and frontier controls, and existed for over 15 years with only a meagre degree of institutionalization.

In the area of immigration and asylum, de Lobkowicz (Head of Unit, General Secretariat, European Commission) writes of 'piecemeal institutional reactions' which resulted from the 'objections of certain member states to the principle of using the legal framework of the Community as an arena in which to tackle the problem of immigration' (de Lobkowicz 1994: 99). Thus, in late 1986, on a British initiative, the Ad Hoc Group Immigration was created to begin dealing with the immigration issues raised by the Single European Act (SEA), which could not be dealt with directly by the Community. Even so, the Ad Hoc Group included representatives of the Commission and Council Secretariat, though the former was more than anything simply an observer. In 1985 the Schengen Agreement made an important, though initially ineffectual, step towards creating a highly institutionalized intergovernmental organization to manage the free movement of persons among the signatory states and to implement measures to compensate for the removal of internal frontier controls (more details below). As in the policing field, the institutional arrangements for cooperating on immigration issues in this period were semi-clandestine.

Policies at the European level were ad hoc, reactive, piecemeal, and duplicative in both policing and immigration. This general incoherence derived in part from the central role of summits in collective policy-making. More often than not the impetus for institutionalized action came from summits of the heads of government. The problem was frequently that domestic practitioners—policing and immigration officials—were not directly involved, nor their interests and expertise taken into account. For example, the Rhodes Summit of 1988 decided that there were too many ad hoc groups dealing with the free movement issue. The heads of state set up the Free Movement Coordinators Group to overcome the policy incoherence, and this group in turn had a significant impact on later developments through its formulation of the Palma Document. This document sought to catalogue the measures needed to deal with the free movement of persons; it designated each recommendation as 'essential' or 'desirable', and set up groups to oversee their implementation. An immigration group received the task of overseeing policy towards foreign nationals. The Madrid European Summit was vital in providing the political endorsement necessary to propel this initiative forward, essentially legitimizing the Ad Hoc Group Immigration as an institutionalized cooperative forum. But as the number of organizations multiplied, the result what was what Bigo (1993: 162) describes as a 'battleground of bureaucracies on a European scale'. In the area of policing, multilateral groups and forums included Trevi, the European Secretariat of Interpol, Schengen, the Police Working Group on Terrorism, and the Comité Européen pour la Lutte Anti-Drogue (CELAD). For immigration and asylum issues, the array of European bodies included Trevi, the Ad Hoc Group on Immigration, the Group of Coordinators for Free Circulation, the Schengen Working Groups, the Council of Europe, Trevi, and the European Political Cooperation machinery of the EC.

For the most part, the various European bodies that were set up to promote cooperation in police and immigration affairs generated informal practices and procedures rather than formal, legal rules. Trevi, for example, was primarily consultative in nature, and its working groups did lead to informal policy co-ordination (Anderson 1994: 12). As an intergovernmental body, the Ad Hoc Group Immigration's decisions took the form of non-binding resolutions and recommendations. However, in the period immediately prior to the 1991 Intergovernmental Conference, the procedure of choice for all cooperation was traditional international law: the convention. The 1990 Dublin Convention on asylum is a good case in point. The Convention establishes procedures for determining which state will be responsible for examining applications for asy-lum filed in one of the Member States. Though criticized for removing rights from asylum seekers,[5] the Convention seeks to alleviate the problem of refugees in orbit by determining that the more a signatory state has allowed an asylum seeker to enter its territory, the more it takes on the responsibility for examining any application for asylum (de Lobkowicz 1994: 111).

2. The Changing European Environment

A pair of major shifts in the European environment provoked a reconsidera-tion of the existing modes of cooperation in immigration and policing; that reconsideration resulted in new ways of framing the policy domains and their place in Europe. The first change had to do with the dynamics of internal insti-tutional development, namely, the Single Market. As a result of efforts to remove internal frontier controls, a number of relevant actors in national cap-itals began to link the Single Market, migration controls, and the fight against transnational crime. In addition to linking these domains, the reframing also began to envision a policy space for them at the European level. The second shift in the environment had its origins outside of the EU and consisted of an immigration 'crisis'. The primary component of the crisis was the fall of the Iron Curtain and the subsequent flood of immigrants into the EC, and espe-cially into Germany, which became the chief protagonist in institutionalizing justice and home affairs cooperation in the EU. What made a new EC policy space appear necessary and appropriate was that the two contextual changes coincided. The abolition of national frontier controls within the EC raised concerns about controlling migration and transnational crime, just as several EC states, especially Germany, confronted an immigration crisis.

2.1. Removal of internal frontier controls

The removal of internal frontier controls, as envisaged in the Single Market and Schengen projects, clearly generated tensions with other policy areas and

---

[5] There was controversy as to whether the Convention guaranteed that a refugee would have an asylum application heard in one Member State or whether it protected signatory states from dupli-cate applications by refugees deported from other signatory states.

with the basic definition of the territorial state. Both the Single Market and Schengen aimed at the free movement of persons across national frontiers within the EC. The elimination of border controls undermined a fundamental cultural frame for the European nation-state. That is, one of the defining features of the nation state was authority over a given population within a given territory, as defined by a national border. To give up the authority to control borders—those within the EC—was to compromise the claim of the nation state to regulate either its population or its territory. The crucial frontiers became the EU's external borders, and this change compelled policy-makers and publics to reconstruct the frame within which policies toward migration and transnational crime took form.

Furthermore, the Single Market and Schengen provoked policy-makers and segments of the public to link issues that had previously been unconnected. The removal of border controls within the European Community would, in the view of many, make it easier for illegal immigrants and criminals to move from country to country, and harder for public authorities to apprehend them. A Eurobarometer survey in late 1992, just as the Single Market was to take effect, revealed that some European citizens feared that it would lead to too much immigration and cross-border crime (see Table 10.1). First, it is important to note that in no country did the prospect of the Single Market provoke fear in a majority of respondents, though France came close. However, among those who feared the consequences of the Single Market, significant numbers cited excessive immigration and trans-border crime among the reasons for their fears.

The Single Market Programme that began in the mid-1980s thus delivered an important impetus to the creation of a European policy space in justice and home affairs. The aim of the SEA, and later of the Schengen Agreement, was to eliminate barriers to the movement of goods, services, capital, and people among the Member States of the European Community. At the 1984 Fontainebleau Summit, the EC heads of state decided to try to balance the economic objectives of the Single Market programme with visible benefits for workers and citizens. The upshot was the Committee on a People's Europe, the 'Adonnino Committee', which identified free movement of people in the EC as its key objective.

The Committee's first report made a number of concrete proposals to bring about the gradual abolition of all police and customs formalities for people crossing intra-Community frontiers (Turnbull 1998: 17). Furthermore, the report recognized that 'abolishing all formalities would presuppose amongst other things . . . the gradual application of a common policy on third country citizens and closer co-operation between the police and judicial services of the Member States', and suggested that the European Council should 'decide to put in hand now work on problems related to the effective co-operation between authorities responsible for the fight against crime, as well as to the definition and gradual application of a common policy concerning the entry, movement and expulsion of foreigners, visa policy and the transfer of control of persons to the external frontiers of the Community' (CEC 1985: 10).

Table 10.1: Public opinion linking the Single Market to fears of immigration and cross-border crime, Sept.–Oct. 1992

	Fear the Single Market (%)	Of those who fear the Single Market the percentage who:	
		Mention too much immigration	Mention no border controls to stop criminals and drugs
France	49	32	26
Belgium	30	37	20
Netherlands	21	29	33
Germany	37	44	43
Italy	33	17	13
Luxembourg	35	31	33
Denmark	34	32	38
Ireland	18	10	23
UK	37	30	28
Greece	23	12	8
Spain	37	16	8
Portugal	24	7	27
EU-12	36	29	25

Note: Respondents were first asked whether the creation of the Single Market made them feel very hopeful, rather hopeful, rather fearful, or very fearful. Data in the first column represent the percentage of respondents who answered either 'rather fearful' or 'very fearful'. Those who answered in either of those categories were then asked to give their main reasons for responding as they did. They were asked to choose up to three items from a list. The data in the second and third columns represent the percentage of those who answered 'rather fearful' or 'very fearful' who named 'too much immigration into our country' and 'no more border control to stop criminals and drugs', respectively.

Source: Eurobarometer, no. 38.

Neither the Treaty of Rome nor the SEA created a competence for the Community regarding the immigration of third-country nationals, that is, immigrants from non-EC countries. However, the reference to the free movement of persons in the former Art. 8a of the EEC Treaty has fundamentally altered the nature and momentum of the debate over police cooperation. The SEA defined the free movement of persons as the absence of internal frontiers and provided a date by which the completion of the internal market was to be achieved: 31 December 1992. However, two Declarations attached to the SEA made it clear that the member governments were not contemplating the creation of a Community competence in policing. One, the 'General Declaration on Arts 13–19 of the Single European Act', stated that 'nothing in these provisions shall affect the right of member states to take such measures as they consider necessary for the purpose of controlling immigration from third countries, and to combat terrorism, crime, the traffic in drugs and illicit trading in works of art and antiques' (European Communities 1987).

The second, the 'Political Declaration of the Member States on the Free Movement of Persons', declared that the Member States 'shall cooperate, without prejudice to the powers of the Community, in particular as regards the entry, movement and residence of nationals of third countries. They shall also cooperate in the combating of terrorism, crime, the traffic in drugs and illicit trading in works of art and antiques'. The Declarations show that national governments were at least cognizant of a possibility that free movement could produce increased transnational crime problems (Benyon *et al* 1993: 18). The Declarations also implied that Member States would retain the initiative in fighting cross-border crime, and suggested that interstate cooperation in these areas would take place outside of EC structures, though 'without prejudice to the powers of the Community' (European Communities 1987).

In some respects, the Schengen agreement, which aimed to create a zone without frontier controls of any kind within the EC, established a blueprint for the institutionalization of police and immigration cooperation. The Schengen initiative was largely a response to the failure of all Member States to fully agree to the free movement of persons in the Single Market programme. In particular, Prime Minister Thatcher had succeeded in retaining Britain's right to keep its frontier controls in place. During the negotiations for the SEA she forcefully stressed the sensitivity of the free movement of persons issue for the British government and secured a *de facto* opt-out for the UK. Britain would be allowed to maintain immigration checks on EC nationals at its seaports and airports. The Schengen Agreement signed in 1985 and the Schengen Implementing Convention signed in 1990 signalled the desire of a 'hard core' of EC Member States[6] to achieve the removal of internal frontiers and procure the full implementation of the freedom of movement of persons.

The Agreement of 1985 also recognized that the achievement of free movement would require 'compensatory measures' by way of police, immigration, and customs cooperation. Negotiations to develop the compensatory measures began in 1985 but, as a result of the innovative and far-reaching nature of the proposals, these were not completed until 1990. Commencing with an original membership of five, Schengen soon expanded to include all Member States except the United Kingdom and Ireland.[7]

The Convention of 1990 is a much more lengthy document than the original Agreement, in part because it addresses the tricky 'compensatory measures'. It also establishes the institutional and decision-making structures for cooperation. The working structure of Schengen was similar to that of Trevi and, through the establishment of an Executive Committee, a Central Committee, and various working groups, it provided for cooperation at ministerial, senior official, and official levels respectively. However, unlike Trevi, Schengen provided for formal institutionalized cooperation and a permanent

---

[6] Both grew out of the 1984 Saarbrücken Agreement between Germany and France which sought to facilitate free movement across the Franco-German border.

[7] It has become increasingly apparent that Ireland would apply for membership of Schengen were it not for the passport-free zone established between the UK and Ireland, and the British government's refusal to countenance any involvement in the Schengen project.

secretariat. The working-group level is divided into Schengen I, addressing police and security issues; Schengen II, addressing the control of persons; Schengen III, dealing with transport; and Schengen IV, covering customs and the movement of goods. The Agreement also provided for the installation of the Schengen Information System,[8] a computerized communications system for use by police, immigration, and customs officials.

The Convention broke new ground, and its formulation was heralded as a key element of the progression towards the codification of justice and home affairs cooperation between European states. The Convention not only provided a framework for the exchange of information and a forum for policy discussion and coordination; it also explicitly enabled operational forms of cooperation. To take just one example, Schengen's key advance in the field of police cooperation lay in its attempts to codify in international public law a number of important innovations. Most fundamentally, it identified situations in which national police authorities can operate in the territory of another state by way of cross-border observation and cross-border pursuit. Prior to this development, practical international police cooperation had been substantially limited (Schutte 1991: 555).

Schengen's development was fairly tortuous and its failings, and occasionally its inevitable demise, were widely reported in the media.[9] A number of very high-profile policy failures, disagreements, and technical difficulties have troubled the history of Schengen from its inception. Persistent acrimonious disputes among the signatory states did little to enhance Schengen's already fragile image. Deadlines for the removal of permanent frontiers controls repeatedly proved over-optimistic; and when the date of 27 March 1995 was finally set for the full implementation of the Convention, including the decisions already taken by the Executive Committee, only seven of the signatory states were able to comply.[10] The lack of judicial and democratic control and accountability was identified by many academic and political commentators as a dangerous element in the Schengen structure (O'Keeffe 1991).

In the process of negotiating the Schengen Agreement and the subsequent Convention, a number of governments came to perceive important linkages between the removal of barriers to movement and problems of migration and policing. The 1990 Schengen Convention formally reframed the issues by linking previously unconnected policy domains—free movement, immigration, and crime—under a single rubric, and by moving them to the European

---

[8] The Central Schengen Information System (CSIS) is based in Strasbourg and is linked to national computers the National Schengen Information System (NSIS) in each of the signatory states.

[9] Headlines detailing the very public failings of Schengen appear regularly in the British and European press. Examples include 'More Setbacks for Schengen', (*European Voice* 1995); 'Greeks Stand Against Schengen' (*Financial Times* 1996); and 'Low Key Optimism over Schengen Agreement' (*European Report* 1995).

[10] Despite its enlargement to include the Scandinavian states, the operation of Schengen regressed in practical terms with the number of states implementing the Convention falling to six. In response to terrorist attacks in Paris in summer 1995, the French government utilized Art. 2(2) of the 1990 Convention to reinstate its national border checks, a policy which in fact continued on the northern borders of France in response to the drugs policy of the Dutch government.

level. The actors involved in the Schengen process would later become the constituency within which Helmut Kohl's appeal for institutionalizing justice and home affairs cooperation in the EU could resonate.

2.2. Crisis of immigration and asylum

Although the form, dynamic, and rationale of migration flows into the Community differed from Member State to Member State, there are identifiable trends from the 1950s to the present day (see Collinson 1993). During the rebuilding of west European economies in the first two decades following the end of World War II, labour shortages meant that it was necessary to recruit foreign workers to fill gaps in the labour market. In the initial post-war period, refugees filled the void. The fall of the Iron Curtain closed off many of the traditional foreign labour markets that had supplied temporary labour for west European states. Later migrants were recruited from the ex-colonies, from southern Europe and the Mediterranean region, or, in the case of the UK, also from Ireland.

In many west European states it was mistakenly believed that these so-called 'guest workers' were temporary immigrants, who would eventually return to their country of origin. In Germany the 1965 Aliens Act made clear the government's intention for foreign labour to be a manoeuvrable resource for solving economic problems (Collinson 1993). In the case of Germany, the absence of colonial ties facilitated the treatment of immigration as a purely economic issue.

Indeed, once the labour market tightened in the early 1970s, recruitment programmes were halted and all west European states introduced immigration controls restricting the circumstances under which primary immigration could occur. However, the new legislative measures which were put in place across western Europe failed to reduce the number of third-country nationals permanently resident in the Community. This is attributable to two phenomena. First, the foreign workers who remained proved reluctant to leave, even though their legal status was often tenuous.[11] Despite various schemes of voluntary repatriation, often involving financial incentives, the vast majority of post-war labour immigrants remained. Second, immigration continued to rise as family reunifications occurred with increasing intensity.[12] Policy-makers in western Europe were learning that public policy could not negate the 'pull factors' that made their countries so attractive to migrants. These included the economic growth of the 1950s and 1960s, the enduring post-war peace, political stability, basic freedoms, and so on.

The 1980s saw a new phenomenon as population explosions and poverty in north Africa and the Middle East led to an intensification of 'push factors'. As

---

[11] *Gastarbeiter* were not given the legal right of residence in the Federal Republic.

[12] As signatories of the European Convention on Human Rights and Fundamental Freedoms, Member States could not refuse immigrants the right to live as families, thus allowing the immigration of additional family members.

a result there was a marked diversification in the origin of immigrants entering western Europe. Immigration did not come solely from north Africa and the Middle East, but migration from those regions came to be seen as crux of the immigration 'problem'. EC countries with traditionally high levels of net emigration—France, Spain, Greece, and Italy—became countries of net immigration as a result of the flow of people from across the Mediterranean. In the mid-1980s the so-called Mediterranean enlargement of the Community to include countries newly experiencing intense immigration placed the issue on the Community's agenda. The southern immigration challenge then interacted with the Single Market Programme that was removing barriers to the movement of people from one EC country to another. It is important to remember in this respect that illegal immigration was not just a question of people crossing the border clandestinely but in the majority of cases involved people entering a country legally, staying beyond their assigned departure dates, and taking employment. The mix of immigration and free movement issues had crucial implications for the notion of borders as effective filters for immigration.

The rise in illegal immigration in the 1980s was accompanied by an increase in the numbers of asylum applications lodged in west European states. It is clear that instability in the developing world and the growth of Islamic fundamentalism led to political and social exclusion. Moreover, refugees showed a lesser propensity to remain within the region of conflict as transcontinental travel became more commonplace. All of these factors contributed to the rise in asylum applications in western liberal democracies. Equally, it was recognized relatively early on that asylum applications were also being submitted by immigrants seeking to circumvent the restrictions on economic, as opposed to political, immigration. This can be identified as a point at which the immigration issue took on a more intense 'security-regulative' dimension. In fact, the Dublin Convention on the Determination of the State Responsible for the Examination of an Application for Asylum Lodged in One of the Member States of the European Communities, signed June 1990,[13] was the most significant legal advance made during pre-Maastricht era of intergovernmental cooperation.[14]

More generally, publics in several EU countries seem to have become much more sensitive than before to immigration as a social and political problem. Four Eurobarometer surveys, from 1988 to 1994, asked people their opinion regarding the number of foreigners residing in their country. Because the wording changed slightly from survey to survey (see the note below Table 10.2), comparisons of the results must be cautious. Still, as Table 10.2 shows, the percentage of respondents who thought that there were too many immigrants

[13] By all Member States except Denmark; the Danish government signed in June 1991, though was the first to ratify the Convention.

[14] Further support was provided by the creation of the Centre d'Information de Réflexion et d'Échanges sur L'Asile (CIREA) by the immigration ministers in June 1992. The Centre, which brought together representatives of the Member States, Commission, and Council Secretariat, was charged with providing a forum in which national asylum practices could be examined.

residing in their country jumped dramatically between 1988 and the early 1990s in nearly every country. For the EU as a whole, the share of respondents who thought there were too many immigrants rose from 39.3 per cent in 1988 to 50.6 per cent in 1991. In several countries, the percentage responding in this fashion declined modestly by 1994.

Furthermore, EC citizens increasingly associated immigrants with criminality. Table 10.3 shows the results of two Eurobarometer polls, one conducted in 1988—before the SEA, Schengen, and the fall of the Iron Curtain—and the other in 1994. Direct comparisons between the two surveys are problematic because the question was phrased differently in each. Still, the number of Europeans who linked immigration to crime appears to have increased dramatically in the period that witnessed the removal of internal frontier controls and the immigration crisis.

Until 1989, migratory flows from eastern into western Europe were primarily sudden movements of refugees responding to particular political events. Already in the public debates of the 1980s, references were being made to the boat being full and the absorption capacity exhausted. A stringent anti-emigration policy in eastern Europe and effective policing of the eastern bloc's border made regular migration almost impossible. As a result, west European states were spared the need to consider the costs and benefits of immigration from the east.[15] After the euphoria of the fall of the Iron Curtain had dissipated, it became clear that an intense reassessment of frontier controls on the Community's eastern flank was required.

2.3. The crisis in Germany and Kohl's EC solution

Germany, with its liberal asylum policy, lay at the heart of this process of reassessment and acted as a key force for change. In stark contrast to the commonly used formula asserting a state's right to grant asylum, Germany's Basic Law afforded the individual the right to seek asylum and placed the onus on the government to disprove the claim.[16] Asylum seekers were permitted to remain in Germany for the duration of the asylum application process and to receive state benefits. They could also take advantage of the opportunity to work illegally. The value of staying in Germany for the period of the asylum procedure far outweighed the costs of repatriation should the application ultimately be refused. As a result, in the early 1990s it rapidly became clear that Germany's constitutionally enshrined right to asylum acted as a magnet to immigrants and refugees alike. Germany's proximity to regions undergoing vast economic, political, and social changes resulted in a geographical vulnerability over which the government had little control. Note also that Germany's policy towards *Aussiedler*—ethnic Germans living in central and eastern Europe—allowed significant numbers of ethnic Germans to enter the

---

[15] In addition, the migration of east European citizens was considered an ideological victory for the 'West'.

[16] *Politische Verfolgte geniessen Asylrecht*, Art. 16(2)2 of the Basic Law.

Table 10.2: Public opinion in the EC regarding the number of foreigners living in one's country

		Too many	A lot but not too many	Not many		Too many	A lot but not too many	Not many
France	Nov-88	46.0	46.4	7.7	Denmark	37.1	46.5	16.4
	Mar-91	55.8	34.2	4.1		42.7	36.4	17.4
	Mar–Apr 92	51.5	35.0	5.7		46.0	33.7	17.8
	June–July 94	54.4	40.2	5.4		38.4	42.4	19.3
Belgium	Nov-88	44.7	46.4	9.0	Ireland	7.6	22.3	70.1
	Mar-91	56.7	31.0	6.3		12.1	26.4	51.7
	Mar–Apr 92	53	32.6	6.2		11.3	26.4	51.9
	June–July 94	62.4	31.6	6.0		9.7	31.4	58.9
Netherlands	Nov-88	31.3	54.2	14.4	United Kingdom	47.0	42.2	10.8
	Mar-91	44.1	43.3	7.5		54.2	30.6	9.4
	Mar–Apr 92	48.7	38.3	8.9		50.2	30.5	12.7
	June–July 94	43.7	44.6	11.7		48.7	39.1	12.1
Germany	Nov-88	48.7	45.6	5.7	Greece	21.5	44.0	34.5
	Mar-91	55.7	34.4	5.0		28.6	46.9	11.8
	Mar–Apr 92	55.0	35.9	4.8		45.1	43.8	6.2
	June–July 94	51.4	41.9	6.7		63.3	32.0	4.7
Italy	Nov-88	35.6	40.7	23.7	Spain	20.0	37.4	42.6
	Mar-91	63.0	29.0	4.5		24.6	41.3	21.3
	Mar–Apr 92	65.0	28.1	3.3		23.4	42.8	21.5
	June–July 94	58.3	35.4	6.3		31.1	46.6	22.3
Luxembourg	Nov-88	30.5	61.4	8.1	Portugal	15.4	37.0	47.6
	Mar-91	20.3	45.6	25.9		18.2	33.0	28.1
	Mar–Apr 92	32.1	45.7	15.4		27.6	42.3	20.6
	June–July 94	26.2	65.3	8.5		26.2	42.4	31.4
	Nov-88				EU-12	39.3	43.3	17.4
	Mar-91					50.6	34.0	9.0
	Mar–Apr 92					50.0	34.4	9.4
	June–July 94					49.8	39.6	10.7

Note: Figures are percentages of respondents. Data for Germany in 1988 exclude the former German Democratic Republic. The question in 1988 read, 'How do you feel about the number of people of another nationality living in our country?' In 1991 and 1992, the question asked, 'Generally speaking, how do you feel about people living in our country who are not nationals of the European Community countries: are there too many, a lot but not too many, or not many?' In 1994 the question read, 'Generally speaking, how do you feel about foreigners living in our country: are there too many, a lot but not too many, or not many?' It is difficult to guess what difference the changes in wording make for the character of responses, though it seems unlikely that the change in wording alone can account for the significant shifts in responses between 1988 and 1991.

Source: *Eurobarometer*, nos 30, 35, 37, 41.1.

Table 10.3: The link between immigration and crime in public opinion

Member State	October–November 1988 (%)	June–July 1994 (%)
France	22.4	62.1
Belgium	23.9	68.4
Netherlands	10.2	53.4
Germany	11.0	62.3
Italy	13.7	53.6
Luxembourg	12.7	32.2
Denmark	18.1	58.8
Ireland	2.7	7.7
United Kingdom	15.9	31.5
Greece	26.0	73.9
Spain	9.3	40.1
Portugal	9.6	36.4
EU-12	14.9	51.5

Note: In the 1988 survey, respondents were asked to identify groups whose presence in the country was one of the causes of delinquency and violence, then permitted to select groups from a list. The first column of data reports the percentage who chose 'people of another nationality' from the list. In the 1994 survey, respondents were asked whether they tended to agree or disagree with the following statement: 'The presence of foreigners is one of the causes of delinquency and violence'. The different wording of the questions suggests that the results should be compared only with caution.

Source: *Eurobarometer*, nos 30, 41.1.

Federal Republic solely on the basis of their German heritage. The massive numbers of asylum seekers and *Aussiedler* arriving threw the German political system into turmoil, as they imposed—certainly in popular perceptions— significant burdens on government budgets and social services. Table 10.4 shows the number of asylum requests in Germany from 1986 to 1992.

Germany's asylum system had been under increasing pressure for a number of years and suffered from the absence of a specific immigration policy. Until recent

Table 10.4: Asylum applications in the Federal Republic of Germany, 1986–92

Year	No. of applications
1986	99,650
1987	57,379
1988	103,076
1989	121,318
1990	193,63
1991	256,12
1992	438,191

Source: Eurostat (1996).

legislative changes, the right to German citizenship could be passed only through blood descent (*ius sanguinis*); nationality was therefore based on the idea of Germanness or belonging to the German *Volk* (Henson and Malhan 1995: 131). The Nationality Law of 1913 remained the official justification for the policy position that Germany was not a country of immigration, a clear irony in view of its nearly seven million foreign residents. The absence of an immigration policy *per se* increased the accessibility of the asylum system and encouraged widespread abuse by so-called *Scheinasylanten*, bogus asylum seekers.

By the early 1990s the asylum system in Germany was on the verge of collapse, with applications taking months, if not years, to process. Recognition rates remained stable at around only 5 per cent, although many more applicants were allowed to remain on humanitarian grounds even if they didn't fulfil the exact criteria for asylum. In addition, others simply disappeared during the application process. The growing impatience of many Germans towards the abuse of the asylum system was clear. A poll conducted in *Der Spiegel* in 1991 found that 76 per cent of respondents supported legislative modifications to prevent the abuse of the asylum provisions, 69 per cent supported a change in asylum provisions altogether, and 96 per cent wanted to exclude economic migrants. Building on these fears, parties of the far right exploited the asylum question for electoral gain; popular support for the German People's Union and the Republican Party peaked at the height of the asylum crisis.[17]

Despite a continuous series of legislative and procedural changes to the asylum process,[18] close to one million asylum seekers arrived between 1989 and 1992. It was clear that the number of applications had to be drastically reduced. Until Art. 16(2)2 of the Basic Law was amended, this objective would remain unachievable. Despite an acceptance that the Basic Law should be *entwicklungsfähig*—capable of development—because it constituted one of the Basic Rights, the right to asylum was supposedly unassailable. Throughout the history of the Bonn Republic, *Verfassungspatriotismus*—the identification of the German public with the Basic Law—has been a profound public sentiment. The act of changing the constitution to stop the flood of refugees could not be approached as a legislative technicality, a reality intensified by the fact that Germany's history added a greater moral burden to the debate.

The difficulties surrounding the future of the right to asylum in Germany embroiled the domestic party political arena in a long and acrimonious conflict. Constitutional change required a two-thirds majority in favour in both the Bundestag and Bundesrat, meaning the ruling Conservative-Liberal coalition (CDU/CSU/FDP), itself divided on the issue, had to secure the support of the opposition Social Democrats (SPD). As the debate progressed it

---

[17] Both parties surpassed the 5 per cent electoral hurdle to gain representation in the state parliaments in Bremen, Schleswig Holstein, and Baden-Württemberg. In the last case, the Republican Party polled 10 per cent of the vote and became the third largest party in the Landtag.

[18] Between 1977 and 1994 there were over 30 laws, decrees, and regulations with the main objective of deterring refugees. Measures have included cutting the right to social security, refusing work permits in the first year of application, and accelerating the application process.

became clear that cleavage lines on the issue cut through parties as well as between them. In general the conservative CDU/CSU favoured amendment but faced the opposition of its coalition partner—the liberal FDP—and the opposition SPD. The debate was complicated by the fact that at times the CSU seemed closer to the SPD on certain issues than to the FDP. In addition, FDP Foreign Minister Genscher made statements clearly at odds with his own party's official line. In late 1991 it appeared as if the party political system was incapable of resolving the problem and references to a 'national state of emergency' were made by Chancellor Kohl.

The German government, facing stalemate and crisis at home, sought solutions in the European arena within the context of the IGC on political union. Jürgen Trittin, then Minister for Federal and European Affairs in Lower Saxony, remarked that the 'trend for a European solution to the asylum problem . . . is primarily motivated by domestic political factors' (Trittin 1993: 191). During the IGC, the German delegation forced the debate on European immigration/asylum policy and police cooperation with highly ambitious policy papers with far-reaching consequences for Art. 16(2)2. As one Council official indicated, 'governments with difficulties in national parliaments found it easier to negotiate regulations in the European Community which had direct effect at home than they did to carry domestic legislation' (Crowe 1993: 174). Although initially presented as two separate proposals in June 1991, by the end of October 1991 the immigration/asylum and Europol issues were combined in one paper recommending the insertion in the EEC Treaty of a new 'Part Four' titled 'Internal Affairs and Judicial Cooperation'. The ongoing fusion of immigration and policing, initially stimulated by the need for 'compensatory measures' in a Europe without internal frontiers, thus found expression in the proposed institutional design of Part Four.

The reframing of the two sectors into a single area of cooperation also reflected German domestic developments. The obvious illegality of *Scheinasylanten*, the increasing phenomenon of trafficking of illegal immigrants by organized criminal gangs with a strong foreign association, and the creation of a distinct category of crimes by foreigners—*Ausländerkriminalität*—within public discourse are just some of the developments that had led increasingly to the linkage of immigration and policing in the domestic arena. Similar patterns were repeated in other Member States.

Remarkably, given the extent of domestic opposition to constitutional change, the government's plans for European cooperation received little if any resistance. A wide range of factors empowered Kohl and his representatives as they sought to impose a European solution on the domestic crisis. Kohl's role as European entrepreneur was supported by his personal strength in EC policy (Paterson 1998) as well as domestic institutional factors, such as the constitutionally defined *Richtlinienkompetenz*—the power of the Chancellor to set policy guidelines. Within Germany, European politics had long been subject to a permissive consensus among the main political parties, the federal and State governments, and the general public. During the 1991 IGC, the federal government's position was widely supported across the political spectrum, even though some of the debates on European harmonization contradicted positions taken on the issue of constitutional change. For instance, the Bundestag's consideration of the Maastricht Treaty emphasized a more restrictive asylum policy than the one allowed by Art. 16(2)2 (Mazzucelli 1995: 67). Furthermore, public opinion was clearly in support of common rules in matters of asylum and immigration. A December 1992 Eurobarometer Report indicated that 81 per cent of Germans polled supported harmonization in these policy domains. The widespread support for European policies should be viewed cautiously however, as at this stage there was little conception or understanding of what common policies or harmonization would entail. It was Kohl's vision and Germany's historical and accepted role as the *Musterknabe*—paragon—of the EC that underpinned German support for European harmonization and opened Kohl's leeway as policy entrepreneur.[19]

3. The New European Migration and Policing Agenda

By 1990, the factors that would bring police and immigration policies together and push them on to the EC agenda were operating. On the one hand, the dominant institutional programme in the EC was the Single Market, which, along with Schengen, envisaged free movement of persons and the removal of frontier controls. A variety of actors at various levels in Member States, and significant segments of the public, started to perceive that the abolition of internal border controls could have an impact on migration and transnational crime. The Schengen Convention represented a first formal effort to link these issues and reframe them at the European level. On the other hand, rising flows of immigrants and asylum seekers highlighted the traditional function of border controls to deal with illegal immigration and transnational crime. The EU's external borders became the relevant ones. Given the flood of immigrants from the east, Germany experienced the crisis most acutely. Helmut Kohl saw a common approach at the EU level as a way to avoid damaging domestic political battles.

Within law enforcement circles, frontiers have provided vital filters in the fight against transnational crime, that is, trafficking of illegal drugs and stolen goods. As markers of nationality and citizenship, frontiers are also inextricably linked to other policies, most notably immigration and asylum (Anderson *et al.*

---

[19] The German asylum crisis was finally addressed with the so-called 'Asylum Compromise' of 6 December 1992. The Christian Democrats, Christian Social Union, Free Democrats, and Social Democrats agreed to amend the asylum provision of the Basic Law and the necessary two-thirds majority in the Bundestag and Bundesrat was achieved. The revised Art. 16 of the Basic Law, though retaining the right to asylum for every persecuted individual, was joined by five sub-clauses that significantly circumscribed this provision. In particular, the right no longer applies to those entering Germany from or through a 'safe third country'—a controversial list was compiled—or from a 'safe country of origin'. Additionally, Art. 16 facilitates the rapid deportation of those deemed to present 'manifestly unfounded' applications.

1995: 124). As a result, the separation between policing functions and immigration policies became muddied, and the perception grew that the two needed to be addressed jointly at the European level. This is not a functional argument that the removal of internal barriers to movement gave rise to twin problems of transnational crime and illegal immigration, which in turn would have to be addressed at the EC level. Police practitioners, for example, have been cautious about drawing an explicit connection between the removal of internal frontier controls and crime levels, recognizing that border controls offer virtually no obstacle to the minimally intelligent criminal (Turnbull 1999: 191).

Indeed, there is little evidence that the elimination of border controls produced a surge in crime and illegal migration. Benyon *et al.*'s lengthy investigation into police cooperation in Europe comes to vigorous conclusions: 'First, there is an inverse relationship between the rhetoric in the statements [about increases in crime] and the evidence offered to support them. Secondly, no attempt is made to differentiate between the fear of crime and the actual risks of criminal victimisation. The fears may be genuine, but they are almost certainly misplaced. Abolishing controls at the frontiers will add little or nothing to the scope for international crime of a serious nature'. They go on to say that 'the removal of internal frontiers will facilitate some criminal activity in a choice of jurisdictions. The removal of border controls in themselves will not produce an automatic increase in rates of serious crime' (Benyon *et al.* 1993: 53).

Furthermore, crime levels had been rising in all of the major industrialized countries except Japan for three decades. It would be difficult, to say the least, to show that the removal of border controls increased crime rates in EU states beyond the underlying trend. What mattered, in this as in other cases, were the perceptions of publics and policy-makers. People act not on what is objectively true but on what they believe to be true. A significant share of the public and of policy-making elites in Europe believed that the removal of internal border controls would lead to problems of immigration and transnational crime (see Table 10.1). A Eurobarometer poll in late 1993 asked citizens what their primary reaction was to the prospect of a complete removal of frontier controls pursuant to the recently implemented Single Market programme. The question, whose results appear in Table 10.5, was asked in only four countries, but the four are at the heart of the EU. In each country, the share of respondents who worried about increased crime was significantly greater than the share of respondents who were pleased that people could travel with fewer restrictions.

In our view, that perception grew out of a significant shift in the cultural framing of borders and their functions. That is, people confronted not the reality of exploding transnational crime but the reconfiguring of traditional social meanings and symbols. In this context of flux and change, various actors could mix the issues of policing and immigration for political advantage.

At its most simple level the implications of the freedom of movement for migration and policing stemmed from the need to substitute tightened

Table 10.5. Reactions in four countries to the removal of frontier controls

	Happy that people can travel without restrictions	Worried about crime rates with open borders	Don't know
France	44.1	49.1	6.8
Belgium	35.9	55.8	8.3
Germany	41.3	55.4	3.3
Netherlands	32.5	64.2	3.3
4-average	42.2	52.8	5.0

Note: Figures are percentages of respondents. The average for the four countries is calculated using the values for each country weighted according to its share of the total EU-12 population. The question reported here was asked only in the four countries listed. Respondents were asked: 'Since the completion of the Single European Market at the beginning of 1993, people crossing internal EC borders, that is border between Member States, are not checked as much as before. In the future, these controls are to disappear completely. Which of the following two opinions comes closest to your own?'

Source: *Eurobarometer*, no. 40.

external frontier controls for dissolving *internal* frontier controls and to increase cooperation within the EU to that end: the so-called compensatory measures. 'Controls at all crossing points of the external frontier should be equally effective in preventing the entry of illegal immigrants so that, within the external frontier, there could be free movement of persons' (Anderson *et al.* 1995: 121). Not surprisingly, a large majority of EU citizens supported the idea that policies on immigration and asylum should be set at the EU level rather than the national level, as Fig. 10.1 shows.

The Palma Document which set out the steps for achieving the free movement of persons objective prior to the TEU made the policing-immigration question clear, calling for increased law enforcement cooperation in addition to the harmonization of procedures governing the crossing of the Community's external frontier.

This linkage strengthened the 'them and us' mentality further, in particular as the majority of the countries on the EU's land frontiers underwent significant economic, political, and social changes, thus experiencing significant push factors for migration. It has also been suggested that for the first time a Community objective actually increased the fears of its citizens: that is, the free movement of persons would also mean the free movement of criminals and illegal immigrants (de Lobkowicz 1994: 104).

Even while cooperation remained intergovernmental, the debate on the many facets of illegal immigration had gathered pace in the late 1980s. In London in November 1992 three texts were adopted, dealing with manifestly unfounded asylum applications, the principle of the first-host country, and countries with no risk of persecution. The collapse of the Soviet Union and the fall of the Berlin Wall undermined the deadly stability of the cold war and left a discursive vacuum in which the previous political and strategic givens were

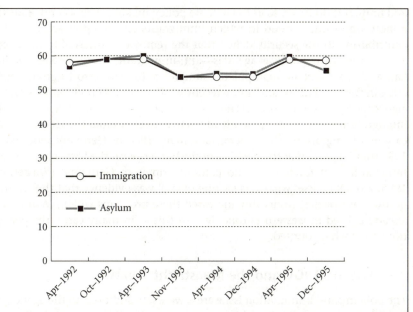

Fig. 10.1. Percentage of *Eurobarometer* respondents who believed that immigration and asylum policies should be decided at the European level

Note: Respondents were presented with a list of policy areas and asked which they thought 'should be decided by the national government and which should be decided jointly within the European Community'. The graph shows the percentage of subjects who said that immigration and asylum policies should be decided by the EC.

Source: Eurobarometer, nos 37–44.

not readily replaced. The sudden disappearance of direct military threats from the east refocused elite and public attention away from traditional security issues threats towards issues of internal security and societal stability. The steady flow of asylum seekers and immigrants who headed into the Member States—most notably Germany, see above—intensified public and elite sentiment that an already strained social equilibrium was in danger of being further undermined.

Fears of a tidal wave of immigrants and refugees were accompanied by concerns that a westward spread of Russian and east European organized crime networks was imminent. The debate has been more pronounced in some countries than others for reasons of both geography—an estimated 60,000 vehicles have been stolen and exported by organized crime groups operating in Germany (Schmidt-Nothen 1995: 34)—and legal terminology—no legal provisions in the UK with which to designate organized crime as an offence *per se*.

The linking of policing and immigration policies has two facets. One relates to the need to understand the interdependence of free movement with crime and immigration issues so as to facilitate policy-making. The second relates to a more unfortunate trend in which immigrants and refugees are viewed as contributing to the security deficit that the removal of internal frontiers creates. Actors with political agendas—anti-immigrant, anti-foreigner, or just 'law and order'—could manipulate examples of foreign terrorist groups operating in western Europe and, more recently, of organized crime gangs with foreign origins or connections. The rise of Islamic fundamentalism and the immigration waves from the south added to concerns about the security implications of migration. The Federal Criminal Office in Germany reported in 1995 that 'in particular the opening of the borders with the East ensures a continual influx of foreigners, who commit crimes in Germany' (Wasserman 1995: 23). Of course, what was lacking overall was evidence that the removal of internal frontiers noticeably increased these problems which, in any case, already existed in western Europe. But, in this as in many cases, the perceptions were what counted.

3.1. The 1991 IGC and the Maastricht Treaty

The policing and immigration issue areas were late additions to the agenda for the Intergovernmental Conferences on monetary union and political union. The heads of state had agreed in June 1989 to convene an IGC on economic and monetary union (EMU); they agreed a year later to conduct a parallel IGC on European political union (EPU). The Germans, in particular Chancellor Helmut Kohl and Foreign Minister Hans-Dietrich Genscher, were the most vigorous proponents of strengthening the EC's political coherence, both through institutional reforms that would streamline the EC legislative process and through the creation of a common foreign and security policy. Kohl in particular saw political integration as the indispensable counterpart to German unification. In his view, a united Germany had to be clearly and firmly bound to a strengthened European Community. Having Germany tightly integrated into a 'deepened' EC would both reassure other European states and constrain Germany (Sandholtz 1993b: 131). Kohl wanted German unification, which in his view required greater monetary and political integration in Europe. This commitment combined with Germany's asylum crisis to make of Kohl the champion of EC cooperation in policing and immigration.

Cooperation on policing and immigration, which would eventually be tied together under the rubric of 'justice and home affairs', did not fit neatly into either of the main headings for the EPU negotiations. As traditional—international—security arrangements in Europe were undergoing a period of intense reassessment, it is unsurprising that the 'new' security agenda of policing and immigration took a backseat at the negotiations. The desire to build new foreign and security policy mechanisms in a changing pan-European landscape made first claim on the attention and energies of the negotiators on the 'political'—that is, non-EMU—side of the IGC. In addition, the low-key, behind-the-scenes nature of international police and migration cooperation in the years prior to the 1991 IGC ensured there was limited pressure from public or media attention. The issue found its way on to the agenda along with a number of other proposed reforms under the heading 'extension of competences' (Turnbull 1998: 19). Neglect of the issue continued throughout much of the initial phase of the IGC. Finally, and perhaps most importantly, the wide divergence of opinions on all aspects of cooperation—its objective, shape, functions, and so on—reinforced the inclination of most negotiators to set policing and migration issues aside.

Thus, immigration and policing made little impact on the IGC's agenda until its cause found a new and vociferous champion. The policy entrepreneur in this case was Helmut Kohl, who was in the thick of a political crisis at home over the issues of immigration and asylum. European cooperation seemed to Kohl to offer a solution to an increasingly stressful domestic problem (Henson and Malhan 1995). Furthermore, during the 1988 German presidency of the EC, Kohl had already spoken of the need for European cooperation in the policing field (Anderson 1989: 30). Germany, in fact, was the only state to submit concrete policy proposals. In response, the Luxembourg European Council asked the ministers responsible for immigration to bring proposals on the harmonization of immigration and asylum policies to the negotiations at Maastricht. At the Conference, there was neither strong support for nor opposition, beyond Britain, to the idea that home and justice affairs could constitute a separate, essentially intergovernmental 'pillar' of the emerging EU structure, alongside to the Common Foreign and Security Policy Pillar. Germany submitted two policy papers, one on immigration and asylum and the other on policing—a proposal to create a Europol—then accepted the first compromises offered by the other delegations (Turnbull 1998: 22).

The substance, and many of the problems, of the Third Pillar, on Justice and Home Affairs, are explicable largely in terms of the pre-existing policy frames in these domains and the institutional structure of the IGC. Title VI of the TEU established the Third Pillar, Justice and Home Affairs. The policy areas to be encompassed within this rubric were enumerated in Art. K.1, which named nine 'matters of common interest' (European Communities 1992: 131).

(1) asylum policy;
(2) rules governing the crossing of the external borders of the Member States and the exercise of controls thereon;
(3) immigration policy and policy regarding nationals of third countries;
(4) combating drug addiction;
(5) combating fraud on an international scale;
(6) judicial cooperation in civil matters;
(7) judicial cooperation in criminal matters;
(8) customs cooperation; and
(9) police cooperation for preventing and combating terrorism, unlawful drug trafficking, and other serious forms of international crime.

This list includes a diverse set of policy problems and institutional actors, which neither the negotiations nor the Treaty attempted to integrate into a coherent policy domain. In fact, the nine areas defining the Third Pillar emerged not from careful study of the policy challenges and linkages among them, but were borrowed more or less directly from existing laundry lists of common concerns.[20]

The institutional forms created for Justice and Home Affairs borrowed heavily from the design of the Second Pillar, Common Foreign and Security Policy. This is a variant of institutional isomorphism, in which institutional patterns created for one policy domain are transferred, with very little reflection or conscious design, to another. The IGC on political union had focused mainly on CFSP and had given it an institutional structure that was connected to the European Community (First Pillar) but was largely intergovernmental—the Commission has a limited role, the European Parliament and the European Court of Justice have virtually none (Smith 1998*b*). The negotiators essentially copied this pattern for Justice and Home Affairs. Pursuant to the Maastricht treaty, in the Third Pillar, the Commission either shared the right of legislative initiative with the Member States or had no right to propose legislation—in policing, criminal justice, and customs—as contrasted with the First Pillar where the Commission retained sole initiative. The TEU granted to the European Parliament no active involvement in policy making under Pillar Three, but only a right to be 'informed' and 'consulted', to 'have its views taken into consideration', and to 'ask questions of the Council or make recommendations'. The ECJ received no explicit role in the Third Pillar at all, its jurisdiction being limited to conventions passed by the Council of Ministers.[21]

Perhaps the most serious single problem, at least with respect to substantive cooperation among national practitioners, was also the product of the institutional structure of the Intergovernmental Conference. The IGCs essentially empower national chiefs of government (COGs) and their personal representatives, and to a lesser degree foreign ministries. In practice, this meant that the negotiations on justice and home affairs were in the hands of non-specialists. Interior and justice ministries were excluded from the formal bargaining, and in fact were in many cases not kept informed on the progress of the negotiations. Of course, the extent of their alienation from the process varied from state to state, and was most noticeable in those countries pushing the maximalist agenda, that is, Germany and France. Reports from Brussels claim that the French interior ministry was left almost entirely in the dark and that the German interior ministry's opinion was equally discounted.[22] Not surprisingly,

---

[20] Interviews with national and Commission officials conducted by Penelope Turnbull in 1996 and 1997.

[21] The ECJ was granted limited entrée into the activities of the Third Pillar when 14 of the Member States 'opted in' to accept judicial review by the ECJ of the functioning of the Europol Convention; this solution was made necessary by Britain's refusal to sign the Europol Convention with ECJ jurisdiction.

[22] Interviews with national and Commission officials conducted by Penelope Turnbull in 1996 and 1997.

interior and justice ministries were in the end hostile to a Third Pillar that was not of their design and which was, in fact, deeply flawed.

3.2. The Amsterdam revisions

The problems encountered in implementing the TEU were institutional, procedural, and substantive. Government officials, practitioners, and analysts alike concluded that the Amsterdam conference, convened to revise and complete the Treaty on European Union, should have as one of its priorities a repair of the Third Pillar. There were, of course, diverse points of view with respect to what specific changes should be enacted. But, as theories of institutionalization would lead us to expect, a return to some version of pre-Maastricht arrangements was impossible. The TEU, despite its problems, had begun the institutionalization of a European policy space in policing and immigration. Institutionalization at one stage shapes the nature of the problems, the range of options, and the institutional possibilities in subsequent periods. The Amsterdam revisions would take place given the institutional changes codified in the TEU.

Interestingly, some of the most important reforms in the Third Pillar worked to bring it more in line with existing Community institutional forms and processes. In particular, some Third Pillar competences were shifted to the First Pillar, the European Community. However, given the sensitive nature of policing and judicial issues, the transfer of Third Pillar policy sectors to the First Pillar was necessarily limited to the free-movement issue. With the new provisions of the Amsterdam Treaty, many facets of the free-movement issue have been 'communitarized'. Under the new title 'Free Movement of Persons, Asylum and Immigration', all policy sectors directly related to free movement—external border controls, immigration, asylum, visas—and judicial cooperation in civil matters will gradually become subject to Community rules and procedures, with the possibility to introduce qualified majority voting after five years following a unanimous vote. Police, criminal judicial matters, and customs issues remain in the reformed Third Pillar, which remains essentially intergovernmental with a 'communitarian gloss'.

4. Conclusions

The formerly distinct areas of policing and immigration, after a brief marriage in the Third Pillar, are once again separate, but with a crucial difference: both have now been institutionalized as policy domains at the European level. Neither area was mentioned in the Treaty of Rome; they became EU policy spaces through processes of institutional innovation. In that respect, the experience in justice and home affairs resembles that of two other policy domains in which the EU has created new authorities and institutions: monetary union and common foreign and security policy (see the chapters in this volume by McNamara and Smith).

Two of the mechanisms of institutional change identified in the introductory chapter played important roles in the construction of new capacities for making common EU policies in migration and policing. First, we argued that endogenous institutional developments brought migration and policing to the attention of national governments and EU officials. These internal developments had to do with the completion of the Single Market, which implied the abolition of national barriers to the movement of persons within the EC. However, the free movement of persons raised questions regarding two of the fundamental capacities of the nation state, namely, the ability to regulate immigration and the ability to combat crime. The Adonnino Committee recognized that removing internal frontier controls suggested a need for common policies in these domains. The hammering out of the Schengen Agreement also led to increased consciousness of the need for 'compensatory measures' in immigration and policing, which the 1990 Schengen Convention began to address. Thus, a number of governments were cognisant of a need for common policies in justice and home affairs. They were not, however, actively placing these issues on the EU agenda.

The second mechanism of institutional change—external crisis—explains how migration and policing did ultimately enter the EU agenda and become institutionalized in the Maastricht Treaty. The end of the Soviet Union's *de facto* dominion over the states of central and eastern Europe unleashed a surge of westward emigration from those countries. The Federal Republic of Germany absorbed by far the greatest share of the newcomers. Politicians and large segments of the public perceived the influx as an unsustainable burden on the German economy and social services, and began to link immigrants with rising crime. But the possibility of changing Germany's liberal asylum law opened deep political fissures within and between parties. Chancellor Kohl saw common EU policies as a potential external solution to Germany's internal crisis, and he began to advocate creation of EU competence in justice and home affairs. Kohl played the role of policy entrepreneur, but he had a receptive audience in the governments of the Schengen states, who had already begun to contemplate cooperation on migration and policing as a necessary complement to the removal of internal frontier controls.

Cooperation in justice and home affairs at the EC level could also be justified in terms of the EC's most fundamental purposes and norms, which had to do with constructing a Single Market. The Single Market programme enjoyed great legitimacy, not just because the member governments had reached a strong consensus regarding its merits, but also because the common market was the central object and primary rationale for the European Community in the first place. Common policies in immigration and policing were framed as necessary to sustain the Single Market project by regulating some of its presumed social consequences.

The extent to which cooperation could be justified in terms of the EC's central purposes differed between immigration and law enforcement; and this difference, we suggest, partially explains the divergent outcomes, with immigration moving toward EC institutional structures—First Pillar—and police cooperation remaining largely intergovernmental—Third Pillar. The introductory chapter to this volume argues for the importance of institutional contexts and legacies. Immigration was a problem of free movement of persons, which had already been cast as part of the Single Market programme. Free-movement issues thus already had a well-developed set of institutions and policy frames, to which immigration could be assimilated, though only gradually and with significant problems. People were already accustomed to thinking of an external EU frontier; it existed, after all, for purposes of international trade. The shift of immigration controls to that EU frontier could be imagined. With policing, the reframing required was more drastic because law enforcement was not so clearly close to the EU's core purposes and norms. Rather, police powers implied the authority to investigate, pursue, and arrest people: functions that were more distant from free movement and the Single Market. Police powers have less to do with explicitly transnational relations like the Single Market and more to do with the core of domestic politics, that is, the relationship between the state and its citizens. In that sense, it is understandable that JHA remained more distant from Community processes, and more intergovernmental.

Finally, we offer some conclusions regarding the extent of institutionalization in JHA, as well as some observations regarding its future course. As argued in the introductory chapter to this volume, one can assess the extent of institutionalization by making judgements with respect to three issues.

1. *The degree to which the phenomenon in question is likely to be reversed.* The current institutional arrangements for cooperation in policing and migration are not likely to be undone. Though the initial framework for JHA, the Third Pillar of the Treaty on European Union, came in for scathing criticism by practitioners and outside observers alike, it was not scrapped. In the first few years after the TEU came into effect, some practitioners would have preferred to abandon the Third Pillar system and return to the pre-Maastricht arrangements.[23] The Amsterdam Treaty revised the institutional structure but did not return it to the *status quo ex ante*. The new treaty resolved some of the organizational problems that had essentially paralyzed the new policy-making arrangements. As a result, various actors have begun to use the committees and forums, and so to develop social networks and practices within the institutions. The more this occurs, the less likely reversals will be.

2. *The extent to which the modes of governance being institutionalized are stable, and thus likely to reproduce themselves.* We would argue, in general, that stability and reproduction of institutions are more likely when an expanding number and variety of actors find in the institutions useful means of pursuing their needs and objectives. In other words, the more the institutions serve the purposes of actors, the more they will be utilized. The more the institutions are utilized, the more actors will adapt to their practices and norms. Actors'

---

[23] Interviews with national and Commission officials conducted by Penelope Turnbull in 1996 and 1997.

socialization to those practices and norms will work to reproduce the institution.

We see some evidence that various actors are becoming more involved in JHA, which implies the beginning of the socialization process. With the creation of many working and steering groups, actors largely excluded from the 1991 IGC are now well established in the Brussels process. Favell (1998: 9) identifies three categories of actors that have been mobilized within the EU's new JHA arenas: 'specialist NGOs campaigning on citizenship and anti-racism issues . . .; cross-national military and policing experts, specializing in security and control issues on a European scale; and, less directly, regional and city-level players . . . via a concern with social policy on integration and inclusion.' In particular, police from the various member countries 'find they have more in common with each other than with their domestic political masters, and have capitalised on this to create more space for action in service of their own independent interests'. As more actors find that they can exploit EU institutions for their own purposes, stable norms and practices will emerge and reproduce themselves.

3. *The degree to which current and future decisions are structured by past ones.* In the broadest sense, the European Community's institutional legacy produced the expansion into justice and home affairs. Specifically, it was the Single Market programme that pushed complementary measures in policing and migration on to the agenda. Furthermore, because migration issues were more closely linked to the internal market process, through free movement of persons, and because the internal market was the central institutional project in the 1980s and 1990s, the migration portion of JHA ended up in closer to the EC and its procedures, in Pillar I. Policing, in contrast, was further from the EC's core mission, and raised different kinds of concerns regarding the relationship between state and citizens; it therefore stayed in the more intergovernmental Third Pillar.

If the previous development of the EU is a guide, actors will exploit any institutional space that opens at the supranational level. To the extent that the justice and home affairs arenas now created in the EU present opportunities for actors—government ministers, civil servants, practitioners, NGOs, and interest groups—to pursue their objectives, those spaces will be increasingly institutionalized.

11

Conclusion: Institutional Logics of European Integration

JAMES A. CAPORASO AND ALEC STONE SWEET

CHANGES in basic forms of political rule are measured in the social science equivalent of geological time. In Europe, the transition from the medieval form, based on personal ties and fragmented authority structures, to modernity, in which sovereignty is exercised through impersonal, institutionalized authority, comprises one such deep change. The move to a 'post-Westphalian' order, if indeed this is occurring, provides another example (Caporaso 1996). The focus of this volume—the consolidation of supranational political spaces in Europe—directs our attention to the transformation of the state system from a relatively 'primitive site of collective governance' (Stone Sweet, Flikgstein, and Sandholtz, this volume, p. 1) to the densely institutionalized system of interrelationships we witness today.

If it is true that we can gain from crafting methodological lenses for the long view, how much of significance will we miss by downplaying or relativizing the near term? If focus on the shifting and grinding of plate tectonics seems the more metaphorically appropriate strategy to institutionalists, how should we view everyday surface manifestations of these forces? In our view, the appropriate time frame is as long as required and possible. It will inevitably be greater for the development of a stable system of interest-group representation (Mazey and Richardson, this volume), which began in the 1950s (Haas 1958) than for monetary policy, where the early 1970s provides one convenient place to start (Cameron 1998; McNamara, this volume); and it will be longer for monetary policy than for development of an EU competence in Justice and Home Affairs (Turnbull and Sandholtz, this volume). Further, such episodes can never be properly told in isolation from the more macro 'integration narratives' that give our subject-matter its historical coherence (Fligstein and Stone Sweet, this volume; Héritier, this volume). Indeed, one of the core messages of this book is that, at virtually every point in time, the processes that constitute European integration have been heavily conditioned by existing institutional arrangements. If this project has been right to conceive of the construction of Europe in institutionalist terms, then the future has been, and will continue to be, meaningfully organized by the ways in which supranational governance has emerged and become real for actors. In any case, it is a brute fact that an increasing number of actors have, over time, invested in these institutions, reinforcing their centrality as loci for future decision-making.

In putting things this way, we are not asserting that we understand all that is important about the EU, or that the end point of European integration is known or predictable with certainty. We start by noting that the European state system has been altered in important ways, from a decentralized balance of power system prior to1945 to the current environment characterized by high levels of interdependence, supranational organization, and dense matrices of hierarchically organized rules. This transformation, whatever it might imply for the Westphalian order, provides us with puzzles in search of explanations.[1] This project addresses these puzzles as if they were a matter for generic social theory. What we collectively assert is that there are patterns to the changes we observe, that new forms of governance did not simply materialize from the thin air, and that there has been an underlying social logic to how supranational arenas have been constituted.

Our use of institutionalist theory to address conventional institutionalist questions is not typical in the study of the EU; counter-examples include Mattli (1999); Olsen (2000); Sandholtz and Stone Sweet (1998); Scharpf (1999). In doing so, we strongly reject the view that Europe or regional integration are somehow *sui generis* objects of inquiry. Instead, the Europe of the past half-century is treated as providing social scientists with rich opportunities for evaluating propositions about how new political systems emerge and evolve. We will return to how the group has done so shortly. Beforehand, we note that the volume also resolutely ignores the standard theoretical reference points in EU studies, which are derived from international relations and integration theory. While we view this orientation as appropriate, given the group's concerns, we think it raises some important issues.

1. Political Integration as International Relations

One implicit claim of this volume is that the processes that have served to institutionalize supranational arenas of governance have also removed Europe from international politics. Generally, institutionalists have good reason to deny essential distinctions between politics within states and politics among states, and then to proceed to the study of the particular rule-based and organizational forms found in international society. Nonetheless, scholars working in the theoretical traditions of international relations have done the most to develop regional integration theory. We wish to make three summary points about these modes of theorizing and research here.

---

[1] Until recently, a comparative social science of integration did not exist. The pioneering study is Mattli (1999).

First, although neo-realist theorists have had something meaningful to say about the conditions leading to the founding of the Communities, they have utterly failed to provide a compelling, even *post hoc*, explanation for the construction of the European polity. In the classic position spelled out by Kenneth Waltz (1979: 70–1), the emergence of the supranational in Europe is treated as evidence supporting the claim that it is the underlying distribution of power among states in the system that determines outcomes of significance. The post-World War II shift from multi-polarity to bi-polarity placed Europe under the American security umbrella, changing the incentives for institutionalized cooperation. While we can all agree that the outcome of World War II made the treaties of the 1950s thinkable and therefore possible, nothing in neo-realism is relevant to how supranational governance has developed subsequent to the treaties, or how Europe impacts upon state-to-state relations today. Indeed, one of the few straightforward propositions derivable from neo-realism would have it that, with the decline of the Soviet threat and American hegemony in the West, Europe would unravel (Mearsheimer 1990). In fact, by any measure, integration has continuously deepened.

Of course, realists can always retreat from the more rigorous Waltzian position and simply invoke state power and concern for relative gains. One possible version might view supranational institutions and organizations as largely meaningless, at best glossing first-order power considerations. The EU is redundant to the expert, who sees that the real action is in the calculation and pursuit of the national interest, and illusory to the non-expert who is comforted by the rosy cooperative glow in a world that would otherwise expose only naked power. A second possible account emphasizes how international organizations both reflect and accentuate the power of states. Just as the Security Council of the United Nations assigned permanent membership to the victorious powers in World War II, so does the European Monetary Union (EMU) reflect the power and interests of Germany. In this view, institutions and organizations are not irrelevant, but neither do they constitute fair and impartial rules for all. Those who are powerful select the rules they consider to be most advantageous to them.

Our response is that institutionalists, too, must recognize that rule systems are never innocent of power, or of attempts by some groups to dominate others (see the introductory chapter to this volume). Rules are not always and everywhere in the interest of all. One bias of the economic literature on institutions is that the dominant focus is on those institutions associated with collective gain. But institutions are not limited to situations where collective action problems exist. They are just as present in circumstances where distributive concerns dominate, and in circumstances where some actors perceive joint gains through cooperative action while others have strong preferences for going it alone. There is nothing unusual about noticing the conflictual aspect of institutions, and focusing on the EU does not make conflict disappear.

Of course, just how much institutions reinforce or mitigate power asymmetries among actors, or channel politics down certain kinds of paths while closing off others, are empirical questions. This volume is partly a response to these questions, and we think that realists are wrong. But these issues also raise tricky conceptual problems that we have not resolved. The neo-rationalists in this project tend to define power and resources instrumentally, as finite commodities that actors deploy in conflict or cooperation with others. At a bare minimum, institutions constitute the rules of the game that serve to stabilize interactions among players, that is, actors conceived as bearers of interests. For others in the group, power is conceived more constructively as 'a dynamic field that enables individuals to define themselves, existentially and in community with others. Normative systems constitute and animate these fields, and therefore also constitute and animate individuals as political actors' (Stone Sweet 2000: 10). In any event, either view takes institutions more seriously than do realists.

Second, neo-liberalism (Moravcsik 1999) and its variant, liberal intergovernmentalism (Moravcsik 1993; 1995; 1998), has proved to be a flexible framework for explaining episodes of intergovernmental bargaining and institutional design. But it has not been very good at identifying or explaining the flow, or the larger patterns, of integration across time. For Andrew Moravcsik, supranational institutions are the codified outcomes of discrete intergovernmental deliberations, which are treated partly as state-to-state bargaining over relative gains. He systematically downplays the extent to which European rule structures, and the spaces they organize, generate institutional innovation within the interstices of the grand bargains with which he is concerned. As with the *European Integration and Supranational Governance* volume, this project recognizes that the decision-making of actors who comprise or represent Member-State governments is often crucial to certain kinds of outcomes. But we also think that larger processes of integration construct the contexts for such decision-making, and that a great deal of importance occurs around and between what governments do. Last, we reject the view that Member-State governments control the pace and scope of integration in any definitive way.

Third, the present status of neo-functionalism is quite ambiguous. If the seminal works of Ernst Haas are still ritually cited, they appear to be less read than invoked and dismissed. Few scholars are willing to bear the neo-functionalist standard, and even fewer engage the actual arguments Haas and his followers made. As with the previous project, some but not all members of our group are quite comfortable being called (modified) neo-functionalists, if labels we must have. The editors of both volumes, for example, think that Haas got most things right, and that the longer the time-frame we adopt, the more prescient his ideas appear. Haas argued that economic interdependence and the growth of transnational society would push supranational organizations, like the Commission, to work creatively to facilitate further integration, at the same time raising the costs of intergovernmental inaction. As important, Haas's conceptualization of positive feedback, through loops of institutionalization connecting actors, organizations, and institutions, was far ahead of his time. Critics (Moravcsik 1993) may rightly insist that neo-functionalists never developed a rigorous theory of positive integration. This problem deserves discussion, not least because it cuts across the intergovern-mentalist-neo-functionalist divide. We take it up again in the next section.

2. Political Integration as Institutionalization

The central problematic of the book is how European political space—'supra-national policy arenas or sites of governance, structured by EU rules, proce-dures, and the activities of the EU's organizations' (introductory chapter, this volume)—emerges and evolves. Institutionalization constitutes the outcome to be explained, and it partially provides part of the explanation. In short, institutions are both exogenous and endogenous. This becomes particularly clear in the more 'sociological' accounts of institutional change where social structure and patterns of agency are more or less co-constituted, or where the actors who have helped to build institutions are then induced to behave in ways that lead to further institutional change (McNamara, Fligstein and Stone Sweet, and Smith, this volume). But even in more economistic accounts, the analyst typically stipulates, for a given institution-building moment, the rele-vant rules of the game (institutions) in order to focus on the interplay of inter-ests and agency (strategy). When the game being played is itself, at least partly, an institutional-design game, distinctions between sociological and rational-choice perspectives on change necessarily weaken. Several chapters of this volume, especially those of Cichowski, Héritier, Le Galès, and Shapiro, demon-strate this point, if only implicitly

One of the book's core messages is that institutional design and change do not take place in an institutional void, or only through the sway of actors' preferences and material resources. A rendering of prior structural facts must always accompany an attempt to explain structural change. The economist's dream of devising an explanation of institutions based solely on relative pref-erences and relative scarcities must be abandoned from the start (Field 1981; 1984). Economic theory can never be complete—all variables included—or closed—no stochastic or error term—as presently formulated, since by definition institutions are outside the basic microeconomic model.[2]

Although the project achieved broad consensus on a wide range of concepts and first-order principles, an eclectic mix of methodological approaches is

[2] The basic economic model is designed to explain allocative decisions, especially allocation of economic resources: land, labour, and capital. The right-hand side of the explanatory equation includes preferences of actors, their resources, and the available technology. Economists such as North (1990) have sought to incorporate institutions into the basic model, allowing the system of rules to interact with other explanatory factors in determining allocation. This move remains con-troversial among many economists because, by endogenizing institutions, North denies that stable outcomes are thereby necessarily efficient, but rather could be the effect of embedded, but sub-optimal, institutional arrangements. Nevertheless, for most economists, institutions are omitted or—what amounts to the same thing—treated as parameters, or constants, in the basic model.

represented in the volume. Chapters draw from economics, political science, law, and sociology, seizing opportunities from comparative politics as well as international relations, and resolutely avoiding paradigm wars in favour of devising successful explanations of institutional change in specific areas. To some extent, this eclecticism is prompted by the very nature of the European Union (EU). William Wallace's (1983) much quoted phrase, 'less than a federation, more than a regime', instructs us as to the difficulties political leaders and scholars have experienced in categorizing the EU. Further, as EU studies have grown, so have opposed disciplinary claims. In political science, early studies—and many contemporary US scholars—have used tools provided by international relations theory, while Europeans have often relied on approaches rooted in policy analysis, public administration, and federalism (Jupille and Caporaso 1999). In law, European scholars have not interacted much with lawyers who focus on parts of national legal orders, even when their respective subject-matters overlap. The European Court, in its jurisprudence on supremacy, has declared that EC law constitutes 'an autonomous legal order', and legal scholarship is still debating whether or not this order is more 'international' than 'constitutional': see the response of Weiler (1999: Ch. 9) to Schilling (1996).

This research project constitutes a denial that the EU's uniqueness precludes the use of more general theoretical materials to identify and explain the central features of the polity and of integration processes. Some may still find it useful to distinguish the 'anarchic' international system, where state power and interests are all that count, from domestic regimes, where rulers govern by law. Such characterizations are not only empirically wrong, they reify disciplinary boundaries, polarizing comparative and international politics, for example. Institutionalists typically bring common elements into the foreground. Contract enforcement is universally problematic, whether in the domestic or the international system, and the problem is basic to the social logic of courts everywhere. The binding nature of agreements, incentives to defect, the ability of parties to signal commitment, and the organizational capacity to implement decisions, monitor compliance, and use threats are variables not fixed parameters of a social setting. It should always be less important to know whether political phenomena occur within or among nation states than to know the institutional properties of the situation within which action occurs.

Of course, at some level of description, every polity is unique; but as we move on to higher levels of abstraction—the domain of theorizing—the system and its parts appear as specific instances of things familiar. This project not only collectively uses previously existing, relatively generic, institutionalist theory to guide its work; but contributors relate their findings to other approaches that are relevant to their respective chapters. The Brussels complex today possesses a system of interest-group representation, for example, so the social science on how interests organize, and with what effects, is salient to Mazey and Richardson's account in this volume. The European legal system may look new and special from some perspectives, but hypotheses derived from the study of other legal systems can generate a productive research programme on the Court and its impact on other policy-makers (Shapiro, this volume; Stone Sweet and Brunell 1998*a*).

2.1. The concept of institutions

The project has sought to draw out some of the consequences of Douglass North's (1990: Ch. 1) earlier, influential formulation of institutions as 'humanly devised constraints that shape human interaction', which include 'rules of the game', 'customs and traditions', 'conventions, codes of conduct, norms of behavior, [and] . . . law' (see also March and Olsen 1989: Chs 1–3). In the introductory chapter to this volume, the authors begin by noting that any rule or rule system will vary along three dimensions, each of which is a defining characteristic of institutions more generally. Rules vary by degrees of precision, formality, and bindingness—also called authority.[3]

Rules provide guidelines for action, of more or less clarity and precision. The rules of traditional diplomatic practice fixed vague standards for dealing with particular conflicts, but provided more detail in terms of the role and treatment of ambassadors and diplomats. As with all modern European constitutions (see Stone Sweet 2000: 41–4), the EU's treaties are paradigmatic examples of what organizational economists refer to as 'relational contracts'. Such agreements seek to frame complex, long-term relationships, broadly rather than in precise detail, by (1) stipulating general purposes and objectives, and (2) establishing procedures and organizational capacity to 'complete' the contract over time (see Milgrom and Roberts 1992: 127). The Treaty of Rome announced certain goals—to guarantee the free movement of productive factors throughout EC territory, and to produce common European policies to regulate the common market—but said less about how to attain these goals. Indeed, when the Treaty entered into force, operational distinctions between what looked to be binding rules, programmatic statements, and policy recommendations were underdeveloped. Today it may seem obvious that ex-Art. 119 EEC was specific and precise, and that women must be paid the same as men for equal work, and that maternity benefits constituted pay (Cichowski, this volume). But before the Court's announcements of the doctrines of direct effect and supremacy, Art. 119 EEC had little operational content. That Art. 119 EEC came to provide the basis for a policy of gender equality owes everything to developments that were unpredictable in 1960 or 1970. Just as important to

---

[3] Some of these points had already been made in light of certain conceptual problems that have afflicted international regime theory (see Kratochwil 1989: Chs 1–2; Stone 1994). Stone (1994) elaborated a continuum on which the rules constituting various regime forms could be situated, with the EC occupying one extreme. The continuum captures three dimensions: degree of normative precision, degree of formality, and degree of organizational capacity to monitor compliance and punish non-compliance. In a special issue of *International Organization* appearing just as this book is going to press, a research project on the legalization of international politics adopts, as an analytical or heuristic device, a continuum that largely reproduces these same elements (see Goldstein *et al.* 2000).

the history of the Community, parts of the Treaty have not been interpreted as requiring action on the part of the EC legislator and are, unsurprisingly, of little consequence. Ex-Arts 2 EEC, 117 EEC, and 118 EEC, for example, set out particular social objectives, but the European Court of Justice has not interpreted them as legally necessary to achieve in order to create the common market (Ball 1996: 338–9).

However important, normative precision can not stand on its own. Some rules may be vague, but higher degrees of formality may enable or require actors to interpret them, authoritatively. It matters that the core rules governing the free movement of goods (ex-Arts 30–6 EEC) are there to be found, as black letter law, in a formal treaty solemnly expressing the will of the contracting parties to be bound. Ex-Art. 36 EEC provides that the Member States can hinder the flow of goods across borders through national regulatory instruments if a legitimate 'public policy' or 'public morality' argument can be mustered. In 1970, no one knew what would constitute a compelling 'public policy' exception to free-movement rules. But traders, whose rights the Court located in ex-Art. 30 EEC, litigated, provoking a long line of ECJ judgements that gradually clarified, by making more precise over time, the terms of ex-Art. 36 EEC and its relationship to ex-Art. 30 EEC (see Poiares Maduro 1998). The high degree of formality of a relatively vague rule undergirded the process through which greater degrees of precision have been achieved. The dynamic is well-known to those who study litigation as public policy, and it features in several chapters of this book—those of Cichowski, Héritier, Le Galès, and Shapiro, for example.

Authority speaks to the issue of obligation. The more any rule is obligatory, or compulsory, the more likely threats and sanctions will come into play. Rules with high levels of precision, formality, and authority may be internalized by the actors, making threats and sanctions less pressing; that is, the rules are more likely to be self-enforcing. Still, the more any rule possesses higher degrees of all three elements, the less difficult it becomes to monitor compliance. Further, organs with the ability to sanction in the name of a rule of law typically have more authority than organs that do not.

There are other dimensions that could have been singled out but were not, such as the coherence of an institutional construct—the degree to which different parts fit together. (In)coherence can be a crucial problem in the legal arena, since legal reasoning commonly values consistency, precedent, and normative hierarchies. It can create tensions among political entrepreneurs, as when the jurisdiction of the various Directorate Generals in the Commission overlap enough on a given issue to bring then into open conflict with one another. The EU is typically viewed as a relatively incoherent polity in institutional terms. The US Constitution propagates the vision of a Greek temple on the hill, with all of its structures balanced in harmonious symmetry; of course, the reality of American governance is far messier. On paper, the European treaty system, however constitutionalized, looks like the hoary Gothic cathedral, slapped together somewhat haphazardly by different architects, at different times, using different materials (for more of this imagery, see the lovely piece by De Witte

1999). But just as normative imprecision begs for clarification, incoherence has led would-be constitution-makers—the Court, skilled social actors operating in Brussels, and academics (Ehlermann and Mény 2000; Weiler 1999: Part II)—to seek to enhance the aesthetics of Europe's institutional architecture. But this issue is not just a cosmetic one, as we will argue shortly.

2.2. The impact of institutions

The contributors to this volume quickly go beyond functional transaction cost and efficiency approaches to institutions. All of the contributors accept that institutions make collective governance possible and more efficient, but emphasize others roles and functions. Fligstein and Stone Sweet demonstrate that institutionalization both constitutes actors and shapes the integration process by forging causal linkages between the activities that take place in otherwise distinct supranational arenas. Since the book is about the emergence and evolution of policy spaces in Europe, some description of the process by which new arenas come into existence, the way older ones change, and how relatively autonomous spaces interact with each other would seem to be critical. The transition from a loosely coordinated balance-of-power system operating with bilateral measures and in an ad hoc way to a dense network of actors and rules in multiple issue areas turns our attention to the formation of issues and arenas. Mark Pollack (1994) has made an important attempt to generalize about how and why new issues and arenas emerged, from the point of view of the Commission. In this volume, Fligstein and Stone Sweet offer a rather different causal account, as well as comprehensive data on economic, interest group, legislative, and judicial activity across the life of the Rome Treaty.

A second way in which institutions have an impact is through their effect on the choice of strategies. Game theorists have demonstrated conclusively that, given a stable set of pre-strategic preferences, altering the institutional context will alter behaviour by inducing a shift in strategy. Under prisoners' dilemma incentives, for example, the dominant strategy is defection, given an environment of anarchy, lack of effective communication, and inability to enforce agreements. But the more an institution allows communication and encourages binding commitments—such as an international organization that carries sanctions, or simply one that increases the value of reputation—the more it will shape preferences in a different direction. Notice that this is true even though, or just because, the preferences are derived and not fundamental. The desire of a country for a trade agreement or arms control agreement may not change at all, but the institutional context could allow for a shift in strategy. In one sense, this is the whole idea behind liberal theories of government, that is, that a proper specification of institutions enables individuals to do what they would want to do in any case. All of the chapters in this volume provide evidence that actors partly seek, in building or seeking to alter institutions, to induce certain kinds of outcomes by altering the rules of game (see especially the chapters of Cichowski, Héritier, and Le Galès).

Third, institutions can change the presumptions of actors concerning the proper arenas within which to solve problems. Certainly Turnbull and Sandholtz, as well as Smith, are correct when they point out that immigration, policing, and national security were dealt with presumptively within the national political arena. The definition of crime, of criminal behaviour, of standards used in prosecuting criminals, had, and continue to have, a strong national stamp on them. Military security and foreign policy were, and continue to be, within the control of national decision-makers and institutions. Nevertheless, in many important areas, including the two mentioned here, significant aspects of problem-solving have migrated to the European level. This is true for the domains of agriculture, competition, trade, aspects of transport, and monetary policy, among other issue areas. While it cannot be denied that most progress has been made in regulatory areas—making laws that regulate or control, set standards, provide guidelines—rather than in the areas of stabilization or redistribution, such regulation is important in its own right. The EU should not be judged only with reference to an image of the state bent on producing the sinews of war, a strong centralized administration, and powerful tax-collecting institutions. It is not a question of which level of government is more powerful, or who would win in a showdown over national sovereignty. The EU is a political construction that is being built on foundations which include the existing nation states; and the division of labour between the EU and these states reflects that elementary fact.

2.3. Feedback effects

Approaches such as the one adopted by this project notice and emphasize feedback loops connecting actors to organizations, to institutions, and back again. These loops are conceived as generic mechanisms of rule innovation and institutionalization (March and Olsen 1989; North 1990; Stone Sweet and Sandholtz 1998). In this volume, a collective concern for positive feedback gives rise to themes that we believe merit summary discussion.

Despite intense debates about how best to explain or assess myriad aspects of European integration, few would deny that there is an overall direction to the EU's development. Competencies have expanded, new members have been added, new systems of rules and procedures have proliferated, controversial moments—and whole domains—of law-making are increasingly judicialized, and so on. Why? The European polity that millions of people now take for granted as providing the basic social context for their activities was not preordained, and no other international organization has experienced the same evolution or impact.

One straightforward way to address this question is through the logic of path dependence (Arthur 1994; North 1990; Pierson 2000). While this term is too often diluted to describe any process affected by its own past, we refer here only to the path dependence generated by increasing returns, through network externalities and lock-in. Since the lock-in mechanism was discussed by

Paul Pierson (1998) and James Caporaso (1998) in *European Integration and Supranational Governance*, we will ignore it here and focus instead on increasing returns in the presence of network externalities.

Once an institutional infrastructure conducive to productive exchange is in place, cooperation obviously becomes easier. The marginal net benefits of cooperation rise, and the marginal costs of additional cooperative efforts will be smaller. The infrastructure in which EU Member States and so many other actors have invested now includes not only its legislative, executive, administrative, and judicial organizations, but a system of property rights and human rights, financial bodies, and a dense and elaborate corpus of hard and soft laws and procedures. Throughout the history of the EC/EU, the infrastructure in place has never been depleted with continued usage; on the contrary, it has been expanded and reinforced through use, more like the growth of muscle mass than the wasting of a finite natural resource such as oil. The chapters in this volume of Cichowski, Fligstein and Stone Sweet, and Shapiro, among others, make these points well.

Nearly all important studies of path dependence made by economic historians (see the reviews in David 1992 and Foray 1997) link increasing returns to positive network externalities through feedback. It is often the case in economics that the utility from consuming a product or service is enhanced as the number of others similarly consuming goes up, and that this networking effect depends critically on the adoption of common standards—of production, behaviour, and so on. This is true for users of a particular type of PC, or for producers of telecommunications equipment, or even for buyers and sellers of a particular type of car. Performances related to compatibility, repair, spare parts, and communication immediately raise issues of how many others are out there in the same situation. A similar logic exists inside institutions which are, after all, standards of behaviour. Institutions are important only in a social context. Variables such as trust, transparency, signalling and communication, credibility, and reputation are salient within institutional settings, although we would not imply that they are non-existent outside of institutions. As a working hypothesis, we would argue that the more an institutional context is used, the more others will be encouraged to use it to, *ceteris paribus*. To the extent that one set of actors—say, Member State governments, or an association of interest groups—exhibits trust, transparency, and commitment within an arena, by adapting to a particular institution, others will be similarly encouraged; such dynamics are more akin to an assurance than a prisoners' dilemma game. Of course, institutions have to show that they facilitate the ongoing resolution of coordination problems, be it in trade, health and safety, or whatever. But often exploitable gains do not occur for purely institutional reasons, even when the objective situation allows profitable transactions. 'Big bills' are indeed left on the sidewalk.

In sum, actors within institutional settings benefit to the extent that rules, understandings, and standard operating procedures are shared. If EU actors, facing a crisis in the environment, have 15 different ways of responding, all unrelated to the others, the exploitation of positive network externalities will not be possible. In this case, we would say that for all practical purposes the EU does not exist in some areas. As the early integration theorists understood, only if a subset of actors shares knowledge regarding definition of problem, expectations regarding other actors, and presumptions about how to deal with the problem within a common institution, are the beginnings of network externalities in place.

We want to stress that path dependence is not a magic wand. It does not logically imply that the EU will forever expand and continue to integrate. Such a prediction could be made only on the basis of observed behaviour, over time, in light of how variables have been specified and operationalized. Increasing returns can stabilize or reverse. Lock-in can work so as to produce gridlock as well as to ratchet up gains. And network externalities can be negative as well as positive. Nothing we have said here necessarily implies an ever-upward, ever-onward view of the EU, whatever that can mean. Instead, given impressive progress in the EU, it is difficult not to entertain the notion that this progress might be profitably viewed through the lens of path-dependence theory. And when we do, we see paths taking shape and pressing forward; we see increasing returns to European institutions; and we see that logics of networking infect more and more domains of action. Not everyone will agree with their conclusions, but the issues of reversibility and deinstitutionalization are address explicitly in this volume in the introductory chapter and in the chapter by Fligstein and Stone Sweet.

2.4. Institutional coherence

While coherence is not treated as a definitional property of institutions, it is treated as a variable worthy of our attention. As we move away from a system based on the material power and interests towards one based on normative or ideational power and rules, the need to include consistency increases. Regarding a particular outcome—say, an environmental agreement—a country cannot simply say 'this should be the outcome because we are more powerful and this is what we want'. Material power obviously still counts, but it works through and is constrained by rules. Interests are always present, but they are more effectively pursued through principled arguments and counterarguments. There is pressure to apply rules evenly, to look upon similar events as requiring similar responses, to think in terms of equity, precedent, and consistency. Shapiro's contribution to this volume shows just how much rules and delegated discretion are intimately linked. Indeed, this tension makes room for judges. As soon as discretion is granted, there is pressure to rein it in, to provide interpretations that limit discretion, to progressively specify the conditions under which such and such will be allowed. All contracts may be incomplete and disputes over the meaning of these contracts may help to fill in the lacunae, but 'the relentless particularity of experience' (Eckstein 1988: 795–6) always produces new political challenges that will renew the cycle.

As critics have noted for some time (Kratochwil 1989; Stone 1994), inter-national-relations scholars have not much dealt with the idea of normative hierarchies, analogical reasoning, and normative consistency. In the international realm, to what would consistency apply? To power and interest? These things are expected to shift. The only kind of consistency expected has to do with a conformity of leaders' actions to underlying national interest. Now we are confronted with a world, a European one, that includes formal and informal systems of rule, doctrine, and precedent, and all of these things have to be taken seriously not because of their intrinsic interest but because they are important for understanding variation in outcomes. Shapiro identifies a process that requires EU administrators first to 'give reasons' for having generated a rule, then to 'give good reasons', and finally to 'give better reasons for the rule than against it'. In this world, material power can be expressed only in the form of a rule-governed, heavily judicialized, discursive politics. Outcomes of this process, of course, are no less political for being generated by normative deliberation. Thus, the idea of institutional coherence is important not only for doctrine, it also plays a role in the politics of institutional innovation and change.

2.5. Institutions and society

Another important theme of this volume concerns the relations between institutions and society, both domestic and international. Political institutions possess some level of autonomy, at least in the sense of being abstract social constructs, but they are also embedded in society or implicated in concrete situations. Some institutions, such as those that sustain highly technocratic or expert modes of governance, may be less generally embedded, but some degree of linkage to ongoing decision-making or problem-solving is required. In this volume, we see this very clearly in the chapters on gender equality policy (Cichowski) and on policing and immigration (Turnbull and Sandholtz). These issue areas provide a strong demand-side component to propel institutional change. Feminist organizations, labour unions, and pressure groups were all quite active in the judicial expansion of gender equality policy, a conclusion shared by everyone who has studied the issue (for example, Alter and Vargas 2000; Caporaso and Jupille 2001; Tesoka 1999). The Rome Treaty and the ECJ's expansive interpretations empowered domestic groups, conferred legal status on individuals, held out the prospect of judicial remedy in light of European law, and contributed to the mobilization of numerous social— mostly women's—groups. It is clear from these and other chapters that where institutions provide mechanisms for their own updating—say, through litigation—they do not simply reflect societal pressures or lock in commitments, they also provide potential for generating ongoing societal change through feedback. To the extent that such feedback loops exist, international institutions are never the analytical endpoint of a narrative that simply runs from demand to mobilization, to official decision-making and public policy, to institutional lock-in. Instead, the creation and day-to-day operation of these institutions provide another convenient point to enter a different debate about the effects of international institutions on domestic politics.

In any case, the new partly comes out of the old through social interactions. This does not happen in a simple way. Institutions are not mindlessly self-reproducing, but are responsive to changes in the environment. Given all the economic arguments one could amass in favour of monetary integration, for example, the resulting form and content of EMU are substantially different from what a team of experts would construct if they were starting from scratch. As McNamara argues in this volume, the EMU and European Central Bank emerged out of a consensus that crystallized in the 1970s. An institutional theory that depended solely on the economic data would not get the story right. McNamara uses a more sociological approach that is attentive to the broader features of the environment as well as to institutional legacies.

2.6. The demand for, and supply of, institutions

Most functional theories of institutions stress the demand side. This is true of classical functionalism of Mitrany as of international regime theory (Keohane 1984). The early functionalists stressed the demands arising from society and the way that institutions responded to those demands. Institutional economists and the regime theorists in international relations stress the role of institutions in terms of locking in bargains, signalling commitments, and monitoring the implementation of agreements. One theme of this book is that institutions have a supply side and an independent impact too. Every chapter in the book is quite explicit about how extant frameworks structure subsequent institutional innovation. How they do so, and the extent to which the demand and supply sides are linked, deserve some attention.

A first issue concerns the project's focus on how processes of institution-building achieve their logics over time. The book contains a wide range of important stories whose endpoints were never known by the relevant actors at any *ex ante* moment. Instead, the authors trace sequences and analyze patterns whose logics are typically unfolding at the same time that actors' strategies, modes of supranational governance, and institutions are also being formed or unmade. The implied assertion is that we miss a great deal of importance if we restrict our attention to what game theorists commonly model as 'institutional design' games, wherein relatively prescient actors, responding to a stable distribution of preferences, bargain among themselves to construct optimal rules to govern their collective future. The fact that, at any given point in time, relevant or potential rules can be hidden or unknown or desired—by some group or individuals, but not others—provides one of the logics of institutionalization the book identifies.

As already noted, many of the chapters explore what the introductory chapter calls endogenous processes of institutionalization, in which actors seek to build new institutions through, among other things, (re)interpreting existing ones, clarifying vague ones, and exploiting institutional voids. Héritier's contribution offers an overview of these techniques, as they have developed over time. She begins with a primary institutional order, that given by the Treaty of Rome, but notes that the restrictive nature of some decision rules, particularly unanimity voting, can freeze the *status quo*. While this voting rule provides assurance that the Pareto principle will not be violated, one can also ask about the forgone welfare of those who want change. From a strictly utilitarian standpoint, there is little difference between a change that worsens someone's utility and a stasis that prevents an equivalent gain from occurring. Yet, for many Council of Ministers' decisions through the life of the EC, one vote was enough to prevent change. From the interplay of demand—the preferences of the members—and the existing supply of institutions, Héritier describes the evolution of informal procedures for making new rules or changing existing ones. Today, running alongside the extant treaty-based rules of legislative procedure, we find ad hoc negotiations, litigation and adjudication, the propagation of soft law, and other informal norms within comitology, among others. Other chapters, of Cichowski, Shapiro, and Smith, take up some of these same mechanisms of institutional change, in light of the development of discrete arenas of governance.

A second issue concerns the interaction between positive and negative integration. Of course, there exists an important literature on this question (for example, Fritz Scharpf 1999: Ch. 2; Weiler 1999: Ch. 2). In it, negative integration—the process through which barriers to cross-border activity within Europe are removed—is taken to be a set of activities that are more or less completely distinguishable from positive integration—the process through which common, supranational public policies are made and enforced. Further, it is commonly asserted that negative integration proceeds more smoothly and less painfully than does positive integration, since it enables Member State governments to reap large and diffuse joint gains; positive integration, in contrast, regularly pits these same governments against one another, to the extent that deciding on one form of regulation or intervention as opposed to another will have distributive consequences for identifiable national constituencies and given restrictive decision rules (Moravcsik 1993; Scharpf 1999).

Scholars have not done a very good job at actually assessing these arguments in light of the actual evidence, and we are somewhat sceptical of the claims made. Building on insights developed by the early neo-functionalists, various contributors to *European Integration and Supranational Governance* argued that negative and positive integration are often causally linked to one another through feedback loops, and that these linkages regularly generate dynamics that serve to expand the domain and scope of supranational governance (for example, Sandholtz 1998; Stone Sweet and Caporaso 1998*a*). We will not repeat these arguments here, since positive integration is one of the topics of this volume. Indeed, one of the tasks assigned to each of the contributors was to explain why we observe so much institutional innovation in the EU despite

powerful forces favouring inertia and stalemate—for example, restrictive decision rules, opposed Member State government interests, and the complexity
of a veto-laden legislative process. The volume, we submit, provides good reasons to think that the distinctions between positive and negative integration
are less absolute than is commonly thought, and that positive integration has
proceeded much further than many of our theories have predicted.

REFERENCES

European Community Legislation

Council Directive 75/117/EEC, *of 10 February 1975, on the approximation of the laws of the Member States relating to the application of the principle of equal pay for men and women.* OJ L 45, 19/2/75.

Council Directive 76/207/EEC, *of 9 February 1976, on the implementation of the principle of equal treatment for men and women as regards access to employment, vocational training and promotion, and working conditions.* OJ L 39, 14/2/76.

Council Directive 79/7/EEC, *of 19 December 1979, on the progressive implementation of the principle of equal treatment for men and women in matters of social security.* OJ L 6, 10/1/79.

Council Directive 86/378/EEC, *of 24 July 1986, on the implementation of the principle of equal treatment for men and women in occupational social security schemes.* OJ L 225, 12/8/86.

Council Directive 86/613/EEC, *of 11 December 1986, on the application of the principle of equal treatment between men and women engaged in an activity, including agriculture, in a self-employed capacity, and on the protection of self-employed women during pregnancy and motherhood.* OJ L 359, 19/12/86.

Council Directive 92/85/EEC, *of 19 October 1992, on the introduction of measures to encourage improvements in the safety and health at work of pregnant workers and workers who have recently given birth or are breastfeeding.* OJ L 348, 28/11/92.

Council Directive 96/34/EC, *of 3 June 1996, on the framework agreement on parental leave concluded by UNICE, CEEP and the ETUC.* OJ L 145, 19/6/96.

Council Directive 96/97/EC, *of 20 December 1996, amending Directive 86/378/EEC on the implementation of the principle of equal treatment for men and women in occupational social security schemes.* OJ L 46, 17/2/97.

Council Directive 97/75/EC, *of 15 December 1997, amending and extending to the United Kingdom of Great Britain and Northern Ireland, Directive 96/34/EC on the framework agreement on parental leave concluded by UNICE, CEEP and the ETUC.* OJ L 10, 16/1/98.

Council Directive 97/80/EC, *of 15 December 1997, on the burden of proof in cases in discrimination based on sex.* OJ L 14, 20/198.

Council Directive 98/52/EC, *of 13 July 1998, on the extension of Directive 97/80/EC on the burden of proof in cases of discrimination based on sex to the United Kingdom of Great Britain and Northern Ireland.* OJ L 205, 22/798.

European Communities (1987). *Single European Act.* OJ L 169, 29/6/87. Full text also available at http://europa.eu.int/abc/obj/treaties/en/entoc113.htm.

——(1992). *Treaty on European Union.* Luxembourg: Office for Official Publications of the European Communities.

European Community Judicial Decisions

CFI (Court of First Instance) (various years). *European Court Reports (ECR)*. Luxembourg: Office for Official Publications of the European Communities.

——(1992). Automec Srl II v. Commission, T–24/90, *ECR* 1992: II 2223.

——(1992). La Cinq SA v. Commission, T–44/90, *ECR* 1992: II 1.

——(1994). Asia Motor France II and others v. Commission, T–7/92 *ECR* 1994: II 671.

——(1995*a*). Detlef Nolle v. Council, [Nolle II] T–67/94 *ECR* 1995: II 2589.

——(1995*b*). SIDE v. Commission, T–49/93, *ECR* 1995: II 2501.

——(1995*c*). Sytraval and Brink's France v. Commission [Sytraval I], T–95/94, *ECR* 1995: II 2651.

——(1999*a*). British Airways and Others and British Midland Airways v. Commission, T–371/94, T–394/94.

——(1999*b*). Buchmann v. Commission, T–295/94.

——(1999*c*). Cascades SA v. Commission, T–308/94.

——(1999*d*). ENS and Others v. Commission, T–374/94, T–375/94, T–384/94.

——(1999*e*). Gruber and Weber v. Commission, T–310/94.

——(1999*f*). ITT Promedia v. Commission, T–111/96.

——(1999*g*). Svenska Journalist Torbundet v. Council, T–174/95.

ECJ (European Court of Justice) (various years). *European Court Reports (ECR)*. Luxembourg: Office for Official Publications of the European Communities.

——(1963*a*). Van Gend en Loos, Case 26/62. *ECR* 1963: 1.

——(1963*b*). Germany v. Commission, Case 24/62, *ECR* 1963: 63.

——(1964). Costa, Case 6/64. *ECR* 1964: 585.

——(1970). Internationale Handesgesellschaft, Case 11/70, *ECR* 1970: 1125.

——(1971). Defrenne v. Belgium (I), Case 80/70, *ECR* 1971: 445.

——(1974). Van Duyn, Case 41/74. *ECR* 1974: 1337.

——(1976). Defrenne v. Sabena (II), Case 43/75, *ECR* 1976: 455.

——(1978). Defrenne v. Sabena (III), Case 149/77, *ECR* 1978: 1365.

——(1986). Bilka, Case 170/84, *ECR* 1986: 1607.

——(1990*a*). Barber, Case 262/88, *ECR* 1990: 1889.

——(1990*b*). Dekker, Case C–177/88, *ECR* 1990: 3941.

——(1990*c*). Hertz, Case C–179/88, *ECR* 1990: 3979.

——(1991*a*). Haupzollamt München-Mitte v. Technische Universität München, [TUM] Case 269/90, *ECR* 1991: I 5469

——(1991*b*). Stoekel, Case C–345/89, *ECR* 1991: 4047.

——(1991*c*). Eugen Nolle v. Hauptzollamt Bremen-Freihafen, [Nolle I] Case 269/90, *ECR* 1991: I 5163.

——(1993). Matra SA v. Commission, Case C-225/91, *ECR* 1993: I 3203.

——(1994*a*). Haberman-Beltermann v. Arbeiterwohlfahrt, Case C-421/92, *ECR* 1994: 1657.

——(1994*b*). Webb, Case C-32/93, *ECR* 1994: 3567.

——(1996*a*). Gillespie, Case C-342/93, *ECR* 1996: 475.

——(1996*b*). P v. S and Cornwall County Council, Case C–13/94, *ECR* 1996: 2143.

——(1997*a*). Larsson, Case C–400/95, *ECR* 1997: 4135.

——(1997*b*). Commission v. French Republic, Case C–197/96, *ECR* 1997: 1489.

——(1997*c*). Commission v. Italy, Case C–207/96, *ECR* 1997: 6869.

——(1998*a*). United Kingdom v. Commission, Case C–106/96, *ECR* 1998: 2729.

——(1998*b*). Commission v. Sytraval and Brink's France, [Sytraval II] Case 367/95, *ECR* 1998: I 1719.

——(1998*c*). Brown v. Rentokil Ltd., Case C–394/96, *ECR* 1998: 4185.

——(1998*d*). Thibault, Case C–136/95, *ECR* 1998: 2011.

——(1998*e*). Boyle, Case C–411/96, *ECR* 1998: 6401.

——(1998*f*). Pedersen, Case C–66/96, *ECR* 1998: 7327.

Other Documents

CEC (Commission of the European Communities) (1985). *A People's Europe: Reports from the ad hoc Committee.* Bulletin of the European Communities, Supplement 7/85. Brussels.

——(1990). *Proposal for a Council Directive Concerning the Protection at Work of Pregnant Women or Women who have Recently Given Birth.* COM (1990) 406. Luxembourg: Office for Official Publications of the European Community.

——(1992). *An Open and Structured Dialogue between the Commission and Interest Groups.* SEC (92) 2272 final. Brussels: Commission of the European Communities.

——(1995). *Commission Report on the Functioning of the Treaty on European Union.* Luxembourg: Office for Official Publications of the European Community.

——(1996*a*). *Commission Report on Reinforcing Political Union and Preparing for Enlargement.* COM (1996) 90. Luxembourg: Office for Official Publications of the European Community.

——(1996*b*). *Directory of Interest Groups.* Brussels: Commission of the European Communities.

——(1997*a*). *Promoting the Role of Voluntary Organisations and Foundations in Europe.* Luxembourg: Office for Official Publications of the European Communities.

——(1997*b*). *Medium-term Community Action Programme on Equal Opportunities for women and men (1996–2000). General Report 1996 of the Legal Experts Group on Equal Treatment of Men and Women. Monitoring Implementation and Application of Community Equality Law 1996.* Commission: Directorate General V. Luxembourg: Office for Official Publications of the European Community.

——(1998). *Equality is the Future.* Congress Summary 21–2 September 1998. Commission Directorate General V. Luxembourg: Office for Official Publications of the European Community.

——(1999). *On the Implementation of Council Directive 92785/EEC of 19 October 1992.* COM (1999) 100. Luxembourg: Office for Official Publications of the European Community.

Council of Ministers (1992). Report to the European Council in Lisbon on the Likely Development of the Common Foreign and Security Policy (CFSP) with a View to Identifying Areas Open to Joint Action *vis-à-vis* Particular Countries or Groups of Countries, Annex I to the Presidency Conclusions. Lisbon European Council, 26–7 June.

——(1995). *Report of the Council on the Functioning of the Treaty on European Union.* Luxembourg: Office for Official Publications of the European Community.

Court of Auditors of the European Communities (1996). *Special Report No. 2/96 Concerning the Accounts of the Administrator and the European Union Administrator, Mostar.* OJ C287/1 (30 September).

Eurobarometer (various numbers). CD-ROM. Zentralarchiv für Empirische Sozialforschung an der Universität Köln. Köln: 1998.

European Parliament (1994*a*). *Report on the Financing of the CFSP* (Willockx Report). EP Documents 209/630 (18 October).

——(1994*b*). *Resolution of the EP on Financing the CFSP*. OJ C 323 (21 November).

——(1995). *Report on Progress Made in Implementing the Common Foreign and Security Policy (November 1993–December 1994) of the Committee on Foreign Affairs and Security* (Matutes Report). EP Documents 211/241 (24 April).

European Union (1995). *Directory of Community Legislation in Force*. Luxembourg: Office for Official Publications of the European Communities.

Eurostat (1996). *Population and Social Conditions: Asylum Seekers*. Luxembourg: Office for Official Publications of the European Communities.

——(1997). *Economic Activities in the European Union*. Luxembourg: Office for Official Publications of the European Communities.

General

Alesina, Alberto, and Grilli, Voter (1992). 'The European Central Bank: Reshaping Monetary Politics in Europe', in Matthew Canzoneri *et al.* (eds), *Establishing a Central Bank: Issues in Europe and Lessons from the U.S.* Cambridge: Cambridge University Press.

Alter, Karen (1998). 'Who are the "Masters of the Treaty"? European Governments and the European Court of Justice'. *International Organization*, 52: 121–47.

——and Meunier-Aitshalia, Sophie (1994). 'Judicial Politics in the European Community: European Integration and the Pathbreaking Cassis de Dijon Decision'. *Comparative Political Studies*, 26: 535–61.

——and Vargas, Jeannette (2000). 'Explaining Variation in the Use of European Litigation Strategies: European Community Law and British Gender Equality Policy'. *Comparative Political Studies*, 33: 452–82.

Allen, D. (1996). 'Competition Policy', in H. Wallace and W. Wallace (eds), *Policy Making in the European Union*. Oxford: Oxford University Press.

——and Smith, Michael (1994). 'External Policy Developments'. *Journal of Common Market Studies*, 32: 67–86.

Ameniya, T. (1985). *Advanced Econometrics*. Cambridge, MA: Harvard University Press.

Anderson, Malcolm (1989). *Policing the World: Interpol and the Politics of International Police Co-operation*. Oxford: Oxford University Press.

——(1994). 'The Agenda for Police Cooperation', in Malcolm Anderson and Monica den Boer (eds), *Policing Across National Boundaries*. London: Pinter.

——and den Boer, Monica (eds) (1994). *Policing Across National Boundaries*. London: Pinter.

————, Cullen, Peter, Gilmore, William, Raab, Charles, and Walker, Neil (1995). *Policing the European Union*. Oxford: Clarendon Press.

Anderson, S. and. Eliasson, K. (1991). 'European Community Lobbying'. *European Journal of Political Research*, 20: 173–87.

————(1993). *Making Policy in Europe*. London: Sage.

Andrews, David (1999). 'History as Destiny: The Committee of Governors and the Origins of EMU'. Paper presented at the 1999 Annual Meeting of the American Political Science Association. Atlanta, GA.

Armstrong, Kenneth A. and Bulmer, Simon J. (1998). *The Governance of the Single European Market*. Manchester: Manchester University Press.

Arthur, Brian W. (1990). 'Positive Feedbacks in the Economy'. *Scientific American*, 262: 92–9.

——(1994). *Increasing Returns and Path Dependence in the Economy*. Ann Arbor: University of Michigan Press.

Aspinwall, Mark and Greenwood, Justin (1998). 'Conceptualising collective action in the European Union', in Justin Greenwood and Mark Aspinwall (eds), *Collective Action in the European Union: Interests and the New Politics of Associability*. London: Routledge.

Auroux, J. (1997). *Réforme des zonages et aménagement du territoire. Rapport au Premier ministre*. Paris: DATAR.

Axelrod, Robert (1986). 'An Evolutionary Approach to Norms'. *American Political Science Review*, 80: 1095–111.

——(1984). *The Evolution of Cooperation*. New York: Basic Books.

Bache, I (1998). *The Politics of European Regional Policy: Multi-level Governance or Flexible Gate-keeping?* Sheffield: Sheffield University Press.

——(1999). 'The Extended Gate Keeper: Central Government and the Implementation of EC Regional Policy in the UK'. *Journal of European Public Policy*, 6: 28–45.

Ball, Carlos (1996). 'The Making of a Transnational Capitalist Society: The Court of Justice, Social Policy, and Individual Rights'. *Harvard Journal of International Law*, 37: 307–88.

Bamforth, N. (1993). 'The Changing Concept of Sex Discrimination'. *Modern Law Review*, 56: 872–80.

Bartle, Ian (1999). 'Transnational Interests in the European Union: Globalization and Changing Organization in Telecommunications and Electricity'. *Journal of Common Market Studies*, 37: 363–83.

Bates, Robert H. (1988). 'Contra Contractarianism: Some Reflections on the New Institutionalism'. *Politics and Society*, 16: 387–401.

Bauer, Michael W. (1999). 'Limitation to Agency Control in EU Policy-Making: The Commission and the Poverty Programmes'. Unpublished Manuscript, European University Institute, Department of Social and Political Sciences, Florence.

Baum, Michael J. (1995/96). 'The Maastricht Treaty as High Politics: Germany, France, and European Integration'. *Political Science Quarterly*, 110: 605–24.

——(1996). *An Imperfect Union: The Maastricht Treaty and the New Politics of European Integration*. Boulder, CO: Westview.

Baumgartner, F. and Jones, B. (1991). 'Agenda Dynamics and Policy Subsystems'. *The Journal of Politics*, 53: 1044–73.

Begg, David, de Grauwe, Paul, Giavazzi, Francesco, Uhlig, Harald, and Wyplosz, Charles (1998). *The ECB: Safe At Any Speed? Monitoring the European Central Bank* (Report No. 1). London: Centre for Economic Policy Research.

Benyon, John, Turnbull, Lynne, Willis, Andrew, Woodward, Rachel, and Beck, Adrian (1993). *Police Co-operation in Europe: An Investigation*. Leicester: Centre for the Study of Public Order, University of Leicester.

Berman, Sheri and McNamara, Kathleen R. (1999). 'Bank on Democracy: Why Central Banks Need Public Oversight'. *Foreign Affairs*, 78: 2–8.

Bigo, Didier (1994). 'The European Internal Security Field: Stakes and Rivalries in a Newly Developing Area of Police Intervention', in Malcolm Anderson and Monica den Boer (eds), *Policing Across National Boundaries*. London: Pinter.

Bini-Smaghi, Lorenzo (1991). 'Exchange Rate Variability and Trade: Why Is It So Difficult to Find any Empirical Relationship?'. *Applied Economics*, 23: 927–37.

Bishop S. (1995). 'State Aids: Europe's Spreading Cancer'. *European Competition Law Review*, 16: 331–3.

Boch, Christine (1996). 'Case Law: Court of Justice'. *Common Market Law Review*, 33: 547–67.

Bolten, J. (1991). 'From Schengen to Dublin: The New Frontiers of Refugee Law'. *Nederlands Juristenblad*, 5: 165–78.

Boyer, R. (1997). 'The Uncertainties of French Statist Capitalism', in C. Crouch and W. Streeck (eds), *The Diversity of Capitalism in Europe*. London: Sage.

Brunsson, Nils (1989). *The Organization of Hypocrisy: Talk, Decisions and Actions in Organizations*. Chichester: Wiley and Sons.

Buiter, Willem H. (1999). 'Alice in Euroland'. *Journal of Common Market Studies*, 37: 181–209.

Burke, Kenneth (1969). *A Grammar of Motives*. Berkeley: University of California Press.

Burley, A.-M. and Mattli, W. (1993). 'Europe Before the Court: A Political Theory of Legal Integration'. *International Organization*, 47: 41–76.

Butt Philip, A. (1985). *Pressure Groups in the European Community*. London: University Association for Contemporary European Studies (UACES).

Calvert, Randall L. (1995). 'Rational Actors, Equilibrium, and Social Institutions', in J. Knight and I. Sened (eds), *Explaining Social Institutions*. Ann Arbor: University of Michigan Press.

——and Johnson, J. (1998). *Interpretation and Coordination in Constitutional Politics* (Working Paper No. 15). Rochester: Department of Political Science, University of Rochester.

Cameron, David (1998). 'Creating Supranational Authority in Monetary and Exchange Rate Policy: The Sources and Effects of EMU', in Wayne Sandholtz and Alec Stone Sweet (eds), *European Integration and Supranational Governance*. Oxford: Oxford University Press.

Caporaso, James A. (1996). 'The European Community and Forms of State: Westphalian, Regulatory, or Post-Modern'. *Journal of Common Market Studies*, 34: 29–52.

——(1998). 'Regional Integration Theory: Understanding our Past and Anticipating Our Future', in W. Sandholtz and A. Stone Sweet (eds), *European Integration and Supranational Governance*. Oxford: Oxford University Press.

——and Jupille, Joseph (2001). 'The Europeanization of Gender Equality Policy and Domestic Structural Change', in Maria Green Cowles, James A. Caporaso, and Thomas Risse (eds), *Transforming Europe: Europeanization and Domestic Change*. Ithaca, NY: Cornell University Press.

Caracciolo di Torella, Eugenia (1999). 'Recent Developments in Pregnancy and Maternity Rights'. *Industrial Law Journal*, 28: 276–82.

Cheyne, Ilona (1994). 'International Agreements and the European Community Legal System'. *European Law Review*, 19: 581–98.

Chowdhury, Abdur R. (1993). 'Does Exchange Rate Volatility Depress Trade Flows? Evidence from Error-Correction Models'. *Review of Economics and Statistics*, 75: 700–7.

Cichowski, Rachel A. (1998). 'Integrating the Environment: The European Court and the Construction of Supranational Policy'. *Journal of European Public Policy*, 5: 387–405.

Cini, M. and MacGowan, L (1998). *Competition Policy in the European Union*. Basingstoke: Macmillan.

Coen, David (1997). 'The Evolution of the Large Firm as a Political Actor in the European Union'. *Journal of European Public Policy*, 4: 91–108.

——(1998). 'The European Business Interest and the Nation-state: Large-firm Lobbying in the European Union and Member States'. *Journal of Public Policy*, 18: 75–100.

Cohen, E. (1989). *L'État-brancardier*. Paris: Calmann-Lévy.

Cohen, E. (1992). *Le colbertisme high-Tech*. Paris: Hachette/pluriel.

Coignez, Veerle (1992). 'A Test Case of Consistency: The San Jose Dialogue', in Reinhardt Rummel (ed.), *Toward Political Union: Planning a Common Foreign and Security Policy in the European Community*. Boulder, CO: Westview.

Collier, J. F. (1973). *Law and Social Change in Zinacantan*. Stanford, CA: Stanford University Press.

Collins, Doreen (1975). *The European Communities: The Social Policy of the First Phase: Vol. II, The European Economic Community 1958–1972*. London: Martin Robertson.

Collinson, Sarah (1993a). *Beyond Borders: West European Migration Policy Towards the 21st Century*. London: Royal Institute for International Affairs.

——(1993b). *Europe and International Migration*. London: Pinter.

Corbett, Richard (1992). 'The Intergovernmental Conference on Political Union'. *Journal of Common Market Studies*, 30: 271–98.

Cowles, M. G. (1998). 'The Changing Architecture of Big Business', in J. Greenwood and M. Aspinwall (eds), *Collective Action in the European Union: Interests and the New Politics of Associability*. London and New York: Routledge.

Craig, Paul and de Búrca, Gráinne (1998). *EU Law: Text, Cases and Materials* (2nd edn). Oxford: Oxford University Press.

Cram, Laura (1994). 'The European Commission as a Multi-organisation: Social Policy and IT Policy in the EU'. *Journal of European Public Policy*, 1: 195–218.

——and Richardson, Jeremy (2001). *Policy Styles in the EU*. London: Routledge.

Cross, M. (1996). 'State Aids: Maturing into a Constitutional Problem', *Yearbook of European Law*, 15: 79–105.

Crowe, Brian (1993). 'Foreign Policy Making: Reflections of a Practitioner'. *Government and Opposition*, 28: 174–89.

Curtin, Deirdre (1993). 'The Constitutional Structure of the Union: A Europe of Bits and Pieces'. *Common Market Law Review*, 30: 17–69.

da Fonseca-Wollheim, Hermann (1996). 'Towards a Coherent European Trade Policy'. Unpublished ms.

Dalton, Russell J. and Eichenberg, Richard C. (1998). 'Citizen Support for Policy Integration', in W. Sandholtz and A. Stone Sweet (eds), *European Integration and Supranational Governance*. Oxford: Oxford University Press.

Damro, Chad (1999). 'Expanding Authority: The European Union and Extraterritorial Competition Policy'. Paper prepared for delivery at the 6th biennial meeting of the European Community Studies Association. Pittsburgh, PA, 2–5 June.

DATAR (Délégation a l'Aménagement du Territoire et à l'Action Régionale) (annual) *Rapport d'activité*. Paris: DATAR.

David, Paul (1992). 'Path-Dependence and Predictability in Dynamic Systems with Local Network Externalities: A Paradigm for Historical Economics', in D. Foray and C. Freeman (eds), *Technology and the Wealth of Nations*. Pinter: London.

De Grauwe, Paul (1996). 'Reforming the Transition to EMU', in Peter B. Kenen (ed.), *Making EMU Happen: Problems and Proposals* (Princeton Essays in International Finance, No. 199). Princeton: International Finance Section, Princeton University.

De La Mare, T. (1999). 'Article 177 in Social and Political Context', in P. Craig and G. De Burca (eds), *The Evolution of European Law*. Oxford: Oxford University Press.

de Lobkowicz, W. (1994). 'Intergovernmental Cooperation in the Field of Migration: From the Single European Act to Maastricht', in J. Monar and R. Morgan (eds), *The Third Pillar of the European Union: Cooperation in the Fields of Justice and Home Affairs*. Brussels: European Interuniversity Press.

Dehousse, Renaud (1994). *La Cour de justice des Communautés européennes* [The European Court of Justice]. Paris: Montchrestien.

——(1997). 'Regulation by Networks in the European Community: The Role of European Agencies'. *Journal of European Public Policy*, 4: 246–61.

Demsetz, Hugh (1988). *Ownership, Control and the Firm*. Oxford: Basil Blackwell.

den Boer, Monica (1994). 'The Quest for European Policing: Rhetoric and Justification in a Disorderly Debate', in Malcolm Anderson and Monica den Boer (eds), *Policing Across National Boundaries*. London: Pinter.

de Schoutheete de Tervarent, Philippe (1997). 'The Creation of the Common Foreign and Security Policy', in Elfriede Regelsberger, Philippe de Schoutheete de Tervarent, and Wolfgang Wessels (eds), *Foreign Policy of the European Union: From EPC to CFSP and Beyond*. Boulder, CO: Lynne Rienner.

De Witte, Bruno (1998). 'The Pillar Structure and the Nature of the European Union: Greek Temple or French Gothic Cathedral?', in T. Heukels, N. Blokker, and M. Brus (eds), *The European Union after Amsterdam: A Legal Analysis*. The Hague: Kluwer Law International.

DiMaggio, Paul (1988), 'Interest and Agency in Institutional Theory', in L. Zucker (ed.), *Research on Institutional Theory*. Cambridge, MA: Ballinger Press.

——and Powell, Walter. (1983). 'The Iron Cage Revisited: Institutional Isomorphism and Collective Rationality in Organizational Fields'. *American* Sociological Review, 48: 147–60.

————(1991). 'Introduction', in W. M. Powell and P. J. Dimaggio (eds), *The New Institutionalism in Organizational Analysis*. Chicago: University of Chicago Press.

Dixit, Avinash (1989). 'Entry and Exit Decisions under Uncertainty'. *Journal of Political Economy*, 97: 620–30.

Docksey, Christopher (1998). 'Community Law and Equal Rights: An Historical Perspective'. *Equality News Quarterly*, 98: 20–2.

Doern, G. and Wilks S. (eds) (1996). *Comparative Competition Policy: National Institutions in a Global Market*. Oxford: Clarendon Press.

Dogan, R. (1997). 'Comitology: Little Processes with Big Implications'. *West European Politics*, 20: 31–60.

Dornbusch, Rudi, Favero, Carlo, and Giavazzi, Francesco (1998). 'Immediate Challenges for the European Central Bank'. *Economic Policy*, 26: 15–64.

Downs, Anthony (1967). *Inside Bureaucracy*. Boston: Little, Brown and Co.

Dudley, Geoffrey, and Richardson, Jeremy (1998). 'Arenas Without Rules and the Policy Change Process: Outsider Groups and British Roads Policy'. *Political Studies*, 46: 727–47.

————(1999). 'Competing Advocacy Coalitions and the Process of "Frame Reflection": A Longitudinal Analysis of EU Steel Policy'. *Journal of European Public Policy*, 6: 225–48.

Dyson, Kenneth and Featherstone, Kevin (1999). *The Road to Maastricht: Negotiating Economic and Monetary Union*. New York: Oxford University Press.

Dumez, H. and Jeunemaître, A. (1991). *La concurrence en Europe: de nouvelles règles du jeu pour les entreprises*. Paris: Le Seuil.

Eaton, M. R. (1994). 'Common Foreign and Security Policy', in David O'Keeffe and Patrick M. Twomey (eds), *Legal Issues of the Maastricht Treaty*. London: Wiley Chancery Law.

Economist (1997). 22 March.

Eckstein, Harry (1988). 'A Culturalist Theory of Political Change'. *American Political Science Review* 82: 789–804.

Edwards, Geoffrey (1984). 'Europe and the Falklands Islands Crisis, 1982'. *Journal of Common Market Studies*, 22: 295–313.

——(1992). 'European Responses to the Yugoslav Crisis: An Interim Assessment', in Reinhardt Rummel (ed.), *Toward Political Union: Planning a Common Foreign and Security Policy in the European Community*. Boulder, CO: Westview.

Egan, Michelle (2001). *Constructing a European Market: Trade Barriers, Regulatory Strategies and Corporate Responses*. Oxford: Oxford University Press.

Ehlermann, C. D. (1995). 'State Aid Control in the European Union: Failure or Success?' *Fordham International Law Journal*, 18: 1212–29.

Ehlermann, Claus Dieter and Mény, Yves (coordinators) (2000). *A Basic Treaty for the European Union*. San Domenico di Fiesole, Italy: Robert Schuman Centre of Advanced Study, European University Institute.

Eichengreen, Barry (1992). 'Should the Maastricht Treaty be Saved?' *Princeton Studies in International Finance* 74. Princeton: Princeton University.

Ellickson, R. C. (1991). *Order without Law: How Neighbors Settle Disputes*. Cambridge, MA: Harvard University Press.

Ellis, Evelyn (1993). 'Protection of Pregnancy and Maternity'. *Industrial Law Journal*, 22: 63–7.

——(1998). *European Community Sex Equality Law* (2nd edn). Oxford: Oxford University Press.

——(1999). 'Case Law: Court of Justice'. *Common Market Law Review*, 36: 625–33.

Elman, Amy (ed.) (1996). *Sexual Politics and the European Union: The New Feminist Challenge*. Oxford: Berghahn Books.

Emerson, Michael and Gros, Daniel (1992). *One Market One Money: An Evaluation of the Potential Benefits and Costs of Forming an Economic and Monetary Union*. New York: Oxford University Press.

European Report (1994). No. 1958, 15 June.

——(1995). No. 2095, 23 December.

European Voice (1995). 12–18 October.

——(2000). 27 January-2 February.

European Women's Lobby (EWL) (1999). *European Women's Lobby Newsletter* (March). Brussels.

Evans, A (1997). *European Community Law of State-aid*. Oxford: Clarendon Press.

——and Martin, S. (1991). 'Socially Acceptable Distortion of Competition: Community Policy on State-Aid'. *European Law Review*, 2: 79–111.

Favell, Adrian (1998). 'The Europeanisation of Immigration Politics'. *European Integration Online Papers* 2 (http://eiop.or.at/eiop/texte/1998–010a.htm).

Fernandez Martin, J. M. and Stehmann, O. (1991). 'Product Market Integration versus Regional Cohesion in the Community'. *European Law Review*,16: 216–43.

Field, Alexander J. (1981). 'The Problem with Neoclassical Institutional Economics'. *Explorations in Economic History* 18: 174–98.

——(1984). 'Microeconomics, Norms, and Rationality'. *Economic Development and Cultural Change*, 32: 683–711.

Financial Times (1996). 15 March.

——(1999). 15 September.

Fligstein, Neil (1991). 'The Structural Transformation of American Industry: An Institutional Account of the Causes of Diversification in the Largest Firms, 1919–1979', in W. M. Powell and P. J. Dimaggio (eds), *The New Institutionalism in Organizational Analysis*. Chicago: University of Chicago Press.

Fligstein, Neil (1997a). *Markets, Politics and Globalisation*. Uppsala: Uppsala University Press.

——(1997b). 'Social Skill and Institutional Theory'. *American Behavioral Scientist*, 40: 397–405.

——(forthcoming). 'Fields, Power, and Social Skill: A Critical Analysis of the New Institutionalisms', in M. Miller (ed.), *Power and Organizations*. London: Sage.

——and Brantley, P. (1995). 'The Single Market Program and the Interests of Business', in B. Eichengreen and J. Frieden (eds), *Politics and Institutions in an Integrated Europe*. Berlin: Verlag-Springer.

——and Mara Drita, I. (1996). 'How to Make a Market: Reflections on the European Union's Single Market Program'. *American Journal of Sociology*, 102: 1–33.

——and McNichol, Jason (1998). 'The Institutional Terrain of the European Union', in W. Sandholtz and A. Stone Sweet (eds), *European Integration and Supranational Governance*. Oxford: Oxford University Press.

Foray, Dominique (1997). 'The Dynamic Implications of Increasing Returns: Technological Change and Path Dependent Inefficiency'. *International Journal of Industrial Organization*,15: 733–52.

Frazer, T. (1995). 'The New Structural Funds, State Aids and Interventions on the Single Market'. *European Law Review*, 20: 3–19.

Fudenberg, D., and Levine, D. (1986). 'The Folk Theorem in Repeated Games with Discounting or with Incomplete Information'. *Econometrica*, 50: 533–54.

Gagnon, J. E. (1993). 'Exchange Rate Variability and the Level of Trade'. *Journal of International Economics*, 34: 269–87.

Garrett, Geoffrey (1992). 'International Cooperation and Institutional Choice: The European Community's Internal Market'. *International Organization*, 46: 533–58.

——(1995). 'The Politics of Legal Integration in the European Union'. *International Organization*,49: 171–81.

——, Kelemen, R. Daniel, and Schulz, Heiner (1998). 'The European Court of Justice, National Governments, and Legal Integration in the European Union'. *International Organization*, 52: 149–76.

——and Weingast, Barry (1993). 'Ideas, Interests, and Institutions: Constructing the EC's Internal Market', in Judith Goldstein and Robert Keohane (eds), *Ideas and Foreign Policy*. Ithaca, NY: Cornell University Press.

Giavazzi, Francesco and Giovannini, Alberto (1989). *Limiting Exchange Rate Flexibility: The European Monetary System*. Cambridge, MA: MIT Press.

Giddens, Anthony (1984). *The Constitution of Society: Outline of the Theory of Structuration*. Berkeley: University of California Press.

Ginsberg, Roy H. (1997). 'The EU's CFSP: The Politics of Procedure', in Martin Holland (ed.), *Common Foreign and Security Policy: The Record and Reforms*. London: Pinter.

Glenn, John K., III (1999). 'Challenger Competition and Contested Outcomes in the Velvet Revolution in Czechoslovakia'. *Social Forces*, 78: 187–211.

Goldstein, Judith, Kahler, Miles, Keohane, Robert, and Slaughter, Anne-Marie (eds) (2000). *International Organization*, 54/3: Special issue on 'Legalization of International Politics'.

Goodman, John B. (1992). *Monetary Sovereignty: The Politics of Central Banking in Western Europe*. Ithaca, NY: Cornell University Press.

Green Cowles, M. (1997). 'Organizing Industrial Coalitions: A Challenge for the Future?', in H. Wallace and A. Young (eds), *Participation and Policy-Making in the European Union*. Oxford: Clarendon Press.

Greenwood, J. (1997). *Representing Interests in the European Union*. Basingstoke: Macmillan.

——and Aspinwall, M. (eds) (1998). *Collective Action in the European Union: Interests and the New Politics of Associability*. London and New York: Routledge.

—, Strangward, Linda, and Stanich, Lara (1999). 'The Capacities of EuroGroups in the Integration Process'. *Political Studies*, 47: 127–38.

Greif, Avner (1989). 'Reputation and Coalitions in Medieval Trade: Evidence on the Maghribi Traders'. *Journal of Economic History*, 49: 857–82.

——(1993). 'Contract Enforceability and Economic Institutions in Early Trade: The Maghribi Traders' Coalition'. *American Economic Review*, 83: 425–48.

Gros, Daniel and Thygesen, Niels (1998). *European Monetary Integration*. London: Longman Press.

Grunert, Thomas (1997). 'The Association of the European Parliament: No Longer the Underdog in EPC?', in Elfriede Regelsberger, Philippe de Schoutheete de Tervarent, and Wolfgang Wessels (eds), *Foreign Policy of the European Union: From EPC to CFSP and Beyond*. Boulder, CO: Lynne Rienner.

Haas, E. B. (1958). *The Uniting of Europe*. Stanford, CA: Stanford University Press.

——(1961). 'International Integration: The European and the Universal Process'. *International Organization*, 15: 366–92.

Hagleitner, Thomas (1995). 'Financing the Common Foreign and Security Policy'. *CFSP Forum*, 2: 6–7.

Hall, Peter (1986). *Governing the Economy*. Oxford: Polity Press.

——(1992). 'The Movement from Keynesianism to Monetarism: Institutional Analysis and British Economic Policy in the 1970s', in S. Steinmo, K. Thelen, and F. Longstreth (eds), *Structuring Politics: Historical Institutionalism in Comparative Analysis*. Cambridge: Cambridge University Press.

——(1993). 'Policy Paradigms, Social Learning and the State: The Case of Economic Policy in Britain'. *Comparative Politics*, 25: 275–96.

——and Taylor, Rosemary (1996). 'Political Science and the Three Institutionalisms'. *Political Studies*, 44: 936–57.

Hancher, L. (1994). 'State Aids and Judicial Control in the European Community'. *European Competition Law Review*, 10: 291–305.

Hancké, Bob (1999). *Revisiting the French Model. Coordination and restructuring in French Industry in the 1980s* (Discussion Paper FS I 99–301). Berlin: Wissenschaftzentrum Berlin.

Hannan, Michael T. and Freeman, John (1984). 'Structural Inertia and Organizational Change'. *American Sociological Review*, 49: 149–64.

Heinz, John P., Laumann, Edward O., Nelson, Robert L., and Salisbury, Robert H. (1993). *The Hollow Core. Private Interests in National Policy Making*. Cambridge, MA: Harvard University Press.

Heisenberg, Dorothee (1998). *The Mark of the Bundesbank: Germany's Role in* European Monetary Cooperation. Boulder, CO: Lynne Rienner.

Heisler, Martin and Kvavik, Robert (1974). 'Patterns of European Politics: The "European Polity" Model', in Martin Heisler (ed.), *Politics in Europe: Structure and Processes in Some Postindustrial Democracies*. New York: David and McKay.

Henderson, P. E. (1977). 'Two British Errors: Their Probable Size and Some Possible Lessons'. *Economic Papers*, 29: 159–205.

Henson, Penny, and Malhan, Nisha (1995). 'Endeavours to Export a Migration Crisis: Policy Making and Europeanisation in the German Migration Dilemma'. *German Politics*, 4: 128–144.

Héritier, Adrienne (1997). 'Policy-Making by Subterfuge: Interest Accommodation, Innovation and Democratic Legitimation in Europe'. *Journal of European Public Policy* 4: 171–89.

——(1999). *Policy-Making and Diversity in Europe: Escaping Deadlock*. Cambridge: Cambridge University Press.

——, Knill, Christoph, and Mingers, Susanne (1996). *Ringing the Changes in Europe: Regulatory Competition and the Transformation of the State: Britain, France, Germany*. Berlin, New York: de Gruyter.

Hill, Christopher (1992). 'EPC's Performance in Crises', in Reinhardt Rummel (ed.), *Toward Political Union: Planning a Common Foreign and Security Policy in the European Community*. Boulder, CO: Westview.

Hooghe, L. (ed.) (1996). *Cohesion Policy and European Integration*. Oxford: Oxford University Press.

——(1998). 'EU Cohesion Policy and Competing Models of European Capitalism'. *Journal of Common Market Studies*, 36: 457–77.

——and Keating, M. (1994). 'The Politics of European Regional Policy'. *Journal of European Public Policy*, 1: 367–93.

Hoskyns, Catherine (1996). *Integrating Gender*. London: Verso.

Hull, R. (1993). 'Lobbying Brussels : A View from Within', in S. Mazey and J. Richardson (eds), *Lobbying in the European Community*. Oxford: Oxford University Press.

Ingram, Helen (2000). *Research Agenda for Public Policy and Democracy* (CSD Working Paper). Irvine, CA: Center for the Study of Democracy, University of California. http://www.democ.uci.edu/democ/papers/ingram2.htm

International Monetary Fund (1984). *Exchange Rate Variability and World Trade* (Occasional Paper 28). Washington, DC: IMF.

Jepperson, Ronald L. (1991). 'Institutions, Institutional Effects, and Institutionalism', in W. M. Powell and P. J. Dimaggio (eds), *The New Institutionalism in Organizational Analysis*. Chicago: University of Chicago Press.

Jobert, B. (ed.) (1994). *Le tournant néo-libéral en Europe*. Paris: L'Harmattan.

Joerges, C. and Neyer, J. (1997). 'From Intergovernmental Bargaining to Deliberative Political Processes: The Constitutionalisation of Comitology'. *European Law Journal* 3: 272–99.

Joerges, Christian and Vos, Ellen (1999). *E.U. Committees: Social Regulation, Law and Politics*. Oxford: Hart.

Jordan, Grant, and Richardson, Jeremy (1982). 'The British Policy Style or the Logic of Negotiation?', in Jeremy Richardson (ed.), *Policy Styles in Western Europe*. London: George Allen and Unwin.

Jupille, Joseph and Caporaso, James A. (1999). 'Institutionalism and the European Union: Beyond International Relations and Comparative Politics'. *Annual Review of Political Science*, 2: 429–44.

Kandori, M. (1992). 'Social Norms and Community Enforcement'. *Review of Economic Studies*, 59: 63–80.

Keatinge, Patrick (1997). 'The Twelve, the United Nations, and Somalia: The Mirage of Global Intervention', in Elfriede Regelsberger, Philippe de Schoutheete de Tervarent, and Wolfgang Wessels (eds), *Foreign Policy of the European Union: From EPC to CFSP and Beyond*. Boulder, CO: Lynne Rienner.

Keck, Margaret and Sikkink, Kathryn (1998). *Activists Beyond Borders: Advocacy Networks in International Politics*. Ithaca, NY: Cornell University Press.

Kenen, Peter B. (1969). 'The Theory of Optimal Currency Areas: An Eclectic yew', in Robert Mundell and Alexander Swoboda (eds), *Monetary Problems of the International Economy*. Chicago: University of Chicago Press.

Kenney, Sally (1992). *For Whose Protection? Reproductive Hazards and Exclusionary Policies in the United States and Britain*. Ann Arbor: University of Michigan Press.

——(1996). 'Pregnancy Discrimination: Toward Substantive Equality'. *Wisconsin Women's Law Journal*, 10: 351–402.

Keohane, Robert (1984). *After Hegemony: Cooperation and Discord in the World Political Economy*. Princeton: Princeton University Press.

——and Martin, Lisa (1999). 'Institutional Theory, Endogenity, and Delegation'. Unpublished ms.

Kiewiet, R. and McCubbins, M. D. (1991). *The Logic of Delegation: Congressional Parties and the Appropriations Process*. Chicago: University of Chicago Press.

Kirchner, E. (1977). *Trade Unions as Pressure Groups in the European Community*. Farnborough: Saxon House.

——(1980*a*). 'International Trade Union Collaboration and the Prospect for European Industrial Relations'. *West European Politics*, 3: 124–37.

——(1980*b*). 'Interest Group Behaviour at the Community Level', in L. Hurwitz (ed.), *Contemporary Perspectives on European Integration*. London: Aldwych.

Kitschelt, H. (1986). 'Political Opportunity Structures and Political Protest: Anti-nuclear Movements in Four Democracies'. *British Journal of Political Science*, 16: 57–85.

Klein, Rudolf and O'Higgins, Michael (1985). 'Social Policy After Incrementalism', in Rudolf Klein and Michael O'Higgins (eds), *The Future of Welfare*. Oxford: Basil Blackwell.

Knight, Jack (1992). *Institutions and Social Conflict*. Cambridge: Cambridge University Press.

——(1995). 'Models, Interpretations, and Theories: Constructing Explanations of Institutional Emergence and Change', in J. Knight and I. Sened (eds), *Explaining Social Institutions*. Ann Arbor: The University of Michigan Press.

——and Johnson, Jim (1994). 'Aggregation and Deliberation: On the Possibility of Democratic Legitimacy'. *Political Theory*, 22: 277–96.

——and Sened, Itai (eds) (1995). *Explaining Social Institutions*. Ann Arbor: The University of Michigan Press.

Krasner, Stephen (ed.) (1983). *International Regimes*. Ithaca, NY: Cornell University Press.

——(1989). 'Sovereignty: An Institutional Perspective', in J. A. Caporaso (ed.), *The Elusive State: International and Comparative Perspectives*. Newbury Park, CA: Sage Publications.

Kratochwil, Friedrich V. (1989). *Rules, Norms, and Decisions*. Cambridge: Cambridge University Press.

Krenzler, Horst-Gunter, and Schneider, Henning C. (1997). 'The Question of Consistency', in Elfriede Regelsberger, Philippe de Schoutheete de Tervarent, and Wolfgang Wessels (eds), *Foreign Policy of the European Union: From EPC to CFSP and Beyond*. Boulder, CO: Lynne Rienner.

Krugman, Paul (1988). *Deindustrialization, Reindustrialization and the Real Exchange Rate* (NBER Working Paper No. 2586). Cambridge, MA: National Bureau of Economic Research.

Lak, Maarten W. J. (1989). 'Interaction Between European Political Cooperation and the European Community (External)—Existing Rules and Challenges'. *Common Market Law Review*, 26: 281–99.

Lange, Peter (1992). 'The Politics of the Social Dimension', in A. Sbragia (ed.), *Euro-Politics: Institutions and Policymaking in the 'New' European Community*. Washington, DC: The Brookings Institution.

Laursen, Finn and Vanhoonacker, Sophie (eds) (1992). *The Intergovernmental Conference on Political Union*. Maastricht: European Institute of Public Administration.

Le Galès, P. (1994). 'Regions Economic Policy: An Alternative to French Economic Dirigism?' *Regional Policy and Politics*, 3: 72–90.

——with Valeria Aniello (2001). 'The Governance of Local Economies in France', in C. Crouch, P. Le Galès, C. Trigilia, and H. Voeltzkow (eds), *The Governance of Regional Economies in Europe*. Oxford: Oxford University Press.

Leibfried, Stephan and Pierson, Paul (eds) (1995). *European Social Policy: Between Fragmentation and Integration*. Washington, DC: The Brookings Institution.

Lenaerts, Koen (1990). 'Constitutionalism and the Many Faces of Federalism'. *American Journal of Comparative Law*, 38: 205–64.

Les Echos (1999). 25 June.

Lesquesne, C. (1993). *Paris-Bruxelles*. Paris: Presses de Sciences Po.

Levi-Strauss, Claude (1966). *The Savage Mind*. Chicago: University of Chicago Press.

Levitt, Barbara and March, James G. (1988). 'Organizational Learning'. *Annual Review of Sociology*, 14: 319–40.

Lévy, J. (1999). *Tocqueville's Revenge*. Boston: MIT Press.

Lodge, Juliet (1989). 'European Political Cooperation: Towards the 1990s', in Juliet Lodge (ed.), *The European Community and the Challenge of the Future*. New York: St. Martin's Press.

Lohmann, Susanne (1999). 'The Dark Side of European Monetary Union', in Ellen Meade (ed.), *The European Central Bank: How Decentralized? How Accountable? Lessons from the Bundesbank and the Federal Reserve System*. Washington, DC: American Institute for Contemporary Germany Studies.

Lopandic, Dusko (1995). 'Les Mémorandums d'Entente: Des Instruments Juridiques Spécifiques de la Politique Étrangère et de Sécurité de l'Union Européenne: Le Cas de l'Ex-Yougoslavie'. *Revue du Marché commun at de l'Union européenne*, 392: 557–62.

Lowi, T. J. (1964). 'American Business, Public Policy: Case-Studies, and Political Theory'. *World Politics*, 16: 677–715.

Majone, Giandomenico (1993). 'The European Community between Social Policy and Social Regulation'. *Journal of Common Market Studies*, 31: 153–70.

——(1995). 'Independence and Accountability: Non-Majoritarian Institutions and Democratic Government in Europe', in J. Weiler, R. Dehousse, and A. Cassese (eds), *Collected Courses of the Academy of European Law*. London: Routledge.

——(1996a). *Regulating Europe*. London: Routledge.

——(1996b). *L'Union européenne, un État régulateur*. Paris: LGDJ.

——(1998). 'Europe's "Democratic Deficit": The Question of Standards'. *European Law Journal*, 4: 5–28.

Mancini, G. F. (1989). 'The Making of a Constitution for Europe'. *Common Market Law Review*, 24: 595–614.

——(1991). 'The Making of a Constitution for Europe', in Robert Keohane and Stanley Hoffman (eds), *The New European Community*. Boulder, CO: Westview.

——and O'Leary, S. (1999). 'The New Frontiers of Sex Equality Law in the European Union'. *European Law Review* 24: 331–53.

March, James G. and Olsen, Johann P. (1989). *Rediscovering Institutions*. New York: Free Press.

Marcussen, Martin, Risse, Thomas, Engelmann-Martin, Daniela, Knopf, Hans Joachim, and Roscher, Klaus (1999). 'Constructing Europe? The Evolution of French, British and German Nation State Identities'. *Journal of European Public Policy*, 6: 614–33.

Marks, Gary, Hooghe, Liesbet, and Blank, Kermit (1996). 'European Integration since the 1980s: State-centric versus Multi-level Governance'. *Journal of Common Market Studies*, 34: 341–78.

——and Doug McAdam (1998). 'Social Movements and the Changing Structure of Political Opportunity in the European Union', in Gary Marks, Fritz Scharpf, Philippe Schmitter, and Wolfgang Streek (eds), *Governance in the European Union*. London: Sage.

Mattli, Walter (1999). *The Logic of Regional Integration*. Cambridge: Cambridge University Press.

——and Slaughter, Anne-Marie (1998). 'Revisiting the European Court of Justice'. *International Organization*, 52: 177–209.

Mayntz, Renate (1993). 'Policy-Netzwerke und die Logik von Verhandlungssystemen', in A. Héritier (ed.), *Policy-Analyse. Kritik und Neuorientierung. Politische Vierteljahresschrift Sonderheft* 24. Opladen: Westdeutscher Verlag.

Mazey, Sonia (1992). 'Conception and Evolution of the High Authority's Administrative Services (1952–56): From Supranational Principles to Multilateral Practices', in *Yearbook of European Administrative History*. Baden-Baden: Nomos.

——(1998). 'The European Union and Women's Rights: from the Europeanization of National Agendas to the Nationalization of the European Agenda?' *Journal of European Public Policy*, 51: 131–52.

——and Richardson, Jeremy (eds) (1993*a*). *Lobbying in the European Community*. Oxford: Oxford University Press.

————(1993*b*), 'Introduction: Transference of Power, Decision Rules and Rules of the Game', in Sonia Mazey and Jeremy Richardson (eds), *Lobbying in the European Community*, Oxford: Oxford University Press.

————(1995). 'Promiscuous Policymaking: The European Policy Style?', in Carolyn Rhodes and Sonia Mazey (eds), *The State of the European Union Vol. 3: Building a European Polity?* Boulder, CO: Lynne Rienner.

————(1997*a*). 'The Commission and the Lobby', in G. Edwards and D. Spence (eds), *The European Commission*. London: Cartermill.

————(1997*b*). 'Policy Framing: Interest Groups and the Lead Up to the 1996 Inter-Governmental Conference'. *West European Politics* 20: 111–33.

————(1998). 'Framing and Reframing Public Policy in the EU: Ideas, Interests and Institutions in Sex Equality and Environmental Policies'. Unpublished paper presented at the European Consortium for Political Research, Joint Sessions of Workshops, Warwick University, 23–8 March.

————(2001). *Filling the Hollow Core? Interest Intermediation in the European Union*. London: Routledge.

Mazzucelli, Colette (1995). 'Germany at Maastricht: Diplomacy and Domestic Politics', in A. Bradley-Shingleton, M. J. Gibbon, and K. S. Mack (eds), *Dimensions of German Unification: Economic, Social and Legal Analysis*. Boulder, CO: Westview Press.

McGlynn, Clare (1996). 'Pregnancy Dismissals and the Webb Litigation'. *Feminist Legal Studies*, 4: 229–42.

McGoldrick, Dominic (1997). *International Relations Law of the European Union*. London: Longman.

McGowan, F. (2000). 'Competition Policy', in H. Wallace and W. Wallace, W. (eds), *Policy-making in Europe*. Oxford: Oxford University Press.

McNamara, Kathleen (1998). *The Currency of Ideas: Monetary Politics in the European Union*. Ithaca: Cornell University Press.

——(1999). 'Consensus and Constraint: Ideas and Capital Mobility in European

252 References

Monetary Integration'. *Journal of Common Market Studies*, 37: 455–76.

——(2001*a*). 'The Culture of Money: Institutional Logics and the European Central Bank'. Unpublished manuscript.

——(2001*b*). 'Globalization, Fiscal Adjustment, and EMU: Race to the Bottom or Room for Maneuver?'. Paper prepared for a workshop on 'Globalization and Governance', UCSD/IGCC, David Lake and Miles Kahler (organizers).

Mearsheimer, John (1990). 'Why We Will Soon Miss the Cold War'. *The Atlantic Monthly* (August): 35–50.

——(1994/1995). 'The False Promise of International Institutions'. *International Security*, 19: 5–49.

Meyer, J. and Rowan, B. (1977). 'Institutionalized Organizations: Formal Structure as Myth and Ceremony'. *American Journal of Sociology*, 83: 340–63.

Milgrom, Paul, and Roberts, John (1992). *Economics, Organization, and Management*. Englewood Cliffs, NJ: Prentice Hall.

Moe, Terry (1987). 'An Assessment of the Positive Theory of Congressional Dominance'. *Legislative Studies Quarterly*, 12: 475–520.

Monar, Jörg (1997*a*). 'The Finances of the Union's Intergovernmental Pillars: Tortuous Experiments with the Community Budget'. *Journal of Common Market Studies*, 35: 57–78.

——(1997b). 'The Financial Dimension of the CFSP', in Martin Holland (ed.), *Common Foreign and Security Policy: The Record and Reforms*. London: Pinter Publishers.

Moravcsik, Andrew (1991). 'Negotiating the Single European Act: National Interests and Conventional Statecraft in the European Community'. *International Organization*, 45: 19–56.

——(1993). 'Preferences and Power in the European Community: A Liberal Intergovernmentalist Approach'. *Journal of Common Market Studies*, 31: 473–524.

——(1995). 'Liberal Intergovernmentalism and Integration: A Rejoinder'. *Journal of Common Market Studies*, 33: 611–28.

——(1998). *The Choice for Europe: Social Purpose and State Power from Massina to Maastricht*. Ithaca, NY: Cornell University Press.

More, Gillian (1999). 'The Principle of Equal Treatment: From Market Unifier to Fundamental Right?', in Paul Craig and Gráinne de Búrca (eds), *Evolution of EU Law*. Oxford: Oxford University Press.

Mosely, Layna (1999). 'Financial Markets and Fiscal Policy in the EU: Permission or Prohibition?' Paper presented at the 95th American Political Science Association Meeting. 2–5 September, Atlanta, Georgia.

Mundell, Robert (1961). 'A Theory of Optimal Currency Areas'. *The American Economic Review*, 51: 657–65.

Nehl, Hanns Peter (1999). *Principles of Administrative Procedure in E.C. Law*. Oxford: Hart.

Neuwahl, Nanette (1994). 'Foreign and Security Policy and the Implementation of the Requirement for "Consistency" Under the Treaty on European Union', in David O'Keeffe and Patrick M. Twomey (eds), *Legal Issues of the Maastricht Treaty*. London: Wiley Chancery Law.

North, D. R. (1981). *Structure and Change in Economic History*. New York: Newton.

——(1990). *Institutions, Institutional Change, and Economic Performance*. Cambridge: Cambridge University Press.

——(1995). 'Five Propositions about Institutional Change', in J. Knight and I. Sened (eds), *Explaining Social Institutions*. Ann Arbor: University of Michigan Press.

Nuttall, Simon J. (1992). *European Political Cooperation*. Oxford: Clarendon Press.

——(1995). 'The European Commission's Internal Arrangements for Foreign Affairs and External Relations'. *CFSP Forum*, 2: 3–4.

Nykios, Stacy A. (1999). 'The European Court of Justice and National Courts: Establishing Legitimacy through Elite Compliance'. Paper presented at the 95th American Political Science Association Meeting, 2–5 September, Atlanta, Georgia.

O'Keeffe, D. (1991). 'The Schengen Convention: A Suitable Model for European Integration?' *Yearbook of European Law*, 11: 185–219.

Olsen, Johan P. (2000). *Organising European Institutions of Governance* (ARENA Working Paper No. 2). Oslo: ARENA, University of Oslo.

Onuf, N. (1989). *World of Our Making: Rules and Rule in Social Theory and International Relations*. Columbia, SC: University of South Carolina Press.

O'Reilly, Dolores and Stone Sweet, Alec (1998). 'The Liberalization and European Reregulation of Air Transport', in W. Sandholtz and A. Stone Sweet (eds), *European Integration and Supranational Governance*. Oxford: Oxford University Press.

Paterson, William E. (1998). 'The Vision Thing'. *German Politics*, 7: 17–36.

Peters, Guy (1992). 'Bureaucratic Politics and the Institutions of the European Community', in A. Sbragia (ed.), *Euro-Politics: Institutions, and Policymaking in the 'New' European Community*. Washington, DC: Brookings Institution.

Peterson, Jon (1995). 'Decision-making in the European Union: Towards a Framework for Analysis'. *Journal of European Public Policy*, 2: 69–94.

Philip, A. B. and Gray, O. (1997). *Directory of Pressure Groups in the EC*. London: Catermill Press.

Pierson, Paul (1993). 'When Effect Becomes Cause: Policy Feedback and Political Change'. *World Politics*, 45: 595–628.

——(1996). 'The Path to European Integration: A Historical-Institutionalist Analysis'. *Comparative Political Studies* 29: 123–63.

——(1998). 'The Path to European Integration: A Historical-Institutional Analysis', in W. Sandholtz and A. Stone Sweet (eds), *European Integration and Supranational Governance*. Oxford: Oxford University Press.

——(2000). 'Increasing Returns, Path Dependence, and the Study of Politics'. *American Political Science Review*, 94: 251–69.

——and Leibfried, S. (eds) (1995). *European Social Policy: Between Fragmentation and Integration*. Washington, DC: Brookings Institution.

Pjinenburg, B. (1998). 'EU Lobbying by Ad Hoc Coalitions: An Exploratory Case Study'. *Journal of European Public Policy*, 5: 303–21.

Poiares Maduro, Miguel (1998). *We, the Court: The European Court of Justice and the European Economic Constitution*. Oxford: Hart.

Pollack, Mark (1994). 'Creeping Competence: The Expanding Agenda of the European Community'. *Journal of Public Policy*, 14: 95–145.

——(1997). 'Delegation, Agency, and Agenda Setting in the European Community'. *International Organization*, 51: 99–134.

——(1998). 'The Engines of Integration? Supranational Autonomy and Influence in the European Union', in W. Sandholtz and A. Stone Sweet (eds), *European Integration and Supranational Governance*. Oxford: Oxford University Press.

Posen, Adam (1993). 'Why Central Bank Independence Does Not Cause Low Inflation: There Is No Institutional Fix for Politics', in Richard O'Brien (ed.), *Finance and the International Economy*, vii. Oxford: Oxford University Press.

Potters, Jan and van Winden, Frans (1992). 'Lobbying and Asymmetric Information'. *Public Choice*, 74: 269–92.

Powell, Walter. M. and Dimaggio, Paul J. (eds) (1991). *The New Institutionalism in Organizational Analysis*. Chicago: University of Chicago Press.

Prechal, S. and Burrows, N. (1990). *Gender Discrimination Law of the European Community*. Brookfield: Gower Publishing Company.

Preston, May E. (1998). 'The European Commission and Special Interest Groups', in Paul-H. Claeys, Corinne Gobin, Isabelle Smets, and Pascaline Winand (eds), *Lobbyisme, Pluralisme et Intégration Européene*. Bruxelles: Presses Interuniversitaires Européennes.

Pretschker, U. (1998). *Public Support to Industry*. Paris: OECD.

Regelsberg, Elfriede (1988). 'EPC in the 1980s: Reaching Another Plateau?', in Alfred Pijpers, Elfriede Regelsberger, and Wolfgang Wessels (eds), *European Political Cooperation in the 1980s: A Common Foreign Policy for Western Europe?* Dordrecht: Martinus Nijhoff.

Regelsberger, Elfriede and Wessels, Wolfgang (1996). 'The CFSP Institutions and Procedures: A Third Way for the Second Pillar'. *European Foreign Affairs Review*, 1: 29–54.

Rhinard, Mark (1999). 'Institutionalisation of Consultation in the E.U. Research Report'. Unpublished manuscript: Cambridge University.

Rhodes, Martin (1995). 'A Regulatory Conundrum: Industrial Relations and the Social Dimension', in S. Leibfried and P. Pierson (eds), *European Social Policy: Between Fragmentation and Integration*. Washington, DC: The Brookings Institution.

Richardson, J. J. and Jordan, A. G. (1979). *Governing Under Pressure*. Oxford: Martin Robertson.

Riker, William (1987). 'The Heresthetics of Constitution-Making'. *American Political Science Review*, 87: 1–16.

——(1996). *The Strategy of Rhetoric. Campaigning for the American Constitution*. New Haven and London: Yale University Press.

Risse, Thomas, Englemann-Martin, Daniela, Knopf, Hans-Joachim, and Roscher, Klaus (1998). *To Euro or Not to Euro? The EMU and Identity Politics in the European Union* (European University Institute RSC Working Paper No. 98/9). Florence: European University.

——————(1999). 'To Euro or Not to Euro? EMU and Identity Politics in the European Union'. *European Journal of International Relations*, 5: 147–87.

Ross, G. (1995). *Jacques Delors and the European Integration*. Cambridge: Polity Press.

Rossilli, Mariagrazia (1997). 'The European Community's Policy on the Equality of Women'. *European Journal of Women's Studies*, 4: 63–82.

Rouam, C. (1998). *Le contrôle des aides d'État aux entreprises dans l'Union européenne*. Paris: Economica.

Sabatier, Paul (1988). 'An Advocacy Coalition Framework of Policy Change and the Role of Policy-oriented Learning Therein'. *Policy Sciences*, 21: 129–68.

——(1998). 'The Advocacy Coalition Framework: Revisions and Relevance for Europe'. *Journal of European Public Policy*, 5: 93–130.

Sack, Jörn (1995). 'The European Community's Membership of International Organizations'. *Common Market Law Review*, 32: 1227–56.

Sandholtz, Wayne (1992). *High-Tech Europe: The Politics of International Cooperation*. Berkeley: University of California Press.

——(1993a). 'Choosing Union: Monetary Politics and Maastricht'. *International Organization*, 47: 1–39.

——(1993b). 'Monetary Bargains: The Treaty on EMU', in A. W. Cafruny and G. G. Rosenthal (eds), *The State of the European Community*. Boulder, CO: Lynne Rienner.

——(1996). 'Membership Matters: Limits of the Functional Approach to European Institutions'. *Journal of Common Market Studies*, 34: 403–29.

——(1998*a*). 'Rule Structures and International Relations'. Unpublished ms. University of California, Irvine.

——(1998*b*). 'The Emergence of a Supranational Telecommunications Regime', in W. Sandholtz and A. Stone Sweet (eds), *European Integration and Supranational Governance*. Oxford: Oxford University Press.

——(1999). 'Dynamics of International Norm Change: The Case of Wartime Art Plunder'. Unpublished ms.

——and Stone Sweet, Alec (eds) (1998). *European Integration and Supranational Governance*. Oxford: Oxford University Press.

————(1999). 'European Integration and Supranational Governance Revisited: Rejoinder to Branch and Øhrgaard'. *Journal of European Public Policy*, 6: 144–54.

——and Zysman, John (1989). '1992: Recasting the European Bargain'. *World Politics*, 42: 95–128.

Sbragia, Alberta (1992). 'Thinking about the European Future: The Uses of Comparison', in A. Cafruny and G. Rosenthal (eds), *The State of the European Community*. Boulder, CO: Lynne Reinner.

——(1993). 'The European Community: A Balancing Act'. *Publius*, 23: 23–38.

——(1998). Institution-Building from below and above: The European Community in Global Environmental Politics, in W. Sandholtz and A. Stone Sweet (eds), *European Integration and Supranational Governance*. Oxford: Oxford University Press.

Scharpf, Fritz W. (1988). 'The Joint-Decision Trap: Lessons from German Federalism and European Integration'. *Public Administration*, 61: 239–42.

——(1996). 'Negative and Positive Integration in the Political Economy of European Welfare States', in Gary Marks, Fritz W. Scharpf, Philippe C. Schmitter, and Wolfgang Streeck (eds), *Governance in the European Union*. London: Sage Publications.

——(1997). 'The problem-solving Capacity of Multi-level Governance'. *Journal of European Public Policy*, 4: 520–38.

——(1999). *Governing in Europe: Effective and Democratic?* Oxford: Oxford University Press.

Schelling, Thomas C. (1963). *The Strategy of Conflict*. New York: Oxford University Press.

Schilling, Theodor (1996). 'The Autonomy of the Community Legal Order: An Analysis of Possible Foundations'. *Harvard International Law Journal*, 37: 389–409.

Schmidt, Susanne (1995). 'The Integration of the European Telecommunication and Electricity Sectors in the Light of International Relations Theories and Comparative Politics'. Paper presented at the European Consortium for Political Research Joint Sessions of Workshops, Bordeaux.

Schmidt,V. (1996). *From State to Market? The Transformation of French Business and Government*. Cambridge: Cambridge University Press.

Schmidt-Nothen, Rainer (1995). 'Cross-border Organised Crime in Germany', in Cyrille Fijnaut, Johan Goethals, Tony Peters, and Lode Walgrave (eds), *Changes in Society, Crime and Criminal Justice in Europe: A Challenge for Criminological Education and Research*. The Hague: Kluwer Law International.

Schmitter, P. C. (1969). Further Notes on Operationalizing Some Variables Related to Regional Integration'. *International Organization*, 23: 326–36.

——(1970). 'A Revised Theory of Regional Integration'. *International Organization*, 24: 836–68.

Schneider, A. L. and Ingram, H. (1997). *Policy Design for Democracy*. Lawrence: University of Kansas Press.

Schön, Donald A. and Rein, Martin (1994). Frame Reflection: Towards the Resolution of Intractable Policy Controversies. New York: Basic Books.

Schutte, J. (1991). 'Schengen: Its Meaning for the Free Movement of Persons in Europe'. Common Market Law Review, 28: 549–70.

Scott, R. W. (1996). Institutions and Organizations. Beverly Hills, CA: Sage.

——and Meyer, John W. (1994). Institutional Environments and Organizations. Thousand Oaks, CA: Sage.

Sewell, William H. (1992). 'A Theory of Structure: Duality, Agency, and Transformation. American Journal of Sociology, 98: 1–29.

——(1994). A Rhetoric of the Bourgeois Revolution: The Abbé Sièyes and What is the Third Estate. Durham, NC: Duke University Press.

Shapiro, Martin (1968). The Supreme Court and Administrative Agencies. New York: Free Press.

——(1988). Who Guards the Guardians: Judicial Control of Administration. Athens, GA: University of Georgia Press.

——(1992). 'The Giving Reasons Requirement'. University of Chicago Legal Forum 1992: 179–220.

Shepsle, Kenneth (1989). 'Studying Institutions: Lessons from the Rational Choice Approach'. Journal of Theoretical Politics, 1: 131–47.

Sidjanski, D. (1970). 'Pressure Groups and the European Economic Community', in C. Cosgrove and K. Twitchett (eds), The New International Actors: The United Nations and the European Economic Community. London: Macmillan.

Simon, S. (1999). 'Recent Developments in State Aid Policy'. European Economy Reports and Studies, 3: 46–61.

Slaughter, Anne-Marie, Stone Sweet, Alec, and Weiler, Joseph (1998). The European Court and the National Courts—Doctrine and Jurisprudence: Legal Change in its Social Context. Oxford, UK, and Evanston, IL: Hart Press and Northwestern University Press.

Smith, Michael E. (1998a). 'What's Wrong with the CFSP? The Politics of Institutional Reform', in Pierre-Henri Laurent and Marc Maresceau (eds), The State of the European Union, Vol. 4: Deepening and Widening. Boulder, CO: Lynne Rienner.

——(1998b). 'Rules, Transgovernmentalism, and the Expansion of European Political Cooperation', in Wayne Sandholtz and Alec Stone Sweet (eds), European Integration and Supranational Governance. Oxford: Oxford University Press.

——(1998c). 'Beyond Bargaining: The Institutionalization of Foreign and Security Policy Cooperation in the European Community, 1970–1996'. Ph.D.thesis: University of California, Irvine.

Smith, P. M. (1996). 'Integration in Small Steps: The European Commission and Member-state Aid to Industry'. West European Politics, 19: 563–82.

——(1998). 'Autonomy by the Rules: The European Commission and the Development of State Aid Policy'. Journal of Common Market Studies, 36: 55–78.

Snow, David A. and Benford, Robert D. (1988). 'Ideology, Frame Resonance, and Participant Mobilization'. International Social Movement Research, 1: 197–217.

Snyder, F. (1989). 'Ideologies of Competition in European Community Law'. The Modern Law Review, 52: 53–87.

Stavridis, Stelios (1997). 'The Democratic Control of CFSP', in Martin Holland (ed.), Common Foreign and Security Policy: The Record and Reforms. London: Pinter Publishers.

Stewart, Richard (1975). 'The Reformation of American Administrative Law'. Harvard Law Review, 88: 1667–813.

Stone Sweet, Alec (1994). 'What Is a Supranational Constitution? An Essay in International Relations Theory'. Review of Politics, 55: 441–74.

Stone Sweet, Alec (1998). 'Rules, Dispute Resolution, and Strategic Behavior: Reply to Vanberg'. *Journal of Theoretical Politics*, 10: 327–38.

——(1999). 'Judicialization and the Construction of Governance'. *Comparative Political Studies*, 32: 147–84.

——(2000). *Governing with Judges: Constitutional Politics in Europe*. Oxford: Oxford University Press.

——and Brunell, Thomas (1998a). 'Constructing a Supranational Constitution: Dispute Resolution and Governance in the European Community'. *American Political Science Review*, 92: 63–81.

————(1998b). 'The European Courts and the National Courts: A Statistical Analysis of Preliminary References, 1961–95'. *Journal of European Public Policy*, 5: 66–97.

————(1999). Data Set on Preliminary References in EC Law (1958–98).

——and Caporaso, James (1998a). 'From Free Trade to Supranational Polity: The European Court and Integration', in W. Sandholtz and A. Stone Sweet (eds), *European Integration and Supranational Governance*. Oxford: Oxford University Press.

————(1998b). 'La Cour européenne et l'intégration [The European Court and Integration]'. *Revue française de science politique*, 48: 195–244.

——and Sandholtz, Wayne (1998). 'Integration, Supranational Governance, and the Institutionalization of the European Polity', in W. Sandholtz and A. Stone Sweet (eds), *European Integration and Supranational Governance*. Oxford: Oxford University Press.

Süddeutsche Zeitung (1999a). 8 September.

——(1999b). 12 September.

——(1999c). 15 September.

Swarze, Jürgen (1994). 'The Procedural Guarantees in the Recent Case-law of the European Court of Justice', in D. Curtin and T. Henkels (eds), *Institutional Dynamics of European Integration*. Dordrecht: Martinus Nijhoff.

Tarrow, Sidney (1998). *Power in Movements: Social Movements and Contentious Politics* (2nd edn). Cambridge: Cambridge University Press.

Taylor, Michael (1989). 'Structure, Culture, and Action in the Explanation of Social Change'. *Politics and Society*, 17: 115–88.

Taylor, P. (1983). *The Limits of European Integration*. New York: Columbia University Press.

Tesoka, Sabrina (1999). 'Judicial Activism in the Community Social Space'. Ph.D. thesis, European University Institute, San Domenico di Fiesole, Italy.

Thielemann. E. (1999). 'Institutional Limits of a "Europe with the Regions": EC State Control Meets German Federalism'. *Journal of European Public Policy*, 6: 419–35.

Thygesen, N. (1979). 'International Coordination of Monetary Policies—With Special Reference to the European Community', in J. Wadsworth and F. Leonard de Juvigny (eds), *New Approaches in Monetary Policy*. The Netherlands: Sijthoff and Noordhoff.

Tietje, Christian (1997). 'The Concept of Coherence in the Treaty on European Union and the Common Foreign and Security Policy'. *European Foreign Affairs Review*, 2: 211–33.

Trittin, Jürgen (1993). 'Schengen, Dublin, Maastricht: Marksteine auf dem Weg zur Wohlstandsfestung Europa', in Christoph Butterwegge and Siegfried Jaeger (eds), *Europa gegen den Rest der Welt? Flüchtlingsbewegungen—Einwanderung—Asylpolitik*. Cologne: Bund-Verlag.

Trousset, P. (1998). *Pour une efficacité renforcée des politiques struturelles communautaires*. Paris: DATAR.

Tsebelis, George (1990). *Nested Games: Rational Choice in Comparative Politics*. Berkeley: University of California Press.

Turnbull, Penelope (1998). *Understanding the 1991 Intergovernmental Conference and its Legacy: 'New Institutions' and the Flaws of the Third Pillar* (Manchester Papers in Politics: European Policy Research Unit Paper No. 5/98). Manchester: University of Manchester.

——(1999). 'The Fusion of Immigration and Crime in the European Union: Problems of Cooperation and the Fight against the Trafficking in Women'. *Transnational Organized Crime*, 3: 189–213.

US Supreme Court (1978). *Vermont Yankee Nuclear Power Corp. v. Natural Resources Defense Council*, 435 U.S. 519.

Vanberg, Georg (1998). 'Abstract Judicial Review, Legislative Bargaining, and Policy Compromise'. *Journal of Theoretical Politics*, 10: 299–326.

Vanhalewyn, E. (1999). 'Trends and Patterns in State Aids'. *European Economy Reports and Studies*, 3: 32–45.

van Miert, K. (1998). 'L'approche de la Commission en matière d'aides d'État'. *L'observateur de Bruxelles*, 27 May.

van Praag, Nicholas (1982). 'Political Cooperation and Southern Europe: Case Studies in Crisis Management', in David Allen, Reinhardt Rummel, and Wolfgang Wessels (eds), *European Political Cooperation: Towards a Foreign Policy for Western Europe*. London: Butterworths.

van Schendelen, M. P. C. M. (1998). 'Prolegomena to EU Committees as Influential Policymakers', in M. P. C. M. van Schendelen (ed.), *EU Committees as Influential Policymakers*. Aldershot: Ashgate.

von Sydow, H. H. (1988). 'The Basic Strategies of the Commission's White Paper', in R. Beiber (ed.), *1992: One European Market?* Baden-Baden: Nomos.

Waldron, Jeremy (1996). 'Legislation, Authority, and Voting'. *Georgetown Law Journal*, 84: 2185–214.

Wallace, H. and Young, A. R. (eds) (1998). *Participation and Policymaking in the European Union*. Oxford: Clarendon Press.

Wallace, William (1983). 'Less than a Federation, More than a Regime: The Community as a Political System', in H. Wallace, W. Wallace, and C. Webb (eds), *Policy-Making in the European Community*. New York: John Wiley.

Waltz, Kenneth (1954). *Man, the State, and War*. New York: Columbia University Press.

——(1979). *Theory of International Politics*. New York: McGraw-Hill.

Warner, Harriet (1984). 'EC Social Policy in Practice: Community Action on Behalf of Women and its Impact in the Member States'. *Journal of Common Market Studies*, 23: 141–67.

Wasserman, Rudolf (1995). 'Kriminalität und Sicherheitsbedürfnis Zur Bedrohung durch Gewalt und Kriminalität in Deutschland'. *Aus Politik und Zeitgeschichte*, 23: 3–10.

Webster, R. (1998). 'Environmental Collective Action', in J. Greenwood and M. Aspinwall (eds), *Collective Action in the European Union: Interests and the New Politics of Associability*. London and New York: Routledge.

Weiler, Joseph. H. H. (1981). 'The Community System: the Dual Character of Supranationalism'. *Yearbook of European Law*, 1: 268–306.

——(1991). 'The Transformation of Europe'. *Yale Law Review*, 100: 2403–83.

——(1994). 'The Quiet Revolution: The European Court and Its Interlocutors'. *Comparative Political Studies*, 26: 510–34.

——(1999). *The Constitution of Europe: 'Do the New Clothes Have an Emperor?' and Other Essays on European Integration*. Cambridge: Cambridge University Press.

Weingast, B. and Marshall, W. (1988). 'The Industrial Organization of Congress'. *Journal of Political Economy*, 96: 132–63.

——and Moran, Mark J. (1983). 'Bureaucratic Discretion or Congressional Control? Regulatory Policymaking by the Federal Trade Commission'. *Journal of Political Economy*, 91: 765–800.

Wessel, Ramses A. (1997). 'The International Legal Status of the European Union'. *European Foreign Affairs Review*, 2: 109–29.

Wessels, W. and Rometsch, D. (1996). 'German Administrative Action and the European Union: The Fusion of Public Policies', in Y. Meny *et al.* (eds), *Adjusting to Europe*. London: Routledge.

Wilson, J. Q. (1979). *American Government: Institutions and Policies*. Lexington, MA: D.C. Heath.

Windhoff-Héritier, Adrienne (1987). *Policy-Analyse. Eine Einführung*. Campus: Verlag.

Winter, J. A (1993). 'Supervision of State Aid: Article 93 in the Court of Justice'. *Common Market Law Review*, 30: 311–39.

Wishlade, F. (1993). 'Politique de la concurrence et cohésion communautaire'. *L'événement Européen*, 21: 119–29.

——(1998). 'Competition Policy or Cohesion Policy By the Back Door? The Commission Guidelines on National Regional Aid'. *European Competition Law Review*, 6: 343–57.

Wood, Pia Christina (1993). 'European Political Cooperation: Lessons from the Gulf War and Yugoslavia', in Alan W. Cafruny and Glenda G. Rosenthal (eds), *The State of the European Community, Vol. 2: The Maastricht Debates and Beyond*. Boulder, CO: Lynne Rienner.

Young, A. (1998). 'European Consumer Groups', in J. Greenwood and M. Aspinwall (eds), *Collective Action in the European Union: Interests and the New Politics of Associability*. London and New York: Routledge.

NAME INDEX

SUBJECT INDEX